WARM
ASHES

WARM ASHES

Issues in Southern History at the
Dawn of the Twenty-First Century

Edited by

Winfred B. Moore Jr.,
Kyle S. Sinisi, *and* David H. White Jr.

University of South Carolina Press

© 2003 University of South Carolina

Published in Columbia, South Carolina, by the
University of South Carolina Press

Manufactured in the United States of America

07 06 05 04 03   5 4 3 2 1

Library of Congress Cataloging-in-Publication Data

Citadel Conference on the South (7th : 2000)
  Warm ashes : issues in southern history at the dawn of the twenty-first century / edited
by Winfred B. Moore Jr., Kyle S. Sinisi, and David H. White Jr.
    p. cm.
  Selected papers from the 7th Citadel Conference on the South.
  Includes bibliographical references (p.) and index.
  ISBN 1-57003-510-5 (alk. paper)
  1. Southern States—Historiography—Congresses. 2. Southern States—Social
conditions—Congresses. 3. Southern States—Race relations—Congresses. 4. United
States—History—Civil War, 1861–1865—Social aspects—Congresses. 5. Group
identity—Southern States—History—Congresses. I. Moore, Winfred B., 1949–
II. Sinisi, Kyle S., 1962– III. White, David H., 1945– IV. Title.
F208.2 .C58 2000
975'.041—dc21

                                                                    2003013278

For Jan M. Moore, Christina S. Sinisi,
and Dale C. White

CONTENTS

PREFACE

"The old South was plowed under. But the ashes are still warm."
Henry Miller, *The Air-Conditioned Nightmare*, 1945

Columbia, South Carolina
July 1, 2000
Noon

"Two cadets from The Citadel, one black and one white, climbed into the dome to take down the flag," the Charleston *Post and Courier* reported. They were carrying out the first part of the compromise recently adopted by the South Carolina General Assembly. Under its terms, the Confederate battle flag that had flown over the capitol since 1962 was to be taken down and sent to the state museum. A smaller, square version of the battle flag was then to be raised atop a flagpole, thirty feet high, at the Confederate Soldiers' Memorial on the east lawn of the statehouse grounds. Nervous legislators hoped that the new arrangement would bring an end to the NAACP's economic boycott of South Carolina and the year's worth of bitter controversy it had triggered over what the flag meant and where, if at all, it could legitimately be displayed.[1]

"I think this is a victory for all reasonable South Carolinians," said Arthur Ravenel, a white Republican from Mount Pleasant. "Everybody got something they wanted." Robert Ford, a black Democrat from Charleston, agreed. "If that soldier can be there," he pointed toward the Confederate monument, "his flag can. If African-Americans were in power, and we had people in our past who did something that caused others pain, would we still love them, would we still want to remember them? I think yes." One of Ford's white friends, Republican Glenn McConnell of Charleston, nodded his approval: "We did what nobody else could with bipartisan, biracial support. Only the hard-liners are objecting."

Perhaps—but if so, more than a few of them were among the 3,000 people who had gathered on the statehouse grounds to make their feelings known. "Shouldn't he [Ford] be ashamed of this?" asked one angry young African American, as he looked at the smaller version of the battle flag about to be raised at the Confederate Memorial. "What do I call him? Sell-out, Uncle Tom." Meanwhile, members of the NAACP marched past. "Your people have divided this state forever," one of the marchers told a boisterous defender of the battle flag. Emblazoned across the marcher's shirt were the words: "Don't start shopping till the flag starts dropping."

Not far away, members of the "Million Rebel March" also felt betrayed. Some of them strummed guitars and sang "The Night They Drove Old Dixie Down." Others wore T-shirts with the inscription: "NAACP Sucks." "This is just another way for the blacks to chisel away all the Southern pride we have left in this country," said one of the rebels. "Personally it breaks my heart."

Across the street the "Step-Daughters of the Confederacy" assembled. They looked, marveled one curious bystander, "like a cross between 'Rocky Horror Show' extras and a 1970s country music group." The Step-Daughters (led by Misses "I. Emma Throwback," "Shalla Jean Pool," and "Vanna Very White") had been "Working to Keep S.C. Bass-Akwards since 1860" and were in town to present the "Lawn Jockey Award for Cultural and Racial Insensitivity" to the members of the General Assembly who championed the flying of the flag.

"Hey," one flag-waving spectator asked, "are you making fun of us?"

"Yankees!" another exclaimed. And so it went.

The crowd looked up when the two Citadel cadets, pulling in tandem, started the big banner above the capitol on its final descent. "As the battle flag disappeared into the roof of the Statehouse dome," the reporters noted, "the cheers and boos mixed into a roar." It had been "billed as a day of healing but it became a day of rancor."

❧

The "flag controversy" was the backdrop against which The Citadel Conference on the South was held in Charleston, South Carolina, from April 6 to 8, 2000. The first call for papers was issued in the spring of 1999—just before the South Carolina chapter of the NAACP asked for a national boycott. The program for the conference was finalized in February 2000, just after the boycott began. And those who attended from throughout the United States arrived as Joseph P. Riley Jr., the mayor of the host city, was in the midst of a well-publicized one-hundred mile march to Columbia to ask that the flag be removed. In sum, the subject, and all it symbolized, was never far away from the thoughts of those who organized and took part in the meeting.

Southerners and those who study them never, of course, need much of a stimulus to think about the past and draw conclusions about what it means. Still, we think the circumstances surrounding the most recent Citadel Conference on the South made it a particularly fertile environment for that exercise. More than a hundred scholars from throughout the United States presented and commented on papers dealing with aspects of Southern history from the colonial era to the present. Not surprisingly, slavery, the Civil War, religion, race relations, public memory, and the characteristics of regional identity were recurring themes in a large percentage of the presentations.

The eighteen essays that follow are among the best of those presentations. While stoking the "warm ashes" of regional history, the authors cast light on the Southern experience and illuminate some of the directions scholarship seems to be headed at the beginning of a new century. It is with those objectives in mind that this volume is offered.

The conference that gave rise to this volume would not have been possible without a generous grant from the South Carolina Humanities Council. Its director, Randy Akers, and its grants officer, Bob Ellis, were consistently helpful to us throughout the process. Indispensable financial assistance for this symposium, as for past ones, was also provided by The Citadel Foundation. The Citadel's dean of undergraduate studies, Suzanne Ozment, and its vice-president for academic affairs, Harry Carter, gave encouragement and support without which the project could never have been undertaken—much less completed. As always, our colleagues in the history department also gave us much needed support before, during, and after the meeting. A final note of thanks should be given our cadets. They enthusiastically offered their time and helped with all the myriad logistics of the conference. Without them— especially the cadet-in-charge, Brian Maloney—the conference would have been a chaotic experience. These and the large number of other folks who participated in the conference deserve much of the credit for the merits of this volume. Its shortcomings are ours alone.

NOTE

1. Rachel Graves and Brian Hicks, "Emotions Run High as Flag Comes Down," *Charleston Post and Courier,* 2 July 2000. All quotations that follow are from this source.

PART I

Forward to the Past

Against the backdrop of public debate over Confederate symbols, the opening essay of this volume, Emory M. Thomas's "Clio at Climax: Apocalypse and the American Civil War," probes the current state of the historiography for clues to what the future study of that conflict needs to examine. While noting the ever-present popularity of the war, Thomas describes, first, what Civil War historians need no longer write. According to Thomas, gone are the days when historians could either dismiss the importance of slavery in causing the war or write biographies and monographs based solely in the *Official Records*. Conversely, Thomas describes a number of areas ripe for the historical plucking. It is a list largely lacking military topics. According to Thomas, cities, off-year elections, religion, marriage, slavery, and the United Daughters of the Confederacy all offer exciting possibilities. Thomas also identifies gaps in the literature that historians have long noted and bemoaned. Still applicable after sixty years are Charles W. Ramsdell's lament for administrative histories of the Confederate War Department and Douglas Southall Freeman's call for investigations of refugees, wartime farm management, and female factory workers. Beyond these fairly specific calls for research Thomas sees a much more important agenda to be filled. With racial conflict an ever present theme in the histories of both the war and the Southern experience, he insists that future historians investigate the confluence of race in shaping past events and culture. Only when this is done, and the war ceases to have relevance to contemporary issues, can the last book be written on the Civil War.

1

Clio at Climax

Apocalypse and the American Civil War

EMORY M. THOMAS

It has been done. Someone had already written the last book about the American Civil War. Thomas L. Connelly, then writing under the pseudonym T. Lawrence Connelly, published his first book in 1963, *Will Success Spoil Jeff Davis?* His subtitle was *The Last Book about the Civil War.*

For a little while I suspect Connelly and others actually believed that this would be the last book about the war for quite some time. By the time *Will Success Spoil Jeff Davis? The Last Book about the Civil War* rolled off the presses of McGraw-Hill on November 22, 1963, American consumers were obsessed with more recent history. Connelly's little book is a delight, a wickedly clever spoof of Civil War, and especially Confederate, buffs. But very few people have ever read it. I purchased my copy for ninety-eight cents at a remainder sale. And subsequent publishing history has rendered Connelly's subtitle far more ridiculous than anyone knew in 1963.[1]

How long, O Lord, will this plethoric outpouring of books about the American Civil War continue? The best estimate of the number of books about the Civil War in existence is 60,000, and that estimate is more than thirty years old (1969). Will readers ever be sated? Will anyone ever *really* publish the last book about the Civil War? My answer to these queries is—yes, but not yet.[2]

Allow me to expand on this assertion. To understand why so many materials continue to pour into the marketplace, I believe that it is vital to learn why so many people seem so hell-bent to buy every last scrap of history about the period of the Civil War—good, bad, and indifferent. What is the source of this national obsession?

Here is Robert Penn Warren in 1961 from his book, *The Legacy of the Civil War: Meditations on the Centennial*—a passage worth reading, whatever the context:

The Civil War is, for the American imagination, the great single
event of our history. Without too much wrenching, it may, in fact,
be said to be American history. Before the Civil War we had no
history in the deepest and most inward sense. There was, of course,
the noble vision of the Founding Fathers articulated in the Declaration and the Constitution—the dream of freedom incarnated in
a more perfect union. But the Revolution did not create a nation
except on paper; and too often in the following years the vision of
the Founding Fathers, which men had suffered and died to vali-
date, became merely a daydream of easy and automatic victories, a
vulgar delusion of manifest destiny, a conviction of being a people
divinely chosen to live on milk and honey at small expense.[3]

Warren speaks to the great issues the war involved and emphasizes their persistence. Americans have not yet resolved the questions they raised in
1861–1865. Borrowing a line from Herman Melville, Warren asks, "Have we
been 'instructed' by that catharsis of pity and terror? Sadly, we must answer
no. We have not yet achieved justice. We have not yet created a union which
is, in the deepest sense, a community. We have not yet resolved our deep dubi-
eties or self-deceptions." Warren continues to note that individuals caught up
in the war, "despite failings, blindness, and vice, may affirm for us the possibility of the dignity of life." And however tragic their stories, some of their
"grandeur . . . may be what we yearn for after all."[4]

If Warren is correct, and I believe he is, Americans and others continue to
revisit the period of the Civil War because that period continues to speak to
contemporary questions—questions about race, community, and identity.
Moreover, the Civil War as human drama continues to evoke interest and fas-
cination. That Warren wrote his analysis about four decades ago does not seem
all that important: his thoughts continue current. His understanding seems as
valid now as it was in 1961.

So the simple answer to the question of how long people will continue to
lust after books and other materials about the American Civil War is as long
as the issues raised by the war continue to resonate in the American experience. We will "get over" the Civil War when we resolve the questions the war
provoked and that still remain unresolved.

I believe that during the century just begun the American people will
resolve the principal issues and questions related to their civil war that now
embroil them. But these resolutions will take time. And in the interim,

scholarship devoted to the mid–nineteenth century will continue to proliferate. Let me address this interim—the immediate extension of the present—before I suggest some ways in which historians and others might answer questions posed by the war that still concern the American psyche.

First let me offer ideas about the sorts of books we do not need but can anticipate anyway. And face it, the American Civil War has always generated an incredible amount of genuinely bad history. Indeed, it has been some of this very bad history that has prevented us from resolving the deep and abiding issues that sprang from the war.

We do not need any more ideological polemics purporting to prove that the war had nothing to do with slavery or race. I think most literate people now know that most Americans were racists during the nineteenth century, so we do not need any more tu quoque arguments as a veneer for Southern apology. Most literate Americans also know that Nathan Bedford Forrest was a vicious man and that what happened at Fort Pillow was a massacre. I would like to believe that the scholarship associated with the war has risen above attempts to revise Andersonville, Saltville, et al. into inconsequence. The same goes for Federal "atrocities," although the literature of "low-rape war" deserves a long second look.

We do not need historiographically challenged graduate students and "talented amateurs" to rewrite books already on the shelves of research libraries. Later in this essay I will suggest that someone should write a new study of Confederate politics. But that someone had better read, mark, and inwardly digest the works of Nathaniel W. Stephenson, Thomas B. Alexander, Charles W. Ramsdell, Rembert W. Patrick, and John Brawner Robbins before he or she does the scholarly equivalent of reinventing the hula hoop.[5]

Long ago Frank E. Vandiver lamented the "potboiler biography (often written by journalists with pretensions to be Nevines, Cattons, or Freemans), which says nothing new, is based on no real sources, but abounds in blood and gore."[6] Let me expand on this thought. Once upon a time, graduate students could write acceptable theses and dissertations grounded essentially in published sources—the *Official Records* and memoir materials. That time is gone. The potential and extant databases available electronically have and will continue to expand the research capacity of scholars indefinitely.

In a similar vein, anyone who now believes that he or she can write a respectable unit history from the *Official Records,* a manuscript diary or two, and a previous published unit history is very much mistaken. My response to such a work is two words: Warren Wilkinson. His *Mother, May You Never See the Sights I Have Seen,* a history of the 57th Massachusetts infantry, has established a new standard for this genre, and Wilkinson's "two words" are National Archives.[7]

Another once upon a time, scholars could be content to produce monographs that were in essence published research notes. Other scholars then made use of this material, and sooner or later someone wrote history, that is, offered ideas about what the facts in the research notes meant. That time, too, is gone. History requires an answer to the question, so what? Why should anyone care about the facts or data that the research unearths? History is about answers to questions; it is about the present. Anything less is not history. Bare facts, exclusive of analysis or understanding, are not history but antiquarianism. We do not need raw, undigested facts about the American Civil War; we need history.

However worthless are the tomes and topics described above, I predict with certainty that this material or similar sorts of studies will continue to crowd our bookshelves during the near future. Indeed, it is more likely than not that the less worthy works will be most likely to make the transit from print to video, e-book, and so forth. But what about good books (and other media) about important topics? What sorts of works can we anticipate during that period before Americans and others become sick of the Civil War, before the questions raised by the war no longer need answers in the present?

I have long been fascinated with the impact of the American Civil War on institutions, people, and peoples. War is by definition a crisis. And people(s) reveal themselves in crises more so than in circumstances of peace and ease. Our culture acknowledges, even celebrates this fact in such traditions as extra innings, "sudden death," presidential debates, deadlines, job interviews, and "talk radio." So I believe that topics that assess the effect of the war on people individually and corporately are significant.

The Confederate State of Richmond: A Biography of the Capital was my maiden effort in this profession, and in a recent reprint edition of my dissertation-turned-book, I lamented in print that no scholar had taken up my topic and revised my work. I still consider cities—and not only Confederate cities— to be intriguing subjects for research, and I hope students will undertake research and writing on the urban impact of the Civil War.[8]

Phillip S. Paludan has suggested a significant connection between single-parent (mother) households produced by the war and the Social Gospel

movement in American churches during the late nineteenth and early twentieth centuries. A number of the leaders of the movement, Paludan discovered,
came of age in households headed by women. He speculates that the influence
of the "feminine" values within these households generated the kinds of consciousness that led these people into religious emphasis on selfless service to
others. This is but one example of the creative opportunities available in the
study of the generation of Americans who endured the national trauma.[9]

What about the impact of the war on marriages? Carol Bleser and Joan
Cashin in separate articles have demonstrated that the experience of the war
produced major transformations in relationships within two marriages.[10] The
correspondence is extant to examine other marriages and eventually to posit
some conclusions about the effect of war, separation, and such on human relationships.

For some time I have with limited success been trying to interest students
in the response of religious groups to the crisis of war. How did a parish, diocese, association, conference, presbytery, synagogue, or other unit of organized
religion react to the war? How did the clergy explain the role of God, providence, or whatever in victory or defeat? Such questions might have important
answers.[11]

Conventional wisdom has long held that Jefferson Davis and his administration suffered significantly in the "off-year" elections of 1863. I am not
sure. I do know that an investigation of each contest will reveal much about
the will, mood, and convictions of the Confederate people. I also believe
that similar studies of the elections of 1862 and 1864 in the United States—
district by district, senate seat by senate seat—would turn up interesting insights about the ways people in the United States attempted to act out their
hopes, visions, and fears. Abraham Lincoln seemed to have taken a huge risk
by proclaiming emancipation only six or seven weeks before the "off-year"
elections of 1862. But did he, in fact? Or did the exodus of Southern senators
and congressmen assure the President a working majority in all but the most
disastrous circumstances? I do not know. And I do not believe that anyone
will know until historians study the individual elections.[12]

Slavery had a lot to do with provoking the American Civil War. But what
about the fate and function of slavery *during* the war? Clarence Mohr has
found considerable volatility within the institution of slavery in Georgia during the war. Historians applaud Mohr's book and cite his research, but someone needs to study other states. How did the war affect this supposedly vital

Southern institution? Did slaves act out and anticipate their freedom, even while they were still slaves?[13]

And what about the response of white people to slavery in the Confederate South? Long ago Bell Wiley offered evidence that a reform movement gained support in the Confederacy. Is Wiley's the last word? And how about what Robert Durden called "the great emancipation debate" within the Confederacy from the fall of 1864 to the passage of the act that authorized the enlistment of 200,000 African Americans in the Confederate army? To date, Durden's book *The Gray and the Black: The Confederate Debate on Emancipation* is the only book on the subject, and this work is almost thirty years old. Is there more to say about this extremely important topic?[14]

The Lost Cause has inspired very fine books by Charles Reagan Wilson and Gaines Foster.[15] But these books are aging. Is there no more to say? How about the United Daughters of the Confederacy? There have been dissertations about the U.D.C., but where are the books? One might ask the same question about the Sons of Confederate Veterans, the Southern Historical Society, and the Children of the Confederacy.

The icons (in the traditional sense of icon) of the Confederate States have been much in the news of late. The song "Dixie" and the battle flag of the Army of Northern Virginia have provoked—and, alas, will continue to provoke—cultural conflict. The debate in Southern legislatures and within all manner of national and regional organizations has often been loud and acrimonious. But this debate has less often been informed by serious scholarship. There is a crying need for the study of culture and symbols, and we need such studies yesterday.[16]

In preparation of this essay, I consulted several other essays written in the past by established scholars on the same or a similar topic. What I found is interesting indeed. Much of the proposed research agenda in these older works remains undone.

Instructive is a piece by Charles W. Ramsdell, "Some Problems Involved in Writing the History of the Confederacy," read before the first-ever annual meeting of the Southern Historical Association in October 1935 and later published in the *Journal of Southern History*. Ramsdell observed what most professional historians have "discovered": that "very few of the narratives of participants can be relied upon; for some had forgotten much before they began to write; others wrote primarily to defend their own reputations; others, still, merely to meet public demand or to gratify a very human desire to leave a record of their own achievements."[17] We are still learning this lesson sixty-five years after Ramsdell taught us.

Many of the "problems" Ramsdell discerned involved gaps in our knowledge of the Confederacy. And many of these gaps remain for the Confederacy—and for the Union as well. Ramsdell lamented the lack of authoritative works about the subsistence, quartermaster, and medical bureaus of the Confederate War Department. He called for studies of "such local industries as tanneries, wagon shops, shoe shops, and the like." Ramsdell was himself interested in the work of Confederate Secretary of the Treasury Christopher G. Memminger and wished for more work on "the development of the Confederate tax system as well as the tax systems and financial operations of the several states and their repercussions upon Confederate finances." He tried to interest his hearers and readers in Confederate politics. He called for studies of churches, army hospitals, relief organizations, and medicines. And none of these topics yet have adequate works about them.[18]

In 1939 Douglas Southall Freeman published *The South to Posterity: An Introduction to the Writing of Confederate History.* Most of this book was an account of the significant early works about the Confederacy and the Civil War; but Freeman's final chapter, "Yet to Be Written," contained suggestions for future works. Freeman mentioned topics such as a biography of James Longstreet, studies of the Nitre and Mining Bureau, and Quartermaster Bureau, and "war-time farm management." He termed "strange" the lack of more work on the roles of women in the war. Specifically, Freeman called for long looks at refugees, female factory workers, and clerks—topics that continue to be "ripe." Freeman also insisted that "the unwritten part of the civil history of the Confederacy lies more in the realm of social psychology other than that of politics." He pointed to the "development of the 'war spirit' in 1859–61," and suggested that a systematic examination "may disclose a clinically perfect case in the psychosis of war."[19]

David M. Potter's *Impending Crisis, 1848–1861* is an exciting and insightful book; still Potter does not quite achieve Freeman's "clinically perfect case in the psychosis of war." In fact, I have some designs on this topic, albeit with a modest format. I propose to expand a series of essays I did some years ago entitled *Travels to Hallowed Ground,* in which the historian (me) goes to places where history happened, tells stories, and reflects on the transcendence between past and present in those places. This sojourn to Charleston, and a series of trips to Fort Sumter with visiting friends and relatives, has inspired me to attempt a "travel" to the decision for war that occurred in Charleston Harbor. I introduce this project here to affirm the vitality of topics and studies in this already overworked realm of scholarship.[20]

Here is what I have in mind for this "travel" in response to Freeman's suggestion. First a text:

> What king, going out to wage war against another king, will not sit down and consider whether he is able with ten thousand to oppose the one who comes against him with twenty thousand? If he cannot then, while the other is still far away, he sends a delegation and asks for terms of peace. (Luke 14:31–32)

Most literate Americans know that the Civil War began at Fort Sumter on April 12, 1861. Those people who made the decisions that led to violence believed with reason that they had no acceptable options. Had they had the foresight to realize the consequences of their decisions, they might, indeed, have found some other option and pronounced it acceptable. I cannot believe that anyone actually willed four years of brutal fighting that cost well over six hundred thousand lives—and these only the obvious consequences. I take no comfort from the fact that the overwhelming majority of people in the United States and the Confederate States endorsed the decision for war by supporting their respective side with enthusiasm, treasure, and blood. Why did no one seriously count the cost and consider terms of peace?

I find several sorts of fantasy abroad in mid-nineteenth-century America. Among the speeches, sermons, editorials, and other forms of discourse that attended the secession crisis was an awful lot of nonsense disguised as truth. Some people, especially in the South, seemed to embrace a romantic vision of Armageddon: if the slave-plantation civilization were doomed, then better to end with a bang than with a whimper. On both sides was the conviction that the other side would not fight, and hence the decision for war involved only picnics and parades. The war, if it did occur, would be brief and victorious. A third theme, especially prevalent in the North, was the proposition that this war would be "good for us"; it would restore moral fiber among the people.

I believe that there is a lesson here. The "dogs of war" once unleashed go where they will, and warfare defies the efforts of either side to control the devastation. Quick and painless victories may appear secure before combat begins; but they rarely happen. I can remember a time when I believed the word "Kurd" applied only to a quality of cottage cheese.

Americans still have much to learn from their civil war. And I hope that seriously good works of history will drive out ephemeral works and foolishness. The best guide to these books and to possible scholarship in the future is James M. McPherson and William J. Cooper, *Writing the Civil War: The Quest to Understand,* published by the University of South Carolina Press in 1998. This book contains historiographical essays by twelve significant scholars about the state of historical writing on the war period.[21]

As I promised some pages ago, let me now attempt to speculate upon the circumstances that will finally sate the American appetite (and presumably other people's as well) for more books, tapes, DVDs, and so forth about the Civil War. When the issues and quandaries raised and remaining unresolved in the Civil War cease to resonate, stop being "current" in American national life, then perhaps this period will become quaint and cease to engage Americans and others so primally. Robert Penn Warren, in his *Legacy of the Civil War,* seemed most concerned with three issues—race, community, and identity. Let me now suggest one possible way in which historians and other scholars might contribute to a resolution. I propose here no less than a new, or at least renewed, "burden of Southern history."

For the greater part of four centuries, the interactions and relationships of European Americans and African Americans have been grounded in conflict. Historians quite rightly have portrayed whites and blacks as living in a state of war, and especially has this been true in the histories of the American South. I suggest—no, insist—that the time will come when historians and other scholars will think, not of conflict, but of confluence when writing or speaking about race in the American South. The reasons for my conviction are many, but they reduce to one fundamental fact of Southern life—black people and white people in the South have shared an enormous amount of the substance of life. Whatever is "Southern" is an amalgam of black and white, African American and Southern American. And sooner or later, both black and white Southerners will realize the degree to which they share.

Already a thin but expanding rank of historians and other scholars are playing upon this theme. James McBride Dabbs, *The Southern Heritage;* Mechal Sobel, *The World They Made Together: Black and White Values in Eighteenth-Century Virginia;* Philip D. Morgan, *Slave Counterpoint: Black Culture in the Eighteenth-Century Chesapeake and Lowcountry;* and Charles Joyner, *Shared Traditions: Southern History and Folk Culture,* all speak to the degrees to which whites and blacks appropriated each other's culture.

I am afraid none of us here will or could live long enough to tell the complete story. To do so will require research into all manner of interchanges—speech, religion, work rhythms, family life, dress, dance, music, folk tales, games, and much, much more. It is a matter of observation and not speculation that black and white Southerners share large amounts of common blood as well as culture. I am convinced that research that emphasizes confluence instead of conflict will reap huge rewards. I believe that accumulated evidence before this present century is more than one generation old will change minds and attitudes both within and outside the American South.

In 1865 Abraham Lincoln wrote that blacks and whites, then mostly slaves and slaveholders, would have to "live their way out of their former relationship" with each other. Now, after 135 years of living, Lincoln's words still offer the best hope of social harmony within a biracial society. And Southerners would seem to have need of still more living their way out.

But ideas have consequences. The old burden of Southern history as proclaimed so eloquently by C. Vann Woodward almost a half-century ago challenged Southern historians to counter the great American success myth, the facile assumption that Americans were destined to innocence, victory, prosperity, and righteousness. Southerners, Woodward insisted, should know that history is not something unpleasant that happens to someone else. The experience of the American South, like the experiences of the rest of the world's peoples, demonstrates that guilt, defeat, poverty, and evil are alive in human experience, and that tragedy blends with triumph in human affairs.[22]

The "new" burden of Southern history that I suggest begins where Woodward stopped. All that Woodward proposed is still valid, and Southern historians still have the burden of reminding Americans that history happens. But in addition, Southern historians might well remind themselves that "Southern" was never a "white only" adjective. "Southern" applies to African Americans, European Americans, and especially in recent decades, to Latin Americans. This is Southern history whole—the experience of people adopting, exchanging, and sharing with each other. And one indication that this idea has consequences would be a corporate expression of what is supposed to be a classic Southern virtue—good manners. Southerners like to believe that they care about the feelings and welfare of other people. If that is so, then South Carolinian Southerners should take that battle flag of the Army of Northern Virginia down from the capitol in Columbia.

I know that these last several pages contain a lot of wishful thinking. But I have to hope even while I know that at some level Tom Connelly was correct in *Will Success Spoil Jeff Davis? The Last Book about the Civil War* when he concluded:

> The war will never be over. Let minié balls corrode, Confederate money crumble, and imitation battle flags rot. As long as there is a tearjerking poem to be read, a droll statue to be unveiled, a cannon ball to be unearthed, a fast buck to be made—then there will always be a Confederacy. Grant, Sheridan, Sherman—they could whip Marse Robert Lee and Retreating Joe Johnston. But they will never whip that long gray line of genealogists, antique dealers, historians, promoters, and roundtable buffs—marching to the Gray Nirvana.[23]

NOTES

1. T. Lawrence Connelly, *Will Success Spoil Jeff Davis? The Last Book about the Civil War* (New York: McGraw Hill, 1963).

2. Allan Nevins, James I. Roberton Jr., and Bell I. Wiley, eds., *Civil War Books: A Critical Bibliography,* 2 vols. (Baton Rouge: Published for the U.S. Civil War Centennial Commission by Louisiana State University Press, 1967–1969), 2:v.

3. Robert Penn Warren, *The Legacy of the Civil War: Meditations on the Centennial* (New York: Random House, 1961), 3.

4. Ibid., 107–9.

5. This sample of seminal works includes: Nathaniel W. Stephenson, *The Day of the Confederacy* (New Haven: Yale University Press, 1919); Thomas B. Alexander, "Persistent Whiggery in the Confederate South, 1860–1877," *Journal of Southern History* 27 (1961): 305–29; Charles W. Ramsdell, *Behind the Lines in the Southern Confederacy* (Baton Rouge: Louisiana State University Press, 1944); Rembert W. Patrick, *Jefferson Davis and His Cabinet* (Baton Rouge: Louisiana State University Press, 1944); and John Brawner Robbins, "Confederate, Nationalism: Politics and Government in the Confederate South," (Ph.D. diss., Rice University, 1964).

6. Frank E. Vandiver, "The Civil War: Its Theory and Practice," *Texas Quarterly* 2 (1959): 107–8.

7. Warren Wilkinson, *Mother, May You Never See the Sights I Have Seen: The Fifty-Seventh Massachusetts Veteran Volunteers in the Army of Potomac, 1864–1865* (New York: Harper and Row, 1990)

8. Emory M. Thomas, *The Confederate State of Richmond: A Biography of the Capital* (Austin: University of Texas Press, 1971; Baton Rouge: Louisiana State University Press, 1998).

9. Paludan offered these ideas in a paper presented at a meeting of the Wisconsin State Historical Society in Madison, Wisconsin, on 2 May 1998.

10. See Joan Cashin, "'Since the War Broke Out': The Marriage of Kate and William McLure," in Catherine Clinton and Nina Silber, eds., *Divided Houses: Gender and the Civil War* (New York: Oxford University Press, 1992), 200–212; and Carol Bleser and Frederick M. Heath, "The Impact of the Civil-War on a Southern Marriage: Clement and Virginia Tunstall Clay of Alabama," *Civil War History* 30 (1984): 197–220.

11. See Randall M. Miller, Harry S. Stout, and Charles Reagan Wilson, eds., *Religion and the American Civil War* (New York: Oxford University Press, 1998) for samples of the most recent work on the topic, and the works of Samuel S. Hill Jr. for seminal ideas.

12. One study of a wartime election is William Alexander Percy, "Localizing the Context of Confederate Politics: The Congressional Election of 1863 in Georgia's First District," *Georgia Historical Quarterly* 79 (1995): 192–209. Recent biographies of the rival presidents are disappointing on this subject. See David Herbert Donald, *Lincoln* (London: Simon and Schuster, 1995), 382; and William J. Cooper Jr., *Jefferson Davis, American* (New York: Alfred A. Knopf, 2000), 461–65.

13. Clarence L. Mohr, *On the Threshold of Freedom: Masters and Slaves in Civil War Georgia* (Athens: University of Georgia Press, 1986). Also outstanding is Barbara Jeanne Fields, *Slavery and Freedom on the Middle Ground: Maryland during the Nineteenth Century* (New Haven: Yale University Press, 1985).

14. Bell I. Wiley, *Southern Negroes, 1861–1865* (New Haven: Yale University Press, 1938); Robert F. Durden, *The Gray and the Black: The Confederate Debate on Emancipation* (Baton Rouge: Louisiana State University Press, 1972).

15. Charles Reagan Wilson, *Baptized in Blood: The Religion of the Lost Cause, 1865–1920* (Athens: University of Georgia Press, 1980); Gaines M. Foster, *Ghosts of the Confederacy: Defeat, The Lost Cause, and the Emergence of the New South, 1865 to 1913* (New York: Oxford University Press, 1987).

16. Promising beginnings are Grace Elizabeth Hale, "Granite Stopped Time: The Stone Mountain Memorial and the Representation of Southern Identity," *Georgia Historical Quarterly* 82 (1998): 22–44; and John Walker Davis, "An Air of Defiance: Georgia's State Flag Change of 1956," *Georgia Historical Quarterly* 72 (1998): 305–30.

17. Charles W. Ramsdell, "Some Problems Involved in Writing the History of the Confederacy," *Journal of Southern History* 11 (1936): 133–47.

18. Ibid.

19. Douglas Southall Freeman, *The South to Posterity: An Introduction to the Writing of Confederate History* (New York: C. Scribner's Sons, 1939), 197–204.

20. David M. Potter, *The Impending Crisis, 1848–1861* (New York: Harper and Row, 1976).

21. James M. McPherson and William J. Cooper, eds., *Writing the Civil War: The Quest to Understand* (Columbia: University of South Carolina Press, 1998).

22. C. Vann Woodward, "The Irony of Southern History," *Journal of Southern History* 19 (1953): 319, reprinted and revised in the several editions of Woodward's *The Burden of Southern History* (Baton Rouge: Louisiana State University Press, 1960, 1968, 1993).

23. Connelly, *Will Success Spoil Jeff Davis?* 143.

PART II

Enslaved

Evidence of Professor Thomas's notion of the confluence of race can be found in the second section of the book, where three authors present microhistories of slavery and its impact upon both whites and blacks. In this section's first essay, "A Reassessment of the Volume of the Post-Revolutionary Foreign Slave Trade to North America, 1783–1810," James McMillin returns to a basic, yet important, question of just how many Africans were imported into the United States. Of specific concern to McMillin is the period from 1783 to 1810 when, according to both national mythology and older scholarship, British merchants brought only 70,000 new slaves to America. McMillin takes aim at this figure as well as others advanced in more recent years by Allan Kulikoff, Robert W. Fogel, and Stanley Engerman. Despite their more realistic estimates of slave trafficking, these studies, McMillin believes, suffer from errant statistical assumptions and a reliance upon questionable Customs enumerations. McMillin reconstructs the volume of importation in three ways. First, he assumes a new and varied natural growth rate of the native slave population when analyzing census data. Second, he uses surviving ship records to document large numbers of slaves that slipped past Customs officials. Third, and finally, McMillin examines the slave trading fleet to estimate its carrying capacity. When the numbers are then added decade by decade, McMillin estimates that 170,000 new slaves arrived in America. This new number occupies something of a middle point between Philip Curtin's low figure of 70,000 to Fogel's and Engerman's high calculation of 291,000. Consequences of this oft-ignored population increase were great. The new slaves represented the largest immigrant group to arrive in America between 1783 and 1810. This massive influx of people thus fueled an increase in the South's congressional representation and a much needed labor supply to keep up with the antebellum cotton boom.

The next two essays examine aspects of the social system that was constructed to manage the relationship between that large group of black slaves on the one hand and the small group of white owners on the other. Since Eugene Genovese first published *Roll, Jordan, Roll* in 1976, the idea of slaveholder paternalism has remained the focus of scholarly contention. Kirsten E. Wood reinvigorates the debate over paternalism and takes it in a fresh direction in her essay. Her concern is slaveholding widows, and she believes them to have been just as paternalistic as the men they replaced. Absent a male head of the household, widows assumed control over the traditional male responsibilities of agricultural labor, discipline, and the mechanics of getting goods marketed and sold. Here also, according to Wood, the women assumed the paternalistic attitudes and practices that had secured the slave system. Discipline, production incentives, and careful attention to their slave's personal lives all characterized the widows in the same way they had characterized their deceased husbands. Wood does note, however, that these women did more than just mimic male paternalism. Given their very femaleness and their lifelong experience in making accommodations running the domestic household, the widows may have been better suited to balancing the force and persuasion that was at the heart of paternalism.

Whether widowed or not, antebellum white women lived with the perpetual possibility of slave insurrection. Patrick H. Breen offers a fascinating look into how these women reacted to a threat that would not provide any special mercy to women or children. Quite simply, Breen argues that male and female slaveholders reacted in culturally acceptable ways to the threat of insurrection. Men projected indifference, while women panicked. This fright, Breen concludes, had the unintended consequence of chipping away at both the institution of slavery and the norms of female behavior in Southern society. Women fled the plantations looking for safety in larger communities thus contradicting the male faith in the security of their homes and a system of paternalistic control. Perhaps more importantly, Breen notes that women's reactions to a possible insurrection did not stop with their frightened entrance into a community stronghold. Not only did they prepare to defend themselves in the absence of male protection, but they also assumed a public political role to minimize potential rebellions in the first place. Countless numbers of women petitioned governments and lobbied politicians seeking remedies that included Northern censorship of abolitionists, the colonization of slaves, or—far more radically—the outright extermination of the slaves themselves. Such public activism and the fear it manifested, Breen contends, revealed a society that failed to live up to its ideal of providing a safe haven for its families.

2

A Reassessment of the Volume of the Post-Revolutionary Foreign Slave Trade to North America, 1783–1810

James McMillin

In 1999 the South Carolina legislature erected a historical marker near Charleston on Sullivan's Island to commemorate the arrival of tens of thousands of captives from the shores of Africa. The marker was long overdue. The significance of the site—Charleston is African Americans' Ellis Island—has largely been ignored for more than a century.[1]

Despite the good intentions of the legislators, however, the marker reinforces a popular misconception. By stating that captives arrived "between 1700 and 1775," the authors imply that the American Revolution marked the end of foreign slave imports into Charleston. This was not the case, however. The Revolution only interrupted the trade. As soon as the war ended in 1783, it reopened, and large numbers of enslaved Africans continued to arrive in Charleston and other North American ports until December 31, 1807.

A number of factors have contributed to this mistaken conviction. One is that scholars have tended to view the slave trade to North America as a colonial event. After all, the colonial trade lasted much longer, and participation was more widespread.[2] A second is that much of the British colonial trade to North America was well documented and most of the records were deposited in London, whereas the meager extant evidence of the post-Revolutionary trade is widely dispersed throughout Western Europe and the Americas. A third is that in their studies of the post-Revolutionary slave trade, most historians have tended to view the Founding Fathers in a positive light. According to this approach, after the American Revolution, British merchants revived the trade to its former colonies, but the Founding Fathers intervened and engineered its swift demise.[3] And finally and most importantly, Philip D. Curtin's numerical analysis of the transatlantic slave trade, *The Atlantic Slave Trade* (1969), buttresses this scholarship. In this influential study, he estimates that only about 70,000 Africans were imported into the United States from 1783 to 1810.[4]

This chapter is an effort to reassess and revise this prevailing view. In Part I previous estimates of the number of foreign slaves imported are analyzed, and in Part II different assumptions and recent research on the dimensions of the post-Revolutionary slave trade are used to revise the volume of the foreign slave trade upward.

PART I

Curtin bases his estimate on calculations performed in the 1850s by H. C. Carey. Because it is still repeated by contemporary authorities, it is important to see just how Carey arrived at his figure. To his credit, Carey based his estimate on a reliable source, United States censuses. He used the censuses to calculate the slave population increase from 1790 to 1810 for South Carolina and Georgia. From this figure he subtracted the number of slaves he estimated migrated with their masters from states north of South Carolina and Georgia, and the increase in the black population he attributed to natural growth. He credited the resulting figure of 47,000 to the foreign slave trade. However, in a discussion of the nation-wide growth of the black population during the period, Carey correctly concluded that more people must have been imported. Consequently, he raised the importation volume to 52,000. To this total he added 1,400 which he claimed was the number of slaves imported from 1782 to 1790.[5] These estimates should add up to 53,400; but a few pages later, when totaling the number of slaves imported into North America from the colonial era through the nineteenth century, with no explanation, Carey lists 70,000 as "import subsequent to 1790."[6]

Carey's estimate is flawed by questionable assumptions. He erroneously assumed that from 1783 to 1790 only 1,400 Africans were imported and that from 1783 to 1810 no foreign slaves were taken to North Carolina, Kentucky, Tennessee, Louisiana, or Mississippi; no Chesapeake slaves were sold and sent West or South without their masters; and no slaves were manumitted. He also used an overly optimistic natural growth rate for the slave population—25 percent decennial—and ignored the possibility that newly imported African slaves could have died before census workers could count them. All these mistaken assumptions, when combined, caused Carey to grossly underestimate

the volume of the United States foreign slave trade, both in his explicit calculations of just over 50,000 and his more familiar general estimate of 70,000.[7]

In spite of its inaccuracy, Curtin uses Carey's estimate in *The Atlantic
Slave Trade*. Aware that the entire North American traffic before and after U.S.
independence represented only a small portion of the whole picture, he
includes only a few sentences on the post-Revolutionary trade in the study. In
one, he succinctly concludes that "Carey's further estimate of 70,000 for the
period 1791–1807 would complete the period of the legal slave trade at a total
in the vicinity of 345,000."[8] Curtin does note that the 70,000 figure does not
include imports into Louisiana during the French and Spanish periods; and
toward the end of the book in a table summarizing his findings, he lists the
total U.S. imports from 1781 to 1810 as 92,300.[9] Nevertheless, the 70,000
figure is still the most widely quoted estimate.

Only a handful of historians have questioned Carey's and Curtin's estimates of the North American post-Revolutionary trade. Among the most
notable are Robert William Fogel, Stanley L. Engerman, and Allan Kulikoff.
In *Time on the Cross* (1974), Fogel and Engerman argue that Carey overesti-
mates the natural growth rate. Instead of 25 percent per decade as Carey
argues, they maintain that the slave population increased at a much slower
natural growth rate of 2 percent per year. Using the slower rate, they calculate
that 291,000 Africans were imported between 1780 and 1810.[10] Certainly, in
some regions of the South the annual growth rate equaled 2 percent or was
even lower, but overall, as is argued in Part II, it surpassed their figure.[11]

Kulikoff's estimate (116,000 people) falls between those made by Fogel
and Engerman and Carey. To arrive at his estimate, Kulikoff uses similar calculations and makes many of the same assumptions as Carey. The difference
in their results arises from Kulikoff's allowances for slave manumissions and
for domestic and foreign slave forced migrations to Tennessee, Mississippi, and
Louisiana. Also he includes an estimate for the years from 1782 to 1790
(20,000 people) and for West Indies slaves imported into Louisiana in the first
decade of the 1800s (3,000 people). Although Kulikoff's calculations are more
sophisticated than Carey's, he also bases his calculations on certain questionable assumptions. He uses a slave population natural growth rate of 2.5 percent for all the Southern regions throughout the period, and he assumes that
Charleston customs officials accurately enumerated arrivals of foreign slaves.
Moreover, he is wary of straying too far from Curtin's estimate. Despite his
reluctance to alter overall estimates, Kulikoff provides valuable insights on

natural growth rates and on the volume of the domestic slave trade between 1790 and 1820.[12]

As we have seen, questionable assumptions have contributed to inaccurate estimates of the post-Revolutionary foreign slave trade to North America. The most widely quoted of these, Carey's estimate of 70,000, was based on the erroneous calculations. Relying more on conjecture than on fact, Carey, as will be seen, underestimated the volume by a wide margin.

PART II

Since the North American foreign slave trade records are notably spotty, I have used three different approaches to revise estimates of the volume: re-examining the census data using different natural growth rates, drawing on incomplete extant arriving ship records to compile the number of captives imported, and estimating the carrying-capacity of the North American slaving fleet.

To re-examine the census data, a number of assumptions are made. First, following other scholars, the numbers provided for black Americans in the first, second, third, and fourth U.S. censuses are assumed to be reasonably accurate.[13] Second, except for foreign and domestic migrants and Louisiana, South Carolina, and Georgia populations, a natural growth rate of 2.5 percent per year for Southern free blacks and slaves is assumed.[14]

Third, for South Carolina and Georgia lowcountry slaves on rice plantations, a much lower rate of natural increase is assumed—indeed, no growth at all for the 1780s, and 0.5 percent for the 1790s and the first decade of the 1800s. Rice plantation slaves suffered intensely in the pernicious lowcountry swamp environments of Georgia and South Carolina. Malaria, yellow fever, cholera, dysentery, respiratory diseases, and exposure were just a few of the afflictions attacking the health of slaves in what one member of the Constitutional Convention called "the sickly rice swamps."[15] Harsh work conditions were also the norm. Tidal rice cultivation demanded arduous work in extreme conditions. Slaves often toiled under the broiling sun in the summer and in freezing conditions in the winter, cultivating rice and building and maintaining levees, dams, trunks, canals, and ditches in estuary swamps often while standing in water.[16]

An influx of male captives in the post-Revolutionary era further slowed natural growth. When the Revolution ended, lowcountry rice planters purchased large numbers of Africans to repair, renovate, and cultivate their plantations.[17] Because the overwhelming majority of these slaves were men, the influx of foreign slaves upset the ratio of adult males to females.[18] Inevitably, disproportionate ratios decreased birthrates in slave populations. Moreover, newly arrived Africans died at an alarming rate within the first ten years after arriving in the New World.[19] The combination of lower birth rates and increased mortality in the region depressed the rate of natural growth in the 1780s and quite possibly in the first decade of the 1800s.[20] Although some evidence suggests lowcountry slave life was improving by the turn of the century, an influx of newly arrived African slaves in the late 1790s and the first decade of the 1800s would have offset any increases in the natural growth rate until the 1810s.[21]

Fourth, for lowcountry cotton plantation slaves, an annual natural growth rate of 1.0 percent is assumed. Lowcountry cotton slaves were not forced to work in such extreme conditions as those on rice plantations, but they contracted many of the same diseases that shortened rice slaves' lives. Also, cotton planters purchased many Africans for their lowcountry plantations.[22] An 1810 inventory of Colonel John Stapleton's St. Helena Island plantation indicates that nearly half of the adult workers were newly arrived Africans. The influx of African workers combined with the adverse health environment reduced the overall growth rate.[23]

Fifth, for states and territories that received a large volume of migrants, an annual natural growth rate of 2.2 percent is assumed. Philip D. Morgan, Edward Countryman, and Allan Kulikoff have each argued that forced migration had enormous human consequences. A combination of physical and psychological stress, and the influx of African male migrants increased mortality rates and reduced births in Kentucky, Tennessee, South Carolina, Georgia, Louisiana, and Mississippi.[24]

And sixth, for Louisiana it is assumed that during the 1780s and 1790s the black population experienced no natural growth, and that for the first decade of the 1800s it grew at the annual rate of 1.0 percent. Curtin, Gwendolyn Midlo Hall, and Paul LaChance argue that the black population growth rate in Louisiana was significantly lower than the rate of North American slaves in general. Citing bad health conditions, they estimate the rate of reproductive change ranged from much less than 2.2 percent annually to an annual *decrease* of 2.0 percent.[25]

Using all these assumptions, the following calculations were performed. For the years 1783 to 1810, the natural increase of the black population was calculated for the Southern states and territories using several different rates of increase as outlined above. The projected natural increase was then subtracted from the sum of the growth in the slave population as calculated from censuses and population estimates that are available during the period of this study. In addition, the total number of slaves manumitted during these years was subtracted from the growth of the slave population.

For Virginia and Maryland, the calculations suggest that 117,532 enslaved workers in the region either migrated with their owners to Southern and Western states and territories or were sent to the regions after being sold. For the remaining Southern states and territories, the calculations suggest that these regions experienced a positive inflow of 305,375 blacks. When the number of domestic migrants (117,532) is subtracted from the positive inflow (305,375), the remainder (187,843) is the estimated number of foreign slaves imported from 1783 and 1810. A breakdown of the estimate by decade, state, region, and territory is shown in Table I.

Despite the fact that the new estimate and those made by Carey, Curtin, Fogel, Engerman, and Kulikoff are all based on census records and are calculated in a similar way, they vary widely. The estimate of 187,843 is 2.7 times greater than Carey's, 2.0 times greater than Curtin's, and 1.7 times greater than Kulikoff's. Fogel's and Engerman's estimate is 1.6 times greater than the new estimate.

To provide further insight as to the preciseness of the estimates, new and more thorough research into the extant records of the post-Revolution North American foreign slave trade have been compiled. A breakdown by year, state, region, territory, and colony is shown in Table II. The total of 109,760 people derived from these records of foreign slave arrivals represents 58 percent of the estimate of 187,843 that was calculated using census records. The primary reason for this wide discrepancy is the limited scope of surviving arrival records. Extant contemporary observations, slave trade documents, duties and customs records, and newspaper reports and advertisements recording the volume of the post-Revolution slave trade to North America document much, but not all, of the foreign slave trade.

Extant duties and customs records and newspaper reports reveal the extent of the problem. Only two sets of duties and customs records exist today that could be considered anywhere near complete: the "Duties on Trade at Charleston, 1784–1789," and a Charleston customs house officer's 1820 report on slave vessel arrivals at Charleston from 1804 to 1807.[26] "Duties on Trade

TABLE I: Conjectural Estimates of Net Slave Migration
to and within North America, 1783–1810

	1783–1790	1790–1800	1800–1810	Total
Virginia	<18,000>	<23,582>	<31,423>	<73,005>
Maryland	<12,000>	<14,497>	<18,030>	<44,527>
Kentucky	15,847	8,266	31,005	55,118
Tennessee	–0–	13,584	28,621	42,205
North Carolina	2,500	5,230	–0–	7,730
South Carolina	22,981	27,010	33,445	83,436
Georgia	13,585	27,457	34,327	75,369
Florida	<2,516>	1,000	4,000	2,484
Mississippi	1,000	1,185	12,760	14,945
Louisiana	6,166	3,000	14,922	24,088
Total	**29,563**	**48,653**	**109,627**	**187,843**

Sources: Evarts B. Greene and Virginia D. Harrington, *American Population before the Federal Census of 1790* (New York: Columbia University Press, 1912), 123–86; the United States Bureau of Census, First, Second, Third, and Fourth Censuses; Gwendolyn Midlo Hall, *Africans in Colonial Louisiana: The Development of Afro-Creole Cultures in the Eighteenth Century* (Baton Rouge: Louisiana State University Press, 1992), 280–81; Paul F. LaChance, "Politics of Fear: French Louisianians and the Slave Trade, 1786–1809," *Plantation Societies* 1 (1979): 196–97; David C. Rankin, "The Tannenbaum Thesis Reconsidered: Slavery and Race Relations in Antebellum Louisiana," *Southern Studies* 18 (1979): 21; Patrick Riordan, "Finding Freedom in Florida: Native Peoples, African Americans, and Colonists, 1670–1816," *Florida Historical Quarterly* 75, no. 1 (summer 1996): 34–40; Edwin L. Williams Jr., "Negro Slavery in Florida," *Florida Historical Quarterly* 28, no. 2 (October 1949): 93–110; Daniel H. Usner Jr., *Indians, Settlers, and Slaves in a Frontier Exchange Economy* (Chapel Hill: University of North Carolina, 1990), 112–16; William Dusinberre, *Them Dark Days: Slavery in the American Rice Swamps* (New York: Oxford University Press, 1996), 460–64; George K. Holmes, *The Rice Crop of the United States, 1712–1911* (Washington, D.C.: Unites States Department of Agriculture, Bureau of Statistics, Circular 34, 1912); Edmund Ruffin, *Report on the Commencement and Progress of the Agricultural Survey of South-Carolina, for 1843* (Columbia, S.C.: A. H. Pemberton, 1843), 21–25; and Joyce E. Chaplin, *An Anxious Pursuit: Agricultural Innovation and Modernity in the Lower South, 1730–1815* (Chapel Hill: University of North Carolina Press, 1993), 246–50.

TABLE II: Arrivals of Foreign Slaves in North America, Based upon
Incomplete Newspaper and Port Records for the Years 1783–1810*

	North Carolina	South Carolina	Georgia	Florida	Mississippi	Louisiana	Total
1783	–0–	1,339	270	–0–	–0–	160	1,769
1784	–0–	4,724	530	–0–	–0–	160	5,414
1785	8	4,060	346	–0–	–0–	160	4,574
1786	145	1,623	480	–0–	–0–	–0–	2,248
1787	222	1,066	482	–0–	–0–	381	2,151
1788	13	160	51	–0–	–0–	674	898
1789	40	150	185	–0–	–0–	500	875
1790	2	100	302	–0–	–0–	310	714
Total	430	13,222	2,646	–0–	–0–	2,345	18,643
1791	–0–	–0–	63	–0–	–0–	–0–	63
1792	–0–	450	1,438	–0–	–0–	43	1,931
1793	–0–	150	839	160	–0–	–0–	1,149
1794	–0–	–0–	114	–0–	–0–	–0–	114
1795	–0–	–0–	1,836	–0–	–0–	225	2,061
1796	–0–	160	3,920	–0–	–0–	–0–	4,080
1797	–0–	274	2,022	–0–	–0–	–0–	2,296
1798	–0–	67	1,215	–0–	–0–	–0–	1,282
1799	–0–	45	330	–0–	–0–	20	395
1800	–0–	180	–0–	50	–0–	–0–	230
Total	–0–	1,326	11,777	210	–0–	288	13,601

TABLE II *continued*

1801	–0–	66	–0–	–0–	–0–	–0–	66
1802	–0–	2,654	750	466	–0–	–0–	3,870
1803	–0–	400	717	200	–0–	463	1,780
1804	–0–	8,368	766	235	–0–	737	10,106
1805	–0–	9,519	–0–	192	200	50	9,961
1806	–0–	18,964	150	3	100	708	19,925
1807	–0–	23,787	504	–0–	–0–	880	25,171
1808	–0–	1,177	–0–	–0–	150	288	1,615
1809	–0–	–0–	–0–	–0–	–0–	3,450	3,450
1810	–0–	–0–	–0–	1,281	–0–	291	1,572
Total	**–0–**	**64,935**	**2,887**	**2,377**	**450**	**6,867**	**77,516**
Total 1783–1810	**430**	**79,483**	**17,310**	**2,587**	**450**	**9,500**	**109,760**

Note: For arrivals where the number of slaves is not known, the following informed assumptions have been made. When the number was listed as "several," "few," or "parcel," twenty slaves were landed; when the term "a number" was listed, 30, "small cargo," 35, and "cargo," 50. When the type vessel is known but not the number landed, averages were drawn from data where more facts were known: 80 for a sloop, 100 for a schooner, 150 for a brig, 160 for a snow, and 225 for a ship. For arrivals where neither the number of slaves nor the type vessel is known, 160 was used for arrivals in the 1780s and 1790s and 200 for the first decade of the 1800s. These numbers were arrived at by averaging the number of slaves per vessel for the 1780s, 1790s, and first decade of the 1800s.

at Charleston, 1784–1789" appears to be the most reliable; however, it lists arrivals and clearances for only thirty-five months (May 1784 through March 1787) out of the forty-seven months in the 1780s when South Carolinians could legally import slaves. Also, newspaper advertisements for slave sales and local observations indicate that state officials under-reported arrivals. During 1785, for instance, state officials failed to record a minimum of five of the forty-two known slave vessel arrivals, or at least 12 percent of the total.[27] And finally, although it appears that duties officials were responsible for reporting all of the state's imports and exports, they listed only a few arrivals and clearances for South Carolina ports other than Charleston. Although more than a hundred vessels entered Beaufort and Georgetown annually in the 1780s, duties officials recorded only five arrivals for the four years the report covered. One of these recorded vessels was the *Brothers,* arriving from Gambia with slaves, but others apparently went unrecorded. Records show that credit was advanced to merchants for duties on at least 453 foreign slaves who arrived in Beaufort during these years.[28]

Customs officials also invariably under-reported the number of slaves imported. During 1806, for example, customs officials under-reported the number of arriving captives in thirteen of twenty-four weekly reports. In most cases the reports erred by more than 50 percent.[29] Newspapers fill some of the gaps left by duties and customs records, but unfortunately, they too are often an inconsistent and incomplete (and therefore misleading) source. Newspapers often survived for only a few years—or in some cases, a few months. In the smaller port towns such as Beaufort and Georgetown, South Carolina, where slavers also landed cargoes, local newspapers did not even appear until decades after the legal slave trade ended.[30] Even when newspapers prospered, many editions are missing, or extant copies are unreadable. Other factors further limit the inclusiveness of newspaper data. Reports of clearances to Africa from Northern ports were reduced from the 1790s onward as federal and state legislation against participation in the slave trade began to induce concealment of the true purpose of slave voyages.[31] Moreover, it appears that newspapers were largely dependent on the inaccurate daily and weekly reports of customs officials for information on the trade. In 1785, for instance, the *State Gazette of South Carolina* failed to report thirty-eight out of a total of fifty-four, or 70 percent of known Charleston arrivals.

Slave sale advertisements further cloud the picture. Between the time a vessel first appeared in port and a sale was conducted, it was not unusual for a sizable percentage of a slave cargo to disappear. After ships arrived, slaves who had managed to survive the extreme conditions of the middle passage were physically exhausted, emotionally depleted, and dangerously susceptible to disease. Often the most ill or vulnerable died before they could be sold. Other slaves, called "privileged slaves," were awarded as remuneration to the master and officers of a vessel who could sell them without paying the usual import duty. Of the remainder, a large number often went to planters or traders who had placed an order with the merchant handling the sale before a ship departed for Africa.[32] Deceased, privileged, and pre-sold slaves were, of course, not available for sale and were therefore not listed in advertisements. In 1807, for example, Customs reported 350 slaves arriving on the *Ann*, while an ad listed only 250 available for sale.[33]

For Louisiana and Mississippi from 1783 to 1810, even fewer extant records document the arrival of foreign slave ships.[34] According to colonial Louisiana historians Gwendolyn Midlo Hall and Paul LaChance, French and Spanish colonial officials failed to record slave imports. This is especially troublesome because, during the French and Spanish colonial periods, census records suggest that merchants and planters imported more than 30,000 foreign enslaved workers into Louisiana, Mississippi, and Florida.[35]

Documenting smuggling activities also presents a challenge. Census calculations suggest that during the 1790s the volume of the foreign slave trade may have approached 48,653 slaves, which is more than three times the 13,601 persons documented through extant records. Some of the discrepancy can be explained by lost and destroyed records and incompetent customs officials, but bits and pieces of evidence indicate that smuggling was widespread during the 1790s and 1800s.[36]

Smuggling was condoned, especially in and around Charleston and Savannah. Several months after the Georgia legislature enacted a ban against further imports in 1798, an advertisement in a Savannah newspaper boldly announced the sale of 330 "New Negroes from Angola."[37] Later that year, South Carolina officials seized the schooner *Phoebe* with its cargo of forty-five Africans.[38] During the last six months of 1799 alone, officials filed six actions for breaking the federal law of 1794 that prohibited U.S. participation in the foreign traffic. Despite the seizures and filings, officials failed to stop or even slow smugglers. When the schooner *Hannah* was seized on August 30, 1803, near Savannah, a local official lamented that "this business of smuggling the Negroes of St. Domingo into this state . . . is becoming truly alarming."[39]

In a letter to his employer (James D'Wolf, the owner of the brig *Nancy*), on January 7, 1802, Charles Clark described how he and other slavers smuggled foreign slaves into Charleston:

> When I wrote you before, I was bound out of the city after my cargo, which had been on the beach to the northward of Charleston. I found them all well, and much better than I expected, for the weather was cold. They had no clothes, and no shelter except for the sandhills and cedar trees, and no person, to take care of them. I arrived in Charleston with them on the 14th of Decr. [1801] without being troubled. . . . I don't see that the Trade stops much, for they come in town 2 or 3 hundred some nights. I believe there has been landed since New Years as much as 500 slaves. They land them outside the harbor and march them in at night. 2 or 3 vessels has come in from Africa in ballast. The revenue cutter seized one brig bound from N. Orleans to Charleston. She was cleared from N. O. by calling them passengers. They clear out from there and go into Havana "in distress," and ship from there to the U. States, or sell if the price is high. I think there will be more distressed vessels this winter than ever before. I left on the [African] coast 14 vessels belonging to the U. States, a great part of them for Charleston.[40]

To help in overcoming the obstacles presented by lost and destroyed records, undocumented voyages, and misleading extant records, a third means of calculating North American foreign slave imports in the first post-Revolutionary generation used here is estimating the slave-carrying capacity of the North American slave ships employed in the transatlantic slave trade. Many scholars prefer this method because much more consistent evidence exists on the number of ships involved in the slave trade than on individual voyages.[41] For a breakdown of incomplete documented North American slave voyages and carrying-capacity, see Table III.

To estimate the slave-carrying capacity, three different sources—extant records of individual voyages, other scholars' research, and contemporary observations—are used. In the 1780s, for example, Table III indicates that North American merchants sponsored ninety-six voyages. However, in 1789 a

TABLE III: Annual North American Slaving Voyages and Carrying Capacity Based on Incomplete Newspaper and Port Records for the Years 1783–1810*

Year	Number of Voyages	Tonnage	Carrying Capacity
1783	3	176	299
1784	6	462	768
1785	15	1,174	1,941
1786	20	1,368	2,274
1787	13	734	1,189
1788	12	703	1,197
1789	14	852	1,947
1790	13	842	1,430
Total	**96**	**6,311**	**11,045**
1791	24	2,355	3,516
1792	31	3,333	4,996
1793	27	2,862	4,293
1794	28	2,828	4,242
1795	43	4,285	6,428
1796	47	5,436	8,154
1797	21	2,095	3,143
1798	18	1,646	2,469
1799	43	3,230	4,848
1800	25	2,065	3,098
Total	**307**	**30,135**	**45,187**
1801	16	1,663	1,996
1802	24	3,008	3,610
1803	20	2,474	2,869
1804	54	7,105	8,526
1805	109	14,486	17,383
1806	120	17,165	20,598
1807	119	15,890	19,068
1808	11	1,565	1,878

TABLE III *continued*

Year	Number of Voyages	Tonnage	Carrying Capacity
1809	–0–	–0–	–0–
1810	–0–	–0–	–0–
Total	473	63,356	75,928
Totals	876	99,802	132,160

Note: To estimate the carrying capacity of the North American slavers, the following assumptions have been made following the work of Roger Anstey and Stephen Behrendt. First, for vessels where the type is known, during the 1780s slave "ships" averaged 110 tons and carried 187 people, brigs averaged 61 tons and carried 104 people, snows averaged 76 tons and carried 129 people, schooners averaged 50 tons and carried 85 people, and sloops averaged 45 tons and carried 77 people. For those vessels that the type and number of slaves disembarked are not known, they averaged 66 tons and carried 255 people, brigs averaged 103 tons and carried 155 people, snows averaged 100 tons and carried 150 people, schooners averaged 77 tons and carried 116 people; and sloops averaged 62 tons and carried 84 people. For those vessels that the type and number of slaves disembarked are not known, they averaged 96 tons and carried 144 people. For the 1790s, slave "ships" averaged 190 tons and carried 255 people, brigs averaged 103 tons and carried 155 people; snows averaged 100 tons and carried 150 people, schooners averaged 77 tons and carried 116 people, and sloops averaged 62 tons and carried 84 people. For those vessels that the type and number are not known, they averaged 96 tons and carried 144 people. For the first decade of the 1800s, slave "ships" averaged 202 tons and carried 242 people, brigs averaged 117 tons and carried 140 people, snows averaged 216 tons and carried 260 people, schooners averaged 84 tons and carried 100 people; and sloops averaged 65 tons and carried 74 people. For those vessels that the type and number of slaves disembarked are not known, they averaged 130 tons and carried 156 people. Also, it should be noted that many vessels were active in the trade for more than one year; therefore, they were counted each year they were in service.

British official estimated that as many as forty vessels had been fitted out in New England in that year alone for the African trade.[42] Based on this observation and others, the carrying capacity of North American vessels in the 1780s is increased by 20 percent to 13,254 people. Allowing for known and foreign disembarkations, North American slavers would have landed an additional 4,460 people in the United States.[43]

During the 1790s, North American involvement in the Atlantic slave trade increased despite the fact that most states and the federal government banned participation in the trade. As we have seen, instead of withdrawing from the trade as the lawmakers had hoped, slavers began concealing their activities. In doing so, they made documenting the slave trade during that period all the more difficult. However, by combining information from Table III with the research of Roger Anstey and Herbert S. Klein, a more accurate estimate of the size of the 1790s American slaving fleet can be made. Table III reveals that American merchants sponsored at least 307 slaving voyages to Africa during this decade. However, Klein documented 111 voyages to Cuba alone in 1797, and Anstey conjectured that 375 American ships landed Africans in the Americas in the 1790s.[44] To compensate for the difference between the number of American slavers that Table III suggests were operating during the decade and Klein's and Anstey's numbers, the estimated carrying capacity is raised by 30 percent to 58,743 people for the 1790s. Allowing for known and foreign disembarkations, North American slavers would have landed an additional 13,720 people in the United States.[45]

In the first decade of the 1800s, American participation continued to increase. When South Carolina officials lifted the prohibition on foreign slave imports, the number of documented voyages skyrocketed from 20 in 1803 to 120 in 1806. To compensate for unreported voyages and lost records, the estimate of the carrying capacity is revised upward by 10 percent to 83,521 people. Allowing for known and foreign disembarkations, North American slavers would have landed an additional 24,603 people in the United States.[46]

On the basis of the varied approaches to population data given above, it is now possible to put together revised figures for the overall North American slave imports for each decade after the Revolution. From population censuses, it is estimated that during the 1780s, merchants and planters imported 29,563 foreign slaves into North America. Documented arrivals suggest that a minimum of 18,643 people arrived. The most problematic region is Louisiana.

Spanish censuses indicate that the black population increased by 6,166 people during the seven years. Assuming that the black population experienced no natural growth, then imports would have accounted for all of the increase in population from 1783 to 1790.[47] Taking into consideration the fact that Spanish officials recorded few slave ship arrivals, the Louisiana import total is increased to 6,166 to compensate for the discrepancy. It is also estimated that Spanish slavers landed an additional five hundred African captives in Florida and five hundred in Mississippi.[48] The 1780s slave-carrying-capacity calculations suggest that North American slaving vessels landed 4,460 more captives in the United States than incomplete records of arrivals indicate. When this figure and the adjustments to Louisiana, Mississippi, and Florida are added to the total of documented arrivals, they produce a new estimate of 27,924 for the decade.

The 1790s present a much greater challenge. Census calculations suggest imports increased to 48,653, but documented arrivals total only 13,601. The carrying capacity of the American slave fleet can help fill a portion of the gaps created by the lack of extant records, but not all. Census calculations suggest that during the 1790s American slaving vessels carried 13,720 more African captives to North America than incomplete records of arrivals indicate. Part of the problem lies with the Spanish colonies. As they did in the 1780s, census records indicate many more slaves arrived than extant records document. To compensate for the difference, the Florida import total is raised 2,000 captives, Mississippi 1,000, and Louisiana 2,000. When adjustments to United States arrivals, Louisiana, Mississippi, and Florida are added to the total of documented arrivals, they produce a new estimate of 32,321 people for the decade.

In the first decade of the 1800s, census calculations, documented arrivals, and carrying capacity are much more in agreement. Census calculations suggest that 109,627 African and Caribbean slaves arrived in North America. Documented arrivals total 77,516 people, or 71 percent of the census estimate. The estimate of the carrying capacity of American slavers suggests that an additional 24,603 people landed in the United States. In the deep South during the French and Spanish periods, officials continued to ignore slave ship arrivals. Therefore, based on census records, the volume of Louisiana, Mississippi, and Florida shipments is increased by 7,500 people. The adjustments to the United States, Louisiana, Mississippi, and Florida volumes raises the total number of foreign imports totals 109,619 people for the first decade of the 1800s.[49] When the estimates of all three decades (27,924 for the 1780s,

32,321 for the 1790s, and 109,619 for the first decade of the 1800s), are combined, they total 169,864 foreign slaves. For a breakdown of the revised estimate of foreign slave imports by state, territory, and colony, see Table IV.

The new estimate of nearly 170,000 is much larger than earlier projections by Carey (70,000) and Curtin (92,000), and much smaller than the one made by Fogel and Engerman (291,000). It is also more accurate because calculations are based on more exact black population growth rates. Moreover, the appraisal is augmented by the use of North American slave trade records of arrivals as well as slave-ship carrying capacities. And finally, new estimates of French and Spanish imports are included.

This reassessment has important demographic, economic, political, social, and cultural implications. Conservative estimates of the number of Africans landed in North America during the colonial and post-Revolution eras total 430,000.[50] When the new post-Revolutionary estimate of 170,000 people is factored into the overall total, it appears that North American imports exceeded 500,000 persons during the period. This appraisal also bears on the overall volume of the transatlantic trade. Curtin estimated that from 1451 to 1870, 10 million African captives were imported into the Americas.[51] The difference (78,000) between the new estimate (170,000) and Curtin's (92,000) totals less than 1 percent of Curtin's overall estimate of imports into North America from 1783 to 1810. However, when one considers the fact that numerous regions outside of the Caribbean and Brazil, like North America, imported Africans, and several carriers besides the British, French, and Portuguese, such as the United States, transported captives, it becomes obvious that more inquiries regarding peripheral importers and carriers could raise the overall figure above Curtin's 10 million projection.

The estimate also indicates that from 1783 to 1810 Africans were by far the largest ethnic group of immigrants who arrived in North America. Based on the 170,000 figure, foreign slaves made up nearly 45 percent of the 380,000 immigrants who arrived during the period.[52] Although these Africans did not constitute as high a proportion in the Lower South's total population as they had in the colonial era, they had a significant impact on the South and on the nation. By importing Africans, white Southerners increased their representation in the lower house of Congress and electoral college votes.

Importing enslaved Africans also aided the Southern economy. The reopening of the slave trade after the Revolution allowed lowcountry planters to re-entrench and sustain slavery in the lowcountry. Planters and farmers were

TABLE IV: Estimate of Foreign Slave Trade to North America, 1783–1810

State, Territory, or Colony Where Disembarked	Number Disembarked			Total Disembarked
	1783–1790	1791–1800	1801–1810	
North Carolina	430	–0–	–0–	430
South Carolina	15,149	11,406	79,796	106,351
Georgia	5,179	15,417	7,562	28,158
Florida	500	2,210	4,071	6,781
Mississippi	500	1,000	5,517	7,017
Louisiana	6,166	2,288	2,673	21,127
Total	27,924	32,321	109,619	169,864

also able to extend slavery to the backcountry regions of Georgia and South Carolina. Moreover, the inexpensive labor that the foreign slave trade provided helped fuel the cotton boom. Without foreign slave imports, farmers and planters would have had to rely solely on domestic imports during the 1790s and 1800s. A limited supply of labor would have increased slave prices quite possibly to such high levels that most farmers and planters could not have afforded to purchase slaves.[53]

And finally, this reappraisal suggests that in the Lower South and South-west the long period of evolution of slavery and black society did not end in 1790 as some have argued.[54] Indeed, any understanding of African American societies and cultures in the nineteenth-century South should begin with an appreciation of the fact that Africans continued to arrive in large numbers until 1810. Undoubtedly, their presence in black communities had an impact on the lives of slaves.

NOTES

1. Peter H. Wood, *Black Majority: Negroes in South Carolina from 1607 through the Stono Rebellion* (New York: W. W. Norton, 1974), ix.

2. See Norman K. Risjord, *Jefferson's America, 1760–1815* (Madison, Wis.: Madison House Publishers, Inc., 1991), 178; and John B. Boles, *The South through Time,*

A History of an American Region, 2 vols. (Englewood Cliffs, N.J.: Prentice Hall, 1995), 1:35–41.

3. See William W. Freehling, "The Founding Fathers and Slavery," *American Historical Society* 77, no. 1 (February 1972): 93; and Winthrop D. Jordan, *White over Black: American Attitudes towards the Negro, 1550–1812* (New York: W. W. Norton, 1968), 324.

4. Philip D. Curtin, *Atlantic Slave Trade: A Census* (Madison: University of Wisconsin Press, 1969), 73, 140.

5. Henry Charles Carey, *The Slave Trade, Domestic and Foreign: Why It Exists, and How It May Be Extinguished* (Philadelphia: John A. Norton, 1859), 16–21.

6. Ibid., 18.

7. Ibid., 16–21.

8. Curtin, *Atlantic Slave Trade,* 72.

9. Ibid., 75, 216.

10. Robert William Fogel and Stanley L. Engerman, *Time on the Cross: The Economics of American Negro Slavery,* 2 vols. (Boston: Little, Brown, 1974), 1:20–29.

11. For discussions of Fogel and Engerman's estimate, see Roger Anstey, "The Volume of the North American Slave-Carrying Trade From Africa, 1761–1810," *Revue française d'Histoire d'Outre-Mer* 62, no. 2 (1975): 63; and Philip D. Morgan, "African Migration," in *Encyclopedia of American Social History,* ed. Mary Kupiec Cayton, Elliot J. Gorn, Peter W. Williams, 3 vols. (New York: Charles Scribner's Sons, 1993), 2:802.

12. Allan Kulikoff, "Uprooted Peoples: Black Migrants in the Age of the American Revolution, 1790–1820," in *Slavery and Freedom in the Age of Revolution,* ed. Ira Berlin and Ronald Hoffman (Urbana: University of Illinois Press, 1986), 143–74. Kulikoff estimates that more than 20,000 foreign slaves were imported into South Carolina, Louisiana, and Mississippi from 1782 to 1790; 30,000 Africans were imported in the 1790s; and 63,000 more arrived in the 1800s. Of the 63,000, Kulikoff suggests that 39,000 were imported legally into Charleston between 1804 and 1808 and that 24,000 were smuggled into South Carolina, Georgia, and along the Gulf coast in the 1800s.

13. Kulikoff, "Uprooted Peoples," 168–69. Although scholars have discovered a number of discrepancies in the censuses, most agree that the rate of under- or over-recording of the 1790, 1800, and 1810 censuses was insignificant.

14. Allan Kulikoff, "A 'Prolific' People: Black Population Growth in the Chesapeake Colonies, 1700–1790," *Southern Studies* 16 (1977): 409–14.

15. Oliver Ellsworth and Max Farrand, eds., *Records of the Federal Convention of 1787,* 4 vols. (New Haven: Yale University Press, 1937) 2:371.

16. Julia Floyd Smith, *Slavery and Rice Culture in Low Country Georgia, 1750–1860* (Knoxville: University of Tennessee Press, 1985), 130–32; William Dusinberre, *Them Dark Days: Slavery in the American Rice Swamps* (New York: Oxford University Press, 1996), 48–83. Dusinberre estimates that in the mid–nineteenth century the slave populations on tidal swamp rice plantations experienced a 4 percent decennial growth rate (p. 415). This was far below the slave norm of the whole South of 26.6 percent. He claims rice slave mortality rates were even worse in the eighteenth century and early nineteenth century before the reform movement of 1820. The 4 percent decennial rate equals less than a 0.5 annual natural growth rate.

17. Sylvia Frey, *Water from the Rock: Black Resistence in a Revolutionary War* (Princeton: Princeton University Press, 1991), 210–14.

18. Kulikoff, "Uprooted Peoples," 153–57.

19. Ibid., 169.

20. Philip D. Morgan, "Black Society in the Lowcountry, 1760–1810," in *Slavery and Freedom in the Age of Revolution,* ed. Ira Berlin and Ronald Hoffman (Urbana: University of Illinois Press, 1986), 84–89. Morgan calculated that the natural growth rate of South Carolina's black population was 2.2 in the 1780s and 1790s and 2.0 percent in the first decade of the 1800s. He attributed the low rate (in the Chesapeake it averaged 2.5) to the large number of Africans in the population and to the harmful living and working conditions in the lowcountry. The natural growth rates Morgan used in "Black Society" were slightly higher than the rates used here, and thus his estimate of the number of foreign and domestic imports were slightly lower. For instance, he estimated that between 1801 and 1810, 30,195 slaves were imported into South Carolina (p. 87). For the same period, lower growth rates produce a new estimate of 33,445 slaves (see Table I). However, apparently Morgan later reassessed his previous estimates of slave natural growth rates and slave migrants. In an article published in 1993, Morgan posited that many more Africans arrived after the Revolution than previously thought, about 140,000 in the first decade of the nineteenth century alone. He based his new estimate on the work of Fogel and Engerman (see Morgan, "African Migration," 802).

21. Morgan, "Black Society," 91–92.

22. To estimate the number of lowcountry cotton slaves, the number of lowcountry rice workers was subtracted from the total slave population of the lowcountry counties. To arrive at an estimate of the number of rice slaves, the lowcountry annual rice production was divided by the average of clean rice produced per slave. For rice production, see Dusinberre, *Them Dark Days,* 460–62; Edmund Ruffin, *Report on the Commencement and Progress of the Agricultural History of South-Carolina, for 1843* (Columbia, S.C.: A. H. Pemberton, 1843), 21–25; and George K. Holmes, *Rice*

Crop of the United States, 1712–1911 (Washington, D.C.: United States Department of Agriculture, Bureau of Statistics, Circular 34, 1912). For rice worker output, see Joyce E. Chaplin, *Anxious Pursuit: Agricultural Innovation and Modernity in the Lower South* (Chapel Hill: University of North Carolina Press, 1993), 246–50.

23. Smith, *Slavery and Rice Culture*, 131–32; and Inventory of slaves belonging to Colonel Stapleton on his Plantation at St. Helena Island, South Carolina, John Stapleton Papers, Caroliniana Library, University of South Carolina, Columbia, South Carolina.

24. Morgan, "Black Society," 84–90; Kulikoff, "Black Migrants," 153–57; and Edward Countryman, unpublished paper on Antebellum Black Migrants.

25. Curtin, *Atlantic Slave Trade*, 83; Paul LaChance, "Politics of Fear: French Louisianians and the Slave Trade, 1786–1809," *Plantation Society* 1 (1996): 196–97; and Gwendolyn Midlo Hall, *Africans in Colonial Louisiana: The Development of Afro-Creole Cultures in the Eighteenth Century* (Baton Rouge: Louisiana State University Press, 1992), 280–81.

26. "Duties on Trade at Charleston, 1784–1787," South Carolina Department of Archives, Columbia, South Carolina; and *Annals of the Congress of the United States, Sixteenth Congress, Second Session; Comprising the Period from November 13, 1820 to March 3, 1821, Inclusive* (Washington, D.C.: Gales and Seaton, 1855), 70–78.

27. For newspaper reports of arrivals not found in "Duties on Trade at Charleston, 1784–1789," see *State Gazette of South Carolina*, 25 August and 13 October 1785. The *Prudent* arrived on August 25 and the *Greyson* on October 13. For local observation, see Nathaniel Russel to Joseph and Joshua Grafton, 2 July 1785, quoted in *Documents Illustrative of the History of the Slave Trade to America*, ed. Elizabeth Donnan, 4 vols. (1930–1935; reprint ed., New York: Octagon Books, 1969), 4:478–80.

28. "Duties on Trade at Charleston, 1784–1789," 360; and Lark Emerson Adams, ed., *Journals of the House of Representatives, 1785–1786* (Columbia: University of South Carolina Press, 1979), 567.

29. *Annals*, 73–74; and appendix A.

30. For information on extant newspapers for the period 1783–1810, see Clarence S. Brigham, *History and Bibliography of American Newspapers, 1690–1820*, 2 vols. (Worcester, Mass.: American Antiquarian Society, 1947).

31. Roger Anstey, "The Volume of the North American Slave-Carrying Trade from Africa, 1761–1810," *Revue française d'Histoire d'Outre-Mer* 62, no. 2 (1975): 52.

32. "Journal of the Ship *Mary,* 1795–1796," in Donnan, *Documents*, 3:360–78; "Duties on Trade at Charleston," 16 October 1784; and Robert Mackay, *Letters of Robert Mackay to His Wife, Written from Ports in America and England, 1795–1816,* (Athens: University of Georgia Press, 1949), 302–3.

33. *Charleston Courier,* 24 July 1807. Captains reported to customs officials the number of slaves onboard when they entered Charleston harbor. Irregularly, this information was passed on to the local newspaper and included in the "Marine List."

34. Foreign slave ships are defined as slave vessels neither registered in North America nor owned by North Americans.

35. Hall, *Africans in Colonial Louisiana,* 277–82; and LaChance, "Politics of Fear," 196–97.

36. W. E. Burghardt Du Bois, *The Suppression of the African Slave-Trade to the United States of America, 1638–1870* (Baton Rouge: Louisiana State University Press, 1965), 230–46. When the Revolution ended in 1783, the three lower Southern states, North Carolina, South Carolina, and Georgia, permitted the importation of foreign slaves. The South Carolina legislature prohibited the trade in 1787, North Carolina in 1794, and Georgia in 1798. From 1798 until 1804, no states allowed the importation of foreign slaves. South Carolina lifted its prohibition in 1804, and foreign slaves were imported until the federal government banned the trade in 1808. In Louisiana the slave trade was open from 1782 until the Spanish governor prohibited further imports in early 1795. The prohibition remained in effect until 1800 when the prohibition was lifted for *bozals,* or slaves imported directly from Africa. When the United States took possession of Louisiana in 1804, it banned the direct shipment of Africans but allowed the trans-shipment of newly arrived Africans from Charleston. Mississippi became part of the United States in 1797, six years earlier than Louisiana. Through New Orleans and Natchez, foreign slaves were imported into Mississippi from 1782 to 1790 and from 1797 to 1803. After 1803, Natchez, like New Orleans, received trans-shipments of newly arrived Africans from Charleston.

37. *Columbia Museum and Savannah Advertiser,* 19 March 1799.

38. Helen Tunnicliff Catterall, ed., *Judicial Cases Concerning American Slavery and the Negro,* 5 vols. (Washington, D.C.: Carnegie Institute, 1932) 2:390.

39. *Providence Gazette,* 20 August 1803.

40. Charles Clark to James D'Wolf, 7 January 1802, quoted in George L. Howe, *Mount Hope: A New England Chronicle* (New York: Viking, 1959), 122–23. Newspaper "Marine Lists" report several vessels entered Charleston and Savannah from Africa "in ballast." Evidently, as Clark infers, slave vessel masters smuggled slaves ashore and then entered Charleston or Savannah. This strategy would have allowed them to settle accounts with local merchants, take on much-needed provisions, and repair their vessels.

41. For previous estimates of the North American carrying capacity, see Curtin, *Atlantic Slave Trade,* 212; Anstey, "Volume of the North American Slave-Carrying

Trade," 61–65; and Tommy Todd Hamm, "The American Slave Trade with Africa, 1620–1807" (Ph.D. diss., Indiana University, 1975), 279–84. For methodologies and estimates using slave vessel carrying capacities, see Anstey, "The Volume and Profitability of the British Slave Trade, 1761–1807," 10–12; David Richardson, "The Eighteenth-Century British Slave Trade: Estimates of the Volume and Coastal Distribution in Africa," *Research in Economic History* 12 (1989): 151–95; Joseph E. Inikori, "Measuring the Atlantic Slave Trade: An Assessment of Curtin and Anstey," *Journal of African History* 17 (1976): 197–223; and Stephen D. Behrendt, "The Annual Volume and Regional Distribution of the British Slave Trade, 1780–1807," *Journal of African History* 38 (1997): 187–211.

42. Petition of Bristol (England) merchants, 12 May 1789, quoted in Elizabeth Donnan, "New England Slave Trade," *New England Quarterly* 3 (1930): 255.

43. This estimate was arrived at by increasing the carrying capacity of the vessels for which the disembarkation point is unknown (6,195) by 20 percent, and then multiplying the product (7,434) by .60 to allow for shipments to foreign ports.

44. Anstey, "Volume of the North American Slave-Carrying Trade," 60–65.

45. This estimate was arrived at by increasing the carrying capacity of the vessels for which the disembarkation point is unknown (21,107) by 30 percent and then multiplying the product (27,439) by .50 to allow for shipments to foreign ports.

46. It appears that between 1804 and 1807, newspapers and customs officials reported most of North American slave voyages. Therefore, the carrying capacity is raised by only 10 percent to allow for illegal voyages between 1801 and 1803 and between 1808 and 1810. This estimate was arrived at by increasing the carrying capacity of the vessels for which the disembarkation point is unknown (31,952) by 10 percent and then multiplying the product (35,162) by .70 to allow for shipments to foreign ports.

47. For Spanish census data, see LaChance, "Politics of Fear," 196. For Curtin's discussion of Louisiana black population, see Curtin, *Atlantic Slave Trade*, 83.

48. Because only a fraction of the foreign slave imports to Spanish and French colonies in North America during the years of this study have been documented, I will rely mainly on estimates of imports generated from census reports.

49. LaChance, "Politics of Fear," 162–97; and Appendix A.

50. Curtin, *The Atlantic Slave Trade*, 268. Curtin estimated that about 288,000 Africans were imported during the colonial era: 92,000 from 1783 to 1810, and 50,000 from 1811 to 1861.

51. Ibid., 265–73.

52. Marcus Lee Hansen, *The Atlantic Migration, 1607–1860* (Cambridge, Mass.: Harvard University Press, 1940), 77; Michael Kraus, *Immigration, the American Mosaic: From Pilgrims to Modern Refugees* (Princeton, N.J.: Van Norstrand, 1966),

19; and David M. Reimers, "Immigration," in *Encyclopedia of American Social History,* ed. Mary Kupiec Cayton, Elliot J. Gorn, and Peter W. Williams (New York: Charles Scribner's Sons, 1993), 1:579–81. The scholars estimate that from 1783 to 1815 about 250,000 English, French, and Irish immigrants landed in North America. Hansen and Kraus ignore Africans in their estimates and discussions of immigration during the period. Reimers discusses African immigrants, but argues that immigration during the period was limited.

53. For discussion of slave prices and the foreign slave trade, see Fogel and Engerman, *Time on the Cross,* 1: 86–94.

54. Donald R. Wright, *African Americans in the Colonial Era: From African Origins through the American Revolution* (Arlington Heights, Ill.: Harlan Davidson, Inc., 1990), 3–5.

3

"Old Miss Sho' Was Good to Us . . . 'Cause She Was Raisin' Us to Wuk for Her"
Widowed Planters and Paternalism in the Old South

KIRSTEN E. WOOD

In early July 1840, a South Carolina cotton planter participated in a ritual familiar to all historians of the Old South: inspecting slaves and disbursing their provisions. While this instance of the ritual resembled countless similar performances of command and dependence in the records of the Old South, it seems particularly poignant because it occurred on July 4th. More importantly, in one key particular it departed from what historians have considered the norm: in this case, the planter was a woman, newly widowed Natalie Sumter of Sumter County. Like many a male planter, Natalie Sumter handed out food allowances to the slaves and "spoke to them" while they were assembled, a ritual of provisioning and instruction that demonstrated the planter's supposedly parental care for her bondpeople. Sumter also paid particular attention to the "negro children," most probably because she recognized that future prosperity depended at least in part on capital accumulation, in which slave children figured largely. Her financial interest in her slaves becomes even more clear if we consider the final stage in her performance, when she distributed and "wrote down all their new hoes." Distributing the hoes to the slaves assembled as a group underlined their collective obligation to labor for their owner, while assigning each hand to a particular hoe made each individually responsible for his or her work and for the loss or damage of a hoe, the most common tool in cotton agriculture. The activities of widowed planters in the eastern portion of the Old South reveal the availability of paternalism to female slaveholders and provide new insights into its impact on slaveholding in the oldest states of the Old South: Virginia, the Carolinas, and Georgia.[1]

As generally used in the history of the Old South, *paternalism* signifies slaveholders' attempts to control their slaves' characters and work habits not just through coercion but also through the use of incentives and rituals in which owners appeared to be kindly but stern parents to their slaves. As Charles Joyner has argued, "The real source of the master's power rested less on his use of brute force than on his ability to get the slaves to recognize his authority. And the remarkable extent to which the master was able to do that was in large part due to his ability to exploit symbolic behavior as an instrument of power." Paternalist thinking idealized slavery as a reciprocal exchange of benevolent but firm rule on the part of the owner and grateful submission on the part of the slave. Paternalism called for moralistic interventions into slaves' sex lives, health, religious observances, parenting, and cleanliness. It rationalized owners' profit mongering, violence, the institution of slavery, and the Southern social order as a whole as being in the best interests of all members of a plantation community. Paternalistic rituals like Sumter's distribution of provisions highlighted slaves' dependence on their owners, expressed vertical power relations, and provided a stage for reciprocal performances of benevolence and gratitude. Occasionally, such rituals gave slaves an opportunity to satisfy some of their own needs as well.[2]

The term paternalism reflects the patriarchal assumptions of mainstream early American society: possessing the ultimate authority in the household, the father was at once protector, provider, master, and judge of all his dependents. (As William Gilmore Simms suggested in 1850, this included his wife, to whom the husband should be as a father.)[3] Building on this image of paternal authority, which shaped the legal and economic as well as the social position of white women, numerous historians have argued that the Old South effectively prevented slaveholding women from wielding any independent authority over households and slaves—that is, authority not proximately and explicitly backed up by their fathers or husbands. According to Elizabeth Fox-Genovese, for example, a woman could not "aspire to be the head of a household." Because a woman could embody neither the physical nor the political attributes of the presumptively male master, Fox-Genovese continues, a woman could not be a master. In his study of the eighteenth-century lowcountry, Robert Olwell agrees that a female master was a contradiction in terms. Similarly, Philip Schwarz characterizes widows (and spinsters) as legally and socially "weak," a characterization that might work for the socioeconomically marginal but does not capture the power and authority of widowed planters.[4]

A number of other scholars, however, have begun to complicate this picture in several ways. Cynthia Kierner points out both the tension and the variability within Southern gender ideology, and both she and Elizabeth Varon, among others, document not just the physical presence but also the conceptual importance of women (usually married ones) in several aspects of the public sphere, including sociability, politics, and reform. Among slaveholders, widows operated less visibly than other women in the realms of reform, politics, and sociability, but considerably more so in law and the economy. And through their adoption of paternalistic rituals and beliefs, they demonstrated the strength and flexibility of early national and antebellum proslavery ideology despite the centrality of patriarchal power over women within the construct itself. Their paternalism also illuminates the complex structural and interpersonal factors that shaped slaves' actions.[5]

Like slaveholding wives, widows oversaw the domestic production and housework of enslaved women and children, which often included making and distributing slaves' clothes and sometimes their food. Widows also assumed new tasks that were usually the province of male slaveholders: they inspected fields, directed agricultural labor, bought and sold crops and supplies, and oversaw or administered discipline. This expanded mandate vastly increased widows' control over slaves, even over slaves they only held for life or managed for their minor children.[6] As heads of households, widows made decisions about when, where, and how their slaves would labor and their crops would be marketed and about whether slaves would be sold, hired out, or permitted to marry off the plantation. Planter widows also decided where their children would go to school, investigated the backgrounds of potential spouses, and helped their sons begin their careers as planters, lawyers, merchants, or politicians. As such, they were, in fact, fulfilling paternal, not maternal functions. Even if the term *maternalism* did not already mean something quite particular in the history of welfare and feminism, it would not be the right word for planter widows' conception of slavery.[7]

During widowhood, planter women's managerial practices reflected their increased responsibility for the daily enforcement and profit making of slavery. Influenced by new necessities and old prejudices, they thought quite detachedly about their slaves' profits and costs, and they constructed themselves within a gender paradigm that increasingly stressed feminine benevolence, rarely if ever seeing the two as incompatible. Events immediately following their husbands' deaths helped widows cultivate this detachment. (Beginning to cope with their managerial responsibilities while still in the first stages of mourning, itself a very gendered experience, helped slaveholding widows feel certain of their essential femininity even as they undertook increasingly masculine-identified tasks.) In particular, the process of inventorying, valuing, and dividing slaves focused slaveholders' attention on slaves' price tags even as they also recognized individuals' humanity through special legacies from, or remembrances of, the dead. The language of sale and distribution itself bespoke this reification: slaveowners put slaves in their pocket or put them in a hat. These were not so much metaphors as they were testaments to the fungible nature of human chattel. In this context, widows' conduct, particularly their use of incentives, reflected the desire to maintain stability and at least the semblance of harmony, for the sake of profit and their own material and emotional comfort. Dosia Harris understood this implicitly: "Old Miss sho' was good to us . . . 'cause she was raisin' us to wuk for her."[8]

During their marriages, slaveholding women used incentives chiefly to shape and reward house slaves; in widowhood, they both continued this practice and sought ways to influence the entire household, especially in the antebellum decades. Georgia planter Martha Jackson gave small gratuities to domestic slaves: twelve and a half cents "to Polly in Athens for sleeping in Martha's room" and twenty-five cents "to Emma to purchase a little present for [her] children." Natalie Sumter provided her old slaves with a special feast of "soup & meat & baked apples & peaches." Old soldier Tom received some of her husband's old clothes, while Old Venus got "a new cotton flannel gown," Priscilla a new frock and black apron. Sumter also permitted Delia, the two Sallys, Matilda, Esther, and Hampton to attend a wedding on another plantation.[9] In addition to these gifts to individuals, widows also made more systematic gestures. Planters frequently gave some kind of Christmas treat to their slaves, which might include extra food, some whiskey, and a break from the usual work regimen. Sylvia Cannon's mistress would "kill hogs en a cow every Christmas an give us all de eggnog en liquor we want dat day." Lacking the resources to give her slaves much by way of special rations, Annie Poore granted an unusual two weeks' holiday from field work, along with permission to hunt possums and rabbits. Frederick Douglass concluded that planters gave their slaves alcohol at Christmas to make them sick of liberty.[10] While such may not have been the conscious or unconscious intent of most planters, the general practice of Christmas privileges clearly linked planters' favors to slaves' productivity.

More importantly, many slaveholders allowed their slaves to sell crops they grew on the side or purchased livestock or produce, especially chickens and eggs, from their slaves in a tacit recognition that if they did not trade with their own slaves, others would. Less commonly, some planters permitted their slaves to grow some cotton for themselves, which their owners sold on their behalf. While few slaves amassed much money in these ways, at least one ended up in the interesting position of being his owner's creditor. In 1851 Martha Jackson "received of my Negro man John Clark seven gold pieces, . . . as part of the money for which his cotton sold. . . . For this money I am to pay him interest at 7 percent." Martha Jackson's monetary debt to Clark put her under a moral or social debt to him as well, but this could confirm rather than challenge her paternalistic performance. Her willingness to place herself under a formal obligation to him—a debt that she could abrogate with little risk of legal consequences, at least—suggests her belief that slaveholders operated in a consistent moral system, were bound by its rules just as dependents were, and could not redefine its terms at their own pleasure.[11]

Widows also sought to use incentives in managing field work. In the early 1850s, Martha Jackson experimented with ways to motivate her slaves, offering cash rewards to her cotton pickers. In the first week of September 1851, her slaves picked cotton in "companies of four." The company that picked the most cotton received thirty cents each, and Mary received the 50-cent prize "put up for the highest Picker." The members of the remaining two companies received twenty cents each, since they were nearly tied, while Bob and Hooker received the second and third prizes for individual picking. The following week, Jackson adopted a different system. Every slave would receive fifteen cents for picking 400 pounds, forty cents for 800 pounds, and 60 cents for 1000 pounds, and an additional ten cents for every hundredweight over 1000. Perhaps in consequence of her scheme, most of her hands picked over one hundred pounds a day each, while three hands picked well over 1,000 pounds apiece over six days.[12]

The actual amounts of money these slaves earned reflect a further wrinkle in Jackson's schemes. Take William Hooker, who picked 972 pounds during the second week's competition. He received forty cents for 800 pounds, and an additional fifteen cents for the next 150. He added his remaining twenty-two pounds to his wife's total of 385. This raised her yield to 407 pounds, which entitled her to fifteen cents. If she had weighed in with less than 400 pounds, she would have received no money at all for her picking. If Hooker had been paid at all for his twenty-two pounds at the rate of ten cents per 100 pounds, he would have received less than two-and-a-half cents, so transferring his extra cotton to his wife earned them at least an extra twelve cents. These transfers occurred repeatedly throughout the picking season on the Jackson place, and they always occurred within families. In addition to sharing his cotton with his wife, William Hooker also gave some to his son. Bob gave his surplus to his wife Harriet, and the same kind of exchanges happened between sisters Fanny and Emma, sisters Mary and Eliza, and Eliza and her mother, Daphne. Unlike some attempts to manipulate an owner, in this instance the slaves needed her awareness and approval to gain extra advantage from her scheme. Committed to regularizing slave families as much as possible within the context of slavery, Martha Jackson may have agreed to the exchanges precisely because they occurred along family lines. Although her general tendency toward miserliness makes it somewhat surprising that she would consent to anything that would add to her outlay, she may have received some valuable emotional gratification from being able to benefit her slaves in this way. For their part, Hooker, Bob, and the rest of the Jackson slaves had their families' interests in mind in redistributing their cotton amongst themselves, but they also knew their owner well enough to guess that she would be amenable to a plan that honored family ties among her slaves—ties she herself had sanctioned.[13] Martha Jackson had reason to be satisfied with her experiment for economic reasons as well: it cost her nearly thirty dollars up front, but the successful cotton harvest mitigated that cost, and the scheme itself suggested that her and her slaves' interests harmonized. As Christopher Morris has argued, slaves' and slaveholders' interests did indeed articulate at times, but the planters' ability to invent that intersection in particular cases supported their more general claims of slavery's overall beneficence.[14]

On a more regular basis than Jackson's picking rewards, widows indicated their concern for their demesnes and dependents through personal inspections of the cabins, storage buildings, fences, and fields. Like male planters, they knew full well the potential dissonance between slaves' and overseers' reports, as well as the value of being seen to pay scrupulous attention. Thus, when James Proctor Screven left his plantations under his aunt's supervision during a trip north, she took care to collect reports both from the slaves themselves and from the overseer.[15] Just two weeks after her husband's death, Natalie Sumter toured the fields, issued "tous les ordres," visited the sick and the slave children, and inspected the mill. While in the fields, she looked over the cotton and corn crops, noting the presence of disease, the unfavorable weather, and the progress of cotton-picking. Over the next thirteen months as recorded in her diary, Sumter made at least thirty separate visits to the fields and outbuildings.[16] If former slaves are to be believed, this level of surveillance often accompanied a hands-on approach to discipline. According to Clara Cotton McCoy, her owner also made regular inspections of the fields, and she "tended to things an' handled de niggers same as a man." Jerry Hill recalled another slaveholding woman who "used to carry a bullwhip around her neck when she walked out on the farm, and would apply it herself to any slave she thought needed it." Another former slave memorialized his widowed owner as her "own whuppin' boss": "Miss Annie didn't need no jail for her slaves. She could manage 'em widout nothin' lak dat."[17]

While paternalism told slaveholders that disciplining unruly dependents was their duty, it did not require them to wield the whip themselves. Accordingly, if slaveholding widows chose not to, or even felt unable to do so, that did not necessarily undermine their authority. In some ways, it could even enhance it. Georgia planter Mary Downs rode out "evvy mornin'" to check on her plantation, but she also employed an overseer, who did most of the beatings. With John Akins in charge of punitive violence, Mary Downs could represent herself as the kind mistress, remembered by a former slave for the little gifts of gingercake she brought to the quarters. Yet Downs's daily visits also highlighted her position as the sponsor of Akins's violence and thus the ultimate authority on the place. Finally, her regular presence amongst them enabled slaves to come to her with complaints. Planters often allowed—and heeded—these complaints; doing so reflected the customary prejudice against overseers, but it also illustrated their concern for their human property and demonstrated their superiority to and authority over their white employees. For widows, this practice also perpetuated the intercessory role that many had filled during their married lives.[18]

Slaveholding widows' basic assumption that the head of the household carried the largest burden of any on the plantation—a key element of slaveholding paternalism—could also rationalize the feelings of a widow whose overseer's violence sincerely troubled her. In 1799, Lucy Thornton of Virginia witnessed the brutal beating of one of her slaves: "Indeed I feared it might be attended with fatal consequences as the Wounds were on his head and the blood gushed out of his eyes, attended with great swelling of the head." The sight of the bleeding and bruised slave may truly have horrified Thornton, but in her letter the incident serves chiefly to highlight her own sensitivity as a viewer. More important than the slave's suffering was his recovery "with only the loss of three or four days work." Even more important, however, was her own emotional state: "My apprehensions are so great that my life is a burden to me."[19] Supremely self-centered, Thornton's reaction defied the common-place prescription of feminine self-abnegation; despite her expressions of dis-comfort, even fear, at this particular moment, at least, she acted more like a prototypical male planter, considering herself the center of her household, her universe.[20]

Slaveholding widows' treatment of families further illuminates the mutual reinforcement of slaveholders' self-interested benevolence on the one hand, and of slaves' dual status as humans and as chattel on the other. Like slavehold-ing men, widows could claim the prerogative of permitting or forbidding slave marriages, naming slave children, and dictating residence patterns in the slave cabins. These invasive practices acknowledged slaves' humanity, but planters themselves often saw this humanity as a quality they had to educate slaves about—part of a civilizing mission—not as something that slaves inherently possessed and moreover insisted that their owners acknowledge. The simul-taneity of slaves' chattel and human status becomes particularly clear in the way some owners honored slaves' family ties by buying and selling individuals in an effort to keep husbands, wives, and children together. Fannie Berry recalled that "if you wanted to marry one on 'nother plantation," Sarah Ann Abbott would investigate the other slave, rather like a planter would search out the background and prospects of a potential daughter- or son-in-law. If she approved, she "would try to buy him so husband an' wife could be together." Being sold in order to be united with family resembles the strange experience some fugitive slaves faced in the North: securing their liberty only by being sold to someone who would free them.[21]

Financial and familial calculations shaped slave sales in other ways, too, as Martha Jackson's negotiations with Thomas Mitchell suggest:

> I am willing to let *you* have [Betsy and her children] still at the appraisement price . . . although the children are a year older, & the eldest one is more large & strong enough to be very useful. . . .

I sincerely hope you will be able to purchase the negroes, as Betsy is very anxious to go to you, & it will be a great satisfaction to me in parting with her, to see her settled with her husband.[22]

Apparently of equal importance to Jackson (and, she hoped, to Mitchell) were Betsy's desire to live with her husband and the increased value that one year's growth had added to their children. Slaves' and owners' interests could coincide, in this case, but only if the interests of the two slaveholders also intersected.[23]

Of course, if slaveholders could unite families by sale, so too could they break families apart. In 1849, for example, lowcountry South Carolina planter Eliza Wilkins sold Billy out of state, having "borne his insolence and neglect of duty" until she was entirely out of patience. Even if she sold Billy in a moment of rage, paternalistic thoughts need not have troubled her conscience afterwards. Like many slaveholders, she could interpret his conduct as a sign of bad character, not as opposition to bondage or a reflection on her management. It was her prerogative and even—if she chose to reason thusly—her duty to rid her household of a troublemaker who could poison the supposedly wholesome plantation community. Referring to slaveowner paternalism as a "flawed mystique," Michael Tadman has argued that Upper South slaveholders usually sold their slaves without much compunction. He suggests that slave sellers did not simply forget their claims to paternalism; rather, he posits that paternalism was mere propaganda, not a strong belief that could mold its adherents. In fact, selling slaves was not at all incompatible with paternalism, because the concern of the paternalist was initially and ultimately the good of the entire household, defined from the top down, not the good of any individual slave or even of the individual slave family.[24]

The assumption that slaveholders were like parents to their slaves had a further function besides allowing slaveholding widows to feel generous, explain away their own shortcomings, and perhaps motivate their slaves. It also helped widows feel safe living among slaves, often without any white men in the immediate vicinity. The paternalistic depiction of slaves as rowdy but loyal children made the possibility of rebellion or violence seem remote. Widows' trust in their slaves occasionally extended even further. Some widows treated individual slaves as trusted advisers, alongside, or instead of, an overseer.[25] For example, Natalie Sumter consulted with several enslaved men about plantation affairs. Edmund advised her about how the crops and slaves were faring, and she sought his input on whether to hire some of her male slaves to the railroad. After several discussions, she reported that "he persuaded me to send them." Daniel also met with Sumter to receive orders and report on the plantation. On October 4, 1840, for example, she "talked with Daniel a long time about plantation affairs." Arrie Binns of Georgia reported that her widowed mistress "turned off" her overseer "an' put my Pa in his place to manage things and look after the work." The deferential performances that a widow could exact from her slaves made them appealing as advisers; relying on slaves had the additional advantage that they could be whipped for acting "biggity," while an overseer could only be fired. Slaves also had a stake in her financial success that an outsider, even an overseer, did not: their physical survival and the integrity of their community depended on her solvency. During the Civil War, slaveholding wives and widows relied on male slaves even more than they had previously. The George family left William Johnson in complete charge of their household in Albemarle County because they knew he "could be trusted to protect Mistress Nancy and her two daughters." Although Confederate women grew increasingly nervous about slaves in their midst as the war dragged on, some still preferred a black man's protection to no male help at all.[26]

Former slaves who had acted as drivers tended to speak fairly kindly of their widowed owners; female house slaves, however, commonly offered up different memorials. Slaveholding widows often developed extremely fractious relationships with their female house slaves. Overlapping workspaces combined with a desire to intervene in slave women's family and romantic lives, making at least some slaveholding women feel emotionally intimate with their female house slaves. Accordingly, slaveholding women tended to take the disobedience of house slaves especially personally, feeling betrayed and often reacting violently when they encountered sloppy work or rude demeanors. When her house was in disarray and she was entertaining guests, Natalie Sumter felt strained and impatient: "My house is full & servants sick. I don't know what to do."[27] The diary of South Carolinian Keziah Brevard contains numerous references to disobedient female domestics who regularly provoked her:

> I wish to be kind to my negroes—but I receive little but impudence from Rosanna & Sylvia—it is a truth if I am compelled to speak harshly to them—after bearing every thing from them I get impudence. . . . At my death it is my most solemn desire that

Tama, Sylvia, Mack, Maria & Rosanna to be sold. I cannot think
of imposing such servants on any one of my heirs.[28]

Regarding their slaves' resistance as a personal insult or a sign of their slaves'
backwardness, slaveholding widows diminished its political and systemic significance and perhaps made themselves feel more secure about being outnumbered by those they held in bondage. Brevard's reference to selling troublesome
slaves, meanwhile, bespeaks the disproportionate power that slaveholders
could unleash against unruly slaves if they so chose. Whenever they did not do
the maximum they were legally allowed, they could congratulate themselves
for their restraint.

Any discussion of what widowhood reveals about slaveholding in general
and paternalism in particular must also address slaves' relation to their owners'
widowhood. Transitions in the life cycle of their owners often posed risks for
slaves. Slaveholders might require slave mothers to nurse white infants at their
own children's expense. When planters' children went to school, personal servants sometimes accompanied them, an opportunity to see more of the world
(or at least of the South) at the cost of separation from family and friends.
Slaveholding parents gave slaves as wedding presents; migration and sale further ravaged slave communities and families. Uprooted en masse to serve in
the rising generation's quest for wealth or sold off singly to pay for a marriage-
able girl's new dress, slaves bore the brunt of their owners' aging in ways most
slaveholders barely noticed. This disruption tended to be particularly acute
after slaveholders died. The deaths of slaveholding husbands dramatically
reshaped their wives' lives but often caused even worse disruptions in the lives
of slaves. Few slaveholding widows, but many enslaved women, faced involun-
tary separation from their children after their husbands' or owners' deaths. A
slaveholding husband's death rendered his wife both less protected and more
independent, but it made his slaves more valuable and more vulnerable than
ever.[29]

In describing how their masters' deaths changed their bondage, ex-slaves
rarely observed that violence declined, but they often remembered material
deprivation and the threat of sale and separation. Whether slaves were sold off
or divided immediately or years after such a death, the anticipatory dread and
the long-term consequences were enormous. Ex-slaves' recollections serve as a
potent reminder that noncorporal coercion and retribution could be at least
as effective as physical punishment in frightening the slaves and obtaining a

functional degree of obedience. As Nancy Williams told it, "De real trouble start for us when ole marsa died." Rereading Natalie Sumter's "Lady Bountiful" act with this in mind, and remembering that it occurred just weeks after Thomas Sumter's death, we would likely be justified in suspecting that these slaves felt more than usually unsure about their immediate and long-term prospects, and perhaps as a result also felt more inclined than usual to act out their part in accordance with Sumter's version of the script. Because of the aftermath of an owner's death, slaves had even more reason than usual to accept their bondage as a practical fact and to work within the system to alleviate its worst abuses, even if they contested a widow's authority on the grounds of her femaleness.[30]

At the heart of slaves' accomodationist behaviors lay the hope of masking themselves, manipulating their owners, and getting something valuable out of them. Like slaves everywhere in the Old South, widows' slaves sought to improve their condition not just in material ways but also in the predictability of their relations with their owners and managers, which was arguably even more important to their individual and collective survival. For reasons of their own, then, slaves might claim to be contented and boast that they would make large crops for their owners. Before his death in 1840, Henry Jackson's slaves often sent ingratiating messages to him and his wife. During Martha Jackson's widowhood, such messages came even more frequently, probably reflecting the slaves' awareness that she worried constantly about debt and had had to give her overseer a slave in lieu of wages. Small wonder, then, that most of her overseer's letters concluded with some variation on the message, "The Negroes all send a bundance [*sic*] of Love to all the family." Playing up their emotional connection to their owners, slaves turned the image of "my family, white and black" on its head. By inscribing themselves within slaveholders' families, slaves could make it more difficult, if only marginally so, for owners to consider selling them. References to the crop served also as a tacit reminder that an owner needed her slaves' labor to meet her debts as much as they needed her favor to shield them from arbitrary sale.[31]

The recurrent threat of being sold or exchanged in payment of debt also lay behind slaves' self-presentation as willing and industrious workers. After relaying the slaves' complaints about short rations in 1845, Vincent Pierson assured Martha Jackson that "they know if times was not so hard that you would giv [*sic*] them a plenty of every thing." Assuming the slaves actually said any such thing, they may have maintained the fiction of benevolence in the hopes that Martha Jackson would become more generous when she had the means. For more desperate reasons, the slaves also wanted Jackson to know "that they will gett [*sic*] out as much cotton for you as they can." Under the circumstances, their actions were pragmatic, taking maximum advantage, however small that might be, of their owner's sensibilities. Of course, overseer Vincent Pierson had his own motives in relaying these messages to his employer. Promises of an excellent crop from the slaves made him look like a good overseer, and they permitted him to be more measured in his optimism, while holding out the possibility of the 100-bale crop, which was something of a financial grail for Martha Jackson.[32]

Playing the loyal servant to their widowed mistresses garnered slaves some significant benefits, but that exchange was limited, in part by the script of generosity and gratitude itself. Even a widow as conscientious as Martha Jackson sometimes neglected her slaves' welfare, particularly when it came to spending money on them. On several occasions someone white had to remind her that the slaves were, for example, "suffering . . . from the want of blankets." Slaves often tried to make the favors of their paternalist masters into binding promises, but they had few good choices when their owners neglected these commitments.[33] Had Jackson's slaves complained more vigorously when she mistreated them, they might have created more leeway for themselves in the system of slavery, but they might also have been suffered a greater incidence of sales, beatings, and other forms of abuse that they were usually spared. To put it simply, slaves often suffered when their owners conserved money, and widows were especially likely to feel the need to economize.[34] Undeceived by the cant of kindness that dominated slaveholders' images of the Southern lady, slaves understood that their widowed owners could manipulate their lives as terribly as could any male slaveholder. Moreover, because the death of a master tended to make his slaves more vulnerable to disasters like sale and separation, slave communities often presented themselves as more or less willing allies in a widow's attempt to preserve her household from bankruptcy and eventual dissolution.[35]

For their part, while widowhood prompted some nineteenth-century slaveholding women to see some parallels between their own bereavements and those suffered by slaves and thus to empathize with them, most did not. Even those who genuinely felt concern for their slaves' welfare did so as a part of a larger, often paternalistic self-conception, in which their finances and their legal responsibilities figured largely and their commitment to their own children, their other kin, or even their class were paramount. Paternalistic beliefs thus helped slaveholding widows reconcile their various roles as mothers, plantation mistresses, household heads—and, sometimes, as executors, administrators, or guardians. Paternalistic tactics, meanwhile, facilitated their performance of these roles. Bearing the ultimate responsibility for overworking slaves, stinting their rations, selling them away from their spouses and children, and whipping them rarely challenged widows' sense of themselves as moral and kindly women. Widows could justify many cruelties—if they even recognized them—as necessary to protect their own children's interests and to fulfill their ethical and legal obligations. That, indeed, formed the heart of paternalism, and it worked especially well for slaveholding women, who had been accustomed to not being their own masters. For them the sense of obligation, of responsibility to and for their slaves and their entire households that paternalism inculcated in many antebellum slaveholders meshed neatly with their conventional gender roles.[36]

Slaveholding widows' comparative success in keeping rebellion at bay and turning a profit despite a formal gender ideology that said they could do neither, suggests that while widows' gender always mattered, it was far from being the only or even the most relevant category in their interactions with slaves. Confronting a male slave, few widows saw someone whom they could not dominate because he was a man. Instead, they saw someone who was black and a slave, to whom they could give orders and from whom they could demand obedience. Widows' usual complacence at living in a household of slaves, especially slave men, speaks loudly to the inextricability of race, gender, and legal status. Moreover, the "design for mastery" suggested by paternalism could be adapted to and by female planters in a way that the republican-oriented version of mastery could not. Thus, when Ada Bacot described her intention to assert her control over some unruly slaves, she referred to herself as their mistress, not their master. But the rest of her words indicate no doubt in her mind that she both should and could make her authority felt by her bondpeople: "I hope I may be able to make them understand without much trouble that I am Mistress & will be obeyed." In fact, it was her duty as much as her prerogative to dominate her slaves, even if it caused her some "trouble."[37]

The ideal master of the Old South was a man of implacable will who received willing obedience from all his subordinates and unquestioned respect from his peers.[38] No slaveholder, male or female, ever achieved that ideal, but slaveholding men generally came closer to an approximation of the ideal than did women, even widows, simply because they had greater access to the many different forms of power. No slaveholding woman, married or single, could reasonably hope to achieve either the autonomy or the power that supposedly constituted white Southern manhood. However, identifying the interests of their families as their own, slaveholding women grew up knowing what some slaveholding men never accepted: that they did not single-handedly determine their own destinies. Indeed, the very thought was surely anathema to women, who understood their own embeddedness in family life as the source of their social position and their identities.[39]

In this light, it seems possible that when faced with the responsibility of running a household, widows might have had a more realistic definition of successful slave management than men did. Their version of mastery was probably closer to the "art of the possible" than the ideal version after which so many white Southern men hungered.[40] In the Old South, slaveholding widows were surprisingly well equipped, not simply to handle their inevitable failures in slave control, but also to craft the delicate balance of force and persuasion that over time seems to have been one of the most effective ways to manage slaves. Femininity and femaleness shaped widows' actions, identities, and access to paternalism; but neither prohibited them from using legal, cultural, and economic powers over slaves any more than masculinity or maleness guaranteed white men's mastery.

NOTES

I would like to thank Douglas Egerton and Catherine Clinton for their comments on the paper I presented at The Citadel conference, and Robert E. Lockhart for his timely feedback during the revisions of the expanded essay.

1. Natalie de DeLage Sumter Diary, 4 July 1840, South Caroliniana Library, Manuscript Division, University of South Carolina (hereafter SCL); Eugene Genovese, *Roll, Jordan, Roll: The World the Slaves Made* (New York: Vintage Books, 1972), 545; Drew Gilpin Faust, *James Henry Hammond and the Old South: A Design for Mastery* (Baton Rouge: Louisiana State University Press, 1987), 99–104; Agnes Hairston to Ruth Hairston, 28 February 1844, and Sterling Adams to Ruth Stovall Hairston, 9 June 1854, Wilson and Hairston Family Papers, Southern Historical Collection, University of North Carolina (hereafter SHC); John Berkeley Grimball Diary, 17 August 1834, SHC. In my ongoing work on slaveholding and widowhood, I look at a wide spectrum of slaveholders, from women like Susan Davis Nye Hutchison, who taught school to support herself, and Caroline Burke, who sought

to survive on a small farm with the help of her son and a small number of sickly and young slaves, to women like Martha Richardson and Ruth Hairston, who owned considerably more than fifty slaves apiece.

This chapter focuses on planter widows because their households yield the clearest evidence of paternalism, a function of planter culture itself and of the particular managerial concerns and distance from most field slaves that large slaveholdings often produced. Christopher Morris suggests that large plantations in long-settled areas tended to display the structural conditions necessary for the articulation of owners' and slaves' interests. Under those conditions, the ideology of paternalism could be, but was not necessarily, conducive to articulation. See Christopher Morris, "The Articulation of Two Worlds: The Master-Slave Relationship Reconsidered," *Journal of American History* 85 (December 1998): 996, 1005–6.

2. Eugene Genovese's classic study *Roll, Jordan, Roll* has many critics, but it is still a core text in the literature on paternalism. For more recent works, see Jeffrey R. Young, *Domesticating Slavery: The Master Class in Georgia and South Carolina, 1670–1837* (Chapel Hill: University of North Carolina Press, 1999); Morris, "Articulation of Two Worlds"; Kathleen Brown, *Good Wives, Nasty Wenches, and Anxious Patriarchs: Gender, Race, and Power in Colonial Virginia* (Chapel Hill: University of North Carolina Press, 1996); Charles Joyner, *Shared Traditions: Southern History and Folk Culture* (Urbana and Chicago: University of Illinois Press, 1999). For scholars who argue against the paternalist interpretation, see James Oakes, *The Ruling Race: A History of American Slaveholders* (New York: Vintage Books, 1982); Ann Patton Malone, *Sweet Chariot: Slave Family and Household in Nineteenth-Century Louisiana* (Chapel Hill: University of North Carolina Press, 1992); Michael Tadman, *Speculators and Slaves: Masters, Traders, and Slaves in the Old South* (Madison: University of Wisconsin Press, 1989).

3. William Gilmore Simms, review of Elizabeth Ellet's *Women of the Revolution, Southern Quarterly Review* (July 1850): 323–24.

4. Elizabeth Fox-Genovese, *Within the Plantation Household: Black and White Women in the Old South* (Chapel Hill: University of North Carolina Press, 1988), quotation at 203, see also 22–25, 97, 111–12, 140, 202–7; Philip J. Schwarz, *Twice Condemned: Slaves and the Criminal Laws of Virginia, 1705–1865* (Baton Rouge: Louisiana State University Press, 1998), quotation at 160; Robert Olwell, *Masters, Slaves, and Subjects: The Culture of Power in the South Carolina Low Country, 1740–1790* (Ithaca: Cornell University Press, 1998), 198–9; Anne Firor Scott, *The Southern Lady from Pedestal to Politics, 1830–1930* (Chicago: University of Chicago Press, 1970), x, chap. 2, esp. 34, 37; Catherine Clinton, *The Plantation Mistress: Woman's World in the Old South* (New York: Pantheon Books, 1982); Brown, *Good Wives,* 9, 32, 77, 90, 109, 170.

5. Stephanie McCurry, "Two Faces of Republicanism: Gender and Proslavery Politics in Antebellum South Carolina," *Journal of American History* 79 (March 1992): 1245–64; Fox-Genovese, *Within the Plantation Household,* 25–6, 115, 128–29; Genovese, *Roll, Jordan, Roll,* 83; Marli F. Weiner, *Mistresses and Slaves: Plantation Women in South Carolina, 1830–1880* (Urbana: University of Illinois Press, 1998); Cynthia Kierner, *Beyond the Household: Women's Place in the Early South, 1700–1835* (Ithaca: Cornell University Press, 1998); Elizabeth R. Varon, *We Mean to Be Counted: White Women and Politics in Antebellum Virginia* (Chapel Hill: University of North Carolina Press, 1998); Suzanne Lebsock, *Free Women of Petersburg: Status and Culture in a Southern Town, 1784–1860* (New York: Norton, 1984); Young, *Domesticating Slavery;* Scott, *Southern Lady;* Stephanie McCurry, *Masters of Small Worlds: Yeoman Household, Gender Relations, and the Political Culture of the Antebellum South Carolina Low Country* (New York: Oxford University Press, 1995); Bertram Wyatt-Brown, *Southern Honor: Ethics and Behavior in the Old South* (New York: Oxford University Press, 1982); Drew Gilpin Faust, *Mothers of Invention: Women of the Slaveholding South in the American Civil War* (New York: Vintage Books, 1996); Victoria Bynum, *Unruly Women: The Politics of Social and Sexual Control in the Old South* (Chapel Hill: University of North Carolina Press, 1992); Catherine Clinton, *The Plantation Mistress;* Cara Anzilotti, "'In the Affairs of the World': Women and Plantation Ownership in the Eighteenth Century South Carolina Low Country" (Ph.D. diss., University of California, Santa Barbara, 1994); Christine Jacobson Carter, ed., *The Diary of Dolly Lunt Burge, 1848–1879* (Athens: University of Georgia Press, 1997); Larry Eldridge, ed., *Women and Freedom in Early America* (New York: New York University Press, 1997).

6. On widows' property rights in slaves, see Cushing, ed., *Laws of North Carolina,* 2:488–92; Cushing, ed., *Laws of Georgia,* 1:313; Marylynn Salmon, *Women and the Law of Property,* 153, 157, 170–72, 177; *Acts of the General Assembly of the State of Georgia, Passed in Milledgeville at a Biennial Session in November, December, January, and February, 1853–4,* compiled by John Rutherford (Savannah: Samuel T. Chapman, 1854), 71. On the work of plantation mistresses—almost always understood as wives—see Weiner, *Mistresses and Slaves;* Fox-Genovese, *Within the Plantation Household.*

7. On maternalism, see for example, Seth Coven and Sonya Michel, eds., *Mothers of a New World: Maternalist Politics and the Origins of Welfare States* (New York and London: Routledge, 1993).

8. George P. Rawick, *The American Slave: A Composite Autobiography* (New York: Greenwood Press, 1972) [hereafter *AS*], vol. 12, pt. 2, 107.

9. "Daily Expenditures for 1842," Plantation Accounts, 1841–1842, folder 95, Jackson and Prince Family Papers, SHC; Natalie de DeLage Sumter Diary, 12 July,

22 July, 11 August, 4 October, 19 December, 24 December, 26 December, all in 1840. The evolution of widows' slave management between 1790 and 1860 is subtle: like other slaveholders, antebellum widows made more explicit defenses than their predecessors of slavery as a positive good and likewise made more strategic use of incentives in their slave management.

10. Frederick Douglass, *Narrative of the Life of Frederick Douglass, a Slave* (1845; reprint, New York: New American Library, 1968), 84.

11. Personal Account Book of Martha and Henry Jackson, 1819–20 (also includes plantation accounts from the 1840s–1850s), Jackson and Prince Family Papers, SHC; *AS*, vol. 2, pt. 1, 190, 206; vol. 12, pt. 2, 132; vol. 12, pt. 1, 320; vol. 14, 105; Joseph Jackson to Sarah Jackson, 1 January 1847, Jackson and Prince Family Papers, SHC; John Berkeley Grimball Diary, 25 December 1832; Carter, ed., *Dolly Lunt Burge;* Morris, "The Articulation of Two Worlds," 987, 994–99; Betty Wood, *Women's Work, Men's Work: The Informal Slave Economies of Lowcountry Georgia* (Athens: University of Georgia Press, 1995); Larry E. Hudson Jr., *To Have and To Hold: Slave Work and Family Life in Antebellum South Carolina* (Athens: University of Georgia Press, 1997); Roderick A. McDonald, *The Economy and Material Culture of Slaves: Goods and Chattels on the Sugar Plantations of Jamaica and Louisiana* (Baton Rouge: Louisiana State University, 1993).

12. Plantation Day Book, 1851, Jackson and Prince Family Papers, SHC.

13. For the Jacksons' behavior toward slaves who formed families without their owners' approval, see Martha Jackson to Henry Rootes Jackson, n.d., folder 48, Jackson and Prince Family Papers, SHC.

14. Faust, *James Henry Hammond,* 72–73, 99–104, 369–70, 381–82. On variations in picking rates, see John Blassingame, *The Slave Community; Plantation Life in the Antebellum South* (New York: Oxford University Press, 1972), 182. On incentives to slave workers, see William Kauffman Scarborough, *The Overseer: Plantation Management in the Old South* (Baton Rouge: Louisiana State University Press, 1966), 180. William Hart, William Hooker, Bob, and Mary were consistently the highest pickers that fall. Over five weeks, William Hooker earned $3.92 1/2, Bob earned $3.75, Mary earned $3.81 1/4, and William Hart, who worked only three of the five weeks, earned $2.70 (Plantation Daybook, 1851, Jackson and Prince Family Papers, SHC).

15. Martha Richardson to James Proctor Screven, 21 April 1833, Arnold and Screven Family Papers, SHC.

16. Natalie de DeLage Sumter Diary, 1–4 July, 10–15 July, 18 July, 25 July, 6 August, 6 September, 16 October, 15 November, 16 November, 28 November, 12 December, 28 December 1840; 3 February, 23 February, 11 June, 8 July 1841.

17. Charles L. Perdue Jr., Thomas E. Barden, and Robert K. Phillips, eds., *Weevils in the Wheat: Interviews with Virginia Ex-Slaves,* 1st ed., 1980 (Bloomington: Indiana University Press, 1980), quotation at 16 and 190, 273–75; *AS,* vol. 2, pt. 2, quotation at 290; vol. 15, 67, 193, 30; vol. 2, pt. 1, 157; vol. 12, pt. 2, quotation at 130–31, 129, 92–93; vol. 12, pt. 1, 169–70; *AS,* vol. 2, pt. 2, quotation at 290; vol. 15, pt. 2, 67, 193; vol. 2, pt. 1, 157; vol. 12, pt. 2, quotation at 130–31, 129, 92–93; vol. 12, pt. 1, 169.0; Catherine Lewis to Emma Speight, 9 August 1838, John Francis Speight Papers (SHC).

18. *Weevils in the Wheat,* 16, 63, 94, 194–95, 274, 285, 307, 309–10; *AS,* vol. 12, pt. 2, 108–9, 130–31; vol. 2, pt. 1, 11, 157; vol. 2, pt. 2, 136. On overseers, see for example "Overseers," *Southern Agriculturalist* (October 1837): 505–7; *Southern Cultivator,* 26 June, 10 July, 24 July, 7 August, 2 October, 16 October, 30 October, 13 November, all in 1844; J. D. B. De Bow, "Plantation Life—Duties and Responsibilities," *De Bow's Review, Agricultural, Commercial, Industrial Progress and Resources* 29 (September 1860): 357–68.

19. Lucy Thornton to [Miss Mary Robinson], 15 November 1799, Jackson and Prince Family Papers, SHC.

20. Faust, *James Henry Hammond,* 100; Brown, *Good Wives,* 327, 350–61.

21. *Weevils in the Wheat,* 40; Harriet A. Jacobs, *Incidents in the Life of a Slave Girl: Written by Herself,* edited originally by L. Maria Child; edited and with an introduction by Jean Fagan Yellin (Cambridge: Harvard University Press, 1987). On the discourse of civilization, see for example Brown, *Good Wives,* chap. 1, and Gail Bederman, *Manliness and Civilization: A Cultural History of Gender and Race in the United States, 1880–1917* (Chicago: University of Chicago Press, 1995).

22. Martha Jackson to Thomas Mitchell, 1 and 5 December 1841; Thomas Mitchell to Martha Jackson, 3 December 1841; Martha Jacqueline Rootes Jackson to Martha Jackson, 21 June 1846, Jackson and Prince Family Papers, SHC; Tadman, *Speculators and Slaves,* 211 and passim.

23. Morris, "The Articulation of Two Worlds," 1002.

24. John Berkeley Grimball Diary, 9 September 1849, SHC; Malone, *Sweet Chariot,* 88–89, 211–16, 269; Brenda Stevenson, "Gender Convention, Ideals, and Identity among Antebellum Virginia Slave Women," in *More than Chattel: Black Women and Slavery in the Americas,* ed. David Barry Gaspar and Darlene Clark Hine (Bloomington: Indiana University Press, 1996), 169–90. My reading of paternalism here converges on Jeffrey Young's "corporate individualism" and, like Young, I suspect that the slaveholder's concern for individual slaves often ceded the field to his (or her) concern for the entire household defined from the top down in a way that prioritized interests of the slaveholder and his (or her) own co-resident kin and perhaps a few favored slaves (Young, *Domesticating Slavery,* 9–15 and passim).

25. I have not attempted to address the thorny question of sexual liaisons, either coerced or consensual, between widows and their slaves in this chapter. We know that some widows formed sexual attachments with male slaves, and some of those who served as trusted advisers may also have had a sexual relationship with their owners. I have no reason to suspect or to doubt that such was the case in the instances I mention here. See Martha Hodes, *White Women, Black Men: Illicit Sex in the Nineteenth-Century South* (New Haven: Yale University Press, 1997); Hodes, "Wartime Dialogues on Illicit Sex: White Women and Black Men," in *Divided Houses: Gender and the Civil War,* ed. Catherine Clinton and Nina Silber (New York: Oxford University Press, 1992), 234–36.

26. Natalie de DeLage Sumter Diary, 1 July, 17 August, 18 August, 19 September, 24 October, 11 November, 12 December, 25 December, 30 December, all in 1840; see also 4 July, 11 July, 12 July, 17 August, 10 December 1840, and 4 January 1841; *Weevils in the Wheat,* 74, 167; *AS,* vol.12, pt. 1, 74; Faust, *Mothers of Invention,* 62. Disputing an older literature, Diane Miller Somerville and others argue that before the end of slavery, whites' identification of blacks as prone to violence, especially sexual violence against white women, did not yet have the enormous power it later had in the era of Reconstruction, Redemption, and especially Jim Crow ("The Rape Myth Reconsidered: The Intersection of Race, Class and Gender in the American South, 1800–1877," Ph.D. diss., Rutgers University, 1995; "The Rape Myth in the Old South Reconsidered," *Journal of Southern History* 61 [August 1995]: 481–518). See also Peter W. Bardaglio, "Rape and the Law in the Old South: 'Calculated to Excite Indignation in Every Heart,'" *Journal of Southern History* 60 (November 1994): 752; Bardaglio, *Reconstructing the Household: Families, Sex, and the Law in the Nineteenth-Century South* (Chapel Hill: University of North Carolina Press, 1995); Jacquelyn Dowd Hall, "'The Mind That Burns in Each Body': Women, Rape, and Racial Violence," in *Powers of Desire,* ed. Ann Snitow, Christine Stansell, and Sharon Thompson (New York: Monthly Review Press, 1983), 328–49; Winthrop Jordan, *White over Black: American Attitudes toward the Negro, 1550–1812* (1968; reprint, New York: W. W. Norton, 1977), 154; Wyatt-Brown, *Southern Honor,* 50; Patrick H. Breen, "'A Storm of Terror': Femininity in the Wake of Nat Turner's Slave Revolt" (conference paper, Citadel Conference on the South, Charleston, S.C., 7 April 2000).

27. Natalie de DeLage Sumter Diary, quotations at 4 February 1841 and 6 December 1840. While historians have long disputed the existence and significance of slaveholding women's fondness for some of their slaves, *expressions* of affection are legion. See, for example, Elizabeth Knox to Franklin Grist, 19 December 1847, Elizabeth (Washington) Grist Knox Papers, SHC; Captain Lea to Henry Jackson, Sarah Jackson to Henry Rootes Jackson, 30 July 1834; Serena Lea to Martha Jackson, 2

January 1840, Jackson and Prince Family Papers, SHC; Weiner, *Mistresses and Slaves;* Fox-Genovese, *Within the Plantation Household.*

For another example of a widow interfering with her domestic slave's family, see Ada Bacot Diary, 8 September 1862, Ada Bacot Papers, SCL. When Old Willie protested her son's beating, she too was whipped. Preventing slave parents from disciplining and protecting their children as they saw fit was an important manifestation of slaveholders' power. Debating who had a right to punish slaves was also a way for slaveholders to contest their authority among themselves (see Ada Bacot Diary, 3 September 1862).

28. Keziah Goodwyn Hopkins Brevard (1803–1886) Diary, 18 September 1860, SCL.

29. *Weevils in the Wheat,* 309; Tadman, *Speculators and Slaves;* Edward E. Baptist, "'Cuffy,' 'Fancy Maids,' and 'One-Eyed Men': Rape, Commodification, and the Domestic Slave Trade in the United States," presented to the McNeil Center for Early American Studies, November 19, 1999; Wills of Tristim Skinner, 1853 and 1857, Skinner Family Papers, SHC; Marriage Settlement between Martha J. R. Jackson and Hezekiah Erwin, Jackson and Prince Family Papers, SHC; *Weevils in the Wheat,* 42; Codicil to the Will of Mary Motte, 17 May 1837, Jacob Rhett Motte Papers, Duke.

30. Occasionally, slaves decided that they would not be whipped by a woman, yet such instances seem to have been rare, and according to my evidence, they concerned wives, not widows. *AS,* vol. 15, pt. 1, 149, 199.

31. Martha Jackson to Sarah Jackson, 27 December 1852; Henry Jackson to Martha Jackson, 29 November 1836, 11 February 1844, 12 July 1845, 7 September 1844, Jackson and Prince Family Papers, SHC; Faust, *James Henry Hammond,* 99–104; Philip Morgan, *Slave Counterpoint: Black Culture in the Eighteenth-Century Chesapeake and Lowcountry* (Chapel Hill: Published for the Omohundro Institute of Early American History and Culture, Williamsburg, Virginia, by the University of North Carolina Press, 1998), 348; Genovese, *Roll, Jordan, Roll,* 609–12; Bertram Wyatt-Brown, "The Mask of Obedience: Male Slave Psychology in the Old South," *American Historical Review* 93 (December 1988): 1228–53. Christopher Morris suggests that the "articulation" of owners' and slaves' interests "probably lessened conflict at the structural level," but "not at a personal and ideological level" ("Articulation of Two Worlds," 1003).

32. Vincent Pierson to Martha Jackson, 11 February 1844, 12 July 1845, 7 September 1844, Jackson and Prince Family Papers, SHC. Sending messages to family members via white folks was often the only way for separated kin to keep in some kind of contact. See, for example, Vincent Pierson to Martha Jackson, 28 May 1844, Jackson and Prince Family Papers, SHC; Margaret Steele to Mary Steele, 7 September 1818, John Steele Papers, SHC; Joan R. Gundersen, "Kith and Kin: Women's Networks in

Colonial Virginia," in *The Devil's Lane: Race and Sex in the Early South,* ed. Catherine Clinton and Michele Gillespie (New York: Oxford University Press, 1998), 90–108.

33. Joseph Jackson to Martha Jackson, 12 January 1847, Jackson and Prince Family Papers, SHC.

34. *Weevils in the Wheat,* 98, 195; Brown, *Good Wives,* 372.

35. The literature on slave resistance is vast and growing; see, for example, John Hope Franklin and Loren Schweninger, *Runaway Slaves: Rebels on the Plantation* (New York and London: Oxford University Press, 1999); Genovese, *Roll, Jordan, Roll;* Charles Joyner, *Down by the Riverside: A South Carolina Slave Community* (Urbana: University of Illinois Press, 1984); Douglas Egerton, *Gabriel's Rebellion: Virginia's Slave Conspiracies of 1800 and 1820* (Chapel Hill: University of North Carolina Press, 1993); Michael Mullin, *Africa in America: Slave Acculturation and Resistance in the American South and the British Caribbean, 1736–1831* (Urbana: University of Illinois Press, 1992); William Loren Katz, *Breaking the Chains: African-American Slave Resistance* (New York: Athenaeum/Maxwell Macmillan International Pub. Group, 1990).

36. On propertied women's financial conservatism, see Lebsock, *Free Women of Petersburg,* 126–29.

37. Ada Bacot Diary, 11 February 1861. For slaveholding women in the Civil War, and their ultimate conclusion that slaves were no longer controllable, see, for example, Drew Gilpin Faust, *Mothers of Invention;* George C. Rable, *Civil Wars: Women and the Crisis of Southern Nationalism* (Urbana: University of Illinois Press, 1989); Weiner, *Mistresses and Slaves,* chap. 8; Lee Ann Whites, *The Civil War as a Crisis in Gender: Augusta, Georgia, 1860–1890* (Athens: University of Georgia Press, 1995), 120–24. On the inextricability of gender, race, and class, see Nancy Hewitt, "Compounding Differences," *Feminist Studies* 18 (summer 1992): 313–27.

38. Faust suggests that having failed in his quest for total mastery over his slave laborers, Hammond learned instead "the art of the possible." He achieved better results—a healthier and more compliant slave force—using "persuasion and manipulation" in addition to the coercion he had previously employed, even though the incentives he offered as a further display of his power quickly became, in the slaves' eyes, rights (*James Henry Hammond,* 89–99).

39. Fox-Genovese, "Family and Female Identity in the Antebellum South: Sarah Gayle and her Family," in *In Joy and in Sorrow: Women, Marriage, and Family in the Victorian South, 1830–1900,* ed. Carol Bleser (New York: Oxford University Press, 1991), 16, 19; "A Prayer for a Woman who has lost her Husband," Archer Family Papers, VHS.

40. Faust, *James Henry Hammond,* quotation at 99.

4

In Terror of Their Slaves

White Southern Women's Responses to Slave Insurrections and Scares

Patrick H. Breen

If one looks at the letter of Joseph Davis to his son Wilbur, Christmas season 1856 in North Carolina was "dull enough." After spending the holiday quietly at their Murfreesboro home, the Davises used a trip to drop off a relative at the train station as a chance to pay social calls. In excruciating detail, Joseph Davis told his son about his week-long excursion, even his company on carriage rides. On New Year's Day he went on a horse ride made "perilous" by a winter snowstorm. Later, "Joe + self put his buggy down on runners and we and the ladies took some notable slay [sleigh] rides." After another day of visiting, the winter vacation ended as everyone returned to their homes. "And so ended one of the most pleasant trips I ever took," Joseph confided to his son. "Night and day we had fun! fun!! fun!!! . . . It will be long remembered by me."[1] Few letters seem less memorable.

Interestingly, there is a strikingly different description of the week. The same day that Wilbur's father wrote describing the "fun! fun!! fun!!!" his mother wrote an account of what seemed most newsworthy to her about their trip: rumors of a slave insurrection. "Upon arriving at Garysburg on last Monday," Anne Beale Davis wrote to her son, "we were informed that the whole neighborhood was in a state of great consternation, on account of an insurrection having been commenced near this place." This was no fleeting rumor, but one taken seriously by the residents at the time: "About 75 white men had assembled at Garysburg, on the previous night, all well armed; and some 40 at Weldon." Before nightfall Sunday, the towns of Garysburg and Weldon were teeming with refugees seeking protection. At the Gray's, the Davises arrived to find "that some 4 families had spent the night there on Sunday, and all had sat up during the night in great alarm."² By Monday night, the word was out that there had been no insurrection. The neighborhood was as safe as usual. In choosing to describe the slave-insurrection scare, Anne focused on what her husband had deemed worthy of not one word.

Anne Beale Davis was not the only Southern white woman who wrote about a slave-insurrection scare that male relatives ignored. In July of 1822, the news reached Savannah, Georgia, that Denmark Vesey's plot had almost caught Charleston, South Carolina, unaware. At the same time, Dr. W. C. Daniel managed to write a seven-page letter to his brother-in-law James Screven, then in Europe, that went on in endless detail about yellow fever but failed to mention Vesey. Martha Richardson, writing from the same house only a day later, spent the majority of her letter relating the details of the failed insurrection and the "awful commotion" that it produced. She even copied at length from a letter from Charleston's Intendant (read: "Mayor") James Hamilton about this most serious slave scare.³

The stark difference between the letters of these men and these women reflected a large difference between the sexes in the South. Women were prone to pay attention to the threat posed by slaves. Conversely, men were expected to suppress their fears. Fanny Kemble—the English actress whose short-lived marriage to the slave baron Pierce Butler gave her, as an outsider, an especially intimate look at the South—noticed this difference. In her letters from Georgia written in 1839, she commented: "Southern men are apt to deny the fact that they do live under a habitual sense of danger; but a slave population, coerced into obedience, though unarmed and half-fed, *is* a threatening source of constant insecurity, and every Southern *woman* to whom I have spoken on the subject has admitted to me that they live in terror of their slaves."⁴

Women's terror for their own lives was only accentuated by their fear for the safety of their families. Southern white women's responses to the news of slave rebellions were fundamentally affected by their concern for their children. Women understood that infants and children, their special charges, were especially vulnerable to slave rebels. When the British threat made slave unrest more dangerous during the War of 1812, John Randolph of Roanoke informed Congress: "I speak from the facts when I say, that the night bell never tolls for fire in Richmond, that the mother does not hug the infant more closely to her bosom." The threat to children was not simply something imagined by hysterical white women; desperate slaves were prepared to take their revenge on even the most vulnerable members of white society. In the

confession taken down by Thomas Gray, Nat Turner remarked that the instiga-
tors of the rebellion quickly agreed that "neither age nor sex was to be spared."
This comment was emphasized by Gray, who noted that the decision "was
invariably adhered to." As if to underscore the significance of this decision,
Gray retold one of the most famous moments of the insurrection, when two
rebels returned a mile to a house where the men had left a sleeping baby alive.
If the special trip to kill "a little infant sleeping in a cradle" were not enough to
highlight the dangers to which women and children were exposed, the list of
white casualties during Nat Turner's Rebellion made the same point perfectly
clear: on the list at the end of Gray's pamphlet, forty-five of the fifty-five dead
—more than 80 percent—were identified as either women or children.[5]

Usually the concerns of the women for their children exacerbated
women's fear of slaves, but on occasion the sisters, daughters, and mothers had
other concerns so pressing that the terror provoked by stories of slave rebels
waned. Littleton Tazewell, for instance, commented on how composed his
wife and daughters were during the bedlam that followed Nat Turner's insurrection. He suspected that their relative calm related to the fact that his son
had fallen sick before the rebellion began. "The anxieties of my wife and
daughters concerning John, absorbed in great degree the distress they would
probably have experienced, from the tales of the horrid scenes lately acted
in Southampton."[6] Most women, however, did not have a child, parent, or a
sibling in a critical state that demanded a woman's full attention during a
slave-insurrection scare. Rather, concern for self and family preservation most
often combined to make women especially nervous when the rumors spread.

In another one of the numerous ironies of Southern history, these thoroughly reactionary responses revealed one of the greatest weaknesses of the
paternalistic system. Like flood waters after a storm, women's often visceral
responses to the slave threats rarely stayed within the levies of appropriate
behavior for Southern women erected by Southern theorists. Because there
was no sanctuary safe from the threat of slaves, women were forced to respond
by emerging into the public sphere. They ran from their homes that were supposed to be safe, fleeing to the woods or seeking protection in the community
strongholds. They became involved in politics, urging myriad solutions to the
problem of racial slavery. At times, even the most dignified women readied
themselves to fight for their lives. Despite often deep commitments to their
roles in the world of slavery and paternalism, Southern women's trust weakened when the news came that the slaves had risen.

When news of a slave-insurrection scare spread through a Southern town, no action was more certain than that the nearby women (and some men) would flood the community's stronghold. Rather than depending only on the protection of their fathers, husbands, and brothers, women left their households and sensibly ran to the safest place they could find. Anne Davis described to her son one woman, who upon hearing the frightening rumors "ran off some three or four miles, until she reached the Railroad," which she then took to the nearest town. During Nat Turner's Rebellion, large numbers of women fled to the biggest town in Southampton County, the county seat, Jerusalem. By one estimate, roughly 20 percent of Southampton's adult women were refugees in the town. One unnamed correspondent in Jerusalem described the scene: "Every house, room and corner in this place is full of women and children, driven from home, who had to take to the woods, until they could get to this place." Helen Read told her friend about the pandemonium in nearby Norfolk, the biggest town in Southeast Virginia: "O my Louisa, through all my long life and two wars I never witnessed such scene before[,] women and Children with their baggage coming to us for protection." According to another observer, Halifax town and Murfreesboro each held no fewer than one thousand refugees.[7]

Moses Ashley Curtis, an Episcopalian priest, described the responses of the women in Wilmington, North Carolina, to the news that an army of two hundred slaves stood within ten miles of Wilmington: "The women were all flying or fled with their trinkets + mattresses to the garrison." More curious than gallant, Curtis went to the armory to check out the scene. "When I reached the garrison there were 120 women packed in a small dwelling half dead with fear. One was stretched out on a mattress in hysterics, a number fainted, + one was jabbering nonsense in a fit of derangement." Petersburg, Virginia, suffered much the same when the bells tolled and rumors spread about a slave army of five hundred ready to attack. One woman took particular note of the surprise. The tavern filled with "women half dressed," some fresh from their beds. One lady, whose husband was out on patrol, came down the street "in a dress 'quite light and airy.'" In a society that valued propriety as much as the South, the image of immodestly clad women fleeing their homes was a powerful one, suggesting the profound fright that led the women to run.[8]

Those who could not reach a city tried to find a sanctuary in the South's vast hinterland. When rumors of a slave uprising swept through the region near

Fayetteville, North Carolina, women and children fled to the swamps, from which, according to one report, "after a day or two they emerged, wet, muddy and half starved." Perhaps no one endured greater indignities than the women described by Anne Davis to her son. While they were out riding, a group of ladies learned that "all the whites in Murfreesboro had been killed." The slave who told them this advised that the women "had better dismount and run for their lives." They did not need to be told twice. Even though it was January, they quickly dismounted and "ran in a small Creek and went up to the knees in ice and water to secrete themselves, where they remained from 11 o'clock until 4," when they were rescued.[9]

Present in both the town and the country, the fear of slave insurrections also transcended class lines. When oral historians in the 1930s asked those who were alive before the Civil War about slavery, the responses indicated fears of a slave threat not unlike those recorded by the affluent diarists and letter writers whose correspondence has survived a century. One sharecropper's wife remembered how her neighbors reacted to the news of a slave uprising: "Most of our neighbors took quilts and blankets and spent several nights in thickets." This woman said that she did not leave home but admitted that "I never slept none for a night or two." Of course, she had her own plan for escape if the marauders were to appear. "I remember plannin' if we heard the niggers comin' we'd run and hide in my butter-bean vines; they was real thick that year."[10]

To protect themselves from slave threats, many women tried to have the best possible defense at hand. On Monday night, one day after Nat Turner began his historic rebellion, reports came to Jerusalem that the rebels had established a camp at Major Ridley's. According to a report later filed by General Eppes, once he was apprised of their situation, his first impulse was to attack. But lobbying on the part of "families" who "were strongly opposed" to such an attack made him pause. If he went out and the rebels decided to attack Jerusalem at the same time, the slaves might pass Eppes and enter Jerusalem unhindered. Listening to these arguments, Eppes decided to wait for morning to engage the battle.[11] Because of lobbying, the militia decided to remain the night in Jerusalem doing its best to protect the gathered women and children.

More commonly, women found themselves afraid of the danger posed by slaves when the militia was not assembled. At these times, women were not bashful about sounding the alarm. In 1835, a widow who lived on her own heard a slave comment that "she was tired of waiting on the *white folks* and wanted to be her own mistress the balance of her days, and clean up her own house." Convinced that this comment signaled an imminent rebellion, the widow spread the word that there was a slave conspiracy afoot. Madison County, Mississippi, erupted in what the historian Bertram Wyatt-Brown described as "a genuine, full scale frenzy."[12] Not until later did the men learn the flimsy basis for the rumored insurrection. By then, however, the militia was out, and the blood of innocent slaves reminded potential insurrectionaries of the steep tariff placed on the entire black community at any sign of insubordination.

At times of extraordinary panic, women were glad to have the militia mustered and ready for action. More often, the best defense women could hope for was to have a man capable of bearing arms in the house. Not surprisingly, some women balked when their husbands tried to leave them alone during a panic. When court was called to hear the cases of slaves tried for participating in Nat Turner's Rebellion, county court clerk James Rochelle took his family to stay with a friend in Portsmouth until the trials ended. Later that same month, Peyton Harrison told John Cocke, "I have been very anxious to see you lately and if my wife will consent for me to leave her a night, I will ride down [to] your house before long. . . . But I fear she will [not] readily grant me this permission as [she] partakes in no small degree of the general alarm which pervades her sex at this time." In Alabama, state representative John Gayle explained to his wife that he did not run for U.S. Congress because he had an "aversion to separating from you so long." He did not explain the basis of his aversion, but a month before receiving that letter, Sarah Gayle gave one reason. Writing about the "rumors concerning the slaves," she commented, "I dread the winter, spending [it], as I shall without protection."[13] John may have believed that he was compromising by staying in Alabama, but Sarah had her doubts, wondering if the capital in Tuscaloosa were close enough to their Greensborough home.

Wives whose husbands traveled from their homes feared that their husbands would not be able to fulfill their duty to protect them in an emergency. Despite this drawback, single Southern women still saw marriage as the best way to ensure a safer home. For most women living in the slave South, marriage was the foundation of public safety. Five months after Nat Turner's Rebellion, Mary Robertson made an unusual proposal to the other young women of Norfolk. Robertson told her friends that "it will be an excellent thing to have a town meeting called to make a new law, that no young gentleman that has been living in Norfolk five years shall go out of town to get a wife." Mary McPhail mocked this suggestion when she noted that "no young lady would second that resolution, unless she was in great want of a husband."[14] Nevertheless, even the sarcastic McPhail did not dispute the premise behind Robertson's outlandish proposal: men had a responsibility to marry to ensure the safety of otherwise unprotected single women.

Women without husbands or fathers to protect them tried to arrange for other men to act as their defenders. When Peggy Nicholas wrote about visiting a friend, she alluded to one condition she would like to have met: "I must say that it will be rather scary to be all the Winter so near a Vagabond place as Milton without a gentleman in the house. Would it not be possible to keep Ben with you. With him and a gun or two, I should defy all danger." Susan Bowdoin apparently felt less compunction when she wrote her nephew, Joseph Prentis, only weeks after the Southampton slave insurrection. In her letter, she asked him to take her, "one who feels herself very unprotected in the World," in for the rest of her life. However, instead of offering to move to his home in Suffolk, she tried to bribe him to move himself, his family, and his law practice to Norfolk. Should he do that, she assured him, "at my death, I should give you at least enough . . . to prevent any regret for affording your only Aunt an asylum."[15]

Women turned to other women when no male champions were available. During an 1844 scare in North Carolina, Frances Bumpas noted in her diary: "Got L. Davies to sleep with me during Mr. B's absence. She thought once timid is quite courageous." Likewise, Mary Chesnut and her sister Kate ended up sleeping together when suspicion of the slaves in South Carolina was particularly acute. Emily Burke described a lady in Georgia in the 1840s who invited her to stay with her while her husband was away. As it turned out, there had been a slave plot on that plantation in the past, and the woman survived only because a loyal slave had betrayed the rebels.[16]

Women might have wanted other women nearby to increase their safety, but some Southern white women were ready to defend themselves if need be. According to Burke, the unnamed Georgian lady never retired at night without "an axe so near her pillow she could lay her hand upon it instantly." She would have preferred a gun, but she felt unable to wield a pistol effectively. Other women had more confidence in their marksmanship. "I have known ladies who wouldn't dare to go to sleep without one or two pistols under their pillows," Burke recalled. One such woman nearly sent her husband to his eternal reward when he tried to surprise her after returning home from a trip early and at night. These Georgian ladies were not the only ones who were ready to defend themselves by force if need be. When Mary Chesnut and her sister Kate found themselves alone on a plantation except for slaves, they doubted their safety. Kate's maid Betsey, "a strong-built mulatto woman," entered these discussions when she brought her own mattress into Kate's room. Betsey's actions led Kate to wonder, "Is this to protect me or to murder me?" Kate never made up her mind about Betsey's loyalty, deciding instead that "she could manage Betsey, who was so 'fat & scant of breath' (like Hamlet) & she so noisy."[17]

Elizabeth Fox-Genovese has argued that Southern "women had no business to bear arms," but such gender conventions were a moot point at the times of extraordinary crisis. Ignoring strictures against bearing arms, women looked for anything to defend themselves from the specter of slave rebels. Almost anything could serve as a weapon when a crisis occurred. The unnamed woman who ran through the streets of Petersburg dressed in only a "light and airy" dress clearly did not have much time to gather herself before leaving. But she did have time to collect one thing before she abandoned her house: her husband's razors. Others took more time to consider their weapons. One wonders if any woman put as much thought into the means of defense as Julia LeGrand's hostess, Mrs. Norton. During the Civil War, rumors spread about a possible slave uprising in New Orleans. The concern was so great that the federal provost marshal allowed former Confederates to rearm to secure the city from the slaves. The white women of New Orleans hoped that such provisions would provide for their safety, but Mrs. Norton, an elderly resident, had prepared her own defense. According to Julia LeGrand, she had "a hatchet, a tomahawk, and a vial of some kind of spirits with which she intends to blind all invaders."[18]

While some women made sensible plans for escape and others more chimerical plans, some Southern women realized that there was nothing that could be bottled that would guarantee their safety from those slaves who were determined to kill. At the start of the Civil War, one South Carolina widow remarked, "I fear twould take very little to make them put me out of the way." Given the often inescapable vulnerability to slave attack, many women's planning focused less on how to survive a slave rebellion and more on how to make sure they would never have to endure such a scare. One sure way to escape the threat posed by human property was to migrate to a place without slavery. In the wake of Nat Turner's Rebellion, Eliza Prentis confessed to her sister, "I often fear that I shall never feel happy or comfortable again, in the state of Virginia. I would gladly remove to any spot on earth that is not a *slave state*." After Denmark Vesey's conspiracy was uncovered in Charleston, South Carolina, Anna Hayes Johnson remarked in a letter, "I wish I could act for myself. . . . I would not stay in the city another day."[19] Such expressions were not uncommon after a serious insurrection scare. Like most other Southern women, however, these women believed that their ties to their families made a unilateral decision to leave the South impossible.

Commitment to their families did not mean that these women saw themselves as helpless, condemned to live and die in the slave South. Many women lobbied their husbands and fathers to move the entire family to a free state. Jane Randolph explained to her friend Sarah Nicholas, "I am using all my efforts with Jefferson to quit at once." While she admitted that it would be "a dreadful sacrifice for us to leave our home," she insisted, "I would make it without hesitation to be freed from the horrors that surround us here." Randolph's lobbying failed, but others apparently had more success. Delia Hurd, for an example, wrote that "I hardly dare to think of Virginia, for so many ties cling around the recollection of that sweet place." Nonetheless, six months after Nat Turner's Rebellion, she indicated that her family would move, probably to Ohio. "We wish to live in a free state," she explained.[20]

Since most women did not persuade their families to leave the South, many Southern women focused their energies on making the South a safer place to be. Lobbying powerful men was one way women tried to improve their world. For example, in the aftermath of Nat Turner's Rebellion, many Southerners believed that the newly established *Liberator* played a key role in inspiring Virginia's slaves to rebel. As a result, Southerners looked for ways to silence Massachusetts's most famous abolitionist. Unable to get William Lloyd Garrison extradited to a Southern state to face a trial for inculcating insurrection, traditional politicians—working in the courts and legislatures— were powerless to muzzle the *Liberator's* editor. Even the most powerful proslavery men could do little but plead their case and hope that sympathetic Northerners would silence a man safely beyond their reach. South Carolina's Senator Robert Y. Hayne, for instance, wrote a plea to Boston's Mayor Harrison Gray Otis less than two months after Nat Turner's insurrection, hoping that the mayor might put Garrison out of business.[21] In the corridors of the Capitol, Hayne was a powerful figure, but he was powerless to stop Garrison from afar.

Women, whose usual access to political power was through lobbying, were not afraid to make similar pleas. Three days after Hayne petitioned Otis to stop Garrison, Ellen Lewis took her pen and wrote to Otis. Appealing to him as a family friend, Lewis used the idea that men had a responsibility to protect women as a fulcrum on which to leverage her demands to silence Garrison. In her letter, Lewis noted that the victims of future slave rebellions were bound to be "our young & lovely females, infant innocent, & helpless age[d]," just as they had been in Southampton. Lewis's letter acted as a not-so-subtle rebuke of the mayor and all the honorable men of Boston who had not silenced Garrison. This failure, she implied, cost scores of Southampton women and children their lives. The men of Boston, because of their inaction, bore the blood of Southampton's dead. Lewis minced no words in describing how she believed the men of Boston should respond: "I think he merits *Death*. . . . He inculcates insurrection, murder, cruelty, & baseness, in every shape."[22] Lewis's call for Garrison's head failed to silence the crusader, but she used the notion that men should protect women as the basis for her emotionally charged appeal.

While some women, such as Lewis, appealed to Northern men to make sure that abolitionists did not incite insurrection, others focused on removing the danger that surrounded them in the South. If slaves and free blacks were removed to Africa or Haiti, the threat they posed to Southern women and children would vanish. As a result, many Southern women turned to colonization, not simply as a humanitarian program designed to help the slaves, but as a policy that would protect whites, especially white women and children. Jane Randolph—who vigorously lobbied to convince her husband to move their family from the South—kept the pressure on her husband to work to relieve her of her fears. Her husband refused to move the family but became one of the leaders of the floor fight for a program of gradual emancipation and colonization. While he led the doomed fight for colonization, she kept the pressure on her husband, writing letters that expressed her distress over the threat of slave insurrections. He took a break from the colonization debates in Richmond to calm his wife, whose letters indicated to him that she was making herself "worry about the negroes."[23] One may fairly ask how much of the fear scripted into the letters of Jane Randolph was simply her way of reinforcing her husband's commitment to a cause dear to her heart.

Colonization was widely supported by Southern white women, especially during the legislative debates about emancipation and colonization that followed Nat Turner's Rebellion. While some school girls vowed "to do all that lies in our power . . . to promote the cause of colonization," the young women at Miss M. Mercer's Seminary in Cedar Park, Maryland, put their knitting needles to work. They formed the "Liberian Free-School Society" and worked on behalf of the American Colonization Society. At the end of the school year, the girls' labors earned the society ten dollars, which they passed along to the national organization. Most donations to the American Colonization Society came through churches, and most donations given to the American Colonization Society through their churches are lost to the historical record, as are the names of the individual students at Miss Mercer's school. Nevertheless, direct gifts from women and from female auxiliaries were an important source of funding for the American Colonization Society. The Fredricksburg and Falmouth [Virginia] Female Auxiliaries of the Colonization Society gave one hundred dollars to the American Colonization Society; the Georgetown, D.C., female Auxiliary of the American Colonization Society took up Gerritt Smith's challenge and promised to donate one thousand dollars over ten years. In the month after Nat Turner's Rebellion, Mrs. Elizabeth Greenfield donated $429.94, enough to send a large family to Liberia from New Orleans. The smallest donations also reveal a deep-seated commitment to colonization on the part of some of the country's the poorest women. In the spring of 1832, the American Colonization Society received from an anonymous woman thirty-seven cents, money she had earned selling the socks she made.[24]

While emancipation and colonization was a popular cause for women, colonization was not the only way to rid the South of slaves. If all the slaves were killed, then there would be no chance of a slave rebellion. Along these lines, one Petersburg woman was heard commenting "that she would willingly cast her own slaves into the street, there to be shot, provided others, who had slaves, would agree to do the same." Certainly she was not alone in contemplating such evil. These ideas were not unusual at the times of greatest terror, when people killed unarmed black men and women without due process and often with little or no basis for suspicion. Most understood that were there another major insurrection scare on the heels of Nat Turner's Rebellion, all nearby blacks—not just those involved—might be put to the sword. One newspaper contended, "Let the fact not be doubted by those whom it most concerns, that another such insurrection will be signal for the extirmination [sic] of the whole black population in the quarter of the state where it occurs."[25] In this atmosphere, even ordinary activities of women, such as providing moral support for the troops, had an important political role. When women presented colors to militia units, or when they expressed their thanks to the soldiers for a job well done, they also provided an important defense for the men who at times got out of line. Even barbarity could be defended when done to protect vulnerable Southern white women and children.

Involvement in the traditional type of influence politics easily bled into a new type of activism, one where women took to the public stage to support their favorite causes. Women not only sewed a flag for the Petersburg militia but also selected speakers from among themselves to give a speech as they presented the colors. When the gallery at the emancipation debates filled with women, a different level of public activity than simply lobbying husbands can be detected.[26] The actions blended easily because this new activism was so much like the old politics. After all, women were concerned about the domestic sphere. No doubt slavery was the single most important political question of the day, but women spoke about the ways that slavery threatened them at home. Their pleas stood out against a landscape where men such as Joseph Davis did not even mention a slave-insurrection scare when he wrote to his son.

No actions more clearly displayed this new found political involvement than the petition drives in Virginia after Nat Turner's Rebellion. Women had always been free to petition the government when they were looking for special action: women petitioned the government when seeking divorce; wives wrote governors pleading hardship as grounds for leniency for their jailed husbands. But these petitions were accepted and understood as simply personal, not as policy statements on the major questions of the day. After Nat Turner's Rebellion, women decided that they would petition the government for relief from the threat of slave insurrections. These women could not pretend that they were acting as Southern women always had. In her petition, Mary Blackford wrote, "We are tremblingly alive to the fear of appearing too forward in this matter." Despite these fears, Blackford insisted that it was "not out of our place" to petition, not least because of "our defenseless state in the absence of our Lords." Mary Blackford got only one woman's signature on her petition before she lost her nerve and pulled it. Other petitions, however, made it all the way to the House of Delegates. In the months after Nat Turner's Rebellion, 215 women signed an Augusta County petition. They invoked "the late slaughter of our sisters and their little ones" in Southampton. This massacre revealed to them the fragility of "the peace of their homes," and on these grounds women called for a "decisive and efficient measure" that had as its object "the extinction of slavery, from amongst us." In these carefully crafted petitions, women passed the point of no return, where they could no longer pretend to be uninterested and uninvolved in the world of politics.[27]

As these conservative women turned to active politics, one can see a serious flaw in the world the slaveholders made. Slaveholders—male and female—hoped and prayed for a sanctuary in which the family would be free from the corruption of the world at large. Women and children would be safe at home, living in what Christopher Lasch calls "a haven in a heartless world."[28] But such a haven was an impossibility in a world full of slaves who sometimes killed. Rather than live with the lie—and pretend that they lived in perfectly safe place—Southern white women did what they could to protect themselves. The fear of slaves drove women to action, even political action, undermining the principle of an incorruptible home. But their actions could not dissipate a threat that was real. The slave South remained a place without refuge.

NOTES

1. Joseph H. Davis to Wilbur Fisk Davis, 5 January 1857, Folder 16, Beale-Davis Family Papers, Subseries 1.1, Southern Historical Collection, University of North Carolina (hereafter cited as SHC).

2. According to Mrs. Davis, the screams came from "a young lady who is subject to screaming fits from temporary mental derangement." Anne Beale Davis to Wilbur Fisk Davis, 5 January 1857, Folder 16, Beale-Davis Family Papers, Subseries 1.1, SHC.

3. W. C. Daniel to James Screven, 5 July 1822; and Martha [Proctor] Richardson to James Screven, 6 July 1822, Folder 34, Screven Family Papers, Subseries 2.1.2, SHC.

4. Fanny Anne Kemble, *Journal of a Residence on a Georgian Plantation in 1838–1839,* John A. Scott, ed. (Athens: University of Georgia Press, 1984), 342. Emphasis in original.

5. Herbert Aptheker, *American Negro Slave Revolts* (Columbia University Press, 1943; New York: International Publishers, 1963), 23; Thomas R. Gray, *The Confessions of Nat Turner, the Leader of the Late Insurrection in Southampton, Va.* (Baltimore, 1831), 12, 22.

6. Littleton Waller Tazewell to John Wickham, 23 September 1831, Box 2, Wickham Family Papers, Virginia Historical Society (hereafter cited as VHS).

7. A. B. Davis to W. F. Davis, 5 January 1857, Beale-Davis Family Papers; Richmond *Enquirer,* 30 August 1831, quoted in Henry Irving Tragle, compiler, *The Southampton Slave Revolt of 1831: A Compilation of Source Material* (Amherst:

University of Massachusetts Press, 1971), 44; Helen Read to Louisa Cocke, 17 September 1831, Box 67, Papers of the Cocke Family, Special Collections, University of Virginia (hereafter cited as UVA). See also Gray, *Confessions,* 20; Richmond *Constitutional Whig,* 29 August 1831, quoted in Kenneth S. Greenberg, *Confessions of Nat Turner and Related Documents* (Boston: Bedford Books, 1996), 64; Robert S. Parker to Rebecca Mannet, 29 August 1831, Folder 2, Box 1, John Kimberly Papers, SHC. The estimate of a percentage of the adult female population is derived from the Southampton County Personal Property List. If one assumes a fairly even split between men and women among the adults in Southampton County, then there were about 1,600 white women over sixteen years old. That means the refugees amounted to between 19 and 25 percent of the total adult female population of the county. See *Southampton County Personal Property Books,* Library of Virginia (hereafter cited as LV).

8. 12 September 1831, Moses Ashley Curtis Diary, vol. 6, Moses Ashley Curtis Collection, SHC; Eliza Kennon Mordecai to Rachel Mordecai Lazarus, 9 October 1831, Folder 56, Box 4, Mordecai Family Collection, SHC. Eliza emphatically rejected any suggestion that the immodest woman was culpable for her actions. She vouched that this woman was not "a silly woman, for she is a great friend of mine."

9. Robert N. Elliot, "The Nat Turner Insurrection as Reported in the North Carolina Press," *North Carolina Historical Review* 38 (1961): 13; A. B. Davis to W. F. Davis, 5 January 1857, Beale-Davis Family Papers, Subseries 1.1, SHC.

10. Tom E. Terrill and Jerrold Hirsch, eds. *Such As Us: Southern Voices of the Thirties* (Chapel Hill: University of North Carolina Press, 1978), 239–40.

11. Richmond *Compiler,* 3 September 1831, quoted in Tragle, *Southampton Slave Revolt,* 61.

12. Bertram Wyatt-Brown, *Southern Honor: Ethics and Behavior in the Old South* (New York: Oxford University Press, 1982), 415.

13. Richard Blow to George Blow, 5 September 1831, Folder 5, Section 4, Blow Family Papers, VHS; [Payton Harrison to John H. Cocke], 24 September 1831, Box 67, Cocke Family Papers, UVA; John Gayle to Sarah Gayle, 3 December 1831, Folder 6, Box 24, typescript, and Sarah Haynesworth Gayle Journal, 1827–1831, Folder 4, Box 725, typescript, Gorgas Family Papers, W. S. Hoole Special Collections, University of Alabama.

14. Mary Elizabeth McPhail to Mary Carrington, 30 January 1832, Carrington Family Papers, VHS.

15. Peggy Nicholas to Jane Hollins Randolph, 9 October 1831, Box 7, Edgehill-Randolph Papers, UVA; Susan Bowdoin to Joseph Prentis, 13 September 1831, Box 5, Webb-Prentis Collection, UVA.

16. Frances Bumpas Diary, August 15, 1844, Folder 15, Bumpas Family Papers, Series 3.1, SHC; C. Vann Woodward, *Mary Chesnut's Civil War* (New Haven: Yale University Press, 1981), 199; Emily P. Burke, *Reminiscences of Georgia* ([Oberlin, Ohio], 1850), 156.

17. Burke, *Reminiscences*, 156, 158; Woodward, *Mary Chesnut's Civil War*, 199; C. Vann Woodward and Elizabeth Muhlenfield, eds. *The Private Mary Chesnut: The Unpublished Civil War Diaries* (New York: Oxford University Press, 1984), 181.

18. Elizabeth Fox-Genovese, *Within the Plantation Household: Black and White Women of the Old South* (Chapel Hill: University of North Carolina Press, 1988), 195; Eliza Kennon Mordecai to Rachel Mordecai Lazarus, 9 October 1831, Mordecai Family Collection; Kate Mason Rowland and Mrs. Morris L. Crozall, eds. *The Journal of Julia LeGrand, New Orleans, 1862–1863* (Richmond: Everett Waddey, 1911), 59.

19. Drew Gilpin Faust, *Mothers of Invention: Women of the Slaveholding South in the Civil War* (Chapel Hill: University of North Carolina Press, 1996), 57; Eliza B. Prentis to Margaret Prentis Webb, 13 September 1831, Box 9, Webb-Prentis Collection (emphasis in original); Richard C. Wade, "The Vesey Plot: A Reconsideration," *Journal of Southern History* 30 (1964): 145–46.

20. Jane Hollins Randolph to Sarah E. Nicholas, n.d., Box 7, Edgehill-Randolph Papers, UVA. Virginia Trist suggested that Jane had selected Cincinnati as the place to, which she wanted to relocate, Virginia Trist to [Nicholas P. Trist], 19 September 1831, Folder 59, Nicholas P. Trist Letters, Series 1.3, UVA. Delia Hurd to John Hartwell Cocke, 3 March 1832, Box 69, Cocke Family Papers. J. D. Paxton of Danville, Kentucky, hoped that the "fears excited" by Nat Turner's Rebellion would help him sell an empty property; see J. D. Paxton to John Hartwell Cocke, 23 February 1832, Box 69, Cocke Family Papers, UVA.

21. Robert Y. Hayne to Harrison Gray Otis, 14 October 1831, quoted in Samuel Eliot Morison, ed. *The Life and Letters of Harrison Gray Otis, Federalist, 1765–1848* (New York: Houghton Mifflin Company, 1913), 2:278–80.

22. E[llen Custis] P. Lewis to Harrison Gray Otis, 17 October 1831, quoted in Morison, *Life and Letters of Harrison Gray Otis*, 260.

23. T[homas] J[efferson] Randolph, Richmond, to Jane N. Randolph, 29 January 1832, Box 7, Edgehill-Randolph Papers, UVA.

24. Lucy [W. Oliver?] to Sally Cocke, n.d., Bremo Recess Papers, UVA; *African Repository and Colonization Journal* 8 (July 1832): 160; 8 (May 1832): 95–96; 7 (November 1831): 287; 8 (April 1832): 64.

25. *Liberator*, 1 October 1831; *Richmond Constitutional Whig*, 3 September 1831, both quoted in Tragle, *Southampton Slave Revolt*, 106, 69. Ellen Lewis made much

the same point in her letter to Harrison Gray Otis. If Northern abolitionists made "the blacks miserable, discontented, & rebellious," she feared this would "force the whites to exterminate them" (Morison, *Life and Letters of Harrison Gray Otis,* 260).

26. Lebsock, Suzanne, *Free Women of Petersburg: Status and Culture in a Southern Town, 1784–1860* (New York: Norton, 1984), 231. On women attending slave debates, see Elizabeth R. Varon, *We Mean to Be Counted: White Women and Politics in Antebellum Virginia* (Chapel Hill: University of North Carolina Press, 1998), 52.

27. Blackford was sure that she "could have gotten [signatures] if I had persevered," Mary Blackford Petition, n.d., typescript, Blackford Family Papers, SHC; Legislative Petitions, Augusta County, 19 January 1832, Fluvanna County, LV. Elizabeth Varon has examined women's political involvement in the 1840s and found a new ideal of feminine civic duty: "Whig womanhood," the belief that "women could—and should—make vital contributions to party politics." Perhaps "Whig womanhood" emerged in the 1840s, but women's political involvement in the 1840s echoes their highly political responses to the Nat Turner's Rebellion. See Varon, *We Mean to Be Counted,* 72 (quote), 49–51.

28. Christopher Lasch, *Haven in a Heartless World: The Family Besieged* (New York: Basic Books, 1977).

PART III

War and Southern Identity

Just as the institution of slavery continues to shape the interests of historians of the South so too does the issue of Southern identity. The third section of the book thus explores the nature of Southern identity before, during, and after the Civil War. Although there is certainly no shortage of works on Southern identity, few have sought to extend that identity in the direction of Missouri. This is odd given Missouri's ties to a conventionally defined "South" and the quantity of blood it shed on behalf of the South and its causes. In "The Southernization of Missouri: Kansas, the Civil War, and the Politics of Identity on the Western Border," Christopher Phillips considers Missouri's Southern identity in his exploration of the state's emotional and political drift toward the Confederacy in 1861. Key to this drift, according to Phillips, was "Bleeding Kansas." Previously, Missourians identified much more closely with the West and its hyper-allegiance to democratic individualism. Abolitionist rhetoric and actions in Kansas struck them as a fanatical expression of majoritarian tyranny. For many Missourians, it was then no small leap of faith to accept a Southern understanding of minority rights. "Bleeding Kansas" and the triumph of free soilism represented nothing short of a failure of democracy and federal governance. Phillips concludes that by 1861 Missourians who had once defined their liberty in terms of the West now looked toward the South to preserve what had been lost to a Northern conspiracy.

In much the same fashion as Christopher Phillips, Brian R. Dirck, in "Jefferson Davis, Abraham Lincoln, and the National Meaning of War," wrestles with identity in an unconventional way. He is concerned, more precisely, with how Jefferson Davis and Abraham Lincoln used language to define their countries. It is a fresh comparison of two leaders that historians have long stopped comparing. Lincoln, Dirck believes, spoke frequently and eloquently because of an intellectual uncertainty over God, slavery, and the meaning of the war. Dirck finds Davis a complete contrast. Confident in his relationship with God and the meaning of the war, Davis saw little need to talk publicly, and repeatedly, about these issues. Perhaps more importantly, Davis made little use of slavery in his speeches, preferring instead to stake the Confederacy's identity on the terrible experience of war rather than the peculiar institution. Davis knew already the hard meaning of war and assumed that the citizens of his country agreed with him. He did not then have to rationalize the war or find some transcendent explanation for it, as did Lincoln. Dirck ultimately believes that while Jefferson Davis did not lack any oratorical ability, he did indeed lack the need of convincing himself and his country of the war's meaning.

Christopher Waldrep finds language no less important in his provocative essay on "The Politics of Language: The Ku Klux Klan in Reconstruction." Waldrep reminds us of the centrality of language in the postwar struggle for control between Democrats and Republicans. Both parties sought to shape, and benefit from, popular support by using particular words to describe people and actions. Wielding terms such as scalawag, carpetbagger, and redeemer, Southern Democrats won not only a war of words but also the near term battles for political power and historical memory. Klan violence was also very much a part of this linguistic shaping of reality. As Waldrep notes, Klan directed violence permeated Reconstruction, but it faded from historical memory due to simple turns of language. Only beginning in the 1880s did the word lynching come to characterize Klan, or white, violence. As lynching appeared infrequently before then, so too did the historical ability to recognize violence committed during Reconstruction. The problem in terminology, according to Waldrep, owes itself in no small measure to Republicans who sought to de-legitimize Klan violence. As lynching then implied an orderly expression of community sovereignty, Republicans preferred terminology that proclaimed Klan violence to be the work of a fanatical minority. The word outrage therefore worked best to describe violence that lacked widespread community support. Waldrep concludes that Democratic successes in the late 1870s ended race-based violence as something only committed at night by men wearing sheets. An emerging political and social consensus on white supremacy now gave community legitimacy to violence directed toward blacks. With legitimacy bestowed, what had been before called an outrage could now safely be called a lynching. The words had changed, but the violence had not.

5

The Southernization of Missouri
Kansas, the Civil War, and the Politics of Identity on the Western Border

CHRISTOPHER PHILLIPS

Historians have long regarded Kansas as the seedbed for the American Civil War. Both as a source of national debate over slavery's extension and as the scene of violence that laid bare the fiction of popular sovereignty, Kansas broadened the already wide sectional divide. No academic study—or for that matter, no college course—on the antecedents of the Civil War can ignore the controversy over Kansas as an integral installment to the series of political crises that gripped the nation for the duration of the 1850s.

Nor can historians overlook its dramatis personae, with John Brown, James Montgomery, James Lane, and David Rice Atchison being only the lead players of a wide cast who themselves have become legendary characters, each having found the windswept prairie to be fertile ground for their zealotry. One need only view John Steuart Curry's evocative mural of John Brown in the Kansas statehouse in Topeka to appreciate his—and Kansas's—historical value. Popular histories of territorial Kansas abound, as writers have been drawn to the narrative value of Brown's and others' often violent exploits. Indeed, the 1999 opening of the motion picture *Ride with the Devil* hoped to capitalize on this interest. Clearly, set against the backdrop of the epic struggle between slavery and freedom, the story of "Bleeding Kansas" is indeed high drama.[1]

Apart from the most popular depictions, scholars have focused largely on the political events surrounding territorial Kansas, from the Kansas-Nebraska Act to the Lecompton Constitution, making them central to the broader tale of the fracturing Union. Sweeping works of the entire era, from Allan Nevins's *Ordeal of the Union* to James McPherson's *Battle Cry of Freedom,* among others, have regarded the Kansas conflict as rehearsal for civil war, while a number of important articles and monographs have placed the Kansas issue at the forefront of national politics during the critical decade of the 1850s. Of course, modern scholars have no lock on proclaiming Kansas a national political watershed; they merely take their cue from contemporary political luminaries. When Lincoln and Douglas squared off in their famed senatorial duel on the Illinois prairie during the hot summer of 1858, the Kansas issue formed the core topic of their "Great Debates."[2]

Ironically, a gap is evident in the coverage of the Kansas struggle. In focusing on either the Kansas violence or the place of Kansas in the national political arena, both historians and popular writers have either ignored or denigrated leading characters in the local drama. Missourians, who formed the largest portion of the Kansas population until well into 1855, are nearly uniformly dismissed as "border ruffians" and "pukes," undemocratic savages who ravaged a virgin Kansas to perpetuate slavery in the West. The unwillingness of historians to legitimate the worldview of these Missourians amid the Kansas furor (both during and well after the actual conflict) caused an exasperated Floyd Shoemaker, long-time director of the State Historical Society of Missouri, to complain in 1954, singling out the topic of the Kansas struggle, for which those Missourians are known most notoriously:

> It has been bypassed by Missouri historians almost in inverse ratio
> to its heavily volumed treatment by Kansas and Northern writers.
> . . . Whereas a score of such works favorable to the free-soil settlers
> of Kansas are still preserved in the research libraries of historical
> societies, universities, and other public collections, I have not
> found a single contemporary volume favorable to Missouri. . . . It
> is one of the few examples I know of of one side being simon-pure
> and the other side being simply poor, of one side having all the
> proof and the other side getting all the punishment, of one side
> receiving the bravos and the other side, the Bronx cheers.[3]

In part, Shoemaker's charge that scholars have offered uneven treatment of the Kansas issue—focusing instead on the abolitionist New England emigrants—appears well aimed. By portraying Missourians monolithically, if at all, scholars have thus missed their—and their region's—complexity. Despite recent studies that have corrected the oversight somewhat, with authors Gunja SenGupta and especially the late Bill Cecil-Fronsman lending depth to proslavery Missourians in Kansas, scholars continue routinely to employ Daniel Crofts's *Reluctant Confederates* as the modern standard—whether of politics or ideology—on the secession crisis in the Upper South ("North of South" as one Ohio observer described the region in 1861), despite its complete omission of those border slave states from its interpretive scope.[4]

Yet Shoemaker's obvious pique suggests even more. A native Missourian, he appears to have written in defense of his own misunderstood regional heritage, one in which, ironically, he assumed shades of Southern leanings against which he castigated "Northern" historians for assuming themselves. His bald charge of a Northern regional bias in academics' treatment of Missouri offers as much about his own misconception of that region or regions as of any misapplication of regional status to his own Missouri. Clearly, the intersection of these misplaced regional perceptions—now as well as then—lay in the Kansas-Missouri conflict, the historical "border war" now manifest most obviously in the annual intercollegiate football contest between the two states' flagship universities for which Missouri residents, more even than those in Kansas, gear up. For Missourians, the violence on the gridiron is emblematic, an opportunity to regain, if temporarily, a paradise lost by punishing the modern Yankees in Eden. What the historians against whom Floyd Shoemaker railed seem not to have recognized is that, at least for Missourians, the Kansas conflict was a cardinal component in the process by which the border was created, one employed by many contemporaries in their creation of a pronounced Southern identity.

Missourians' intensity surrounding the Kansas issue has deep roots. From the summer of 1849 to the spring of 1854, the state's politics, in one contemporary's recollection, were "characterized by a bitterness of invective and popular excitement without parallel in the history of Missouri." The maelstrom swirled about Missouri's leonine senator, Thomas Hart Benton. Allegiance or opposition to Benton defined the camps within Missouri's Democratic legion, largely a result of Benton's apparent defection to the free-soil cause. Having opposed the annexation of Texas and maintained a moderate stance on the issue of slavery's extension, Benton found himself assailed by an aggressive proslavery faction in Missouri led by Claiborne Fox Jackson. In 1849 Jackson had taken credit for a set of resolutions enacted by the Missouri legislature that instructed Benton to vote consistently for any congressional legislation that supported slavery's extension in the West. Benton savagely countered Jackson and his followers, as well as his old nemesis John C. Calhoun, from whom the state's proslavery "Central Clique" took inspiration, leading the Jefferson City *Metropolitan* to speculate: "Colonel Benton has lost his reason and is now the prey to his wicked and ungovernable passions. . . . [H]e is every day losing the respect and confidence of his friends, he seems determined on self-ruin." The newspaper predicted correctly. With the state's Democrats hopelessly fractured over Old Bullion and the so-called "Jackson Resolutions," the party was unable to unite on any issue, much less Benton's seat. In August 1850, after forty ballots, Henry S. Geyer, a proslavery Whig (until recently a Democrat) from St. Louis emerged the winner, ending the then-longest consecutive reign of any U.S. senator.[5]

The bitter struggle for Benton's senate seat in Missouri was no mere contest between legislative rivals or even cabals for an election-year plum. Rather, this was by 1850 a jihad, a holy war for the state's—indeed, for the West's—soul. The truest nature of the conflict, one refined or even altered by the very tumult that surrounded the coup, centered on slavery, by now an ironic shibboleth in Missouri. The language of power employed during Benton's long torment points clearly toward a transition of mind in Missouri with regard to the place of slavery in the state and the region. Old Bullion's damning sin had been neither his wayward party demeanor nor his imperious nature (earning him the derisive nickname "the great I AM"); each of these infelicities had been in place well prior to his precipitous fall from grace. His immolation resulted from his apparent outright embrace of the free-soil doctrine that in itself signaled a sea change in his philosophy of the West.[6]

Missouri's newly risen star—David Rice Atchison—ascended to the Senate by adopting Calhoun's rhetoric, though not his world. An able confederate of Calhoun who assisted in the drafting of the Southern Address and then was the lone Missourian to sign it, Atchison actively championed it in his home state. To his own Platte Countians, he avowed that he "expect[ed] always to be found acting with the southern men in the Senate chamber and out of it, in defence of the rights of the southern States." Moreover, Atchison publicly supported Missouri's Jackson Resolutions, the General Assembly's refraction of Calhoun's address to the Senate, claiming that "as a Senator from Missouri and as a citizen of a Slave State, it is my duty to resist every attempt to change her institutions, and every assault upon her rights."[7]

However fiery his words, Atchison was no planter—not in Missouri's reckoning, much less that of the plantation states. He was not even a farmer, but a bachelor lawyer and circuit court judge prior to attaining the Senate. Atchison, son of a small slaveholding Bluegrass yeoman, had removed from Kentucky, not to Missouri's Boon's Lick, the state's slaveholding heart, but to far western Clay and Platte Counties, vestibules to the slaveholding Missouri River counties. Atchison quickly became seignior of the region's common whites and, if judged by his words—and ultimately his deeds—in defense of slavery in the West, he proved indistinguishable from the fire-eaters of South Carolina and Mississippi. Yet one incontrovertible fact set him decidedly apart from the rabid cotton-state defenders of the peculiar institution: Atchison owned at most one bondman.[8]

Atchison was anything but alone as a small or even non-slave-owning Missourian. Missouri's year of meteors—1850—coincided with a precipitous proportional downturn in the state's slave holdings. In that year, slaves represented 12.8 percent of its total population, down from more than 15 percent a decade before. By 1860, after the waves of immigrants had poured into the state, Missouri slaves accounted for just 9.6 percent of its residents, the smallest of the slave states save Delaware. More to the point, in that year slave-owning families represented just 18.4 percent of the state's total, lowest of any of the slave states save Delaware and a far cry from South Carolina, where more than half of all free white families owned bondpeople. By 1860, Missouri's 24,000–odd slaveholders would comprise just 2.3 percent of its total free population; they and their families represented just 12.5 percent of Missouri's white families.[9]

Clearly, Atchison's peculiar crusade for the peculiar institution was no mere charade designed to win political support among slaveholders or anyone else—his ultimate relinquishment of his Senate seat over the issue settled that question. That Missouri's most ardent defender of slaveholding was himself barely if at all the master of slaves offers a revealing insight into the complex evolution that the issue of slavery had undergone in the minds of Missourians, slaveholding and not. The dualistic nature of slavery in the state only complicated the issue further. Rather than signaling any death knell in the state, raw slave numbers in Missouri actually increased during the same period, and they did so far more dramatically than their proportion within the state's overall population declined. Between 1830 and 1850, Missouri's slave population more than tripled to 87, 422; by 1860, that number had increased by another third to 114,931, an all-time high. More than thirty-five thousand of these labored in the central river counties. Inflated prices of slaves offered no indication that chattel bondage was waning in Missouri. (Prime field hands fetched routinely as much as $1,500 in Howard County, while annual prices for hired laborers caused one resident of Prairieville to write, late in the decade,

"Every thing is rising in value—especially negro property—hirelings went at most exorbitant prices on New Year's day—men generally at about $230 for the year. . . . Slave labor has never been any thing like so high.") Nor should they have; in the last antebellum decade, slavery was thriving.[10]

Given the proliferation of slavery in Missouri, the storm clouds that gathered with the abolitionists' assault on the peculiar institution became a tempest during the debate over Texas, Mexico, free-soil, and Benton. With roots sunk firmly into a bedrock of individual and democratic rights, these Westerners found it easy to construct an active response to the threat posed to their peculiar institution by the antislavery host. Armed with the battle-cry of liberty, they waged war first against Garrison's undemocratic minions, then against any of their own who turned against the cause. In this new sectional realm, Missourians targeted those they knew best, their free-state antagonists —now including Benton, who advocated a Northern president—who sought to subvert democratic ascendance in the West. "It was the fixed design of the Free States," Atchison howled, "not only to prevent the Slave States from any further participation in the Territories of the United States, but by a series of measures to reduce the latter to a state of *helpless inferiority*, and to subject them and their institutions to the mercy of Abolitionism. And that Missouri would be the first victim sacrificed upon the altar of this infernal spirit." Echoing this sentiment, state supreme court justice William B. Napton wrote in 1850 that "the persistence of the North is regarded as a proof of her fixed and settled purpose, not only to prevent the increase of slave territory but gradually to undermine and ultimately to destroy the institution itself. This will be resisted as an unconstitutional interference with our domestic concerns." Recognizing slavery's power in Missouri's consciousness, artist George Caleb Bingham remarked astutely in 1854 that "the slavery agitation is too convenient an instrument in the hands of demagogues to be dispensed with."[11]

As abolitionists within and without attacked Missouri's democratic right, an alarmed populace quickly parroted proslavery arguments articulated by Calhoun and other positive good apologists. Napton was one of the state's most ardent polemicists; the justice accused Free-soilers of duplicity as well as hypocrisy "in trying to shut up slavery within the old states and exclude it from the new territories, which shows clearly their motives to be not of a philanthropic character—but merely based upon a thirst for political power." A rock-ribbed agrarian utopian, Napton promoted the classical republican image of superior slave-based societies, including Missouri, arguing that slavery "has the effect of ridding society of a great many evils which infest countries where free labor alone is found and tolerated. . . . Hence a certain degree of dependence and loftiness of sentiment pervades even the poorer and humbler classes of citizens, which among the idle and higher classes, is united with intelligence, taste, and refinement. . . . We are clear of these evils here. . . . To slavery we owe this distinction.[12]

Ironically, while Napton's rhetoric on slavery and social progress might have invoked the language of Deep South apologists, Missourians yet clearly considered the South a distinct place of which Missouri was not a part. While their culture might have derived largely from a slaveholding heritage sectionalized now to the extent that in common parlance their institution was "peculiar," Missourians still considered themselves and their state part of the West, or now—in the sectional era—more specifically the Middle West, "the heart of the American continent." Embodied in town names such as Westport, Weston, and even the German-Americans' Westphalia, this conscious regional identity was articulated best by Boone County proslavery politico James S. Rollins, who cautioned his son, a cadet at West Point, to "say to the Northern and Southern cadets—that you belong to *neither section*—that you are a true son of the great West." In their language, rural Missourians—even those in the Boon's Lick—regarded the South—and certainly the North—as distinct, even foreign regions from their own. One proposal submitted to the Missouri House as an alternative to the Jackson Resolutions claimed that Missouri, "being one of the most north western Slave States . . . occupies a central portion in this grand valley of the Mississippi [whose] geographical position in this Union presents a unity in interest, whether considered commercially, socially or politically—such a unity of interest can never be permanently severed." Even Atchison, responding to arguments linking Missouri with the South, quickly reminded a middle-western colleague in the Senate who had differentiated his region from those that practiced slavery that Missouri was indeed "one of the northwestern States, although it is generally, from its institutions, classed as one of the southwestern States." True to its Western identity and to its pledge to "take a just and conservative position . . . and arrest the fire brands hurled by the violent and fanatical portion of the North and the South," Missouri sent no representatives to a "Southern convention" held at Nashville in 1850, though the topic of debate concerned the maintenance of slavery.[13]

As the national debate over slavery drew the West into its scope in the wake of the war with Mexico, Missourians saw the debate over their own statehood rekindled and thrust into the national forum. The very boundary that was their state's southern border—the 36° 30' parallel—became alternately the seed of harmony and discord between slavery's restrictionists and extensionists. As Congress debated afar the future of the vast territories taken from Mexico, and as the nation's politicians contorted over it in the subsequent electioneering mayhem, the sacred parallel became a regular topic as a practical compromise line upon which to organize the entire region. Just as the debate laid the state's name yet again on the lips of the nations' leaders, so did it isolate Missouri as potentially the only slave state situated above the parallel. The Compromise of 1850 essentially sidestepped the issue by avoiding the Louisiana Purchase entirely, allowing all the remaining portion of the Mexican cession save California to organize on the murky principle of popular sovereignty. Missouri was thus segregated even further, the only state allowed to have slavery in a north-western region that, by permanent decree, forbade the institution. More confusing, Missouri was now situated alongside the remaining northern expanse of the Louisiana territory, whose future was barred from slaveholding by the very act that had breathed life into Missouri. As Missourians did all in their power to maintain their allegiance to the democratic Middle West, the nation's newest paradox over slavery forced them glaringly into the role of regional outsiders.[14]

Yet Missourians refrained from adopting the language of power emanating with increasing volume from the cotton states. Cries of disunion and secession, grown louder during the territorial debate, met with stony silence in Missouri. Claiborne F. Jackson was forced to fend off widespread attacks as a "nullifier"—a once-democratic hallmark now linked to the Calhoun camp and thus condemned as being disunionist—a charge that he was unable to shake, costing him his seat in the Missouri Senate as well as his candidacy for the U.S. House of Representatives. More important, in their defense of slavery, Missourians embraced a strangely selective, even contradictory stance on federal and state power within the republic, one that accepted Congress's authority to legislate on slavery while accommodating the states' rights to protect its residents' property, so long as neither interfered with individual liberties, of which slaveholding was one. "I take the ground, that neither Congress, nor even the state in convention have anything to do with slave property, any more than any other species of property," wrote John J. Lowry, a legislator from Fayette. "I assume that there is no such thing as *absolute state sovereignty*, because, even in a state convention, such convention can only make fundamental regulations, which rules are guides for subsequent Legislatures whereby to shape their state laws. . . . I am satisfied with the 'Missouri compromise,' or any other compromise, if the people acquiesce in them, & they will sement [*sic*] the Union of these states . . . This is high ground . . . but it is the only tenable ground, which I can discover in accordance with the true rights of property."[15]

Indeed, Missourians remained vigilant against those, proslavery and not, who manipulated to their own advantage the already-blurred lines surrounding the debate over slavery's extension into the West. The editor of the *Glasgow Weekly Times* cautioned readers that "whilst we are as decidedly and as unalterably opposed to Abolitionism, 'Freesoilism' and all sorts of slavery agitations as any *live* man on the face of the earth, we, nevertheless, regret to hear the charge of Abolitionism and Freesoilism applied indiscriminately to all men who do not feel disposed to threaten 'blood and thunder' against every man hailing from a free State, and especially against those who, whilst they believe that Congress has the constitutional power to legislate upon the subject of slavery in the Territories, are yet decidedly opposed to its exercise." Indeed, in 1853, Claib Jackson found himself forced to explain his understanding of the term "Free-Soiler" on the floor of the state senate, after having used the charge ubiquitously against political opponents. Jackson quickly equivocated, claiming that "he did not consider a man who believed Congress had the power to exclude slavery from the Territories of the United States a free-soiler; but those who advocated the *exercise of the power*, were free-soilers."[16]

Seeking a middle ground in the growing struggle, Missourians maintained steadfast loyalty to the Union while supporting the democratic process as the foundation of liberty. In 1855, Boon's Lickers called for a Union state convention for the purpose of "averting the calamities which a separation of the States would bring upon us." A year before, residents of Weston had called a "Law and Order" meeting and declared unwavering fidelity to the government, taking as their motto "The Union First, Union Second, and Union forever." Yet because of the past decade's debates, the politicized issue of slavery had become for its residents democracy's litmus test, making unfirm the ground on which slavery and liberty had coexisted peacefully.[17]

In an attempt to keep their footing as slaveholders and as Unionists, Missourians sought to convince the nation that a fourth section of the country existed, apart from the North, South, and West—one that ameliorated the antagonistic influences in their daily lives and that, if recognized, could do so with the country as a whole. The middle, or border states formed a natural alignment, whether of culture, heritage, climate, or geography. More important, all were slaveholding states, but of conviction rather than of economy. As Senator Henry S. Geyer noted before the U.S. Senate, "South of 36° 30' is the cotton region, where slave labor may be profitably employed, . . . There, soil & climate settle the question; . . . but in the latitude above that and below 41° is the debatable ground. That is the latitude of the middle states—Virginia, Maryland, and Kentucky." Able to separate themselves from the sectional debate over slavery, the middle border states, as Geyer saw them, "the heart of the American continent, containing at this time nearly one half of the population of the U.S. should, and must, at no distant day, exercise a potent influence in giving tone, character and direction to our national legislation." The concept of a middle confederacy of sorts as healer of the ailing nation appealed to many Missourians who felt caught in the increasingly vituperative sectional climate. More important, the concept vindicated their place as virtuous slaveholders within the republic.[18]

Yet as the nation divided over the issue of chattel slavery, Missourians heard well, in the Northern condemnations of the institution, the heavy tolls of an accepted superiority—both moral and economic—of a free society over a slave society. Though in the sectional arena the abolitionists directed these jeremiads largely at those in the South, Missourians found themselves squarely in two lines of fire, one the abolitionists'—aimed at slaveholders—and another the free-soilers'—directed at slaveholding Westerners. Abolitionists such as William Lloyd Garrison condemned slaveholders indiscriminately as "murderers of fathers, and murderers of liberty, and traffickers of human flesh, and blasphemers against the Almighty," vowing Old Testament retribution and trumpeting that "the motto enscribed on the banner of Freedom should be NO UNION WITH SLAVEHOLDERS," a slogan that soon pealed from the mouths of radical Northern politicians in the halls of Congress. Free labor and free-soil advocates in Washington condemned Southern slave society as socially stagnant, without incentive, and degrading to laborers, and touted the West as holding the future greatness of America—a vista achieved only by the prohibition of slavery from the region. One of the Old West, Ohioan Salmon P. Chase, held that a free West, removed of slavery, would offer "freedom not serfdom; freeholds not tenancies; democracy not despotism, education not ignorance . . . progress, not stagnation or retrogression." To Missourians, Frank Blair proclaimed boldly that "the wealth and the political power of the country will in a little time reside at its Geographical centre," adding almost wistfully that once crossing the river into Illinois, one could not view "the splendid farms of Sangamon and Morgan, without permitting an envious sigh to escape him at the evident superiority of free labor."[19]

More offensive to proslavery Missourians, the Northern assault on slavery and the restrictionist effort intrinsically relegated slaveholders to the status of inferiors, whether moral or numerical. Indeed, Atchison became John C. Calhoun's Southern rights standard bearer, not from any longstanding belief in his or Missourians' general Southern heritage, but because of the specter of a Northern majoritarianism. His dead captain's "Disquisition on Government" —which argued that too much liberty in the hands of those unfit to exercise it was democracy's curse—put the matter in language unmistakable to these beleaguered Westerners. The triumph of democracy had, in effect, empowered an unequal yet majority people, extending them the right—the power—by virtue of the mass franchise, to claim the nation's future. Those so unfit, in the sectional era, were antislavery Northerners, especially those now influencing the national government as they sought to "monopolize" the territories. With free states positioned on two of Missouri's community borders—and by virtue of the Missouri Compromise, their third, western border, once populated— Missouri appeared inevitably doomed as a slaveholding peninsula in an angry sea of Free-Soilers.[20]

The charge of inferiority, combined with the attempt to limit slavery's extension, caused Missourians to see the Northern antislavery element as a tyrannical majority intent on oppressing an enlightened minority. In attempting to limit the South's ability to carry their property wherever they chose, the North was clearly limiting their constitutional freedoms. Denying slaveholders their constitutional right to property, to freedom, was in effect the denial of equality—yet another proof that free-soilers, not slaveholders, intended to destroy democracy in the nation. The defense of slavery gave way to one more germane for Westerners: defense of white minority rights within the republic, a concept that both Atchison and Geyer grasped firmly. In the debate over the organization of Nebraska, Atchison the Calhounite vowed to "oppose the organization or the settlement of that Territory unless my constituents and the constituents of the whole South, of the slave States of the Union, could go into it upon the same footing, with equal rights and equal privileges, carrying that species of property with them as other people of this Union . . . I will vote for a bill that leaves the slaveholder and non-slaveholder upon terms of equality." Geyer argued similarly: "The antagonism and hostility between the States and the people, engendered by the agitation of the slavery question," he charged, "is aggravated by hostile legislation and the struggle for political power by a sectional party warring upon the institutions of one half the States of the Union."[21]

Indeed, the defense of individual rights—with slavery at the notion's core—soon drew Missourians into a general acceptance of the concept of Southern rights, which meant defiance against majoritarian authority. More ominously, its sympathetic and widespread use in country parlance suggested a retreat from the Middle-Western identity that had so shaped its past and a move toward a distinctive identity based on separation—party and otherwise—and all over slavery. In the heat of the sectional debate, that identity clearly found sympathy in the plight of the beleaguered South. One Democratic editor saw need to clarify for his Boon's Lick readers the specious political nature of this newfound Southern affiliation: "Many conscientious men both Whigs and Democrats doubted the policy of repealing the Missouri Compromise; but our idea is that all those of every party who *acquiesce* in that *repeal,* and who are opposed to *interfering* with the question any longer, are *good friends* to . . . 'Southern rights,' as they are termed; . . . yea, as good friends as any others; for *therein* consists the *test* of loyalty to the South." In response, one western Missouri newspaper adopted as its moniker, *Southern Advocate.*[22]

Yet Missourians found solace in the imagery of victimization embedded in the concept of Southern rights. As Congress again wrestled over slavery's extension into the Mexican Cession, Missourians, already condemned by abolitionists as moral degenerates, conjured from the moral chords the not-too-distant memory of their own state's natal struggle. The recollection of Northern contempt and diminution inflamed its residents' passions yet again. Clearly, as Henry S. Geyer dutifully reminded his Senate colleagues, "there were some in western Missouri who remembered how little their rights were respected by the North in the memorable struggle of 1820." William B. Napton echoed these sentiments, claiming that "the injustice of the old Missouri Compromise is manifest from its very terms. It recognizes the great principle of popular sovereignty south of the line of 36° 30'—but north of that line establishes a guardianship over the people and imposes an absolute restriction. It is as much adverse to the spirit of our Constitution as the famous Wilmot Proviso."[23]

Anathema to egalitarianism, the North's concert of exclusion against the South quickly conjured among Missourians their ancestors' own revolutionary struggle against a tyrannical majority. Indeed, Napton defended "the great principle of popular sovereignty, for which our ancestors in the revolution fought." Yet this new struggle did not yet signal a new revolution, at least not against the federal government. Rather, democratic Missourians must act as sentinels against antislavery zealots bent upon the Union's destruction. "Certainly it is not the part of a good patriot to do anything, or say anything," Napton cautioned, "by which the tendency to disunion may be hastened—and it is well enough to hold up *in terrorem* all the evils which fertile imagination may conceive, as to the necessary results of such an occurrence." John J. Lowry's condemnations of Benton echoed the same themes: "Col. Benton is the *Disunionist* then, & not the Legislature of Mo. & Mr. Calhoun! . . . He will divide the Democracy of the Union & be the cause of a *Disolution* [*sic*] of the confederated states! No patriotism, no philanthropy, in brief a Calagula [*sic*] in North America in 1849. . . . I am for my country, for the Union & for the constitutional rights of the whole of the people of the confederated states!"[24]

Yet as Northerners united against slavery and the Slave Power by adhering to the free-soil movement, many Missourians heard much more than condemnations of the South; they heard themselves condemned, first as slaveholders, then—by yet another sin, that of association—as Southerners. When Frank Blair, an aggressive free-soil Democrat who would soon take up and wave the Republican banner, received election to Congress from St. Louis in 1856, the *National Era* hailed the victory as harbinger of regional, even national politics, predicting confidently that the border would soon become an antislavery, and thus Republican, bastion. "Our principles have become *aggressive*," trumpeted the paper's editor. "We no longer stand upon the defensive. We have crossed the line, and are upon slaveholding ground." The boast crossed lines indeed, appearing to Missourians a taunt.[25]

More repugnant, Northerners who dishonored Southerners by proclaiming their institutions—and thus their society—as inferior and thus unworthy dishonored Missourians who shared those Southerners' commitment to chattel slavery. Northerners and Middle Westerners, in lumping Missourians together with the South as a result of one lone, shared institution, ignored the "identity of interest, feeling and destiny" that Missourians hoped yet prevailed over the Western states. Considering theirs the freest society in the world, both because of their Western, rural residence and because of their pervasive egalitarianism and commitment to liberty, Missourians opposed the free-soil arguments as slanderous attacks by an undemocratic host upon a free and loyal people. Now, listening to the widespread attacks on the South and on them as well, many Missourians at last began—however cautiously—to consider their interests distinct from those of their once-northwestern neighbors and consistent with those of the beleaguered, slaveholding South. Indeed, a sense of honor was at stake, as William B. Napton observed: "The South regards it as a point of honor not to submit and the North regards it as a point of honor to persist, so it is merely a point of honor upon which we split. This is however enough." Though Napton was a native New Jerseyite and a former Boon's Lick Democratic newspaper editor, his choice of "we" was no mere editorial form. Missouri's southernization was underway.[26]

In direct response to the Northern attacks against the South and slavery, Missourians—proslavery or even free-soil—slowly adopted the mantra of Southerners. Prior to the 1840s, little evidence exists of Missourians having applied the term to themselves, in large part because the nation itself had not yet fully sectionalized so as to create the region in a national consciousness. The term "Southern," as Missourians employed it initially, was a metaphor for slaveholder, regardless of the individual's political stance on slavery's extension. In 1844 the Kentucky-born Benton responded defiantly to his free state antagonists by affirming: "I am Southern by birth; Southern in my affections, interest, and connections. . . . I am a slaveholder, and shall take the fate of other slaveholders in every aggression upon that species of property." Similarly, free-soiler Frank Blair, also a native Kentuckian and slaveholder, proclaimed: "I am a southern man by birth, and identified with southern institutions by my interest and education."[27]

By the time of the Texas debates, however, with the cant of abolitionism well amplified, Missourians took up the cognomen of Southerners more widely, yet largely as a defense of the peculiar institution. More important, Missourians generally reserved its use for the company of either those from the free states (who had so labeled Missourians solely as a result of their slaveholding adherence) or to Northern-born free-soilers in their midst. While Atchison proclaimed his Southernness defiantly in the presence of Northern colleagues in general, he limited usage of the term in the company of fellow proslavery Missourians. To the Democrats of Livingston County, he offered his take on the recent Compromise of 1850: "Although in my opinion the slave States did not get equal and exact justice, yet we escaped dishonor and degradation. Let us hold our northern brethren to a strict observance of all the terms of settlement; they must comply with their part of the bargain." To another group, he affirmed that "as a Senator from Missouri, and as a citizen of the Slave States, it is my duty to resist every attempt to change her institutions, and every assault upon her rights." Atchison's knowingly selective use of language suggests that adherence to slavery did not yet warrant any exclusive Southern identity, at least not to others of the same stripe. The employment of the terms "Southern" or "Southerner" by Missourians was reserved exclusively for the benefit of outsiders, those who now posed a threat to the institution.[28]

Though even the most ardent of Missouri's proslavery adherents refrained from using these terms with one another, the procreation of Southern identity in the state as ligature of the slaveholding imperative had become powerful. By the mid-1850s those who evinced anything short of wholesale support for the institution and its extension to the Western territories were subject to bitter political attack. James J. Lindley addressed the U.S. House in 1856, claiming that Missouri's proslavery Democrats "assume to have taken into special custody the slave interest of Missouri, and freely denounce as Republicans and Abolitionists men of southern education, slaveholders, and all others who do not conform to and maintain every arbitrary tenet which they set up; . . . I am charged by the orators & presses of the anti-Benton faction in Missouri as a Free-Soiler—I who have been raised and educated to believe in the propriety of southern institutions, and who have never uttered one word against slavery, either as it exists or in the abstract."[29]

Those Missourians born in nonslaveholding states proved especially vulnerable. B. Gratz Brown captured this distinction most completely when responding to New York–born state senator Robert M. Stewart's attack on Benton as an abolitionist. Pointing out Stewart's Northern birth, Brown—a Kentuckian—threw doubt on Stewart's proslavery stance based on it. Unlike Stewart, Brown argued, "I am a Southern man, in feeling and in principle, . . . the place of my birth forbids the ridiculous nonsense of abolitionism!" Frank Blair noted that "the absconding abolitionists from the north, who, in my county at least, are the principal leaders of the Anti-Benton party, find it necessary to turn pro-slavery nullifiers to free themselves from the suspicion which attends their place of birth." Blair then added smugly: "I can well afford to entertain the opinions of Washington and Jefferson, upon the subject of slavery, and to express them without incurring the suspicion of disloyalty to the institutions of the south."[30]

Blair was wrong about his own immunity from suspicion attendant with his place of birth. Perhaps more than those in any other state, Missourians of the 1850s now drew the sharpest distinction between their neighbors, not based on sectional hailing, but on their adherence or opposition to slavery. Lying astride two noncontested borders, one North-South the other East-West, these Missourians felt they could not risk granting exemptions to anyone, even those born in slaveholding states. Indeed, with grim irony, William B. Napton took aim at those of Benton's and Blair's ilk while pointing out the imperfection of the new Southern identity swirling about Missouri. "A man's opinions are not to be determined by the place of his birth," he observed:

> Because a man is born and raised in a slave state does not prevent him from being a free-soiler or an abolitionist. . . . Kentucky is a slave state, yet I will venture that one half of the Kentuckians who emigrate here are free-soilers—one fourth out-and-out abolitionists. They are not slave holders though born and raised in a slave state, and wherever they are they still entertain anti-slavery sentiments. . . . The political adjuncts of the northern free-soilers stay scattered here and there throughout the South and "born and raised" in slave states are the most dangerous of the whole tribe.

Atchison concurred: "Put confidence in *no man* for any station of public trust," he cautioned a group of supporters, "who is not known to be true to the institutions of the State and the rights of our citizens."[31]

Against this backdrop, in 1854 Congress debated the Kansas-Nebraska bill, which effectively repealed the Missouri Compromise in that it allowed popular sovereignty into the region long assumed as being forever free from slavery. The bill triggered a congressional debate of a magnitude the nation had not seen since the fracas over Missouri's statehood. More important, the bill unleashed a sectional storm that would eclipse any controversy that surrounded its passage. When Douglas forecast "a hell of a storm" to attend his bill, he spoke exclusively of the legislative fight; what he could not have foreseen was the bitter border war that would ensue in the Kansas Territory, revealing the fiction that was popular sovereignty. And at the center of this national crisis, for a second time in a generation, lay Missouri.[32]

Missourians saw in the opening of Kansas several opportunities for progress. By allowing popular sovereignty to dictate the settlement of territories, Western agrarian settlers would carry to the future their brand of democratic promise and thus triumph over a distant, urban, industrial, and thoroughly inferior East. One Missourian who homesteaded in eastern Kansas immediately after the territory's organization believed that because of proximity and through concerted action, Westerners could stymie "the hosts of the Lazarroni from the Eastern States and Cities and paupers from Europe that will be thrown into this country, . . . a curse equaling, at least, in its pestiferous character, the plagues of Egypt, in being made the unwilling receptacle of the filth, scum and offscourings of the East and Europe." Moreover, the Kansas-Nebraska Act signified to residents that though challenged, even blunted for a time, the practicability of democracy had reasserted itself in its purest form, outside the invasive influence of government, whether national or state. "Let neither Congress, not state conventions," exulted John J. Lowry, "enact any arbitrary laws to regulate property, then will our political institutions smoothly progress, & then will *soil & climate* point out where the slave-holders ought to locate." In Kansas, liberty appeared to triumph over influence.[33]

Beyond its abstractions over slavery and government, Missourians— perhaps more than any other residents of the Union—considered the debate over the Kansas territory in a practical sense. While slave state residents in the Deep South attached symbolic political importance to winning Kansas, the matter offered far more immediate implications to those closest to the storm's center. Indeed, beyond the Southern arguments for the winning of Kansas being "a point of honor," a means of regaining parity in the Senate, or even a last, best hope for the spread of Southern culture and institutions in an expanding nation that had routinely constricted them both, Missourians saw Kansas as a gift to them. The term commonly used by Missourians when debating Kansas—"the Goose question"—connoted the sense of largesse implicit in the Kansas issue, in this case a Christmas goose. By virtue of the natural progress of American westward expansion, Missourians claimed a "natural right" to expand into the territory immediately west of them. Just as Kentucky had been settled by Virginians, Tennessee had been settled by North Carolinians, and Iowa had been settled largely by Illinoisans, so Kansas would be settled by Missourians. As Napton noted in 1850, in the midst of the debate over the Mexican cession, "the natural order of events" would have brought slaveholding Southerners into those regions had not Northern machinations interrupted the process by claiming California.[34]

More pressing even than this was the notion that if Kansas should not become a slave state, Missouri would become the first and only such slave state bordering a free state to its west, effectively sealing slavery from further progress and changing the complexion of westward expansion, likely forever. Napton certainly recognized the implications of this point. "If we cannot carry slavery into Kansas," he reasoned, "it is quite obvious that we cannot succeed anywhere else. The result will be that no more slave states will be created. The majority of the north over the South will in a few years become overwhelming, in both houses of Congress. This majority can mould the Constitution to their own purposes. What will constitutional guarantees be worth under such circumstances?" This precedent held a weighty charge, one that led Missourians to conclude that Kansas, by mandate, was theirs to shape. As Atchison declared to a Northerner who opposed slavery in Kansas, "I and my friends wish to make Kansas in all respects like Missouri. Our interests require it. Our peace through all time demands it, and we intend to leave nothing undone that will conduce to that end and can with honor be performed. . . . We have all to lose in the contest; you and your friends have nothing at stake."[35]

The nearly immediate mobilization of Emigrant Aid societies in New England threw Missourians into a frenzy, in part from the fear that the most dangerous of interlopers would soon entice their bondpeople to escape. Hundreds, even thousands, of these "Hessian band[s] of mercenaries" were to be "sent here as hired servants, to do the will of others" and were poised "to pol[l]ute our fair land, to dictate to us a government to preach Abolitionism and dig underground Rail Roads," William Walker predicted. Indeed, even before Congress authorized settlement in Kansas, Claib Jackson wrote to Atchison: "I say let the Indians have it [Nebraska] *forever*. They are better neighbors than the abolitionists, *by a damned sight*. If this is to be come 'free-nigger' territory, Missouri must become so too, for we can hardly keep our negroes here now." In turn, Atchison wrote Jefferson Davis later in 1854 that "the men who are hired by the Boston Abolitionists to settle and abolitionize Kansas will not hesitate, to steal our slaves," prompting him to counsel one group of prospective emigrants from western Missouri "to give a horse thief, robber, or homicide a fair trial, but to hang a negro thief or Abolitionist, without judge or jury."[36]

While the specter of abolitionists' slave-stealing was bad enough, Missourians found far more detestable the well-publicized method by which the New Englanders organized their swarming. With a capitalization of five million dollars approved by the Massachusetts legislature and plans for mills, a hotel, a newspaper, towns, and tens of thousands of subsidized settlers, the Emigrant Aid Societies intended nothing like squatter sovereignty. Rather, they appeared intent on replicating in the West the North in its entirety, rather than any Jeffersonian vision. Indeed, the rabidly proslavery *Squatter Sovereign,* a territorial newspaper founded by Missourian John H. Stringfellow in Atchison (named conspicuously for Missouri's proslavery champion) forecast Kansas's grim future if invading urban Yankees gained sway, creating "sores in the body politic . . . [with] great wealth gathering in the hands of the few, the toiling millions struggling for bread; the one class is corrupted by luxury, the other debased by destitution." These Northern hirelings, dupes of Eastern money, could never be free, independent men of the land and thus had no legitimate rights in the West.[37]

Most ominous to Missourians was the grim realization that their "vilest enemies" would now use the democratic process to usurp popular sovereignty as the Missourians understood it. As one Missouri Kansan predicted, "The Abolitionists will compass sea and land[,] heaven & hell to prevent the establishment of slavery in this Territory." What Eli Thayer and Amos A. Lawrence intended, even orchestrated, was an invasion, one initiated not so much to populate the region as to subvert the system on which they pinned their futures as well as the nation's. In effect, just as Missourians breathed a sigh of relief that the Southern phalanx had at last dragooned Congress into making liberty and democracy once again consonant by virtue of the principle of popular sovereignty, New Englanders now threatened the vulnerable alloy. Industrial capitalism would now provide the edge over individualism; slavery would be its first casualty. To destroy slavery, not by competition but by the state-making process, free-labor Northerners would use both popular sovereignty —the democratic tool Missourians believed would open the West to slavery— and state sovereignty—the slave states' Cerberus as a minority within the republic—against those very slaveholders who championed these doctrines' theoretical actuality as well as depending on their political viability. Indeed, as Missourians saw it, the democratic process now threatened to consume the West's heart—liberty.[38]

Cornered, unable now to oppose popular sovereignty or to trust the national democratic order, Missourians lashed out with fury at the New England interlopers. "Kansas meetings" held throughout the state quickly led to the formation of "self-defensive societies" and later "blue lodges" and other secret societies that sought to prevent abolitionist emigrants from reaching Kansas. One historian has estimated that as many as ten thousand Missourians pledged allegiance to such organizations, a thousand alone in Platte County.

William Walker wrote to David Rice Atchison from the settlement at Wyan-
dotte, Kansas, just across the Missouri River from Westport, soliciting aid
from the other slave states. "A heavenly time we will have of it if they gain the
ascendancy here!" Walker exclaimed. "I tremble when I contemplate the
threatening prospect. Our Southern friends must be up and stirring. Virginia,
Tennessee, and Kentucky ought to send her hardy sons out to claim their
rights and maintain them too. Missouri, as far as she can, is doing nobly for a
new State."[39]

Walker's plea did not go unheeded; Missourians and other slave state men
formed emigrant aid societies of their own. At Atchison's urging, thousands of
Missourians crossed the Kansas border to claim exemptions or to vote illegally
in territorial elections. Newspapers sounded the call. "We are in favor of making Kansas a 'Slave State' if it should require half of the citizens of Missouri,
musket in hand, to emigrate there," declared the Liberty *Democratic Platform*.
The editor of Howard County's *Glasgow Weekly Times* reminded residents in
the summer of 1854 that "if Missourians desire Kansas to be slave territory,
they must do something more than hold public meeting, and pass high-
sounding resolves; they must be on the move, and that speedily." As the territorial elections approached the following spring, he employed a more urgent
tone. "If we would protect our hearth-stones, and defend our most sacred
principles, we must act promptly," he implored. "Let no one hug any longer
the defensive hope of security, for there is none; already the torch of desola-
tion has been lighted, and is now in the hands of fanatics . . . [and] nothing
but prompt and determined action on our part can avert a catastrophe . . .
Kansas should be a slave State, but it will take slavery votes to make it so. . . .
There is no time for delay—and those who do not expect to go there at present, if at all should assist those who intend, and want to go this spring, in getting off immediately."[40]

Once the voting fraud in Kansas became known, widespread condemnations issued from the Northern states. Missourians did anything but disavow
their activities; in fact, they defended them vigorously as a virtuous defense of
liberty against the undemocratic New Englanders. One Linn County meeting
claimed to "deeply regret the necessity for any action on our part against any
considerable portion of the citizens of the United States; but such has been the
course of the Abolitionists and Freesoilers, that duty to ourselves and families
and a love for the Union of States require it of us, at the present time." A Boone
County Democratic meeting justified the actions of the Missouri voters in

Kansas, claiming they were merely "neutralizing said abolition efforts, and preventing the fraud attempted by the importation of hireling voters into that territory." Similarly, a Kansas meeting held in Fayette offered eighteen resolutions, the second of which "heartily approve[d] the action of our friends who met in Kansas, and defeated the machinations of the enemies of the Union and equal rights, the 'aid society' emissaries, thereby maintaining the principles of the constitution and the Kansas bill, by which that Territory is recognized as common property open to settlement by citizens of all the States."[41]

The Fayettans' statement offers a revealing insight into what had clearly become these Missourians' uniquely sectionalized construction of democracy. Though admitting that the territories, including Kansas, were open to the settlement of all, not all were indeed welcome. Only those who evinced a willingness for slavery to extend into the West would be allowed to settle in the region. This conception now transcended old sectional lines to embrace only those who understood the democratic process, those whom the corruptive influences of industrialized land had not bastardized. Only Westerners and Southerners, the agrarian backbone of the nation, would gain free access to the fruits of Kansas; slavery would be the litmus test. "Companies coming from slave States," wrote John H. Stringfellow in *Squatter Sovereign,* "will be heartily welcomed by our citizens, as well as those from free States who are all 'right on the goose'. . . . There will be many a good citizen settle among us from Illinois, Indian[a], and Ohio, whose notions of slavery are parallel with our own."[42]

To protect liberty, its Missouri defenders targeted New England abolitionists, debauchers of the democratic process, and not free-soil Westerners, procreators of this greatest and most vulnerable of American systems. Drawing great distinction between free-state emigrants, Stringfellow charged, "We are not contending against the honest, but mistaken Free-Soiler, but with *the scum and filth of the Northern cities;* sent here as hired servants, to do the will of others; not to give their own free suffrage." "No one can fail to distinguish between an honest, bona fide emigration, prompted by choice or necessity," he railed, "and an organized colonization with offensive purpose upon the institutions of the country proposed to be settled." Westerners, the virtuous majority, would save democracy from the hands of a conspiratorial, corrupted minority. Kansas offered their best hope.[43]

The bloodshed in Kansas brought ill repute to Missourians. Northerners expanded their condemnations of Missourians from that of slaveholding sinners to that of frontier savages, barbaric bullies, uneducated "pukes." The caning of

Massachusetts senator Charles Sumner in defense of free-state Kansas only confirmed the notions of most Northerners that Missourians were indeed Southerners; the event entwined in public perception the slaveholding perpetrators of the Kansas and Sumner crimes. Condemned as Southerners, many Missourians during the Kansas conflict internalized the characterization in a fuller political sense. Those Missourians looked beyond New Englanders or Northerners as the enemy of liberty and democracy in the West and toward the federal government. An angry group of more than two hundred slaveholders from twenty-six counties assembled in Lexington in July 1855 to condemn abolitionism, but in their language pledged themselves to a conflict that transcended the current one in Kansas. Calling slavery a "God-given . . . Natural right," James Shannon, president of the state university at Columbia, argued that neither individuals nor governments could interfere. "Let us hope for the best, and prepare for the worst;" Shannon implored the audience, "and then having done all that men can do to save the Union, if a dissolution is forced upon us by domestic traitors . . . then I, for one say . . . we will stand to our arms."[44]

As the struggle for Kansas revealed painfully to Missourians, the promise of democracy would not be realized in the West. Constant exertions, including armed forays into Kansas, continued interference with territorial elections, and recurrent violence in the hopes of intimidating abolitionist residents did not stem the tide of what became a floodtide of antislavery migration. This influx came, not from New England, however, but from the Western states, the same pragmatic people that Missourians had predicted would support slavery in Kansas. These free-staters, well outnumbering proslavery settlers in Kansas, waged their own war with the proslavery element in the territory, delegitimizing the legislature and ultimately forcing a congressional showdown when Kansas applied for statehood in 1857. By the time the territorial legislature proffered its ill-fated Lecompton Constitution to Congress for approval—with its infamous option to vote "*for* the Constitution with slavery, or *for* the Constitution without slavery"—even Missourians grudgingly conceded that the proslavery clauses in the document no longer reflected the constituency of Kansas and condemned the document as undemocratic. "All this is . . . the work of a few political demagogues," declared the *Jefferson Inquirer,* "who are seeking to bring about a dissolution of the Union, and are reckless of the means to which they resort to accomplish their purpose." For the sake of the Union, Missourians accepted—however bitterly—Kansas's destiny as a free state, but not before one final act of retribution. In the fall of 1860, nearly six hundred St. Louis volunteers marched again grimly to the Kansas border in a "Southwest Expedition," to campaign against the hated "Jayhawkers" who now occupied Eden.[45]

The democratic process had robbed Missouri of its own progeny. For many of its residents, the events in Kansas pointed out clearly that a new alliance had emerged, one in which the Northern and Northwestern states had united in their conspiracy against slavery. No longer was the West a place of liberty; the democratic process that had once buttressed Missourians' belief in Western independence now threatened the institution that to them embodied those liberties—and not only in the territories, but in the existing states as well. Angry and disillusioned, many Missourians would now begin to question their loyalty to the federal government and to the Union itself. These once-Westerners now looked to the region that now embodied their sense of betrayal—the beleaguered South—for more than comfort. Ironically, while the identity of the South as a whole, in C. Vann Woodward's and others' time-honored arguments, stemmed directly from a postwar culture of "frustration, failure, and defeat," Missouri's Southern identity by 1861 was already well in the making.[46]

NOTES

1. For narrative and popular histories of "Bleeding Kansas," see Alice Nichols, *Bleeding Kansas* (New York: Oxford University Press, 1954); Jay Monaghan, *Civil War on the Western Border, 1854–1865* (Boston: Little, Brown, 1955; reprint, Lincoln: University of Nebraska Press, 1984); Thomas Goodrich, *Black Flag: Guerrilla Warfare on the Western Border, 1861–1865* (Bloomington: Indiana University Press, 1995), and *War to the Knife: Bleeding Kansas, 1854–1861* (Mechanicsburg, Pa.: Stackpole Books, 1998); Judd Cole, *Bleeding Kansas* (New York: Leisure Books, 1999); Jon Sharpe, *Bleeding Kansas* (New York: Penguin Books, 1990). For biographies of Kansas territorial figures, see Stephen B. Oates, *To Purge This Land with Blood: A Biography of John Brown* (New York: Harper and Row, 1970); Kendall E. Bailes, *Rider on the Wind: Jim Lane and Kansas* (Shawnee Mission, Kan.: Wagon Wheel Press, 1962); James C. Malin, *John Brown and the Legend of Fifty-six* (Philadelphia: American Philosophical Society, 1969); Christopher Phillips, *Damned Yankee: The Life of General Nathaniel Lyon* (Columbia: University of Missouri Press, 1990; reprint, Baton Rouge: Louisiana State University Press, 1996).

2. For general works on Kansas in the sectional era, see Allan Nevins, *The War for the Union* (New York: Charles S. Scribner, 1959–60, 1971), 2:408–46; James G.

Randall and David H. Donald, *The Civil War and Reconstruction* (Lexington, Mass.: D. C. Heath and Co., 1969), 97–102; James M. McPherson, *Battle Cry of Freedom: The Civil War Era* (New York: Oxford University Press, 1986), 145–69; David M. Potter, *The Impending Crisis, 1848–1861* (New York: Oxford University Press, 1986), 199–224; William L. Barney, *The Road to Secession: A New Perspective on the Old South* (New York: Praeger, 1972), 6–17; William W. Freehling, *The Road to Disunion: Secessionists at Bay 1776–1854* (New York: Oxford University Press, 1990), 536–65; Kenneth M. Stampp, *America in 1857: A Nation on the Brink* (New York: Oxford University Press, 1990), 266–331. For more focused works on Kansas in national politics, see Don Fehrenbacher, "Kansas, Republicanism, and the Crisis of the Union," in *The South and Three Sectional Crises* (Baton Rouge: Louisiana State University Press, 1980), 46–65; William E. Gienapp, "The Crime against Sumner: The Caning of Charles Sumner and the Rise of the Republican Party," *Civil War History* 25 (September 1979): 218–45; James A. Rawley, *Race and Politics: "Bleeding Kansas" and the Coming of the Civil War* (Philadelphia: J. B. Lippincott, 1969; reprint, Lincoln: University of Nebraska Press, 1979). On the Great Debates, see Robert W. Johannsen, ed., *The Lincoln-Douglas Debates of 1858* (New York: Oxford University Press, 1965).

3. On Missouri "pukes," see Michael Fellman, *Inside War: The Guerrilla Conflict in Missouri during the American Civil War* (New York: Oxford University Press, 1989), 13 (first and second quotes); Floyd C. Shoemaker, "Missouri's Proslavery Fight for Kansas," *Missouri Historical Review* [hereinafter cited as *MHR*] 48 (April 1954 and July 1954): 221–36, 325–40; 49 (October 1954): 41–54, 221 (third quote). For a similar criticism of the delegitimation of antebellum Southern conservatism, see Eugene D. Genovese, *Southern Tradition: The Achievement and Limitations of an American Conservatism* (Cambridge, Mass.: Harvard University Press, 1994), ix–9 and passim.

4. Gunja SenGupta, *For God and Mammon: Evangelicals and Entrepreneurs, Masters and Slaves in Territorial Kansas, 1854–1860* (Athens: University of Georgia Press, 1996); Bill Cecil-Fronsman, "'Death to All Yankees and Traitors in Kansas': The *Squatter Sovereign* and the Defense of Slavery in Kansas," *Kansas History* 16 (spring 1993): 22–33; S. B. Axtell to L. Kerr, 5 April 1861, Vertical File A, Western Reserve Historical Society, Cleveland, Ohio (quote); Daniel W. Crofts, *Reluctant Confederates: Upper South Unionists in the Secession Crisis* (Chapel Hill: University of North Carolina Press, 1989).

5. William M. Meigs, *Life of Thomas Hart Benton* (Philadelphia: J. B. Lippincott Company, 1904; reprint, New York: DaCapo Press, 1970), 411–12 (first quote); *Jefferson City Metropolitan*, 30 October 1849 (second quote); Walter Morrow Burks,

"Thunder on the Right" (Ph.D. diss., University of Kansas City, 1962), 305; Robert E. Shalhope, *Sterling Price: Portrait of a Southerner* (Columbia: University of Missouri Press, 1971), 94–97; William E. Parrish, *David Rice Atchison, Border Politician* (Columbia: University of Missouri Press, 1961), 91–93, 110–14; William Nisbet Chambers, *Old Bullion Benton: Senator from the New West* (Boston: Little, Brown, 1956, 374–77; Perry McCandless, *A History of Missouri: Volume II—1820–1860* (Columbia: University of Missouri Press, 1972), 251–53; Charles H. McClure, *Opposition to Thomas Hart Benton in Missouri* (Nashville, Tenn.: George Peabody College for Teachers, 1927), 211–16.

6. *Columbia Missouri Statesman,* 18 May 1849 (quote).

7. *Liberty Tribune,* 29 June 1849, quoted in Parrish, *David Rice Atchison,* 79–80.

8. Paul C. Nagel, *Missouri: A Bicentennial History* (New York: W. W. Norton, 1977), 126; Parrish, *David Rice Atchison,* 1–5; Harrison A. Trexler; *Slavery in Missouri* (Baltimore: Johns Hopkins University Press, 1914, 43–44. Sixth U.S. Census, 1840, Population Schedule, Clay County, Missouri, NARA (National Archives and Record Administration), Washington, D.C.; Seventh U.S. Census, 1850, Population and Slave Schedules, Platte County, Missouri, NARA; Eighth U.S. Census, 1860, Population and Slave Schedules, Clinton County, Missouri, NARA.

William Freehling offers a description of Atchison's F Street "mess," the Washington boarding house he shared with three fellow senators from slaveholding states, Virginians William O. Goode and James M. Mason and South Carolinian Andrew P. Butler, that included three black domestic servants. No record indicates that any of these slaves belonged to Atchison. Indirect evidence suggests that at this time he might have had a personal servant named George. By August 1865, Atchison clearly had slaves in his possession; indeed, a letter written from Grayson County, Texas, to his brother in Clay County, Missouri, states that "I have all the rest of the Negroes on my hands and know not what to do with them." The letter does not state whether he owned these slaves. If he did, Atchison likely acquired these slaves after retiring from the Senate in 1855 to a 250-acre farm in Platte County. Possibly he had taken one of his brother's slaves in the relative safety of northern Texas while his brother remained in war-torn Missouri. See Freehling, *Road to Disunion,* 550; A[ndrew] P. Butler to Atchison, 5 March 1856, David Rice Atchison Papers, mss. 71, folder 6, Western Historical Manuscripts Collection, Joint Collection—State Historical Society of Missouri/University of Missouri, Columbia [hereinafter cited as SHSM]; D. R. Atchison to William Atchison, 12 August 1865, ibid., SHSM, quoted in Parrish, *David Rice Atchison,* 220–21, and 115.

9. Lewis C. Gray, *History of Agriculture in the Southern United States to 1860,* 2 vols. (Washington, D.C.: Carnegie Institution of Washington, 1932; reprint,

Gloucester, Mass.: Peter Smith, 1958), 1:482; McCandless, *History of Missouri,* 35–36, 59–60; R. Douglas Hurt, *Agriculture and Slavery in Missouri's Little Dixie* (Columbia: University of Missouri Press, 1992), 219–23; Nagel, *Missouri,* 128.

10. Gray, *History of Agriculture in the Southern United States,* 2:650–56; Hurt, *Agriculture and Slavery in Little Dixie,* 222–23; Trexler, *Slavery in Missouri,* 37–43; McCandless, *History of Missouri,* 35–36; 57; P. Carr to C. F. Jackson, 15 January 1859, John S. Sappington Papers, Mss. 1027, box 3, folder 95, SHSM (quote).

11. Parrish, *David Rice Atchison,* 73 (first quote); *Diary of Willam B. Napton,* William B. Napton Papers [hereinafter cited as *Napton Diary*], folder 1, 50–51, Missouri Historical Society, St. Louis [hereinafter cited as MHS] (second quote); McCandless, *History of Missouri,* 270 (third quote).

12. *Napton Diary,* folder 1, p. 77, (first quote); folder 2, pp. 100–101 (second quote) MHS; Larry E. Tise, *Proslavery: A History of the Defense of Slavery in America, 1701–1840* (Athens: University of Georgia Press, 1987), 349–60; William S. Jenkins, *Pro-Slavery Thought in the Old South* (Chapel Hill: University of North Carolina Press, 1935, reprint, Gloucester, Mass.: Peter Smith, 1960), 65–81. For a fuller discussion of the classical republican theories of slavery; see Clyde N. Wilson, *Carolina Cavalier: The Life and Mind of James Johnston Pettigrew* (Athens: University of Georgia Press, 1990), and Robert E. Shalhope, *John Taylor of Caroline: Pastoral Republican* (Columbia: University of South Carolina Press, 1980).

13. *Columbia Missouri Statesman,* 9 March 1849 (first and fourth quotes); James S. Rollins to My Dear Son, 14 November 1858, James S. Rollins Papers, Mss. 1026, box 2, folder 55, SHSM (second quote); *Appendix to the Congressional Globe,* 33rd Cong. 1st sess. (Washington, D.C.: Office of the Globe, 1855), 301 (third quote); Thelma Jennings, *The Nashville Convention: Southern Movement for Unity, 1848–1851* (Memphis, Tenn.: Memphis State University Press, 1980), 187–211; Parrish, *David Rice Atchison,* 101.

14. Michael A. Morrison, *Slavery and the American West: The Eclipse of Manifest Destiny and the Coming of the Civil War* (Chapel Hill: University of North Carolina Press, 1997), 62–63.

15. *Columbia Missouri Statesman,* 14 May 1852 (first quote); J. J. Lowry to M. M. Marmaduke, 8 September 1848, Sappington Family Papers, box 5, MHS (remaining quotes).

16. *Glasgow Weekly Times,* 29 March 1855 (first quote), 19 February 1853 (second quote); *Columbia Missouri Statesman,* 15 June 1855, quoted in Hurt, *Agriculture and Slavery in Little Dixie,* 283.

17. Shoemaker, "Missouri's Proslavery Fight for Kansas," 232; Fellman, *Inside War,* 6–7.

18. *Appendix to the Congressional Globe,* 34th Cong., 1st sess. (Washington, D.C.: Office of the Globe, 1856), 465 (first quote); *Columbia Missouri Statesman,* 9 March 1849 (second quote).

19. William E. Smith, *The Francis Preston Blair Family in Politics,* 2 vols. (New York: Macmillan, 1933; reprint, New York: Da Capo Press, 1959), 1:203 (first quote); James Brewer Stewart, *Holy Warriors: The Abolitionists and American Slavery* (New York: Hill and Wang, 1976), 112 (second quote); Eric Foner, *Free Soil, Free Labor, Free Men: The Ideology of the Republican Party before the Civil War* (New York: Oxford University Press, 1970), 56 (third quote), 55 (fourth quote), 63 (fifth quote), and 46–72 passim.

20. Richard Hofstadter, *The American Political Tradition and the Men Who Made It* (New York: Alfred A. Knopf, 1948; reprint, Vintage Books, 1959) 68–85, 86 (quote)–92; R. K. Crallé, ed., *The Works of John C. Calhoun,* 6 vols. (New York: D. Appleton, 1854), 1:52–59. Calhoun's anti-majoritarian polemicism prompted Hofstadter to offer his now-famous analogy of the proslavery Calhoun as "Marx of the master class."

21. Foner, *Free Soil, Free Labor, Free Men,* 89–94; Morrison, *Slavery and the American West,* 59–62; William J. Cooper Jr., *Liberty and Slavery: Southern Politics to 1860* (New York: Alfred A. Knopf, 1983), 257–58; *Congressional Globe,* 32nd Cong., 2nd sess. (Washington, D.C.: Office of the Globe, 1854), 1111–12 (first quote); *Missouri Republican,* 16 September 1853, quoted in Parrish, *David Rice Atchison,* 126 (second quote); *Appendix to the Congressional Globe,* 34th Cong., 1st sess., 464 (third quote).

22. Stephen C. LeSueur, *The 1838 Mormon War in Missouri* (Columbia: University of Missouri Press, 1990), 57–58; *Glasgow Weekly Times,* 28 March 1855 (quote).

23. *Appendix to the Congressional Globe,* 34th Cong., 1st sess., 465 (first quote); *Napton Diary,* folder 1, 78–79, MHS (second quote).

24. *Napton Diary,* folder 1, 78–79, MHS (first and second quotes); J. J. Lowry to M. M. Marmaduke, 26 July 1849, Sappington Family Papers, box 5, MHS (third quote).

25. *National Era,* 14 August 1856, 14 May 1857 (quote), both in Foner, *Free Soil, Free Labor, Free Men,* 121.

26. Bertram Wyatt-Brown, *Yankee Saints and Southern Sinners* (Baton Rouge: Louisiana State University Press, 1985), 183–213; *Napton Diary,* folder 1, 50–51 (quote), 57, MHS.

27. Chambers, *Old Bullion Benton,* 276 (first quote); *Jefferson Inquirer,* 12 February 1853 (second quote).

28. David Rice Atchison to W. Y. Slack, W[illia]m, Hudgins, and Others, 19 November 1850, in *Missouri Republican,* 7 January 1851, reprinted in *MHR* 31 (July 1937): 443–44 (first quote); Parrish, *David Rice Atchison,* 74 (second quote).

29. *Appendix to the Congressional Globe,* 34th Cong., 1st sess., 673 (quote).

30. Thomas L. Snead, *The Fight for Missouri from the Election of Lincoln to the Death of Lyon* (New York: Charles Scribner's Sons, 1886), 13; *Jefferson Inquirer,* 5 February 1853, quoted in Norma L. Peterson, *Freedom and Franchise: The Political Career of B. Gratz Brown* (Columbia: University of Missouri Press, 1965), 28–29 (second quote); *Jefferson Inquirer,* 12 February 1853 (third and fourth quotes).

31. *Napton Diary,* folder 1, 92–93, MHS (first quote); David Rice Atchison to W. Y. Slack, W[illia]m Hudgins, and Others, 19 November 1850, in *Missouri Republican,* 7 January 1851, reprinted in *MHR* 31 (July 1937): 443–44 (second quote, italics mine).

32. Potter, *Impending Crisis,* 158–59 (quote), 160–77; Barney, *Road to Secession,* 6–17; Freehling, *Road to Disunion,* 552; Rawley, *Race and Politics,* 70.

33. William Walker to David R. Atchison, 6 July 1854, David Rice Atchison Papers, mss. 71, folder 4, SHSM (first quote); J. J. Lowry to M. M. Marmaduke, 8 September 1848, Sappington Family Papers, box 5, MHS (second quote); Cecil-Fronsman, "Death to All Yankees and Traitors in Kansas," 25–27.

34. Fehrenbacher, "Kansas, Republicanism, and the Crisis of the Union," in *The South and Three Sectional Crises,* 53–56; Gienapp, "Crime against Sumner," 238–45; Barney, *Road to Secession,* 6–17; Cooper, *Liberty and Slavery,* 260; William J. Cooper Jr., *The South and the Politics of Slavery* (Baton Rouge: Louisiana State University Press, 1978), 351–56; Morrison, *Slavery and the American West,* 165–67; SenGupta, *For God and Mammon,* 118 (first quote); *Napton Diary,* folder 1, 50–51, MHS (second quote).

35. Parrish, *David Rice Atchison,* 162 (first quote), 165 (third quote), 168; *Napton Diary,* folder 3, 208, MHS (second quote).

36. *Atkinson (Mo.) Squatter Sovereign,* 16 October (first quote), 6 March 1855 (second quote); William Walker to David R. Atchison, 6 July 1854, David Rice Atchison Papers, mss. 71, folder 4, SHSM (third quote); C. F. Jackson to David R. Atchison, 18 January 1854, David Rice Atchison Papers, mss. 71, folder 4, SHSM (fourth quote); Atchison to Jefferson Davis, 24 September 1854, Jefferson Davis Papers, Special Collections, William R. Perkins Library, Duke University, Durham, North Carolina [hereinafter cited as Duke] (fifth quote).

37. *Atkinson (Mo.) Squatter Sovereign,* 13 February 1855 (quote); Shoemaker, "Missouri's Proslavery Fight for Kansas," 226–27.

38. Hurt, *Agriculture and Slavery in Little Dixie,* 281 (first quote); William Walker to David R. Atchison, 6 July 1854, David Rice Atchison Papers, mss. 71, folder 4, SHSM (second quote); Cecil-Fronsman, "Death to All Yankees and Traitors in Kansas," 25.

39. William Walker to David R. Atchison, 6 July 1854, David Rice Atchison Papers, mss. 71, folder 4, SHSM (first quote); Shoemaker, "Missouri's Proslavery Fight for Kansas," 230–33; Elmer Leroy Craik, "Southern Interest in Territorial Kansas, 1854–1858," *Kansas Historical Collections* 15 (1919–21): 376–95; James C. Malin, "The Proslavery Background of the Kansas Struggle," *Mississippi Valley Historical Review* 10 (December 1923): 285–305; SenGupta, *For God and Mammon,* 116–18; Hurt, *Agriculture and Slavery in Little Dixie,* 290.

40. Shoemaker, "Missouri's Proslavery Fight for Kansas," 233–34 (first quote); *Jefferson Inquirer,* 21 July 1860; Monaghan, *Civil War on the Western Border,* 19–20, 147; *Glasgow Weekly Times,* 14 June 1855 (second quote), 19 October 1854 (third quote), 15 March 1855 (fourth quote).

41. *Glasgow Weekly Times,* 28 June (first quote), 14 June 1855 (second and third quotes).

42. *Atkinson (Mo.) Squatter Sovereign,* 20 February (first quote), 29 May 1855; Cecil-Fronsman, "Death to All Yankees and Traitors in Kansas," 25–29.

43. *Atkinson (Mo.) Squatter Sovereign,* 6 March (first quote), 16 October 1855 (second quote); Morrison, *Slavery in the American West,* 169–78.

44. Fellman, *Inside War,* 13 (first quote); Hurt, *Agriculture and Slavery in Little Dixie,* 283–86, 287–88 (second quote); *Glasgow Weekly Times,* 26 July 1855, *Liberty Weekly Tribune,* 20, 27 July 1855; Parrish, *David Rice Atchison,* 175–76; *Columbia Missouri Statesman,* 8 June 1849. Preston S. Brooks, a congressman from South Carolina, attacked Senator Charles Sumner on the floor of the U.S. Senate, days after Sumner had delivered a two-day speech, "The Crime against Kansas," an excoriation of the government's Kansas policy as well as of Senator Andrew Butler (Brooks's cousin) and his recent public apology for the violence in Kansas. The savage caning forced Sumner to absent himself for a three-and-a-half years from the Senate, while Northerners galvanized against "Bully Brooks" and a perceived proslavery extremism. See Gienapp, "Crime against Sumner," 226–29, and Rawley, *Race and Politics,* 125–29.

45. *Jefferson Inquirer,* 5 December 1857 (quotes); Robert E. Miller, "Daniel Marsh Frost, C.S.A.," *MHR* 85 (July 1991): 382–83; Philip T. Tucker, "'Ho, For Kansas': The Southwest Expedition of 1860," *MHR* 86 (October 1991): 22–36; John S. Bowen to Claiborne Fox Jackson, 10 March 1861, Missouri Volunteer Militia Papers, 1860–1865, Duke.

46. Paul M. Gaston, *The New South Creed: A Study in Southern Mythmaking* (New York: Alfred A. Knopf, 1970), 4–13; C. Vann Woodward, *The Burden of Southern History* (Baton Rouge: Louisiana State University Press, 1960; reprint, New York: Mentor Books, 1969), 27 (quote).

6

Jefferson Davis, Abraham Lincoln, and the National Meaning of War

Brian R. Dirck

Jefferson Davis did not deliver a Gettysburg Address. In fact, the Confederacy's president did not deliver a speech or write a letter that even remotely resembles Abraham Lincoln's famous remarks at the Gettysburg dedication ceremonies. By this I do not mean to observe simply that Davis gave no speech that was comparably famous, or that Davis would never have suggested, as Lincoln did, that the Declaration of Independence's guarantee of human equality lies at the heart of the American experiment. I also do not wish to draw any excessive or invidious distinctions between the two men's speech-making skills. While Lincoln was without peer in his use of rhetoric, Davis was a talented and polished public speaker.[1]

Rather, Davis did not feel compelled to engage in what was almost instinctive behavior for Lincoln at Gettysburg and elsewhere: he did not try to pause, stand on a metaphorical high place as his nation's interpreter-in-chief, and explain the Civil War's ultimate meaning for his nation.[2] This is not to say that Davis did not sometimes speak of the war's causes or of the broad political implications of victory and defeat. But his efforts in this regard were rather few and far between, and his tone was often pedestrian, an almost matter-of-fact litany of the very familiar, even threadbare reasons for the secession crisis. Davis produced no high Confederate moments that were even remotely comparable to Lincoln's renowned efforts.

Why? While no historian to my knowledge has asked this exact question, I would venture to guess at what would be the preferred answer: Davis was simply not as talented as Lincoln. One thinks of David Potter's oft-quoted sentiment that "it seems hardly unrealistic to suppose that if the Union and the Confederacy had changed presidents with one another, the Confederacy might have won its independence." Emory Thomas has written that Davis "sadly lacked the charismatic appeal to the mass of people possessed by his Northern rival." In much the same spirit, James McPherson contrasted Lincoln's habit of "express[ing] himself in a clear, forceful manner" and his brilliant articulation of the war's meaning, with Davis's "inability to communicate effectively." Davis's principal biographer, William C. Davis, wrote that "Lincoln was Lincoln, a man of myriad quirks and failings, who yet governed his weaknesses," while "Davis was Davis, and was governed by them."[3]

There is truth in these assertions. Lincoln probably did have more charisma, and he was a more effective politician. But reducing these two complex men to something as vague as talent—let alone "genius" or "greatness"—is a limited and unsatisfying analytical approach. It does not tell us exactly what it was about Davis that made him a less effective—or perhaps merely different—national leader than Lincoln, or precisely what attributes Lincoln possessed that Davis lacked. It devalues Davis as a political and intellectual figure, effectively reading him out of the conversation about the war's broader meaning. Conversely, it makes Lincoln seem too certain, too sure of himself. In the extensive literature that has developed around Lincoln's role in articulating a higher national meaning for the Civil War, the Union president comes across as a remarkably sure-footed, clear-eyed thinker and politician, who knew exactly what the nature of the American experiment was, what his fellow Americans needed to hear, and the precise nature and underpinnings of the American national community.[4]

Many Americans believe that there really was no comparison between the two, making Davis forever the horse chestnut to Lincoln's chestnut horse. The reason is not simply that Lincoln won and Davis lost the Civil War, though this of course plays an important and unavoidable role in any assessment of the two Civil War presidents.[5] There is perhaps a more subtle, powerful force at work: the ubiquitous and vexed matter of slavery. While no scholar says so directly, many probably believe Lincoln was better able to articulate the national meaning of the war because his was the cause of freedom, liberty, and emancipation. There are no viable causal links in such an argument: being antislavery did not necessarily make a given American a better leader than one who was proslavery. But perhaps many scholars feel Lincoln could deliver a gem like the Gettysburg Address because God was on his side, after all, while Davis paid the price for his racist sins by failing to provide adequate leadership at critical moments during the war.[6]

I want to outline a different approach in this chapter. I will focus on the particular strand of thought epitomized by the Gettysburg Address: Americans' understanding of the relationship between the war itself and the nature of national identity and community formation. In doing so, I will offer three broad arguments. First, the differences between Lincoln and Davis were not so much matters of talent as of intellect; that is, of very different intellectual understandings of the way in which war affects a community. Second, when Lincoln did articulate the war's meaning, he did so, not out of a sense of certainty, but rather from a sense of uncertainty, even confusion, concerning the impact of the war on the national polity. Third, when Davis addressed issues of the Confederate nation's viability, slavery was a distinctly secondary matter.

When Davis dictated two brief autobiographical sketches from his sickbed in 1889, he was quick to mention his family's combat record in both. "My father . . . served in the War of the Revolution," he said, "first in the 'mounted gun-men,' and afterward as captain of infantry during the siege of Savannah." He was quite proud of this, and also of his brothers' service during the War of 1812. Three served, while one remained, and Davis took pains to illustrate that this was no reflection on his family honor. "A county court . . . ordered a draft for a certain number of men to stay at home," he wrote. "This draft stopped my brother . . . making him the exception of my father's adult sons who were not engaged in the defence [*sic*] of the country during the War of 1812."[7]

Davis interpreted his nation's founding through the lens of war, suggesting that the Revolution was the defining American community experience. His particular reading of the Revolution had the British visiting "outrages upon the northern Colonies," after which Southerners rose to their defense. "Sympathy, fraternal feeling, and devotion to principle, brought the South to your side in your first step to resistance," Davis told Northern congressmen. War cemented the Union by bridging what Davis apparently believed was a natural gap between North and South. The Revolution formed "a record of the triumphs of our cause, a monument of the common glory of our Union."[8]

For Davis, the Revolutionary War had provided a permanent fraternal foundation for the American national community. He was never very specific about how this worked or why it was so, nor does it seem to have been a matter of romanticizing combat itself. In some rather fuzzy, ill-defined way, Jefferson Davis believed that war could form the glue that bound a people together, and he believed this long before he became the Confederacy's president.

For Lincoln, war and its effect on community bonding was different. When he wrote his own autobiography in 1859, he did not dwell on any ancestral military prowess, and he took pains to separate his family from even the suggestion of combat. "My paternal grandfather . . . was killed by Indians," Lincoln wrote, then added, "not in battle, but by stealth, when he was laboring to farm in the forest." Davis would likely have embellished this incident into something smacking of martial bravery, but not Lincoln, who never was much impressed with the drums and trumpets of warfare, and who felt a lifelong abhorrence for violence in general.[9]

Nevertheless, Lincoln could evoke romantic images of war when the need arose, and like Davis, he saw that shared experiences of war had helped to shape the Revolutionary generation's sense of community. He believed eighteenth-century Americans were able to redirect at Britain the negative emotions —"jealousy, envy, and avarice"—that might otherwise have destroyed any nascent American nationalism. Military service created positive national memories and shared experiences. "At the close of [the Revolution], nearly every adult male had been a participator in some of its scenes," he said in 1838. "The consequence was, that of those scenes, in the form of a husband, a father, a son or a brother, a living history was to be found in every family . . . a history that could be read and understood alike by all."[10]

Both Lincoln and Davis worried that the unifying nationalism of the Revolutionary experience had worn thin during their time. Davis believed the corrosive agent was sectionalism. "If envy, and jealousy, and sectional strife, are eating like rust at the bonds our fathers expected to bind us, they come from causes which our southern atmosphere has never furnished," Davis declared; and he called for the "remembrance of the petty jarrings of today" to be "buried in the nobler friendship of an earlier time." Northerners should keep alive the flame of revolutionary ardor, keep the familial spirit created by the Revolution permanently intact. That some might not do so spoke to a failure of Northern character.[11]

Lincoln thought the community spirit of the Revolutionary War was fading away naturally. The passion produced by the conflict with Great Britain "must fade, is fading, has faded, with the circumstances that produced it." The passions of war and revolution "were a fortress of strength; but, what invading foe men could never do, the silent artillery of time has done." It was unreasonable to expect otherwise. "Like everything else, [the Revolution] must fade upon the memory of the world, and grow more and more dim by the lapse of time . . . [the Founding Fathers'] influence cannot be what it has heretofore been."[12]

Lincoln had less faith than Davis in the abiding sense of national fraternity forged in war, and herein lay a sharp difference between Lincoln's and Davis's antebellum views on the relationship between war and nationalism. Davis believed that a sense of community was created out of war, as during the Revolution, and that this was a more or less permanent feature of American national life. But Lincoln saw in the Revolution a phenomenon that had, at best, temporarily overcome the various petty jealousies and rivalries among the nations' founders.

Lincoln was very reluctant to face the possibility of war in the weeks following his election in 1860. He insisted that white Southerners were not terribly serious about separation and were merely engaged in a particularly divisive attempt to bluff Northerners into acquiescing on the issue of slavery's existence in the territories. "The crisis is all artificial," he told an audience in Cleveland, Ohio. Lincoln reassured Americans that he would not willingly "consent to the destruction of this Union." But this was merely an expression of personal resolve; during his whistle-stop journey from Springfield to Washington, D.C., the president-elect seemed reluctant to mention the impending civil war at all, to the point that some observers believed he was unequal to the task of leading the nation should a war occur.[13]

Unlike Lincoln (and many of his fellow Confederates), Jefferson Davis generally did expect war to come out of the secession crisis. If the Border States entered the Confederacy, he wrote, "there will probably be a peaceful separation." But Davis never had much faith in Border-area Southerners, and he wrote that "if the cotton states are to maintain their position alone, war is probable." A few weeks later he wrote, "My mind has been for some time satisfied that a peaceful solution of our difficulties was not to be anticipated." In late 1862 he told a crowd of Mississippians: "I was among those who, from the beginning, predicted war." While Lincoln was very reluctant to imagine his new presidential duties and national standing in the context of war, Davis embraced from the very beginning the notion that his presidency, his nation, and warfare were inseparable.[14]

Davis did not glorify war. In 1848 he had described as "heresy" the notion that "war is the purifier, blood is the ailment, of free institutions" and declared: "It is true that republics have often been cradled in war, but more often they have met with the grave than the cradle."[15] But his sense of war's costs was leavened by factors of personal and regional pride. "This war is ours," Davis said in 1862. "We must fight it out ourselves, and I feel some pride in knowing that so far we have done it without the good will of any body." He gloried in his nations' reputation for militarism. "In Europe . . . they laugh at us because of our fondness for military titles and displays," Davis told a British visitor, "but the fact is, we are a military people." To a Richmond crowd, he exclaimed that Virginia was "the theater of a great central camp, from which will pour forth thousands of brave hearts to roll back the tide of [Northern] despotism."[16]

Davis openly stated his belief that the war was a good thing for the Southern project of nation building. "This is a new government, formed of independent States, each jealous of its own sovereignty," he told a Richmond crowd in 1863. "It is necessary that it should be tried in the severe crucible in which we are being tested." This was useful political rhetoric, of course, but it provides an interesting contrast to Lincoln. Whereas Davis tended to describe the war as a "severe crucible," a "common and sacred cause," a great "struggle" or "contest"—terms that could imply both positive and negative attributes— Lincoln described war in unreservedly negative terms, as if it had no mitigating qualities.[17]

For Lincoln the Civil War was the "great difficulty," an "affliction" of "casualties and calamities," an "unhappy fraternal war," and a collection of "national difficulties."[18] It was "unnecessary" and "injurious," begun by an act of "madness," and its incidents—such as calls for new volunteers—created not Davis's sense of community, but the potential for "panics and stampedes." "I sincerely wish war was an easier and pleasanter business than it is," he wrote one correspondent, "but it does not admit of holy-days."[19]

Lincoln saw the war as an endless source of new problems. "War, at the best, is terrible," he declared. It had "radically changed[,] for the moment, the occupations and habits of the American people . . . [and] excited political ambitions and apprehensions."[20] He described wartime as "days of dereliction," which seemed to bring out the worst in people who sought jobs and favors, avoided responsibilities, peddled influence—in short, people who wanted to grow fat off the war's tremendous social and economic upheavals. The war complicated foreign relations with other countries, disrupting what he thought was the natural "harmony so necessary and so proper between the two countries [America and Great Britain], and to convert them into enemies."[21]

Ever mindful of economic issues, Lincoln fretted about the war's effects on the nation's finances, observing that the war had "produced a national debt and taxation unprecedented." In his 1864 annual message to Congress, he spoke of the war's unfortunate distraction from beneficial projects like the transatlantic telegraph and stated, "It is hoped that with the return of domestic peace the country will be able to resume with energy and advantage the former high career of commerce and civilization." Even at that late date, with the war nearly won and the Northern economy exhibiting robust growth, Lincoln refused to accede that the war might have provided a positive economic stimulus, stating only that the national economy had proven "adequate" to the task of suppressing the rebellion.[22]

Lincoln equated war with a species of radical surgery in which a limb must be removed—slavery—to save the entire body. "While we must, by all available means, prevent the overthrow of the government," he wrote Secretary of War Edwin Stanton in 1864, "we should avoid planting and cultivating too many thorns in the bosom of society." The war cost too much, diverted valuable resources, and warped Americans' moral sensibilities into placing the need to pursue violent victory above other concerns, such as liberty and civil rights. As early as 1861, he worried about ways in which a relentless pursuit of victory, encompassing measures like property confiscation and martial law, might damage the very nation he wanted to save. "The Union must be preserved," he said, but "we should not be in haste to determine that radical and extreme measures, which may reach the loyal and the disloyal, are indispensable."[23]

At times he also worried about what the war was doing to his personal standing in the eyes of the nation and the world. In response to a letter from a group of New England Quakers, he observed: "Engaged, as I am, in a great war, I fear it will be difficult for the world to understand how fully I appreciate the principles of peace." To a Massachusetts delegation that had presented him with a ceremonial whip, along with some comment about whipping the Confederacy, Lincoln replied, "Let us not think only of whipping rebels, or of those who seem to think only of whipping negroes, but of those pleasant days which it is to be hoped are in store for us, when, seated behind a good pair of horses, we can crack our whips and drive through a happy, peaceful, and prosperous land."[24]

Davis was much less given to expressing such concerns. He did his share of grumbling about the incessant barrage of complaints and requests to which he, like Lincoln was constantly subjected. "Language was said by Talleyrand to be useful for the concealment of one's thoughts," he wrote in exasperation to one man, "but in our day, it fails to communicate any thought. If it had been otherwise, the complaint . . . of which you speak would not have been made." To his wife, Varina, he wrote, "The great temporal object is to secure our independence and they who engage in strife for personal or party aggrandisement [*sic*] deserve contemptuous forgetfulness." Davis also knew that the Confederate people could waiver in their commitment to the cause, particularly in the wake of battlefield reverses. Confederate defeats in the West, for example, "have undermined public confidence, and damaged our cause," he wrote. As the war continued, he also could not fail to notice increasing discontent in some quarters of the Confederacy.[25]

But whereas Lincoln saw the war as the wellspring of such behavior, for Davis it was behavior that ran contrary to the true national patriotism that the war created. Calls for peace and reunion with the North were, he believed, the product of "a knot of traitors who have been conspiring at home" while the majority of Confederates were doing their duty. Davis drew a parallel to his beloved Revolutionary-era nationalism and suggested that in fact the Confederacy had created a stronger sense of national community, which made shirking and speculation very much the exception to the rule. "The tories of the Revolution were immensely more numerous than the disaffected among us," he claimed, and "there was much division of sentiment among the people of the colonies, while we are a united people."[26]

For Lincoln, war should have been expected to expose people's foibles and shortcomings; at best it sometimes produced what he called "relieving coincidents" in the form of the Sanitary Commission and other such benevolent organizations.[27] But Davis felt the war had much more widespread beneficial effects on the South. Battlefield reverses were mere "privations and disappointments" that provided "tests of manly fortitude" for an army that exhibited "entire unanimity and zeal." In direct contrast to the "rich man's war, poor man's fight" complaints of poor whites, he believed the war actually smoothed away distinctions between rich and poor. "We have no cause to complain of the rich," he told his fellow citizens. "All of our people have done well; and, while the poor have nobly discharged their duties, most of the wealthiest and most distinguished families of the South have representatives in the ranks." Davis also thought the war could override state jealousies. "The firm friendship soldiers from different States have formed and cemented by mutual hardships and dangers," he declared, "and the thousand events and associations which have since tended to render us more united by all these causes the existence of jealousies and rivalries will be prevented." Lincoln thought war made shirkers and profiteers. Davis thought it made patriots.[28]

Like Lincoln, Davis proclaimed himself to be a man of peace. "Civil War has only horror for me," he wrote former president Franklin Pierce during the early days of the secession crisis.[29] But he loved military metaphors in his speeches, and he used them in such a way that they gave a heavy accent to the patriotic, positive side of war. Davis referred to Northern "friends of the South" in early 1861, for example, as those "who have in the front rank of the battle been fighting the enemies of the Constitution and therefore of the South."[30] Whereas Lincoln worried about the war's economic impact on national harmony, Davis exulted that the pressures of war were in fact creating a Confederate national economy that was "gradually becoming independent of the rest of the world." The war was a rite of national passage for Davis. "We are becoming independent in many ways," he said, and "if the war continues, we shall only grow stronger and stronger as each year rolls on."[31]

Much of this had the standard, rather jingoistic ring one might expect of a leader trying to rally his people. But in Davis's pronouncements there was something more. He believed the war was making a new national community as it had done for his Revolutionary forefathers. "Distinct as the billows, yet one as the sea," was a favorite metaphor, expressing Davis's belief that the war experience was transcending the jealousies and squabbling that had heretofore separated Southern states. "Upon every hill which now overlooks Richmond, you have had, and will continue to have, camps containing soldiers from every State of the Confederacy," he declared, "and to its remotest limits every proud heart beats high with indignation. . . . There is not one true son of the South who is not ready to shoulder his musket to bleed, to die or to conquer in the cause of liberty here."[32]

Davis drew rhetorical connections between the national bonding prevalent in the shedding of blood during previous American wars and the like shedding of Southern blood in defending the Confederacy: "Well, my friends, I can only say we will make the battlefields in Virginia another Buena Vista and drench them with blood more precious than that shed there. We will make a history for ourselves."[33] This was what war did for a nation; it created a history, a shared sense of personal sacrifice binding formerly disparate peoples together. For Davis, war was not an affliction but an opportunity. "Revolutions develop the high qualities of the good and the great," he wrote Braxton Bragg. Davis acknowledged that the war "cannot change the nature of the vicious and the selfish," but in saying this he betrayed no sense that war made a people any worse: it could only elevate—or, at worse, expose—the characters who could not be elevated.[34]

Slavery is conspicuous largely by its absence in Davis's pronouncements on war and Confederate nation building. Prior to 1860, he had been unequivocal about the central role that protection of the peculiar institution played in uniting Southerners. During the war, however, he placed relatively little emphasis on slavery as a determining factor in creating a sense of Confederate nationalism. He sometimes mentioned emancipation and violations of slave property in the litany of abuses perpetrated by the enemy—as in late 1862 when he referred to Lincoln's newly announced emancipation policy as an attempt to reduce "the white and the negro to an equality," and later when he called the Emancipation Proclamation itself a measure that "encouraged [slaves] to a general assassination of their masters."[35] But Davis was far more likely, when trying to arouse the Southern people to a sense of outrage against the enemy, to use examples and metaphors concerning alleged atrocities committed by Yankee soldiers. References to slavery in these speeches occur almost as an afterthought, with Davis listing emancipation and the training of black Union soldiers rather far down on a list of Union "perfidy" and "madness."[36] The war colored everything for Davis, even shoving into the background the all-important issues of slavery and emancipation.

Of course, one could argue that Davis omitted mention of slavery for a variety of sound political reasons. It was a touchy subject among the British and other potential European supporters.[37] It was a divisive issue for poor Southerners whose ire had been raised by the twenty-slave exemption in the Confederacy's draft laws.[38] This is all true. Yet if we take Davis directly at his word, if we listen to what he himself is saying rather than speculate on motives he may or may not have had, then it seems clear that the Confederate president looked to war more than to the peculiar institution that actually started the war as the primary means by which his fledgling nation could bind itself together and create a strong, viable national character.

Lincoln, in contrast, did not suggest that the war was creating a national character or resolve. Rather, the reverse was true; character was needed to resist the difficulties and temptations caused by the war. Lincoln could, of course, see that the war afforded certain opportunities; it allowed him to vanquish slavery. But he did not see the war as necessary to do so, at least not early on. When he pressed Border State leaders to voluntarily emancipate their slaves, he suggested that in doing so they could mitigate the war's baleful effects. "The change it [voluntary emancipation] contemplates would come gently as the dews of heaven, not rending or wrecking anything," as war was bound to do, he declared.[39]

Lincoln came to realize that the war was a useful—though not indispensable—vehicle for emancipation, and at times he sounded pleased that emancipation had made it all worthwhile, becoming as he put it, "a King's cure for all the evils" of the war. But Lincoln drew from this no tone of grim triumph such as that expressed by, for example, Frederick Douglass. Lincoln's tone was one of quiet, at times perhaps even reluctant, opportunism. Yes, the war was going to destroy slavery; it meant that he could now describe the war as "the nation's day of trials, and also of its hopes" and battlefield death as having "laid so costly a sacrifice upon the altar of freedom." One often senses in Lincoln a pang of regret that it took a war to do this. "The incidents of the war cannot be avoided," he told Border State politicians in 1862. "If the war continue[s] long . . . the institution [slavery] in your states will be extinguished by mere friction and abrasion." This was not John Brown's purifying violence, Frederick Douglass's righteous wrath of God, or, for that matter, Jefferson Davis's supreme test of national will. Lincoln's war was no more good for the country than an earthquake that happened to destroy some antiquated buildings.[40]

Lincoln saw the war as a tool, creating both opportunities and dangers. "The Union must be preserved, and hence all indispensable means must be employed," he said in early 1862. "War has been made, and continues to be, an indispensable means to this end. . . . If, however, resistance continues, the war must also continue; and it is impossible to foresee all the incidents, which may attend and all the ruin which may follow."[41] But war was a very dangerous tool, one which might lead to unforeseen consequences, carrying the nation to who knew what end. "See our present condition," he told a group of African American delegates. "Our white men [are] cutting one another's throats, none knowing how far it will extend."[42]

One suspects that much of Lincoln's point of view was rooted in his very keen emotional appreciation of the war's heavy human cost—what one observer called his "gushing sympathy for those who offered their lives for this country"—and perhaps in particular his close relationship with ordinary Union soldiers and civilians.[43] The old Lincoln mythos about the frontier railsplitter who had an affinity with the common man does contain this grain of truth: Lincoln made strenuous and consistent efforts to see and be seen by large numbers of ordinary Americans, at home and in the field of battle. Scholars rightly see this as evidence that Lincoln was a great communicator, a good steward of national bonding who was cognizant of his people's needs.[44] But perhaps Lincoln also did all of these things because he felt that the bonds being created by the Civil War were as transient as those created among Americans during the Revolution. In the 1830s he had spoken of national bonding from Revolutionary days that had faded away. In his frequent visits to his men, his almost self-destructive willingness to see each and every visitor to the White House, even in the large number—over forty—of likenesses he allowed to be taken of himself during the war, Lincoln implied that he believed the people's national will was a fungible, transient thing with a relatively short shelf life.

Lincoln seemed to feel that he constantly needed to refuel and refresh Northerners' willpower with appearances, speeches, and the like. And as the war ground on, he increasingly found that he needed God. The story of Lincoln's fervent appeals to the higher purposes of the Almighty is, of course, well known. Many have seen in this a surefooted, farseeing Lincoln, invoking God as a way of calling Americans to higher political goals. These scholars see Lincoln as sort of a master architect, one who knew precisely what he wanted to do in creating a new civil religion for America. But we sometimes overlook the fact that Lincoln turned to God, not out of certainty, but out of confusion, a confusion born out of his anxiety over what the war was doing to his country. "Now, at the end of three years struggle the nation's condition is not what either party, or any man devised, or expected," he wrote in the spring of 1863. "God alone can claim it." To a Baltimore audience, he pointed out that "when the war began . . . [Americans did not] anticipate that domestic slavery would be much affected by the war. But here we are; the war has not ended, and slavery has been much affected—how much needs not now be recounted. So true it is that man proposes and God disposes."[45]

Lincoln appealed to a mysterious God rooted in his Calvinist past, whose purposes were unknown to mere mortals like himself. The passage from his Second Inaugural Address on this point is well known: "Both read the same Bible, and pray to the same God, and each invokes His aid against the other. . . . The prayers of both could not be answered; that of neither has been answered fully. The Almighty has His own purposes."[46] What is noteworthy here is not so much what Lincoln says about the nature of God, but what he reveals about the nation and its toils in what was for Lincoln not only a wasteful but also ultimately mysterious military conflict. In a July 1864 proclamation, for example, the war appeared as an awful, unfathomable force, which, if God chose to do so, could be unleashed on a sinful nation. Lincoln implored God "not to destroy us as a people, nor suffer us to be destroyed . . . by obstinate adhesion to our counsels, which may be in conflict with his eternal purposes, and to implore Him to enlighten the mind of the Nation to know and do his will."[47] This is a Lincoln, not just of humility, but, to put it bluntly, of self-styled ignorance: ignorance of God's will and the true national purpose of the war. He does not presume to possess with certainty God's blessing for his administration policies, the Union's battlefield victories, or even emancipation.[48]

Many scholars have suggested that Lincoln gave the Gettysburg Address and other speeches in that vein as a way of reestablishing national faith, of creating links between the war and national purpose.[49] But the unspoken assumption Lincoln brought to these tasks was that Northerners needed him to do this, and to do it repeatedly, in the face of a debilitating civil war that did as much damage as good to the nation's sense of itself as a community, and in the face of what Lincoln believed was the ephemeral quality of wartime national bonding. Lincoln delivered the Gettysburg Address and engaged in similar public musings about the war's higher purpose because he was unsure of what exactly was in his listener's hearts and because he saw whatever might have been the war's redeeming qualities as transitory and temporary at best.

Otherwise, why make the speech? The voluminous literature on the Gettysburg Address and other famous Lincoln speeches never really explores why Lincoln thought his people needed to hear, repeatedly, his words about the national meaning of war. We assume the reason is self-evident: to motivate the troops, to inspire the civilian home front and the soldiers in the field. But in fact, there were serious political risks for Lincoln every time he opened his mouth to say something about what it all meant. He knew this only too well. "Everything I say, you know, goes into print," he told a crowd of well-wishers in April 1865. "If I make a mistake, it doesn't merely affect me nor you but the country."[50] He believed and he hoped that Americans would be inspired by his talk of freedom and equality, but he was not certain.

The truth is, Abraham Lincoln was not certain of anything, and it was this lack of certainty and fundamental lack of faith in the value of war itself that compelled him to run the political risk of repeatedly and publicly trying to speak to the war's higher meaning. He rarely missed an opportunity, formal or informal, to do so, because he imagined the national community to be one where motives, ideas, and ideals needed constant reinforcement and renewal.

For Davis, this was all unnecessary; and in his actions, or lack thereof, we see the road not taken by Lincoln—not because Davis wasn't as bright or as astute as Lincoln, but because Davis just would not have seen the need to do things Lincoln had done. Davis needed no appeals to a higher power to make sense of the convergence of war and Confederate nationalism. Once the war began, he wrote, "I was led to forget the past, and to regard all good and true men now, as belonging to one party of the South, in which all are loyal." To North Carolina governor Zebulon Vance, he wrote: "Like yourself I have hoped that the party distinctions which existed at a former time would be buried in the graves of the gallant men who have fallen in the defence [*sic*] of their birthright." It was the war that had created this "one party" of the Confederacy.[51]

Indeed, Davis believed not only that the Confederacy had been born in the cradle of war, but that it would likely continue to be subject to periodic intervals of hostilities with the North, the prospect of which should keep the Southern people permanently united and vigilant. "Cast your eyes forward to that time at the end of the war, when peace shall nominally be proclaimed," he told an audience in December 1862, "for peace between us and our hated enemy will be liable to be broken at short intervals for many years to come —cast your eyes forward to that time, and you will see the necessity for continued preparation and unceasing watchfulness." He then proposed what amounted to a system of peacetime conscription, with Southerners taking rotations of two or three years in the ranks. This would be a fine thing, Davis believed. "Serving among his equals, his friends, and his neighbors, [the Southerner] will find in the army no distinction of class." Lincoln always saw the war as a temporary aberration in the nation's life and history; for Davis, it was almost a permanent way of life, a "war of the people," which could create a stronger, more durable national community.[52]

Davis was not confused by the war; we find in his speeches and writings no anguished Lincolnian musings about the war's greater meaning or purpose. Nor was Davis terribly confused about God. Lincoln referred to a mysterious and inscrutable Almighty in a paroxysm of apprehension; Davis appealed to a God whom he knew would ratify the purity of Confederate motives. The God "who knows the hearts of men will judge of the sincerity with which we labored," he declared, and "we shall continue this struggle in humble dependence upon Providence from whose searching scrutiny we cannot conceal the secrets of our hearts." Davis was convinced that Confederate hearts were pure, and he was very nearly as certain that God knew this and would act accordingly. "If we perform our duty and are true to ourselves, under the blessing of Providence, our victory [will] be complete, our triumph certain," he said.[53]

"It is written in the book of fate that we shall whip them yet," Davis told his people in the fall of 1863, and he expected all Southerners to "be ready to make every effort, [and] make any sacrifice." "If we [are] unanimous . . . then our subjugation [will] be impossible," he declared.[54] Was this false bravado? Was it a blind expectation of a universal Confederate unity that did not really exist? Yes, and it was part and parcel of a Davis personality that presumed instant agreement with him on all matters. "He . . . has a way of taking for granted that everybody agrees with him when he expresses an opinion, which offends me," Varina Davis once shrewdly observed about her husband.[55]

So as to the question of why Jefferson Davis did not give a Gettysburg Address, or more generally why he was not given to this Lincolnian style of oratory, I must respectfully disagree with Professors Potter, McPherson, and others—Davis was not lacking in talent or ability, and it was not that he was unable to communicate effectively. It was that, given his particular assumptions about the relationship between war and national bonding, he did not think he needed to try to do what Lincoln felt constantly impelled to do: speak to the national meanings of war that might transcend the war itself.

To suggest that Davis lacked Lincoln's uncertainty about what the war meant may seem strange, since the popular vision of the two men suggests a sure-handed Lincoln and a vacillating Davis.[56] But where the war's effect on national identity was concerned, rather the reverse was true. Nor was Davis's assumption that war itself provided the requisite national bonding inherently wrongheaded. It was a reasonable assumption to make. Indeed, given the relative strength of the South's postwar Lost Cause mythology in comparison with the short-lived commitment of white Northerners to African American equality, perhaps Davis was more correct on this score: maybe the war *was* more powerful than the Declaration of Independence.

NOTES

1. On Davis's speechmaking skills, see comments on the subject by observers at his speech at Natchez, Mississippi, 13 June 1844, in Lynda Lasswell Crist, et al.,

eds., *The Papers of Jefferson Davis,* 10 vols. (Baton Rouge: Louisiana State University Press, 1971–1999; hereinafter *PJD*), 2:166; at Port Gibson, Mississippi, 1 July 1844, *PJD* 2:5; and at Vicksburg, Mississippi, 6 November 1843, *PJD* 2:47.

2. There are, of course, many sources on Lincoln's general purpose and vision in delivering the Gettysburg Address, as well as his other major speeches; for a recent treatment of this subject, see Allen C. Guelzo, *Abraham Lincoln, Redeemer President* (New York: William Eerdman, 1999); and, of course, Garry Wills, *Lincoln at Gettysburg: The Words That Remade America* (New York: Simon and Schuster, 1992). Also generally useful are Waldo W. Braden, *Abraham Lincoln, Public Speaker* (Baton Rouge: Louisiana State University Press, 1988); James Hurt, "All the Living and the Dead: Lincoln's Imagery," *American Literature* 52 (November 1980): 352–80; Phillip S. Paludan, "Emancipating the Republic: Lincoln and the Means and Ends of Antislavery," in *"We Cannot Escape History": Lincoln and the Last Best Hope of Earth,* ed. James M. McPherson (Urbana: University of Illinois Press, 1995), 45–62, and the relevant segments of Paludan's *Presidency of Abraham Lincoln* (Lawrence: University Press of Kansas, 1992).

3. James M. McPherson, "How Lincoln Won the War with Metaphors," in *Abraham Lincoln and the Second American Revolution* (New York: Oxford University Press, 1990), 93–94; Emory M. Thomas, *The Confederacy as Revolutionary Experience* (New York: Prentice-Hall, 1971), 60; William C. Davis, *Jefferson Davis: The Man and His Hour* (New York: HarperCollins, 1991), 703; David M. Potter, "Jefferson Davis and the Political Factors in Confederate Defeat," in *Why the North Won the Civil War,* ed. David Donald (New York: Collier Books, 1960), 109.

4. For representative examples of such treatments of Lincoln's leadership, see William E. Gienapp, "Abraham Lincoln and Presidential Leadership," in McPherson, *"We Cannot Escape History,"* 63–85; the various essays in McPherson, *Abraham Lincoln and the Second American Revolution;* and Stephen B. Oates, *Abraham Lincoln, the Man behind the Myths* (New York: HarperCollins, 1984). William C. Davis, *Lincoln's Men* (New York: Free Press, 1999), portrays an almost error-free program pursued by Lincoln in cementing relations with his soldiers.

5. On this matter, see Ludwell Johnson, "Jefferson Davis and Abraham Lincoln as War Presidents: Nothing Succeeds Like Success," *Civil War History* 27 (1981): 128–52.

6. On the pitfalls of using victory and defeat as yardsticks to measure Confederate nationalism, and on the influence of slavery on historians' moral judgements, I have been strongly influenced by Gary Gallagher's excellent observations in his *The Confederate War* (Cambridge, Mass.: Harvard University Press, 1997).

7. Davis, autobiographical sketches, November 1889, *PJD* 1:liii, lxix.

8. *PJD* 4:462–63; speech on Oregon Bill, 12 July 1848; *PJD* 3:366; see also Jefferson Davis, *Rise and Fall of the Confederate Government* (1881; New York: Da Capo Press, 1990), 1:41.

9. Lincoln to Jesse W. Fell, 20 December 1859, in Roy P. Basler, ed., *The Collected Works of Abraham Lincoln* (New Brunswick, N.J.: Rutgers University Press, 1953; hereinafter *CW*), 3:511; on Lincoln's general attitude toward violence and war, see Davis, *Lincoln's Men,* esp. chaps. 1–2; also see his remarks about his own attitude toward battle and war to Noah Brooks in *Lincoln Observed: Civil War Dispatches of Noah Brooks,* ed. Michael Burlingame (Baltimore: Johns Hopkins University Press, 1998), 205.

10. Lincoln, Lyceum Address, 27 January 1838, *CW* 1:115.

11. Davis, speech in the House of Representatives, 6 February 1846, *PJD* 2:462–63.

12. Lincoln, Lyceum address, 27 January 1838, *CW* 1:115.

13. Lincoln, speech in Cleveland, Ohio, 15 February 1861, *CW* 4:216; speech in New York, New York, *CW* 4:227; see also Donald, *Lincoln,* 275–77.

14. Davis to Alexander M. Clayton, 30 January 1861, *PJD* 7:28; Davis to Francis W. Pickens, 20 February 1861, *PJD* 7:55; speech at Jackson, Mississippi, 26 December 1862, *PJD* 7:566.

15. Davis, speech in House of Representatives, 6 February 1846, *PJD* 2:439.

16. Davis, speech at Jackson, Mississippi, 26 December 1862, *PJD* 8:576; interview with Lord Russell, 7 May 1861, *PJD* 7:153–54; speech at Richmond, Virginia, 1 June 1861, *PJD* 7:184.

17. Davis speech at Richmond, Virginia, 5 January 1863, *PJD* 9:14.

18. Lincoln, proclamation of Thanksgiving for victories, 10 April 1862, *CW* 5:186; Lincoln to I. A. Gere et al., *CW* 5:216; reply to Joseph Bertinatti, 30 July 1864, *CW* 7:473; Order for Observance of the Death of Martin Van Buren, 25 July 1862, *CW* 5:340.

19. Davis to Earl Van Dorn, 20 May 1862, *PJD* 8:193. There were, of course, times when Davis referred to war in negative terms; see e.g., Davis to John Forsyth, *PJD* 8:293. Lincoln to Eliza P. Gurney, 26 October 1862, *CW* 5:487; call for new volunteers, 1 July 1862, *CW* 5:297; Lincoln to Thomas H. Clay, 8 October 1862, *CW* 5:452.

20. Lincoln speech to the Great Sanitary Fair, Philadelphia, Pennsylvania, June 16, 1864, ibid., 7: 394; Annual Message to Congress, December 1, 1862, ibid., 5: 519.

21. Lincoln to Queen Victoria, 1 February 1862, *CW* 5:177; Lincoln to John M. Clay, 9 August 1862, *CW* 5:364.

22. Lincoln to Edwin M. Stanton, 18 March 1864, *CW* 7:255; Lincoln message to Congress, 6 December 1864, *CW* 8:139.

23. Remarks at the Great Central Sanitary Fair, Philadelphia, Pennsylvania, 16 June 1864, *CW* 7:394; Lincoln to Albert G. Hodges, 4 April 1864, *CW* 7:281; on Lincoln's sense of the war's tremendous cost, see Lincoln to Henry J. Raymond, 9 March 1862, *CW* 5:152–53; Message to Congress, 1 December 1862, *CW* 5:532; and Message to Congress, 3 December 1861, *CW* 5:49; on the consequences of the war for laboring classes, see Lincoln's address to the New York Workingmen's Democratic Republican Association, 21 March 1864, *CW* 7: 259–60.

24. Lincoln to Samuel B. Tobey, 19 March 1862, *CW* 5:165; remarks to a Massachusetts delegation, 13 March 1862, *CW* 5:158.

25. Davis to Wiley P. Harris, 3 December 1862, *PJD* 7:433; for similar correspondence, see Davis to William M. Brooks, 15 March 1862, *PJD* 8:100–102; Davis to Varina Howell Davis, 16 May 1862, *PJD* 8:179; Davis to Albert S. Johnston, 12 March 1862, *PJD* 8:93.

26. Davis to Zebulon Vance, 29 February 1864, *PJD* 10:268; Davis, speech at Mobile, Alabama, 30 December 1862, *PJD* 8:588.

27. Lincoln, speech at the Great Sanitary Fair, Philadelphia, Pennsylvania, 16 June 1864, *CW* 7:394.

28. Davis to Joseph E. Johnston, 28 February 1862, *PJD* 8:69; speech at Jackson, Mississippi, 26 December 1862, *PJD* 8:569; Message to Confederate Congress, 2 May 1864, *PJD* 10:379; speech at Richmond, Virginia, 5 January 1863, *PJD* 9:14.

29. Davis to Franklin Pierce, 20 January 1861, *PJD* 7:18.

30. Davis to George Lunt, 17 January 1861, *PJD* 7:14.

31. Davis, speech at Richmond, Virginia, 5 January 1863, *PJD* 9:14; First Inaugural, 18 February 1861, *PJD* 7:47; Message to CSA Congress, 18 November 1861, *PJD* 7:412; see also 7:416, where Davis argues that the blockade was in fact serving to "complete the circle" of the Confederate economy; speech at Richmond, 23 July 1861; Annual Message to Congress, 15 February 1862, *PJD* 8:58–59.

32. Davis, speech in Richmond, 1 June 1861, *PJD* 7:184.

33. Ibid., 7:185.

34. Davis to Braxton Bragg, 5 August 1862, *PJD* 8:322.

35. Davis's remarks at Murfreesboro, Tennessee, 13 December 1862, *PJD* 8:548; reaction to the Emancipation Proclamation may be found in James D. Richardson, ed., *Messages and Papers of Jefferson Davis and the Confederacy* (New York: Chelsea House Publishers, 1966), 1:290–94.

36. See, e.g., Davis's speech at Jackson, Mississippi, 26 December 1862, *PJD* 8:566–68; Davis to Joseph Davis, 31 May 1863, *PJD* 8:200; Message to Congress, 15 August 1862, and [?] January 1863, both reprinted by Davis in his *Rise and Fall of the Confederate Government*, 2:599–600; this litany of Yankee outrages continued long after the war; see ibid., 602–6.

37. This point has been made by, among others, Drew Gilpin Faust; see *Creation of Confederate Nationalism: Ideology's Identity in the Civil War South* (Baton Rouge: Louisiana State University Press, 1988), 59–60.

38. Paul Escott makes this point in "Southern Yeomen and the Confederacy," *South Atlantic Quarterly* 77 (1978): 146–50.

39. Proclamation Revoking General Hunter's Order, 19 May 1862, *CW* 5:223.

40. Response to Serenade, 1 February 1865, *CW* 8:254; Lincoln speech to 113th Ohio, 11 June 1864, *CW* 7:388; Lincoln to Mrs. Lydia Bixby, 21 November 1864, *CW* 8:117; appeal to Border State representatives, 12 July 1862, *CW* 5:318.

41. Lincoln, message to Congress, 7 March 1862, *CW* 5:145–46.

42. Address on colonization, 14 August 1862, *CW* 5:372.

43. Interview with Alexander W. Randall and Joseph T. Mills, 16 August 1864, *CW* 7:507.

44. This point is made particularly by Davis, *Lincoln's Men,* esp. chap. 5.

45. Lincoln to Albert G. Hodges, 4 April 1864, *CW* 7:282; speech at Sanitary Fair, Baltimore, Maryland, 18 April 1864, *CW* 7:301; Guelzo, *Redeemer President,* 370–73 makes a somewhat similar point, arguing that Lincoln saw the war as testing an uncertain proposition about equality—as opposed to a "truth"—and that he was unwilling to predict with certainty the war's eventual outcome.

46. Lincoln, Second Inaugural Address, 4 March 1865, *CW* 8:333.

47. Proclamation of a Day of Prayer, 7 July 1864, *CW* 7:431.

48. See also Lincoln to Eliza P. Gurney, 4 September 1864, *CW* 7:535; one rather mild exception to the latter can be found Lincoln's proclamation of Thanksgiving, 20 October 1864, in which he suggests that God "has largely augmented our free population by emancipation and immigration," *CW* 8:55.

49. On this point, see especially Wills, *Lincoln at Gettysburg,* esp. chap. 9; Glen Thurow, *Abraham Lincoln and American Political Religion* (Albany: State University of New York Press, 1976); Hans J. Morganthau and David Heln, eds., *Essays on Lincoln's Faith and Politics* (Lanham: University Press of America, 1983).

50. Lincoln's response to a serenade, 10 April 1865, *CW* 8:394. Lincoln constantly expressed his concerns about being misconstrued or saying anything too divisive; e.g., see his speech of 11 April 1865, *CW* 8:402–3.

51. Davis to Isham G. Harris, 17 July 1862, *PJD* 7:246; Davis to Zebulon B. Vance, 1 November 1862, *PJD* 8:477.

52. Davis speech at Jackson, Mississippi, 26 December 1862, *PJD* 8:573; speech at Savannah, Georgia, 31 October 1863, *PJD* 10:44.

53. Davis, First Inaugural Address, 18 February 1861, *PJD* 7:47; Message to CSA Congress, 18 November 1861, *PJD* 7:419; speech at Savannah, Georgia, 1 November

1863, *PJD* 10:44. For similar remarks on God's ratification of the Confederate cause, see Message to CSA Congress, 18 November 1861, *PJD* 7:412; Davis to Varina Howell Davis, 2 June 1862, *PJD* 8:209; Davis to Robert E. Lee, 8 December 1862, *PJD* 8:533; Message to the Confederate Congress, 2 May 1864, *PJD* 10: 383. It is true that even Davis at times felt his nation should be a bit more humble in face of God and not presume to know his will; see Drew Gilpin Faust's remarks on this point in her *Creation of Confederate Nationalism,* 33.

54. Speech at Savannah, Georgia, 31 October 1863, *PJD* 10:44; speech at Wilmington, North Carolina, 5 November 1863, *PJD* 10:49.

55. Varina Banks Howell to Margaret K. Howell, 10 December 1843, *PJD* 2:52–53.

56. On Davis's vacillation, see Richard E. Beringer, "Jefferson Davis's Pursuit of Ambition: The Attractive Features of Alternative Decisions," *Civil War History* 38 (winter 1992): 5–38.

7

The Politics of Language
The Ku Klux Klan in Reconstruction

CHRISTOPHER WALDREP

Historians have long characterized the period between the 1880s and 1930 as the "lynching era." One historian dates its beginnings to 1889, claiming that as late as 1888 there was little hint of the coming wave. A recent book on lynching concedes that Reconstruction violence "presaged" what came later but differed significantly in that the Ku Klux Klan had a revolutionary intent, while lynchers did not aim to overturn state governments.[1]

This argument for a distinct lynching era seems to fly in the face of evidence from Reconstruction. After the Civil War, crowds of Klansmen broke open jails, seized black prisoners, and hanged them in ways that closely resembled violence later in the century. At least one historian of the Klan now calls these events "lynchings." Another historian, looking at racial violence in Kentucky, insists that Reconstruction "lynchings" must be counted the same as those that came after 1880.[2] In fact, while the underlying violence may not have changed all that much, the time when the Klan rode did differ from the so-called lynching era. The key to understanding the difference is in language. Lynchers did what the Klan did; they and their enemies just used different words to describe racial violence. Changes in language mark the difference between the Reconstruction era's revolutionary violence and that in the Gilded Age when white Conservatives held power more securely.

In a truly revolutionary environment, competitors for power make bids for popular support. With old power structures in disarray, the insurgents have a genuine opportunity to seize power. This happened in Reconstruction, when Republicans and Conservatives articulated, negotiated, and enforced competing claims for public support and popular sovereignty. Across the South, Republicans and Conservatives both presented themselves as the truly legitimate expression of popular will. They shared an ambition to represent "the people," though they disagreed over what people they represented. The Republicans had fought the Civil War to make the United States function as a unified whole. According to the most determined Republicans, a crime against an American citizen's civil rights in the most obscure Southern hamlet outraged the entire republic. Conservatives were more reluctant to surrender the old anti-Federalist understanding of America as a collection of mostly independent communities. They believed that violence condoned by the white people in a neighborhood, community, or state could be legitimate even when condemned by white "outsiders" from other states or black "outsiders" from within their own states.[3]

Since competitors for power try to fix labels on events, actions, and movements that paint themselves as legitimate and their enemies as less so, language becomes critically important in revolutionary situations. While modern historians have denounced Klansmen as "terrorists" and "lynchers," the implications of this powerful language have yet to be explored.[4] Conservatives defended the perimeter around their constituents' popular sovereignty by blasting their enemies in the newspapers and in political speeches as "outsiders," "scalawags," and "carpetbaggers." Their goal was to plant this language in ordinary conversation, in the public consciousness. How Klan violence should be described became a particularly hard-fought battle, one that continues even today. The words *terror, lynching,* and *outrage* have become important weapons in this enduring fight over appropriate language to describe the Klan. In Reconstruction, Republicans fought to persuade the public to conceptualize each Klan act as an "outrage," repugnant to the entire American public, an attack on the public good, defined nationally. If most Americans found such violence outrageous rather than legitimate, white Conservatives had lost an important battle. Republicans and Conservatives battled in language for legitimacy.

Lynching implied a killing carried out by a small community, an expression of localized popular sovereignty of the sort Southern white Conservatives advocated. Western lynching influenced their thinking. When Western writers talked of resorting to Judge Lynch, they meant a town meeting and communal trial followed by consensus and, often, an orderly execution. Lynchers were no mob, "but emphatically the *people*."[5] The Reconstruction Klan aspired to be seen as lynchers because they wanted to "emphatically [be] the *people*." But they never achieved that status. Real lynching came later, in the Gilded Age. The Klan's failure to establish itself as a lynching organization does not mean that the organization did not do exactly what later lynchers did, but it does call into question claims that white Southerners universally favored extralegal racial violence. In this environment, in some places, at some times, the insurgents did have a chance at success.

A major part of the Klan's appeal came from its claims to representing unified white communities, defined as small neighborhoods. It vigorously denied that politics had anything to do with its violence because politics implied division, a splintered and uncertain white community. In 1868 the Pulaski, Tennessee, Klan angrily denied that they were "politicians."[6] Georgia newspaper editor Ambrose Wright insisted that "there was no politics in it, so far as I know." When the Klan claimed to target people who were "a curse to the community," they did not mean a community rent by division. Wright said that every "outrage" he had described in his county was "spoken of commonly as Ku-Klux." His questioner asked him to define "Ku-Klux." Wright answered that "it is synonymous with lynch law," meaning violence carried out on behalf of the community, not as an outrage to the community.[7]

In places where not all whites actually joined the Klan, observers sometimes claimed that all were implicated nonetheless. The Republican postmaster in Tuskegee, Alabama, explained that he did not charge the better people of his county with direct participation in Klan violence, adding, "But I think they are to blame indirectly, because they permitted these things to be done by young men and reckless men, without ever censuring or manifesting any displeasure."[8] In Tallapoosa, Alabama, one white planter estimated that all the "good" citizens in his county opposed the violence. He thought that if all the white people had met together and passed resolutions denouncing the Klan, they could have stopped the violence. These good people did not do so because they feared making themselves "obnoxious." Though they were a minority, Klansmen had very effectively established a feeling of dominance— so much so that their opponents dared not challenge them.

On a more practical level, foes of the Klan also worried that the Klan would burn them out of their homes.[9] An Alabama Republican declared, "A man might as well go and dig his grave as to go to Blountsville and apply against a Ku-Klux or try to warrant him." Another said that "a great many" voters wanted to vote Republican but did not only because of their fears.[10] One Georgia Unionist estimated that most people were not in the Klan but were afraid to speak against it. According to this Unionist, only the lower classes carried out Klan "depredations."[11] Republicans believed many opponents of the Klan failed to speak out only because they feared its violence.

One argument for the universality of Klan violence came from the South's alleged culture of violence. Abolitionists had long argued that slavery had led Southerners to violence. Some observers continued this argument after the fall of slavery. In 1865 the Louisville *Journal* reported that "lynch law" remained as active in Kentucky as it had been before the war. A "large and excited crowd" hanged James Miller after he stabbed Tilford Gregory, the paper reported. Race had nothing to do with the killing, as both Miller and Gregory were white. At least one black newspaper quickly picked up the story and reprinted it as evidence of a continued white Southern tendency to use lynch law.[12]

Despite such reports, the Klan did not actually represent all whites in all neighborhoods as a unified mass. Most whites supported white supremacy, but a significant number preferred to maintain white control without vigilante violence. One Georgia native declared himself a Democrat, but not "one of these fighting democrats." He added, "If we cannot beat them at voting, we cannot beat them at shooting."[13] North Carolina lawyer David Schenck never wavered from his commitment to white supremacy. "I utterly loathe the negro," he candidly wrote, adding that "all my sympathies and hopes are with the white race." Shortly thereafter, he thanked God that "I have been true to my race and color."[14] But Schenck did not feel he had to toe the white line on every issue. When North Carolina Republicans proffered a new state constitution, Schenck favored accepting it as "the best we can do." This stance cost him friends, but Schenck felt he could risk the criticism. Even after he went on record favoring the Republicans' proposed constitution, Klan organizers still wanted Schenck to join their "Invisible Empire." Schenck enlisted only after being assured that no violence would follow. The Klan, he was told, "was purely a secret political society using lawful measures." When the Klan turned violent, Schenck abandoned it, leaving the order entirely in 1870.[15] Schenck's insistence that he never participated in Klan violence might be dismissed as self-serving—except his claims are found on the pages of his private journal and hardly seem to have been prepared for public consumption.[16]

Such sentiments forced the Klan to attack not only blacks but whites who were opposed to their violence. Some members of the Klan had been forced into the order. South Carolinian John S. Millar may have had "kindly feelings" for the Republicans, but he joined the Klan when vigilantes raided his house. In some cases, Klansmen forced reluctant recruits to implicate themselves in serious crimes so that they could not easily oppose the Klan. After Klansmen killed Charley Good, they drafted local whites to place his body in the river. Once they had aided and abetted a murder, they could hardly refuse other assignments for fear of being turned over to authorities themselves.[17]

Frederick Douglass identified three distinct classes in the South. There was, he said, "the intensely loyal class," which included freed slaves for the most part and white "carpetbaggers." A second group included "the more enlightened slaveholders and their friends." Such people still supported slavery and despised black suffrage but had decided to "endure what they cannot cure." As Douglass explained in 1869, "They are not pleased with the sport of butting their heads against a stone wall." Finally, Douglass described "the Ku-Klux stripe" as the third group. He dismissed these people as "the haters," opposed to Northerners, black Southerners, and the very thought of accepting the new order.[18]

Other African Americans agreed with Douglass. No doubt John Roy Lynch voiced an overly sanguine view of white voters when he claimed that whites did not seriously hamper Reconstruction between 1868 and 1872 and accepted it between 1872 and 1874. But Lynch was a skilled political operator, and he did report success in recruiting white voters into the Republican ranks.[19] White Republicans did not always break the South into precisely the same categories as Douglass or express the same optimism as Lynch, but they agreed with the principal point. The U.S. Attorney for the northern district of Mississippi divided native-born whites into two classes. The larger class harbored bitter feelings for Northerners, but the more respectable element, this Mississippi Republican thought, desired harmony and treated Northerners with respect and kindness.[20]

In some places, Republicans stoutly resisted the Klan. In Limestone County, Alabama, a mob tried to break into the jail, only to be repelled by an organized opposition.[21] In Floyd County, Georgia, the Klan was so weak it could kill a nineteen-year-old boy only by masquerading as Union soldiers. They told the boy they needed him to go after the Klan. The ruse worked. He went with the "soldiers" and died, trapped and alone with his enemies.[22] Allen M. Gunn of Gravella, Alabama, courageously confronted a crowd that first denounced him as a Republican and then beat him senseless. Despite such pressure, Gunn would not surrender: "My father's *blood* purchased the american constitution, as a faithful and dutiful son, My blood Shall Seal IT before I yield one inch." Despite such powerful rhetoric, Gunn felt frustrated that pen and ink failed to communicate the depth of his angry determination to resist Klan violence.[23]

The political nature of the Klan proves that few Southerners thought "ku-kluxing" was synonymous with lynch law. Klansmen disarmed blacks and assassinated politically effective black leaders, thus carrying out their adver-tised mission of protecting white society from rampaging blacks. Sometimes, though, they advanced the fortunes of the Democratic party at a time when not all whites had yet signed onto the Democrats' standard. The hearty hatred of Democrats nursed by some old Whigs led some into the Republican party, at least for a time. Even in the York County, South Carolina, Klan stronghold, some whites objected to vigilante violence as political when carried out on behalf of only a segment of white society rather than for the good of all whites.

In some cases, Klansmen forced reluctant whites into their organization. Charles Foster joined the Klan only to avoid a beating. A grocer, he had sold liquor, and Klansmen warned him he would be whipped if he did not join their order.[24] Many more joined the Klan thinking the vigilantes intended to protect whites from black violence, only to leave the order disenchanted. Osmond Gunthorpe grumbled that when he joined the Klan he did not think of it as a political organization: "I understood it was an organization for the protection of each other against . . . the negroes rising."[25] Once Gunthorpe decided the Klan had a political agenda, representing one segment of the white community against another, he quit.

When the Klan first organized, many blacks feared that white neighbor-hoods were as united as the Klan claimed. After the Civil War, some blacks feared a white "reign of terror." At this time, terror meant violence perpetu-ated by established but illegitimate authorities, as in the French Revolution, not violence directed against authority.[26] In 1868 a black newspaper called the *Elevator* worried that "rebel leaders" plotted "a war of extermination against all Union men, white as well as black." If white "rebels" were as united and pow-erful as the *Elevator* feared, then their hangings of blacks and whites could be called lynchings. Black and white Republicans had no claim to authority or legitimate place in the community. The *Elevator* did call whites' violence lynchings, reporting in one instance that "a force of armed Democrats" had attacked a Republican newspaper in Louisiana and *lynched* its editor." The *Ele-vator* implied that whites had so totally united behind violence-prone leaders that Republicans had been squeezed into outsider status. In essence, the *Elevator* conceded that the newspaper had been marginalized, not yet established as a significant part of its community.[27]

≈

Whatever the realities of their support, white Conservatives campaigned through Reconstruction to present themselves as representatives of all whites. They most credibly claimed to "lynch" their victims when they actually attracted the kind following among whites that the *Elevator* feared. In 1868 a crowd of Tennessee men gathered outside their Republican sheriff's door at midnight. They taunted the man by groaning loudly in his yard and called for him to come to his door. J. S. Webb appeared only after they promised not to hurt him. But when he came to his door, they grabbed him and took him to the center of his yard. They cut switches, he reported, "and told me they were going to lynch me if I did not resign the office of sheriff."[28]

By 1869, when Klan violence had attracted national attention, Republicans armed themselves and feared for their lives. They needed strong language to denounce Klan violence, but their denial that all Southerners, or even all white Southerners, supported the Klan made *lynching* the wrong word. When Republican Arthur A. Smith described how members of a white mob had been indicted for lynching after they seized a black man, he quickly added, "Do not understand me to say that these persons were lynched." Authorities had relied on an act passed to suppress lynching. The law had labeled them as lynchers, but that, Smith explained, was a mere legal technicality. They were not true lynchers.[29]

In his great Reconstruction novel *A Fool's Errand,* Albion Tourgee quotes Klansmen as plotting to "execute" a victim.[30] But when they did, a "loud-voiced young man" objected. "we'll all be running our necks into hemp," he warned, adding, "It's what we call murder, gentlemen, in civilized and Christian countries!" (281–82). Tourgee describes the killing of "old Jerry," found hanged from an oak not forty steps from the court house, as a "hanging" rather than a "lynching" (230). In another passage, Tourgee's hero looks keenly at a Klansman and charges, *"you are a murderer!"* The Klansman acknowledged the appropriateness of the term: "It is a hard word. . . ; yet I do not know but I must submit" (298–99). Tourgee's central character worries about being "assassinated," fearing his "individual destruction" (296). The voices echoing from the pages of Tourgee's prose do not cry "lynching"; instead, they shriek "murder," "assassination," "outrage."

As time passed, black Republicans became more and more determined not to call Klan violence lynching. In 1868, the San Francisco *Elevator* had associated a Klan "reign of terror" with "lynching." As late as September 1874, the *Elevator* still complained that whites subjected blacks to "indiscriminate lynching."[31] Thereafter, however, the *Elevator* accused Southern white Conservatives of carrying out "murders," "outrages," "atrocities," and "massacres." The paper headlined, "Shooting, Hanging and Whipping," adding that "The Bullet, Knife, Halter and Torch [are] the Weapons." But there were no more lynchings. As the *Elevator* had explained, things had changed: "Now, however, the case is different." From the *Elevator's* perspective, the key difference was that "the negro is a political power." If African Americans were a political power, and a legitimate part of the community, then the term *lynching* no longer fit.[32]

The word that black and white Republicans preferred when describing Klan violence was *outrage,* not *lynching.* While *lynching* suggested a killing carried out by the community, *outrage* implied a terrible crime against the community. To call a Klan act of violence an *outrage* denounced it as the work of a minority. Republican rhetoric followed a long search conducted by the Abolitionists to find the right word to describe white Southern violence. They had accused Southerners of committing "crimes," "horrors," "atrocities," and "outrages." The word *outrage* worked well because it implied a crime against the nation's conscience. As Philip Hone wrote in 1835, an *outrage* was violence calculated "to make humanity shudder." Riots, tarrings and featherings, and murders all constituted *outrages* according to the abolitionist press.[33] "Another Fiendish Outrage" the Boston *Liberator* headlined on December 3, 1831, after "a mob of slavites" had attacked a Petersburg, Virginia, resident for favoring emancipation. Northerners abused by Southerners proved the need for national citizenship rights. Like postbellum Republicans, the abolitionists understood *outrage* to mean an affront to the national morality. Exciting a riot or a mob, the *Liberator* charged, was treason.[34]

In Reconstruction, opponents of the Klan complained of hundreds, even thousands of "outrages" in Southern states.[35] This rhetoric can be found in Republicans' private correspondence, not just in the newspapers. Governors hoped outrage rhetoric would make federal authorities more amenable to protecting the rights of American citizens everywhere in America.[36] Judges reported ordering Klansmen arrested for outrages.[37] Ordinary citizens had no trouble knowing what constituted an outrage. As one man wrote, when Klansmen robbed loyal men of everything they could take away, even taking the food out of their cooking pots, taking them out of bed "to be hung for voating for Mr Lincolen," that was an *outrage*.[38]

Republican propagandists hammered the word into the minds of its readers. For months in 1871, few issues of the New York *Tribune* rolled off the presses without a column devoted to "Southern Outrages." The paper headlined "Ku-Klux Outrage," "Another Terrible Ku-Klux Outrage," "Recent Outrages," offered "Particulars of Outrages."[39] In New Orleans, the Republican-controlled state legislature investigated whites' "outrages," "massacres," "slaughters," and "murders."[40] Republicans distinguished "outrages" carried out by private citizens, even when "systemic," from the terrorism sponsored by local governments.

The word *outrage* also implied a challenge to white Conservatives' definitions of community as a small, autonomous neighborhood. Republicans wrote laws to define national citizenship and establish rights enjoyed by all citizens. Even the most ordinary of Americans understood this fact. One Ohioan listed a series of "outrages," reminding President Ulysses S. Grant that he had "promised protection to all citizens of the united states."[41] Albion Tourgee, a Union Army veteran, came to North Carolina after the war, becoming a judge. Tourgee found the experience impossibly frustrating. He explained that whites commonly classed the racial violence he confronted as "outrages." Tourgee wrote that all sorts of violence qualified as "outrages." He clearly intended his catalog of horrors to shock Northern readers:

> The entry of the premises, and surrounding the dwelling with threats against the inmates; the seizure and destruction, or appropriation of arms; the dragging of men, women, and children from their homes, or compelling their flight; the binding, gagging, and beating of men and women; shooting at specific individuals, or indiscriminately at inhabited houses; the mutilation of men and women in methods too shocking and barbarous to be recounted here; burning houses; destroying stock; and making the night a terror to peaceful citizens by the ghastly horror of many and deliberate murders,—all these come within the fearful category of "outrages."[42]

In 1871 Congress organized a joint committee to investigate Klan violence. Moderates, like James A. Garfield, explained that they wanted to ascertain whether the state of conditions in the Southern states warranted further legislation. Other Republicans, however, chafed impatiently, insisting that Congress already had all the information it needed about Southern outrages. John Coburn of Indiana wanted to put "the strong arm of the law . . . in motion" and not merely a committee of inquiry into the field. Despite such objections, in April Congress created a joint committee of seven senators and fourteen representatives to investigate the safety of American citizens' lives and property. The committee organized on April 20 and began taking testimony one month later. Witnesses came to Washington, but subcommittees fanned out across the South to hear from the victims of Reconstruction violence as well as from conservative white Southerners sympathetic to the vigilantes.[43] The testimony collected by the committee is a rich source for the study of Reconstruction rhetoric. Witness followed witness from June to December 1871, their words carefully transcribed by patient government stenographers. The resulting thirteen-volume record documents Klan outrages, preserving black and white Southerners' logic, discourse, dissembling, ordinary conversation, taunts, and argument.

Conservatives tried to dismiss the congressional investigation as the "outrage committee," but the term *outrage* stung. Southern Conservatives insisted the Republicans acted from purely partisan motives, but they clearly understood that every Southern "outrage" weakened their argument.[44] The Atlanta *Constitution* fought back with a satirical advertisement headlined, "Wanted, a Liberal Supply of Ku Klux Outrages in Georgia," suggesting that the Republicans falsified outrage stories.[45] Asked about "outrages" by congressional Republicans, Alabaman Edward Clement Sanders objected to such language. Killings carried out on behalf of an indignant community could hardly be classed as "outrages," he insisted. When asked what term he would use, Sanders answered, "I call it justice." Sanders's candor surprised his interrogator: "Murders, do you mean to say; several murders?" Yes, that was what Sanders meant. Killings of disreputable blacks, carried out by mobs, amounted to "justice" and was legitimate, Sanders answered.[46]

Republicans had considerable success inserting the word *outrage* into the language as a description of Klan violence. They did not manage to permanently label acts of Klan violence as outrages, but the word remained in use for at least seventy-five years. The earliest historians, the ones most hostile to Republican Reconstruction, found it hard to resist describing Klan attacks as "outrages."[47] In 1939 Stanley Horn defended the Klan, but even he could not avoid the term *outrage,* even when he encased it in quotes and dismissed the violence it described as "harmless hazing."[48] But while the Republicans changed the language, their effort to use outrage language to discredit the Klan ultimately failed. Most whites decided in the 1870s and 80s that the United States was still a collection of localities, not a unified nation. Republicans could not persuade enough Northerners that assaults on citizens in Southern villages outraged the entire nation.

In 1871 many white Southern opponents of the Klan found a home in the ranks of the New Departure. Proponents of a New Departure pledged themselves to easing racial tensions, promising moderation. In some places, Democrats accepted Reconstruction but kept New Departure Democrats as their party identification. New Departurists opposed a division of the parties along racial lines. Only after the Democrats lost the 1872 election did critics of the New Departure make political headway. To the horror of the New Departurists, white Conservatives' arguments for racial polarization caught hold. In some places this happened when blacks realized whites' worst fears by scoring electoral victories. When blacks armed themselves in self-defense, this too frightened whites and emboldened those calling for a "white line."[49] In Virginia, Nathaniel B. Meade declared that "we must make the issue *White* and *Black* against race" to save the state. He added, "The position must be made so odious that no decent man can support the radical ticket." In 1873 Democrats won an election in Virginia with the white line strategy, but their success in Alabama was more telling. In 1874 white Conservatives defeated Republicans using the "white mans' party" strategy. In 1874 the White League organized in Louisiana, sometimes relying on violence to achieve its ends. In Mississippi the whites-only approach triumphed in the 1875 elections amid violence. In South Carolina whites felt confident enough to apply violence overtly and systematically. This differed from the Klan phase, when the vigilantes had been covert and uncoordinated. With unity achieved at last, whites could operate without fear of their fellows.[50]

Perhaps in the 1880s the same number of white Southerners objected to racial violence as in the 1860s and 1870s. Yet the difference seems as clear as night and day. Gilded Age lynchers rarely donned the masks and robes favored by the Klan and did not act at night. Rather than skulking in the dark, they killed their victims in broad daylight and posed for photographers, freely distributing postcard pictures of themselves and their victims. The Klan's goal of uniting Southern whites behind racial violence had not necessarily been entirely achieved, but the Invisible Empire's campaign had achieved considerable success nonetheless. More than the Reconstruction Klan, lynchers credibly claimed to act on behalf of all whites. A kind of consensus had been won. Opponents of lawless violence felt constrained to concede that white superiority required violence. Opposition existed, but it had been effectively silenced.

White Conservatives' success at turning Klan attacks into "lynchings" signals the importance of language in Reconstruction. Albion Tourgee, himself a victim of this discourse, ruefully recognized Conservatives' skill. "Scalawag," "carpetbagger," and "redeemer" were all conservative inventions, of course, and white Southern newspapers reinvigorated the old calumny "nigger" as well. White Conservatives called themselves "redeemers," slyly invoking evangelical Christianity. White Conservatives deployed these words with great skill, winning a permanent place for them in the language. These words became so much a part of the language that it became difficult even to talk about Reconstruction without implicitly passing judgment against the Republicans. As one Alabama newspaper explained, white rhetoric had served as an "engine of moral power."[51]

Recognizing the importance of language in Reconstruction allows the restoration of contingency and the recovery of the essential tendentiousness of the period. It requires that we not close the book on white Southerners as hopelessly mired in a racism that did not change from the colonial era until 1964—if then. In the American South at the end of the Civil War, white Conservatives and Republicans fought a war. An important part of this struggle involved language. Republicans fought to label Klan violence as "outrageous." This both challenged Klan claims to represent all white communities, defined as small neighborhoods, and proposed a new, nationalized definition of community. To describe the Klan as guilty of "lynching" not only ignores an important part of Reconstruction history, but it also assumes that all white Southerners opposed Reconstruction or that all accepted the Klan's definition of community.

Understanding why racial violence in Reconstruction was not called lynching helps explain the difference between Reconstruction and the lynching era. Reconstruction was a revolutionary time, a time when power as expressed in language was genuinely up for grabs. Once the white population seized power and rallied itself into a racial bloc, then, and only then, could they kill—confident that they had the support of what they defined as the community. And they understood a community-sanctioned killing to be a lynching.

NOTES

1. Joel Williamson, *The Crucible of Race: Black-White Relations in the American South since Emancipation* (New York: Oxford University Press, 1984), 183–89; W. Fitzhugh Brundage, *Lynching in the New South: Georgia and Virginia, 1880–1930* (Urbana: University of Illinois Press, 1993), 6–7. For the revolutionary implications of Reconstruction, see also Eric Foner, *Reconstruction: America's Unfinished Revolution, 1863–1877* (New York: Harper and Row, 1988).

For the meaning of revolution, I draw theoretical inspiration from François Furet, *Interpreting the French Revolution,* trans. Elborg Forster (Cambridge: Cambridge University Press, 1981), 1–79; Keith Michael Baker, *Inventing the French Revolution* (Cambridge: Cambridge University Press, 1990), 1–58; William H. Sewell Jr., *A Rhetoric of Bourgeois Revolution: The Abbe Sieyes and What Is the Third Estate?* (Durham, N.C.: Duke University Press, 1994), 1–40; Linda Orr, *Headless History: Nineteenth-Century French Historiography of the Revolution* (Ithaca, N.Y.: Cornell University Press, 1990), 145–67.

2. Allen W. Trelease, *White Terror: The Ku Klux Klan Conspiracy and Southern Reconstruction* (Baton Rouge: Louisiana State University Press, 1971), xxi, xliii, and passim; George C. Wright, *Racial Violence in Kentucky, 1865–1940: Lynchings, Mob Rule, and "Legal Lynchings"* (Baton Rouge: Louisiana State University Press, 1990), 19–60.

3. For the persistence of Southern Anti-Federalism, see Donald Nieman, "Republicanism, the Confederate Constitution, and the American Constitutional Tradition," in *An Uncertain Tradition: Constitutionalism and the History of the South,* ed. Kermit L. Hall and James W. Ely Jr. (Athens: University of Georgia Press, 1989), 201–24.

4. Eric Foner has described Reconstruction-era Ku Klux Klan violence as a "wave of counterrevolutionary terror." Michael Fitzgerald has described the Klan as "a broad terrorist movement" dedicated to "systematic terror." Allen Trelease entitled his encyclopedic look at the Klan *White Terror.* Foner, *Reconstruction,* 425, 427, 428–29, 431, 437; Michael W. Fitzgerald, "The Ku Klux Klan: Property Crime and the Plantation System in Reconstruction Alabama," *Agricultural History* 71 (spring 1997): 186–206.

5. Quoted in Frank Soule, John H. Gihon, James Nisbet, *The Annals of San Francisco* (New York: Appleton, 1855), 318; John Phillip Reid, *Policing the Elephant: Crime, Punishment, and Social Behavior on the Overland Trail* (San Marino: Huntington Library, 1997), 139, 197.

6. *Pulaski (Tenn.) Citizen,* 14 February 1868.

7. *Report of the Joint Select Committee to Inquire into the Condition of Affairs in the Late Insurrectionary States,* 42d Cong., 2d sess., 6:280–81. Hereinafter cited as *KKK Report.*

8. *KKK Report,* 9:1039; Trelease, *White Terror,* 363.

9. *KKK Report,* 9:1136–39.

10. Ibid., 9:742–43.

11. Ibid., 6:50.

12. *San Francisco Elevator,* 6 October 1865.

13. *KKK Report,* 7:1101.

14. David Schenck, 11 September 1868, 21 November 1868, David Schenck diary, Southern Historical Collection, University of North Carolina Library, Chapel Hill.

15. Ibid., 30 September 1871.

16. Schenck's statements are confirmed by Fitzgerald, "The Ku Klux Klan," 186–206.

17. Lou Falkner Williams, *The Great South Carolina Ku Klux Klan Trials, 1871–1872* (Athens: University of Georgia Press, 1996), 92–94, 114–15.

18. Frederick Douglass, "We Are Not Yet Quite Free," address delivered at Medina, New York, 3 August 1869, *The Frederick Douglass Papers,* ed. John W. Blassingame, 5 vols. (New Haven, Conn.: Yale University Press, 1979–1992), 4:237–39.

19. John Hope Franklin, ed., *Reminiscences of an Active Life: The Autobiography of John Roy Lynch* (Chicago: University of Chicago Press, 1970), 139–44.

20. *KKK Report,* 12:1148; Williamson disparages this as the "grit thesis" (*Crucible of Race,* 292–95).

21. *KKK Report,* 8:610.

22. Ibid., 1:130–31.

23. Allen M. Gunn to Ulysses S. Grant, 22 June 1871, in *Papers of Ulysses S. Grant,* ed. John Y. Simon, 24 vols. (Carbondale: Southern Illinois University Press, 1967–), 22:15–16.

24. Charles W. Foster testimony, *Proceedings in the Ku Klux Trials at Columbia, S.C., in the United States Circuit Court, November Term, 1871* (Columbia, S.C.: Republican Printing Co., 1872), 200–213. (Hereinafter cited as *Ku Klux Trials.*)

25. Osmond Gunthorpe testimony, *Ku Klux Trials,* 215–17.

26. Nineteenth-century popular writers accused authority figures of "terrorism" when they acted in a dictatorial fashion. Judges, teachers, librarians, nurses, and even butlers were all capable of terror when they used their powers illegitimately. They more closely associated the term *terrorism* with illegitimate government power.

27. *San Francisco Elevator,* 23 October 1868.

28. *Papers in the Contested Case of Sheafe vs. Tillman in the Fourth Congressional District of Tennessee,* House Misc. Document 53, 41st Cong., 2d sess., 214.

29. *KKK Report,* 8:57.

30. Albion W. Tourgee, *A Fool's Errand,* ed. John Hope Franklin (Cambridge, Mass.: Belknap Press, 1961), 281. Page numbers in the text are to this edition.

31. *San Francisco Elevator,* 23 October 1868, 5 September 1874.

32. Ibid., 10, 17, 24, 31 October; 7, 14, 21 November 1874.

33. Allan Nevins, ed., *The Diary of Philip Hone, 1828–1851* (1927; reprint, New York: Kraus, 1969), 167–68; *Boston Liberator,* 9 July 1836, 6 January 1860; *Alton (Ill.) Observer,* 28 December 1837.

34. *Boston Liberator,* 28 January 1842.

35. Allen M. Gunn to Ulysses S. Grant, 22 June 1871, in *Papers of Ulysses S. Grant,* 22: 16.

36. Governor Tod R. Caldwell to Ulysses S. Grant, 20 April 1871, in *Papers of Ulysses S. Grant,* 22:362; Governor Robert K. Scott to Ulysses S. Grant, 17 January 1871, ibid., 21:259; Governor W. W. Holden to Ulysses S. Grant, 10 March 1870, ibid., 20:211.

37. Judge J. L. Henry to Ulysses S. Grant, 27 April 1871 in *Papers of Ulysses S. Grant,* 22:364.

38. M. A. Smith to Ulysses S. Grant, 16 January 1871, in *Papers of Ulysses S. Grant,* 21:410–11.

39. *New York Tribune,* 23 January, 23 February, 10 March, 20 March, 7 April 1871.

40. *Supplemental Report of Joint Committee of the General Assembly of Louisiana on the Conduct of the Late Elections and the Condition of Peace and Good Order in the State* (New Orleans: A. L. Lee, 1869), iv–xl.

41. M. A. Smith to Ulysses S. Grant, 16 January 1871 in *Papers of Ulysses S. Grant,* 21:411.

42. Tourgee, *Fool's Errand,* 246.

43. James A. Garfield, remarks on Southern outrages, *Congressional Globe,* 42d Cong., 1st sess., 16 March 1871, 130; John Coburn, remarks on Southern outrages, *Congressional Globe,* 42d Cong., 1st sess., 16 March 1871, 130–31; *KKK Report,* 1:1–2.

44. Willard Warner, *Congressional Globe,* 41st Cong., 3d sess., 18 January 1871, 570–72.

45. Stanley F. Horn, *Invisible Empire: The Story of the Ku Klux Klan* (1939; reprint, New York: Haskell, 1973), 183.

46. *KKK Report,* 10:1798–99.

47. See, for example, James W. Garner, *Reconstruction in Mississippi* (1901; reprint, Baton Rouge: Louisiana State University, 1968), 345–53

48. Horn, *Invisible Empire*, 17, 176, 183, 217, 232, 236.

49. Foner, *Reconstruction*, 412–21; Christopher Waldrep, *Roots of Disorder: Race and Criminal Justice in the American South, 1817–1880* (Urbana: University of Illinois Press, 1998); Gene L. Howard, *Death at Cross Plains: An Alabama Reconstruction Tragedy* (Tuscaloosa: University of Alabama Press, 1984), 61–74.

50. Michael Perman, *The Road to Redemption: Souther Politics, 1869–1879* (Chapel Hill: University of North Carolina Press, 1984), 147–77.

51. Cal M. Logue, "Rhetorical Ridicule of Reconstruction Blacks," *Quarterly Journal of Speech* 62 (December 1976): 400–409.

PART IV

In the House of the Lord

The Protestant Church was, of course, a pillar of life in most Southern communities in the years after the end of Reconstruction. The four articles in this section examine how selected members of the church approached some of the schisms that fragmented the Christian community and made it all too often, "a house divided against itself."

In "The Color of Skin Was Almost Forgotten: Biracialism in the Twentieth-Century Southern Religious Experience," Paul Harvey investigates the extent to which Holiness and Pentecostal services deviated from the racial practices of the more mainstream Southern congregations. The author's examination of early twentieth-century sources uncovers a "hidden world of biracial services that coexisted with the dominant and completely racially separated world of religion in the region." And although Holiness/Pentecostal groups later separated into different black and white church organizations, they each continued to worship their God in common ways that fused white and black evangelical thought and culture. "Racial interchange in Southern religious culture could not override racism, and it rarely even mitigated it," Harvey concludes. "Yet even outside observers sensed that white and black Southerners carried on religious cultures that bound them together, somehow, even as it marked their separateness."

Another example of Christianity guiding Southerners into more egalitarian directions is chronicled in James O. Farmer Jr.'s "'Doing Contrary to My Raising': Emma Anderson Dunovant and the Woman Suffrage Campaign in South Carolina." As the daughter and daughter-in-law of socially prominent Confederate generals, Emma Anderson Dunovant was not the most likely candidate to lead a crusade for liberal reform—and yet she did just that in 1919 when she started writing a weekly column that championed women's rights. Her conversion grew primarily out of a devout Presbyterian faith and the conviction that God "holds for woman the great privilege" of using the vote to improve the human condition on Earth. "Scholars for whom the church was an agent of oppression of women, or at best a non-factor in the movement for their liberation," Farmer warns, "have to contend with [Southern] women like Emma Dunovant. For her religion was the source from which she drew her hope in this, as in all of the challenging aspects of life."

Dunovant had peers in the Episcopal Church who took on the most challenging aspects of Southern life—the inequities between the races—as Joan

Marie Johnson reveals in her essay, "The Shape of the Movement to Come: Women, Religion, Episcopalians, and the Interracial Movement in 1920s South Carolina." Indeed, the most important leaders of the South Carolina chapter of the Commission on Interracial Cooperation were Episcopal women. In comparison to members of other denominations, the greater wealth, social prominence, and sense of noblesse oblige that Episcopal women tended to have coupled with their church's greater affinity for the social gospel and closer organizational ties to black congregations all made them, Johnson suggests, more logical candidates to pursue racial reform. Although their approach to reform was paternalistic and limited to improving life within the Jim Crow system, it nonetheless did re-establish conversations between blacks and whites on which more meaningful, if much more difficult, change had to be predicated.

These stirrings of change pointed toward a narrowing of the doctrinal differences that had split Protestant denominations along regional lines in the antebellum period. In "Reconciliation and Regionalism: Reunion among Southern Methodists and Presbyterians, 1920–1955," William R. Glass examines the arguments made by opponents of reunification of the Methodist Church in 1938 and the Presbyterian Church in 1955 for insights into how much, and in what ways, regional religious identity persisted a century later. The two most common arguments against reunification, Glass discovers, were the fears that such a move would cause the social gospel to replace evangelicalism as the main theological focus of the church and integration to replace segregation as its position on race relations. "That opponents ultimately were not successful in stopping reunion reveals something of the changing nature of the Southern regionalism," the author concludes. But "that they stalled it for as long as they did suggests the persistence of the pattern of Southern pastors coming to the defense of Southern culture" for a lot longer than some might have predicted.

8

"The Color of Skin Was Almost Forgotten"
Biracialism in the Twentieth-Century Southern Religious Experience

PAUL HARVEY

> God and Negroes and Jesus and sin and salvation are baled up
> together in southern children's minds and in many an old textile
> magnate's also.
>> Lillian Smith, *Killers of the Dream*, 1949

> Negro entered into white man as profoundly as white man
> entered into Negro—subtly influencing every gesture, every
> word, every emotion and idea, every attitude.
>> W. J. Cash, *The Mind of the South*, 1941

July 10, 1895: E. B. Ingram, a general merchandise store owner and church member in Darlington, South Carolina, sorted through his impressions of going to see "the Negro Girl Preacher" then visiting town. That evening there was a "crowded house white and [colored] about 300 mourners don't know what to say," he recorded in his diary. The next week, he "went to hear the Mulattoe 12 year old girl Preach to night don't know what to think. Big crowd white & [colored] white ladies and all sorts." There was at least "good behaviour there to night," he commented, knowing how often young men disrupted church services. When a "colored girl preacher" came to North Carolina and preached in the local African Methodist Episcopal Zion church in New Bern, whites and blacks sat across from each other in the church. The whites remained for a revival service after the star performance.[1] In Selma, Alabama, African Methodist Episcopal (AME) pastor and bishop Winfield Henry Mixon led a camp meeting in 1903, preaching on the theme "Seek ye first the Kingdom of God." There was, he recorded, a "great crowd, many white friends out." In May of that year, AME bishop W. J. Gaines also had visited town, lecturing to a "very good crowd, white and colored."[2]

Since the late nineteenth century, Holiness churches, traveling evangelists, and other religious novelties had attracted biracial interest. Female evangelist and faith healer Maria Woodworth-Etter conducted meetings in Louisville, Kentucky, in 1888, welcoming all classes and colors. White leaders attempted to dissuade her, but Etter had "no desire to drive [the Negroes] away, but felt glad to have the privilege of leading them to Christ. God came in such wonderful power it was not long till they seemed to forget the color. The altar was filled with seekers, white people on one side and colored on the other." A black female evangelist, visiting an Etter gathering, graced one meeting with a spontaneous prayer that "took hold of God in such a way as to shake every member of the congregation and came near raising them all on their feet."[3]

Segregation laws and customs, of course, enforced rigid rules and norms on such informal biracial gatherings. The turn-of-the-century South, moreover, was hardly an auspicious place and time for racial interchange. White Southerners, having just fought bitterly over Populism, engaged in campaigns in nearly every state to enshrine segregation and disfranchisement into state constitutional law. Whites viscerally feared the "new Negro," the first generation of blacks born after slavery coming of age, and expressed those fears in lynchings and petty daily racial harassment. For many black Southerners, it was a time of degradation and terror.[4]

Yet even during this "nadir of race relations" in post–Civil War Southern history, a common evangelical heritage attracted white and black Southerners and led them to the same events—whether for curiosity's sake, for entertainment, or for a meaningful worship experience. What did biracial evangelical events signify in the Jim Crow South? What was the meaning of racial interchange in religious gatherings in this context of de facto and de jure segregation?

White and black Southerners attended separate churches, organized into racially defined denominations, baptized their converted in separate pools, and buried their dead in segregated cemeteries. Their "normal" religious expressions took place in separate institutions. That is an important part of the story, well told by numerous historians. There is another, considerably more hidden aspect to the story: biracialism in this world of segregated Southern religion. White and black Southerners—Christians, spiritual seekers, curiosity hounds, socializers, village atheists—gathered to celebrate, observe, question, and mock their common evangelical heritage. Southern believers, white and black, attended special community occasions, including events such as the child evangelist that drew E. B. Ingram's curiosity, as well as other novelty acts, townwide revivals, and river baptisms. Early-twentieth-century Holiness/ Pentecostalism, involving moments of tactile and cultural connection between black and white, created another part of this world of racial interchange. Southern religious music, with its deep biracial roots, did as well. Within Southern religious culture there existed strata of white and black religious experience seen rarely in the institutional churches (the reigning triumvirate of Baptist, Methodist, and Presbyterian) but evident in the interstices of community life—strata that mixed in imperceptibly with the top layer of religious segregation.

Like religious expression elsewhere, Southern religion has contained both priestly and prophetic sides. It has often undergirded, and less frequently challenged, the social order. If white Southern formalized theology generally sanctified Southern hierarchies, evangelical belief and practice could also subtly undermine the dominant tradition. Segregation in post–Civil War Southern religion was normal. Only in those liminal times—in novelty acts, revivals, and the creation of new religious and musical traditions—did the bars of race come down—and then only temporarily. When they did come down, however, they opened up possibilities for cultural interchange that fed into the "shared traditions" outlined by historian and anthropologist Charles Joyner. Like Huck and Jim on the raft, black and white Southerners, Joyner argues, "continued to swap recipes and cultural styles, songs and stories, accents and attitudes. Folk culture simply refused to abide any color line, however rigidly it may have been drawn."[5] White and black Southern religious folk cultures drew from common evangelical beliefs and attitudes and swapped musical and oratorical styles and forms. On occasion, they shared liminal moments of religious transcendence before moving back into the quotidian Jim Crow world, where color defined and limited everything. This essay explores the meaning of those moments.

The possibility of a biracial worship tradition necessarily raises the long-lived discussion between contending Africanist and Americanist schools of black evangelical roots.[6] Scholarly skeptics of biracialism in Southern religion have raised important challenges. Even if whites and blacks worshipped in the same place, how much did that, could that, really mean? In antebellum churches, white clergymen preached the expected message—submission, obedience, contentment with one's lot in life—to a captive (literally) audience of slaves and their masters. The slave narratives address both directly and slyly the soul-deadening nature of sitting through too many such sermonic rationalizations. The slaves knew it was a ritual: the clergymen (in their eyes) pretended to preach, and they pretended to listen. But whites and blacks in the nineteenth-century South often approached God together, sometimes in the stilted and tense settings of the antebellum biracial church, other times in more informal ways.

In the post–Civil War era, missionaries, travelers, reporters, and early anthropologists presented believers in the region as culturally other—whether exotically primitive, pathetically backward, folkishly quaint, or heroically resistant to the homogenizing trends of corporate capitalist America. For these observers, Southern religion was emotion—overwrought, anti-intellectual, too given to personal experience over formalized understandings of faith. In short, it was too "negro." From national publications such as *Harper's* and *Lippincott's* to regional venues such as *Southern Workman* and the *South Atlantic Quarterly*, they recounted their experiences observing Southern religious services, white and black. Some were missionaries intent on converting Southern Christians to respectability; others were Northern reporters dabbling in exotica; still others were anthropologists collecting material in the field, including black reporters sent out by William Armstrong of Hampton Institute to collect folkloric data before it passed away with the older slave generation.

There were obvious differences in white and black traditions, and class distinctions within each of those, yet a regional style remained identifiable and peculiarly interesting for participants and outsiders. The evangelical enthusiasm pervading regional religious culture provided ample opportunity for ridiculing primitive whites so backward as to practice customs tinged with folk Negritude. Solomon Conser, a Methodist cleric in Reconstruction-era Virginia, described the "extravagant devotions" common among the freedpeople, how they fell into "trances and cataleptic fits and professed to see visions of angels and demons." Such "spasmodic excesses," he pointedly added, punctuated worship services among both white and black believers. This religious "fanaticism," he commented acidly, was "encouraged by a class of zealots and divines of limited physical learning." Myrta Avary, an unsympathetic chronicler of Southern life after Reconstruction, sniffed that Southerners could not believe a conversion was genuine unless it was "ushered in by a good, strong unmistakable fit of hysterics." Observed another reporter at a camp meeting in Augusta,

Georgia, in 1885: "Southern people think nothing is done unless there is a gale of excitement, and they do not think they can seek pardon or purity without this." In the 1930s, an ex-slave witnessed "both white and colored people responding to preaching in much the same way as in his early life," with preachers appealing "to the emotions of their flock."[7]

Such observations fit the tradition of viewing Southern religious expression through the lens of entertainment. In the nineteenth century, whites from both South and North flocked to hear John Jasper, an "old-time" black preacher in Virginia known regionally for his funeral orations, preach his famous sermon "De Sun Do Move." Yet at least some of these cultural tourists recognized a spiritual movement in themselves that shook up their initial ironic bemusement. Jasper's white contemporary in the Virginia Baptist ministry, William E. Hatcher, eulogized the orator in *John Jasper: Unmatched Negro Philosopher*, a genuine but hopelessly paternalistic effort to afford the "old-time" preacher his due: "His sermons had the ring of the old gospel preaching so common in the South. He had caught his manner of preaching from the white preachers and they too had been his only theological teachers. . . . Wherever he went, the Anglo-Saxon waived all racial prejudices and drank the truth in as it poured in crystal streams from his lips." Whites who heard his funeral sermons were "stirred to the depths of their souls and their emotion showed in the weeping." If exaggerated, this is not entirely imagined. Even minstrel shows in Northern cities, with their cruel parodies of slaves and free blacks, sometimes moved white audiences to tears in ways much like Jasper, who was also a figure both of parody and empathy.[8]

References both explicit and cryptic suggest the frequency, and hint at the meaning, of biracially attended religious events. Elizabeth Johnson Harris— mother of nine and devout Colored Methodist Episcopal Church member in Georgia from her girlhood in the 1870s until her death in 1942—provides one example. In her life story, scrawled out in the 1920s, she recounts the aid from both white and colored that built her beloved home church, the Rock of Ages Colored Methodist Episcopal Chapel, in Augusta, after the Civil War. In 1876, when she was nine, she desired immersion, but the Methodist pastor convinced her to "be baptized in the usual way of the Methodist faith. I was young, but proud to be a member of the Church by true conversion and always proud to fill my seat in Church at every opportunity." Her faithfulness earned her the appellation "little pastor." She recalled the time when the Chicago-based mass revivalist Dwight Moody preached in town. Moody generally acceded to local custom in audiences, preaching to all-white crowds as well as mixed ones, depending on the preference of the organizers. In this case, white and black Augustans gathered together to hear the Christian crusader. He was, according to Johnson, "perfectly free and friendly as a man of God, with both white and colored. He extended a free invitation to one and all, to these services. The audience was sometimes mixed, the crowds were great, and the Holy Spirit seemed to be in such control over the house that the color of skin was almost forgotten for the time being."[9]

Harris devoted her life to extending God's kingdom on her postage stamp of soil in Georgia. Accordingly, she seized on any indication of evangelical cooperation, and said little about the racial conflicts that she lived through. Yet her account suggests that biracial religious gatherings provided, on occasion, communal spaces for worship, spectating, and entertainment.

A twentieth-century example comes from Eli Evans's account of growing up Jewish in Durham, North Carolina. Evans felt himself an outsider—white but not really white—and identified closely with black worship. His friends, however, "didn't seem to see any distinction; black and white Christianity was all mixed up in their minds." His friends saw the emotion in the black church as "primitive." It reaffirmed their presumption of the "supremacy of the white culture." Evans saw it differently. As a teenage boy, he "did what most other white boys did on the weekends," going to rural black churches "just to see the holy rollers shake and chant. . . . We bathed in the 'Oh tell it . . . tell it' magic of hypnotic stimulation between preacher and congregation, each driving the other on to mounting excess of singsong sermonizing and jump-up conversions and twitching moments of 'cain't-stand-it-no-more' spiritual release and liberation. For us white boys clustered way in the back where we had to stand to see anything, it was more like going to a performance than to a religious service. It was a special experience for me to immerse myself in a kind of Christianity without fear." For once, he could rest assured that none of his chums "would get swept away and go down front to be saved, and leave me as the only unwashed outsider at the service." After the service he could join in imitating "the Negro preacher, moaning and crying out the 'praise de Lawd' accents of the panting sermons." If white fundamentalist churches, in Evans's young eyes, "churned up resurrection and retribution," black churches "conveyed a sense of gentleness and consolation."[10] Evans respected the African American liturgy more than his white counterparts did, but even his rowdy friends came back for more. In the very act of mockery, they recognized the passionate theater of Southern religious performance styles.

Racial and cultural interchange figured importantly in early Holiness/Pentecostalism. A faith not born in the South but attracting white and black Southern folk disaffected by the embourgeoisement of dominant urban religious institutions, early Pentecostalism functioned much like the early national camp meetings. In both cases, mobile common folk created a democratic religious impulse that impelled close bonds with fellows, a strict moral code forbidding worldly pleasure, and hypnotic worship practices that induced receptivity of bodies to the Spirit. Significantly, both whites and blacks drank in the Spirit together, and blacks delivered a message that, for a time, whites eagerly embraced. Once these initial enthusiasms settled into institutional routines, white and black believers moved into separate and (usually) distinct religious organizations.

Notions of Spirit possession had long been attractive to plain-folk Southern believers, from the eighteenth-century Baptists and the early-nineteenth-century Methodists. Indeed, if Pentecostal fatalism about the irredeemable fallenness of this world came from traditions of white Southern belief, Pentecostal faith in personal transformation through the power of the Spirit closely parallels common African American belief arising from slave religion as well as from the remnants of African practices.

Pentecostalism originally was an offshoot of the Holiness Movement, a Northern evangelical revival and reform tradition that emphasized the total sanctification of the believer and the accompanying "enduement" for Christian service. Holiness made little headway in the South until the 1880s, when Southerners disenchanted with the increasing "worldliness" of respectable Southern denominations turned to Holiness sects. This was especially true of Southern Methodists, who easily could trace Holiness ideas back to Methodism's founders. Methodism itself was a kind of eighteenth-century holiness movement, a gathering of seekers after purity in the Church of England that eventually spawned a separate denomination. By the 1890s, Holiness sects (many of which would later turn to Pentecostalism) sprouted like mushrooms throughout the South. Generally more radically sectarian than their Northern counterparts, Southern Holiness preachers emphasized a "second work of grace" that produced an instantaneous sanctification of the believer's soul. Southern Holiness churches demanded total abstinence from alcohol,

tobacco, worldly entertainments, and fashionable frills, all considered allure-
ments of Satan.

In looking at racial interchange in Southern religious culture, one of
the most interesting early Holiness groups was the Fire–Baptized Holiness
Church. Originating out of the work of a Baptist minister named Benjamin
H. Irwin in Iowa and later carried on by Southerners, adherents held that
God's spirit would baptize the believer with fire, purifying the body and soul
of sin, with emotional rapture following. Those in this proto-Pentecostal
church did not yet preach that speaking in tongues would appear as evidence
of this fire baptism, but it was a short step from fire–baptized holiness beliefs
to this basic tenet of Pentecostalism. "It seems clear to us that history is repeat-
ing itself and that in these last days we are being permitted to witness the same
marvelous and miraculous displays of divine power which the early disciples
witnessed in those first days," wrote an early believer.[11]

The apocalyptic imagery of "fire-baptism" induced the fervent emotional-
ism that later characterized Pentecostal meetings. "When we use the word 'Fire'
in our name we use it as a symbol of the uncompromising God," explained the
original manifesto of the Fire-Baptized Holiness Church. At one gathering in
Beniah, Tennessee, in 1899, a church evangelist recorded, "The Lord put the
holy dance upon a number of the saints. . . . Such jumping, and screaming,
and shouting, and dancing before the Lord, we have seldom seen." From there
this holiness minister traveled to Abbeville, South Carolina, at the invitation
of W. E. Fuller, ruling elder of the Colored Fire Baptized Holiness Association.
Whites in the region scorned Holiness—in part for its theology, and in part
precisely because of the class of people its attracted—lower-class whites, factory workers, ordinary black farmers and laborers. "In this country," the evangelist wrote, "the proud, supercilious, ungodly whites look upon us with scorn
and contempt because we hold meetings for the colored people, and preach
the gospel to their former slaves." White mill workers also flocked to the services. "These poor and needy people are hungry for the pure gospel," he commented, as the "big, proud, worldly church, and the unsaved preachers . . .
have no real interest in them, and do not want them in their 'heathen tem-
ples.'" Others just looked on the Holiness bands as alien: "The people look
upon us and say the Mormons are coming; others regard us as traps, and others are in amazement as to what we are." For black seekers, he held services in
a ramshackle building on the outskirts of town, but the impoverished setting
could not offset the rich spirit: "Such singing, such shouting, such dancing,

such praying, it has never before been our privilege to hear." He found the colored people to "dance before the Lord differently than our white people," a feature of the meeting "peculiarly fascinating" to the Brother leading the service, who was the only white man there. The minister then traveled to Kingstree, South Carolina, where he joined Isaac Gamble, a black Holiness evangelist. The two held meetings there conjointly and constructed a tent for biracial worship, with the salvation altar divided into a white and a black section. The services, by their account, came off harmoniously, with a "profound interest manifested among the people, both white and colored, and a real Holy Ghost awakening." The black evangelist Gamble later led some camp meetings in which blacks and "some of the leading white people of the community came out, and showed much interest."[12]

Frequent reports in the Holiness/Pentecostal press, books, and diaries illuminate this hidden world of biracial services that coexisted with the dominant and completely racially separated world of religion in the region. A. B. Crumpler, a powerful preacher and contentious newspaper editor, pioneered Holiness in Dunn, North Carolina. One convert remembered camp meetings he led in 1896: "Some said the preacher had powder and scattered [it] on the folks and that they fell like dead men and lay for hours. They fell, it was true, but it was by the mighty power of God. . . . Brother Crumpler brought several workers with him, men and women filled with the Holy Ghost. . . . They soon had the town and surrounding country in a stir. Brother Crumpler could be heard preaching on a still night fully two miles, and the Lord was on him so the people could not stand it." Reporting from a Colored Holiness Convention in North Carolina, a reporter noted the effect Crumpler's ministry had on the black saints, who were not "bound down by conventionalities" but full of "blessed liberty." If this represented a fair sample of black holiness, he concluded, then whites would have to "spur up or they'll find themselves behind in this blessed race. May God pour out his Spirit on both the white and colored people in our state." In 1903, the "colored saints" in Dunn invited white Holiness minister Gaston B. Cashwell to preach to them on a Sunday evening. "The house was packed with both white and colored," he recorded, "and the Spirit of the Lord was there, the people rejoiced and God blessed them. They seemed to be filled with the Spirit, and the white people of the community say they live it."[13]

Some of the early holiness groups were initially biracial before later separating into white and black church organizations. William E. Fuller, a native

South Carolinian and pioneer black Holiness preacher in the Southeast, attended the organizing session of the Fire-Baptized Holiness Association of America in 1898 in Anderson, South Carolina. A few years later it organized more officially into the Fire Baptized Holiness Church of God. "We were connected with the white people for ten years" (1898–1908), Fuller later recounted, at which time, "owing to the growing prejudice that began to arise among the unsaved people, it was mutually agreed that we have separate incorporations." In 1908 Fuller formed a separate black organization, the Fire Baptized Holiness Church of God of the Americas (also based in South Carolina) to carry on the work. He served as this church's overseer until his death in 1958, his early biracial preaching services forgotten even in Pentecostal church annals.[14]

Early white and black Southern Holiness/Pentecostal converts experienced the "second baptism" in similar ways. After the Azusa Street revivals in Los Angeles in 1906 (a key originating Pentecostal moment), many believers accepted tongues speech as the initial evidence of the "baptism of the spirit." Theologically, that is, they became Pentecostals. Charles Fox Parham was a key theological innovator. Leading a Bible school in Kansas at the turn of the century, Parham preached that tongues speech would appear as evidence of the baptism of the Holy Spirit. Parham taught his doctrines to a group of seekers in Houston in 1905–6, including a black Louisianan named William J. Seymour, the man who would lead early Pentecostals in Los Angeles, and Lucy Farrow, niece of Frederick Douglass and another key black Pentecostal figure. By the 1910s, Parham himself was haranguing audiences with a loony pseudoscientific racism, but in the first decade of the century, whites and blacks alike took in his theological ruminations. The second baptism of sanctification— the ultimate soul cleansing from sin explained by Holiness theologians—was necessary but not sufficient, he preached. Only the Holy Spirit baptism, sometimes called the third blessing, could complete the initiate's spiritual quest. Tongues speech (glossolalia) was its true signifier, for it evidenced that God's power had suffused the human vessel.[15]

Howard Goss, a native of rural southern Missouri, was one early convert to the new doctrine. His autobiography provides a glimpse at what Pentecostals called the "baptism of the spirit." After a youth spent working in mines, he sold his worldly possessions and followed Charles Parham to Houston, where several early converts gathered to experience the latter-day Pentecost. As Howard Goss progressively accepted Pentecostal doctrines, he witnessed fellow mourners lining up, being touched, and speaking in tongues, all under the guidance of Lucy Farrow. His "heart became hungry again for another manifestation of God. . . . So I went forward that she [Farrow] might place her hands upon me. When she did, the Spirit of God again struck me like a bolt of lightning; the Power of God surged through my body, and I again began speaking in tongues. From that day to this I have always been able to speak in tongues at any time I yielded to the Spirit of God." He remembered the transformation of Addison Mercer, formerly a black Baptist deacon in Texas: "Such spectacular conversions as his . . . were all deeply sincere; they covered up nothing, and held back nothing. This brought everyone under conviction and packed the building." Unlike more established evangelicals, Goss endorsed fervent bodily exhibitions: "I have never seen dancing that was of God that did not touch someone in the audience." Public religious dance in white Holiness and Pentecostal churches, he acknowledged, was "drawn from the colored work, there their freedom from inhibition, one of their most attractive traits made its appeal." Such joyous expressions were, he assured his perhaps discomfited readers, "entirely controlled by the pastor, and stopped or started at his signal. As does any other pastor, he knew his congregation, no doubt, and allowed only what was beneficial."[16]

These early believers—Southerners, Northerners, and Westerners—subsequently organized new religious groups that embraced Pentecostal worship practices along with strict behavioral codes. The Reverend Charles Harrison Mason, a former black Baptist minister in Mississippi converted to Pentecostalism during the Azusa Street revivals, founded the Memphis-based Church of God in Christ (COGIC) as a Holiness band in the 1890s. In his early days, Mason was a tireless itinerant evangelist. In Conway, Arkansas, in 1904, Mason's preaching overpowered a white man named James Delk, one of a substantial crowd standing around a cotton wagon listening spellbound to Mason's sermons and songs. "That day Brother Mason made an impression on me that I have never forgotten and can never forget," Delk later wrote. "Brother Mason attended college very little but has a wide experience with human nature and an understanding of his fellow man such as no other man seems to have. . . . I doubt if there ever has been a minister who has lived since the day of the apostles who has shown the sweet spirit to all people, regardless of race, creed, or color, or has preached with greater power than Brother Mason." Delk founded a COGIC church in Madisonville, Kentucky, suffering harassment there for his work.[17]

In 1906 Mason made his Pentecostal pilgrimage to Los Angeles. There he heard the new doctrines of Pentecostalism from ex-slave and early tongues-speech apostle William Seymour, who himself had been tutored (seated on the other side of a curtain from the white students) by that eccentric future racist demagogue Charles Fox Parham. Seymour's preaching, and the tumultuous services that resulted, had been publicized in the *Los Angeles Times* as well as in Holiness and Pentecostal publications. Word spread quickly, and seekers from around the country (and world) converged on the humble location. Mason joined a number of other Southerners, including the white North Carolinian Gaston B. Cashwell, who would, in the next few years, prove to be instrumental in the formation of the Pentecostal Holiness Church.

At the Azusa Street revival, along with Lucy Farrow and other white and black Southerners, the Mississippian Charles Harrison Mason received "all three operations of divine grace: regeneration, sanctification, and spiritual baptism." He then traveled back home to Memphis. From his pulpit he dispensed supernatural cures and the Pentecostal gospel to crowds primarily of black, but also of some white, seekers. He quickly developed a reputation for spiritual gifts of interpreting "sounds, groans, and any kind of spiritual utterance." He held close ties to a number of early white Pentecostals, and indeed, for a time he led the only officially incorporated church in which Pentecostal ministers could be credentialed (important for obtaining clergy rates for rail passes). Mason spoke to the founding Assemblies of God convention in 1914, blessing this new (white) alliance of Pentecostal groups. In his sermon he employed roots and strangely shaped plants as folk homiletic devices, a practice he followed throughout his career.[18] During these years Mason traveled with a white minister named W. B. Holt, and the two were jailed at times for breaking Jim Crow customs. In Nashville, Tennessee, in 1916, Mason preached to a sizable crowd at a city auditorium. "Many of the best white people of the city attended the meeting. The Holy Spirit through me did many wonderful things," he later recounted. A series of services in Little Rock, Arkansas, in 1919 had the same effect, as "God so wonderfully wrought His power among both white and black, sanctifying, baptizing, and healing." In 1933 the paper of the church, *The Whole Truth,* reported that "both white and colored testified of the wonderful healing power of God" at the COGIC annual convention in Rocky Mount, North Carolina.[19] Until his death in 1961, Mason reigned over the Church of God in Christ, the most significant black Pentecostal movement in twentieth-century America.

The relationship between whites and blacks in early Pentecostalism in some cases incited violence. At an annual state encampment in Hearne, Texas, blacks built a brush arbor as an add-on to accommodate the white people who wanted to attend a camp meeting. People flocked to the meeting, having never heard the full gospel of Pentecostalism before. Because they could not bring themselves to "seek Baptism at a colored altar," whites requested a white Pentecostal teacher to come and "help them into the Baptism." A young minister came, preaching to crowds of whites and blacks in separate services. At his next appointment, he met men with pistols who threatened to shoot him for putting them "on a level with the d—— niggers." While waiting to take the train out of town, another crowd of men beat him with clubs, fracturing his wrist. The young minister proudly reported his Pentecostal martyrdom. Founders of the Assemblies of God also were involved in early biracial Pentecostalism. Traveling around Little Rock, Arkansas, in 1912, M. M. Pinson expressed disappointment with his work with whites but found "quite a work among the colored folks."[20]

In contrast, the Church of the Assemblies of Jesus Christ in Charlotte, North Carolina, under Bishop R. L. Hancock, counted a substantial black membership alongside the white majority. "Each person desirous of becoming a member must vow to be completely void of all prejudice and express a willingness to associate and fraternize with all races," a reporter noted of the church. Here too the racial interchange of Southern Pentecostalism aroused ire among local whites, who attempted to obtain a court injunction to prohibit the worship and later resorted to threatening letters and other acts of intimidation. "A casual visitor may tend to scoff at and find amusement in some of the antics of the worshippers," a black paper noted. "Especially their fervor and complete abandon during service. Yet it isn't necessary to be a student of the Bible to know that Jesus and his handful of followers were at variance with the mores of their day."[21]

Like the "Negro Girl Preacher" seen by E. B. Ingram in the 1890s and the traveling ministry of W. E. Fuller from 1898 to 1907, black Pentecostal evangelists proved to be popular in the 1910s and 20s. Numerous white and black Pentecostal evangelists, songsters, faith healers, and itinerant preachers combed the Southern countryside, attracting racially diverse crowds, sometimes arousing the ire of authorities, and generally existing in a world set apart from the dominant institutions of Southern religion. E. N. Scippio was a class leader of an African Methodist Episcopal Church. After claiming sanctification and divine healing of his cataracts in 1914, he preached for two decades for both white and black listeners in the Southeast. At one meeting in Georgia, he recounted, "white and colored were at the altar. Seeking for Salvation. The meeting was so powerful that men seemingly could not stay on their jobs." Later, in Jacksonville Heights, Florida, he discovered that "the white people throughout that place had great faith in the gospel that was preached to them, until they would send handkerchiefs to the meeting, and God would manifest his power through the prayer of faith." He continued through the 1920s and 1930s, again with what he described as "large gatherings, white and colored," greeting him. In one service in South Carolina, "God began to work, and the power began to fall; one night it fell so, until it fell on a white girl outside the tent, and she began to shake, so they carried her away."[22]

Sister Mary Magdalena Tate, another of the itinerant black Pentecostal apostles, founded The Church of the Living God, the Pillar and Ground of Truth, Inc. Tate felt moved to preach the gospel in 1903. Along with her two sons, she began her work in Steele Springs, Tennessee. From there she preached in Paducah, Kentucky, where "her call to the ministry and commission to go and preach the Gospel was more forcibly shown and made plain to her." Soon she accepted invitations to many churches to "teach and preach what was hailed as a 'new gospel,' for many people had not heard of true holiness and the baptism of the fire and Holy Ghost which she advocated." She was invited "to the homes of both white and colored and invited to preach in a Temple of a Presbyterian Church, colored. Never will it be forgotten how the power of God lifted physically strong men as well as women from off their seats while she preached and taught the people that night in that Temple of the Presbyterian Church in Paris, Tennessee. Grown men shouted, leaped, and wept for joy."[23]

The experience of one early Pentecostal minister shows the degree of (mostly) unacknowledged cultural interchange between white and black Pentecostals. Poorly clothed as a boy, ashamed to attend a regular Baptist or Methodist church, he accompanied his family to Pentecostal tent revivals led by the Church of God, a young Pentecostal organization based in Cleveland, Tennessee. His family represented precisely the kind of ordinary whites that responded to the Holiness/Pentecostal message and worship practices. "The services they held," he remembered, "were something like ours had been up home, but somehow there seemed to be *more power* in their meetin's than we'd ever had. Of course we had seen shoutin' before, but not the kind that they were doin' there." He remembered how "my built-up emotions and feelin's came surgin' out as I sobbed and cried for the blood of Jesus and its cleansing power." Praying for sanctification, he submitted to the Spirit's "every impulse and let Him have His way. What I did I don't remember, but they say I was joyous in the spirit." He later studied elaborate premillennialist schemes and wanted to impart his knowledge to his congregants, but he knew his people would not stand for it; what they wanted was "somethin' to shout about." Millworker Ila Dodson grew up in a Baptist church but moved her allegiance to the Pentecostal Holiness Church. Men from a Bible college came to preach Holiness, she recalled, "and we just liked it." At first she feared the services: "Them women would shout, you know, and their hair'd fall down, and I didn't know what was taking place." Tennessean Leander Huskey recalled the Holiness minister who converted him: "You don't know how happy I was after God had touched me with his Great Spirit. I could feel him working in me and the Spirit caused me to talk in tongues. . . . I ain't never backslid yet."[24] In their experiences, the shared traditions of evangelical emotional expression, spirit possession, and holy dancing are unmistakably present.

Energetic white Pentecostals created small empires of competing churches, publishing houses, academies, and denominational structures. As rural Southerners made their treks from countryside to town in the early twentieth century, and as many of them found their way to Northern cities later in the century, they carried their Holiness/Pentecostal churches with them, marking them for the derision of their metropolitan neighbors. Later in the twentieth century, however, Pentecostalism became one of the fastest growing religious groupings in America, confounding a generation of interpreters who condemned it as the opiate of primitive people unable to adapt to modern life. These primitives instead provided much of the soundtrack for modern life. Like the black Pentecostals in COGIC, white Pentecostal churches served as training grounds for a remarkable number of figures (such as Elvis Presley, Johnny Cash, and Oral Roberts) who left their mark on American popular culture.

The vivid encounters evident in Pentecostal experience strongly influenced Southern evangelical music. From the early intermingling of Protestant hymns and African musical styles into spirituals, to the mixing of white and black country and gospel sounds on radio dials, two streams of musical religious culture flowed beside each other, never merging but often intersecting.

Twentieth-century Southern gospel music illustrates these shared traditions. The gospel music business, according to music historian Bill Malone, evolved from shape-note singing schools and evangelical revivals, but it "drew much of its dynamism and much of its personnel from the Holiness-Pentecostal movement of the late nineteenth century and early twentieth century. By 1900 a great stream of religious songs, fed by the big-city revivals of the era, flowed into American popular culture." Publishing houses both within and outside denominations cranked out paperback hymnals for church meetings and singing schools. White gospel singing groups learned from hearing the shape-note hymnals and instruction in singing schools and from barbershop and black gospel quartets who toured the region and received wide regional radio airplay. And beyond the church walls, white and black secular and religious performers traded licks, vocal styles, and lyrics. Bluegrass pioneer Bill Monroe incorporated black quartet singing into his own gospel renditions, while the white gospel hymn tradition handed down from the nineteenth century was revivified by black gospel music innovators such as Thomas Dorsey (a native Georgian) and Lucy Campbell.[25]

Holiness/Pentecostalism provided fertile ground for musical interchange among white and black Southerners, just as the great camp meetings of the early nineteenth century provided a similar forum for cultural interchange. Guitars, tambourines, and other rhythmical instruments, once seen as musical accompaniments for the devil, found their way into black Pentecostal churches in the early twentieth century. C. H. Mason's Church of God in Christ congregations immediately adopted them. White Pentecostalists soon picked them up, and the two shared hymns and holy dancing back and forth. Not bound by respectable conventions, white Pentecostals borrowed freely from all traditions. Howard Goss remembered the singing in early Pentecostal services as "entirely unpretentious. . . . The very artlessness of these songs . . . created no barriers of antagonism." He recounted how styles borrowed from black Pentecostal brethren (Goss was rather unusual in his free acknowledgment of this borrowing) insinuated themselves into white musical performance. The songs came in at "break-neck speed, we didn't notice the accelerated tempo. Anyway, everyone was jubilantly dancing inside, whether it showed outwardly or not. . . . We were the first, so far as I know, to introduce this accelerated tempo into Gospel singing. . . . 'Jazzed-up hymns' they were sometimes designated by the critical, because this joy of the Lord was so built up on our young people that when they got a chance to sing, they exploded. Every particle of their being was poured into worship as they sang, nothing slowed them down."[26]

The derisive term "holy roller music" referred to gospel hymns, refrains, and chants belted out in an enthusiastic and syncopated style. White and black Pentecostal musical styles remained distinct, but they intersected at many points. Both employed rhythmical accompaniments, enthusiastic hollers, and holy dancing. Pentecostals were among the first white worshippers to incorporate black styles, but hardly the last.

Holiness and Pentecostal preachers and singers were among the most culturally innovative and entrepreneurial of twentieth-century plain-folk Southerners. As Bill Malone explains, "Whether black or white, Pentecostal evangelists . . . armed with guitar and Bible, accompanied perhaps by a mandolin-strumming or tambourine-shaking wife, and preaching on street corners, under brush arbors, in tents, or in storefront churches, took their places alongside the shape-note teachers and gospel quartets as major agents in the fashioning of the southern gospel music repertory."[27]

Brother and Sister George Goings, black Pentecostal singing evangelists, took their Holiness message through Tennessee and Kentucky in the last years of the nineteenth century. They introduced audiences to songs such as "There's a Little Black Train a Coming," a tune that found its way to black churches and rapidly became a gospel music war-horse. It became a staple of a black minister in Atlanta named J. M. Gates, who made over three hundred recordings of his preaching and singing from 1926 to 1941. White and black gospel songs by the hundreds employed the seemingly infinitely malleable metaphor of the train, a vehicle taking sinners to hell, saints to heaven, pilgrims to rest, and prodigal sons home.

As white Pentecostals organized into groupings such as the Pentecostal Holiness Church (centered in the Southeast), The Church of God (Cleveland, Tennessee), and the more conservative and carefully institutionalized Assemblies of God (centered in the midsection of the country, now headquartered in Springfield, Missouri), they seized on the opportunities provided by mass media to spread their message. So did black Pentecostals. Gospel music publishing companies, led by the Tennessee-based Vaughan empire and its numerous offshoots, spread musical literacy and profited from marketing their own tunes by sending out gospel quartet groups that sang the new songs in appealingly innovative styles. In this way, plain-folk Southerners learned new songs (typified by the 1930s hit "I'll Fly Away") that addressed their millennial hopes and daily struggles during the Depression. Among whites, pioneer publishers in gospel music such as the Vaughan family in Tennessee and their rivals, the

Stamps-Baxter company, introduced a whole new catalogue of Southern religious songs that could be adapted by white gospel groups, by bluegrass musicians such as Bill Monroe, or by black gospel soloists, quartets, and choirs. Black publishers and composers were just as aggressive. Many of the black gospel pioneers came out of the Baptist and Methodist churches, but it was clearly the influence of Holiness/Pentecostal performance styles that broke the stranglehold of "respectable" music that had defined urban bourgeois black services. Black gospel during these years developed its own tradition, its favorite touring quartets and choirs, its first star soloists (such as Mahalia Jackson), and its own fierce internal competitions among publishing outfits, composers, and traveling singing groups. In gospel, then, the steams of Southern religious music, white and black, flowed alongside one another, sometimes exchanging tunes and lyrics and styles, while remaining identifiably distinct. Radio became their most effective medium, for it reached out-of-the-way places where many parishioners lived.

Later in the twentieth century, those raised as cultural products of this racial interchange in religious expression entered the public world of broadcasting and performing. Radio orators, barnstorming evangelists, gospel singers, bluegrass pioneers, and pop stars—nearly all with roots in the low-church Southern religious traditions—permanently changed American popular culture. Their familiarity, whether as insiders or even as outside spectators, with Southern religious traditions profoundly affected American culture. Any number of country and soul singers and black gospel stars, from Hank Williams and Bill Monroe to Ray Charles and Sam Cooke, come to mind. Hank Williams's "Honky-Tonk Angels" bore a marked resemblance to the white gospel classic "Great Speckled Bird" made famous by Roy Acuff; Bill Monroe's innovative jamming on mandolin often backed gospel crooning that was obviously influenced by black quartet singing; Ray Charles's "Baby What I Say" was little more than a gospel vamp backing Charles's eroticized refrain; and Sam Cooke set a model for later singers such as Al Green in his move from gospel to soul and back again. Perhaps more than anyone else, however, Elvis Presley illustrates this point.

The young Elvis borrowed freely from sacred performers in creating his own musical persona. Elvis committed to memory an entire catalogue of church music from both the white and black traditions, and he could produce on command church songs of all sorts. Along with his friends in Memphis, Presley enthusiastically sampled African American religious culture both in person and on the radio. Unlike the rowdies (both white and black) who made sport of Southern religious solemnities, Presley was affected by his encounter, particularly with African American Pentecostalism, recognizing its kinship to his own Assemblies of God tradition. He listened to black religious orator Herbert Brewster on the radio and visited local meetings of the Church of God in Christ.

Presley's cultural pastiche emerged from a larger cultural transmission from black to white and back again, seen most clearly in the early history of Holiness/Pentecostalism and its relationship to the evolution of Southern religious music. In both cases, whites and blacks borrowed theologies, performance styles, and cultural practices freely (if often unwittingly) from one another. Presley, for example, absorbed the sounds, the rhythms, and the stage manner (including the leg shake) that shaped his own electric performances. By Presley's time, white and black teenagers were eager to break down the rope lines that segregated them at rhythm and blues events, and white teenagers found black styles alluringly imitable. White secular and religious performers learned from—some might suggest they stole—the doo-wop singing (with its own roots in black gospel quartets), religious "holy-roller" dancing, and the melismatic singing that coursed through African American church music. In the process they created sacred entertainments that shaped American popular culture. Sacred passion, expressed most obviously in white and black Southern Pentecostalism, was at the heart of rhythm and blues, as well as of rock-and-roll.[28]

Racial interchange in Southern religious culture could not override racism, and it rarely even mitigated it. Biracial attendance at religious events was not a necessary or sufficient step to interracialism. Racial separation in Southern religion was the norm, obvious to anyone who attended church on Sunday. Yet even outside observers sensed that white and black Southerners carried on religious cultures that bound them together, somehow, even as it marked their separateness. Sunday morning at 11:00 A.M. may have been the most segregated hour in America, but the religious expressions of Southern common folk emerged from an entangled racial and cultural history.

The parched topsoil of Southern religious racism is evident. But the biracialism and interracialism existing in submerged strata of Southern culture also demand attention. Lillian Smith expressed it best in a letter to Martin Luther King in 1956: "I, myself, being a Deep South white, reared in a religious home and the Methodist church realize the deep ties of common songs, common prayer, common symbols that bind our two races together on a religio-mystical level, even as another brutally mythic idea, the concept of White Supremacy, tears our two people apart."[29]

NOTES

1. E. B. Ingram, diary entries for 10 July 1895 and 17 July 1895, in E. B. Ingram Papers, Special Collections, Perkins Library, Duke University (hereafter cited SCL); Glenda Gilmore, *Gender and Jim Crow: Women and the Politics of White Supremacy in North Carolina, 1896–1920* (Chapel Hill: University of North Carolina Press, 1996), 73.

2. Winfield Henry Mixon Papers, diary entries for 1 August 1903 and 1 May 1903, SCL.

3. M. B. Woodworth-Etter, *Signs and Wonders: God Wrought in the Ministry for Forty-Five Years* (self-published, 1916), 98–101.

4. See Leon Litwack, *Trouble in Mind: Black Southerners in the Age of Jim Crow* (New York: Knopf, 1998), for an absorbing account of the violence meted out to black Southerners during that era, and the limited means blacks had to respond.

5. Charles Joyner, *Shared Traditions: Southern History and Folk Culture* (Urbana: University of Illinois Press, 1999), 25. For the slave era, Mechal Sobel makes a similar argument in *The World They Made Together: Black and White Values in Eighteenth-Century Virginia* (Princeton, N.J.: Princeton University Press, 1987).

6. In recent work, scholars such as John Boles and Sterling Stuckey have revived the debate, Boles stressing the biracial tradition of Southern evangelicalism in the antebellum era and Stuckey grounding black American cultural expression in the African-based ring shout. Mechal Sobel's work *Trabelin On,* if problematic in assuming a monolithic "African cosmos," provides a richly detailed portrait of the large number of black institutional churches before the Civil War, as well as a penetrating analysis inside the visionary travels of black conversion experience narratives, juxtaposing the biracial and African sources of black American religion. More recently, William Montgomery has analyzed the mutual interaction of and tension between the folk church and the institutional church in the late nineteenth century, between African-based religious expressions and Protestant notions of respectability.

For a small sampling of contemporary scholarship on this debate, see John Boles, *Masters and Slaves in the House of the Lord: Race and Religion in the American South, 1740–1870* (Lexington: University Press of Kentucky, 1988); Sterling Stuckey, *Slave Culture: Nationalist Theory and the Foundations of Black America* (New York: Oxford, 1987); Mechal Sobel, *Trabelin' On: The Slave Journey to an Afro-Baptist Faith* (Westport, Conn.: Greenwood Press, 1979); and William Montgomery, *Under Their Own Vine and Fig Tree: The African-American Church in the South, 1865–1900* (Baton Rouge: Louisiana State University Press, 1991).

7. Solomon L. M. Conser, *Virginia after the War: An Account of Three Years' Experience in Reorganizing the Methodist Episcopal Church in Virginia at the Close of the Civil War* (Indianapolis: Batter-Randolf, 1891), 39–40; Myrta L. Avary, *Dixie after the War: An Exposition of the Social Conditions Existing in the South, during the Twelve Years Succeeding the Fall of Richmond* (reprint, New York: Arno Press, 1969), 203–5; Augusta camp meeting quoted in Brian Keith Turley, "A Wheel within a Wheel: Southern Methodism and the Georgia Holiness Association" (Ph.D. diss., University of Virginia, 1994), 283; *The American Slave: A Composite Autobiography*, vol. 17, *Florida Narratives*, ed. George Rawick (Westport, Conn.: Greenwood Press, 1972), 353 (interview with Willis Williams).

8. William Hatcher, *John Jasper: The Unmatched Negro Philosopher and Preacher* (New York: Fleming and Revell, 1908), 98, 36.

9. Elizabeth Johnson Harris, "Life Story, 1867–1923," in Elizabeth Johnson Harris papers, SCL.

10. Eli N. Evans, *The Provincials: A Personal History of Jews in the South*, rev. ed. (New York: Simon and Schuster, 1997), 260–62.

11. *Live Coals of Fire*, 9 February 1900. Extant copies of this periodical were consulted at the Archives of the International Pentecostal Holiness Church, Oklahoma City, Okla. (hereafter PHC).

12. *Live Coals of Fire*, 27 October 1899, 3 November 1899, 26 January 1900.

13. Florence Goff, *Fifty Years on the Battlefield for God: Being a Sketch of the Life of Rev. J. A. Hodges, Coupled with Some of the Lord's Dealings with H. H. Goff and Wife, Evangelists of the Cape Fear Conference of the Free Will Baptist Church* (Falcon, N.C., n.d.,), 19, PHC; *Holiness Advocate*, 16 September 1901, 1 October 1903.

14. *Tenets of the Fire Baptized Holiness Church of God of the Americas* (Atlanta: Fuller Press, n.d.,), pamphlet in PHC; *Discipline of the Fire Baptized Holiness Church of God of the Americas* (1962) (Atlanta: Church Publishing House by the Fuller Press), in box 7, folder 1, of the Dupree Collection, Schomburg Center for the Study of Black Culture, New York Public Library (hereafter cited as DC). The Dupree Collection, a twenty-five-box archival collection, constitutes a remarkably rich resource for the history of black Pentecostalism.

15. For more on the history of Holiness/Pentecostalism in the South, see Vinson Synan, *The Holiness-Pentecostal Tradition: Charismatic Movements in the Twentieth Century*, 2d ed. (Grand Rapids, Mich.: Eerdmans, 1997).

16. Howard A. Goss (as told to Ethel E. Goss), *The Winds of God: The Story of Early Pentecostal Days (1901–1914) in the Life of Howard A. Goss* (New York: Comet Press Books, 1958), 34, 42, 56, 113, 129.

17. Ithiel C. Clemmons, *Bishop C. H. Mason and the Roots of the Church of God in Christ* (Bakersfield, Calif.: Pneuma Publishing, 1996), 5–20.

18. E. W. Mason, *The Man. . . . Charles Harrison Mason* (self-published by Elsie W. Mason, 1979), 19; David M. Tucker, *Black Pastors and Leaders: Memphis, 1819–1972* (Memphis: Memphis State University Press, 1975), 87–100.

19. Paul Conkin, "Evangelicals, Fugitives, and Hillbillies: Tennessee's Impact on American National Culture," in *Tennessee History: The Land, the People, and the Culture,* ed. Carroll Van West (Knoxville: University of Tennessee Press, 1998), 287–322; Elsie Mason, ed., *From the Beginning of Bishop C. H. Mason and the Early Pioneers of the Church of God in Christ* (Memphis, Tenn.: Church of God in Christ Publishing House, 1991), 6; *The Whole Truth,* 6 January 1933, Assemblies of God Archives, Springfield, Missouri.

20. F. F. Bosworth to Mother, 22 August 1911, reprinted as "Beating in Tex. Follows Ministry to Blacks," *Assemblies of God Heritage* 6 (summer 1986): 5, 14; M. M. Pinson, "Trip to the Southwest," *Word and Witness,* 20 August 1912.

21. *Norfolk Journal and Guide,* 28 January 1950, box 10, folder 3, DC.

22. "Partly—Biography of N. Scippio and Wife," (1987), from *A Christian Worker's Handbook,* pp. 9, 15, box 1, folder 16, DC.

23. From *The Constitution, Government, and General Decree Book of the Church of the Living God, the Pillar and Ground of the Truth, Inc.* (Chattanooga, Tenn.: New and Living Way Publishing Company, n.d.); and materials for the 70th Annual General Assembly of The Church of the Living God, The Pillar and Ground of Truth, Inc., both in box 6, folder 8, DC.

24. Federal Workers' Project interviews (FWP), Southern Oral History Program, Manuscripts Department, Southern Historical Collection, University of North Carolina, Chapel Hill (hereafter cited SOHP), box 23, folder 778; Interview with Ila Dodson, 23 May 1980, transcript H-241, SOHP; FWP, folder 957.

25. Bill Malone, *Southern Music, American Music* (Lexington: University Press of Kentucky, 1979), 67–68, 76–78.

26. Goss, *The Winds of God,* 129.

27. Bill Malone, *Singing Cowboys and Musical Mountaineers: Southern Culture and the Roots of Country Music* (Athens: University of Georgia Press, 1993), 32.

28. For a fuller analysis of Elvis's grounding in his religious upbringing, see Peter Guralnick, *Last Train to Memphis: The Rise of Elvis Presley* (New York: Little and Brown, 1994). For more on sacred passion in religion and music, as well as the connection of music and struggles for racial justice, see David Chappell, *A Stone of Hope: Religion, Culture, and Civil Rights* (Chapel Hill: University of North Carolina Press, forthcoming).

29. Lillian Smith to Martin Luther King Jr., 10 March 1956, in *How Am I to Be Heard: Letters of Lillian Smith,* ed. Margaret Rose Gladney (Chapel Hill: University of North Carolina Press, 1993), 193.

9

"Doing Contrary to My Raising"
Emma Anderson Dunovant and the
Woman Suffrage Campaign in South Carolina

JAMES O. FARMER JR.

"Her life was one long act of devotion—devotion to God, devotion to her husband, devotion to her children, devotion to her servants, to the poor, to humanity. Nothing happened within the range of her knowledge that her sympathy did not reach and her charity and wisdom did not ameliorate. [As a result,] she reaped the reward . . . [of the] sympathy and tenderness" of her circle, who "worshiped her." Thus did Thomas Nelson Page describe and pay homage to the Southern Lady of a century ago.[1]

Page was echoing a long line of writers, beyond as well as within the South, who had contributed to a "cult of true womanhood." But nowhere did that cult flower more luxuriously than in the South. In her seminal article in 1966, Barbara Welter noted that the cult of true womanhood was the basis for society's decision as to what were the proper areas of female concern. As the market revolution transformed more and more of the American economy in the nineteenth century, men, in Suzanne Lebsock's words, "gave themselves over to the relentless pursuit of wealth, [and] assuaged their anxiety and guilt by assuring themselves that women, as long as they stayed home, would keep the country's religious faith vital and its moral virtue strong." Women thus became more cherished as mistresses of the domestic realm as the world beyond the home shed more of the "feminine virtues." Yet the elasticity of the concept of "woman's sphere" would allow women to expand their reach and take up various reform campaigns, widening the walls of the home to encompass the community and beyond. This elasticity also accounts, Welter concluded, for the longevity of the cult of true womanhood.[2]

Whatever its status in more rapidly modernizing places, the cult of true womanhood was still strong in Edgefield, South Carolina, in the early twentieth century. Here we find women such as Emma Anderson Dunovant, whose family and friends might well have believed Thomas Nelson Page was thinking of her when he wrote the words that begin this chapter. That this model Southern Lady became a determined worker in the cause of woman suffrage makes her life a case study in the widening of woman's sphere, for at a fairly advanced age (53), she grafted onto her rich but circumscribed personal life the additional role of wordsmith of the suffrage movement in South Carolina.

It was not a role she sought. Rather, she yielded to the entreaties of the leader of Palmetto State suffragists, Eulalie Chafee Salley of Aiken—a woman who serves for us as a foil to Emma Dunovant, placing her peculiar contribution to the cause in sharper relief. The contrast between them suggests the breadth of personalities and perspectives brought together by the movement, while their comfortable partnership in the cause shows how far a woman like Emma Dunovant could come from her origins as a traditional Southern Lady.

The woman suffrage movement in South Carolina was modest in its scope, and while fulfilling to its participants, disappointing in its result. The label attached to South Carolina circa 1915 by the National American Woman Suffrage Association (NAWSA)—"hopeless"—fairly evaluated the record of the movement in the Palmetto State and proved prophetic as to the outcome of the campaign for the ratification of the nineteenth amendment there. The reasons for the movement's weakness in South Carolina, as throughout the South, are not hard to find. Its origins were associated with abolitionism and other "radical" causes, as the career of Charleston's Grimké sisters illustrates. The Radical Reconstruction governments included reforms in the area of women's rights as part of their agenda, thereby cursing the cause in the minds of most white Southerners, male and female. Elizabeth Cady Stanton did not help matters when she issued her "Woman's Bible," in 1895, which deleted sections deemed incompatible with the image of the liberated woman, thus branding her—and by extension the movement—as heretical in the evangelical South.[3] Meanwhile, the "Lost Cause" cult had risen, with its cherished image of the Southern Lady as the symbol and repository of all that was good and pure in the civilization that had flourished before "the war" and that must now be protected from the corrupting forces of modernity. And the Southern Populist movement, after briefly promoting biracial politics, focused on limiting the franchise, as state after state enacted measures to effectively exclude black men from the polls. In combination, these elements so stacked the deck against woman suffrage in Dixie that even those few

women who looked past them were likely to be deterred from actively addressing those concerns.[4]

Yet South Carolina, like the rest of the South, did produce a small woman
suffrage crusade beginning in the 1880s, led by Virginia Durant Young of
Allendale. But Young's death in 1906, during the era labeled by suffragists as
"the doldrums," left a void that was not filled until around 1915, when the
South Carolina Equal Suffrage League began its futile effort to add the state
to the list of those endorsing woman suffrage. With a few exceptions, therefore, students of Southern suffragism, finding little to inspire them in South
Carolina, have bypassed the state in their surveys of the movement.[5]

By the same token, however, surely no suffragists were more "great-
souled," as Carrie Chapman Catt called her Southern comrades, than those
who battled against the odds in South Carolina.[6] That they kept any optimism
at all is a testimony to their tenacity and patience. As if the derision of men
and the scorn of most women were not discouraging enough, they also contended with divisions within their own ranks. Surprisingly, the states' rights
wing of the movement was not prominent in South Carolina. Most Palmetto
State suffragists, after futilely pursuing the vote at the hands of their legislature, shifted with apparent ease to the campaign for a federal amendment. A
more serious split was the tactical one between the majority, who favored
moderate, "respectable" methods, and their more radical sisters, who joined
the National Women's Party and demonstrated more aggressively. Scholars
may bemoan the moderation of the vast majority of Southern women reformers, but most South Carolina suffragists agreed with Suzanne Lebsock's observation that "you do not get the Constitution of the United States amended by
calling yourself a bolshevik."[7] Mainstream suffragists in South Carolina were
therefore at pains to distance themselves from the few radicals in their midst.

While the radicals are not the subjects of this study, it is worth noting that
the feminine political spectrum in South Carolina some eighty years ago was
wider than one might expect. Sidney Bland has illuminated the "radical"
Women's Party activist Susan Pringle Frost, and Amy McCandless has studied
Frost's colleague, Anita Pollitzer. Dedicated as they were to the cause, these
militants were almost anathema to moderates like Emma Dunovant.[8] Their
methods provide part of the explanation, for to the moderates, both pragma-
tism and manners dictated a more respectable course. But perhaps a deeper
cause of concern was Frost's and Pollitzer's rejection of the Democratic Party
(and the Republican as well, of course) for a third party. In the "solid South,"

such a posture suggested radicalism in its true form, going to the roots of things and threatening fundamental structures and norms. As disgusted as Mrs. Dunovant and her allies often were with their Democratic politicians, and despite their rhetorical threats, they never seriously considered abandoning the party of Redemption and social order.[9] Perhaps their opponents intuitively understood this, but by painting the movement with a broad brush, they made it necessary for the moderate suffragists to spend an inordinate amount of time denying that they were anything like the women who picketed the White House and went to jail, or embraced various radical ideas. When the anti-suffrage editor of the Easley *Democrat* sarcastically advised the state's suffrage leaders to "bring Mrs. [Mary Ellen] Lease and Mrs. Victoria Woodhull and some of the Yankee female vigaroes . . . and let them speak for [woman suffrage]," he was acknowledging that the opponents' best weapon was the notion that advocates of votes for women were radicals who rejected the gender conventions of the South.[10] Yet while he no doubt knew better than to link most of his state's woman suffragists with extremists, the editor was not entirely wrong, for the crusade for the vote put some women on a slippery slope toward ideas that even they might have denied any interest in at an earlier stage in the battle.[11]

Like their counterparts elsewhere, South Carolina suffragists had, in addition to their considerable personal endowments, two assets. First, they held prominent social positions by virtue of their family relations, and being thus accustomed to seeing power close up, they could confront it fearlessly. Second, they had previous experience in some form of social activism through their involvement in such groups as the Woman's Christian Temperance Union (WCTU), their church denominational women's organizations, and women's clubs. Their efforts, through these organizations, to bring about social reforms, particularly in areas affecting women and children, had both trained them in the social policy arena and frustrated them with the inadequacy of indirect influence. As a result, they had concluded that they knew better than men what public policies were most needed and that only the vote would enable them to succeed where they had thus far fallen short. As year after year their appeals fell on deaf ears, this conclusion intensified. In contrast to their public politeness, their private correspondence reveals an intensity of spirit and a level of anger toward opponents of votes for women that must have made it hard to maintain their diplomatic façade. They were, in Marjorie Wheeler's words, "respectable radicals."[12]

The historian of the South Carolina League of Women Voters, the organization that evolved from the Equal Suffrage League, notes that "the two dynamos of the South Carolina woman's suffrage movement . . . were Mrs. [Emma] Dunovant and Mrs. [Eulalie] Salley."[13] Other women certainly played important roles, but a reassessment of the cast of characters sustains this conclusion.[14] They lived in neighboring towns in west central South Carolina: Eulalie Chafee Salley in Aiken, some fifteen miles east of Augusta, Georgia; and Emma Anderson Dunovant in Edgefield, about twenty miles north of Aiken. Their partnership in the cause of woman suffrage sheds light on the interpretive model suggested by Elizabeth Hayes Turner in her study of the "white-gloved ladies" and "new women" in the Texas movement. Turner's white-gloved ladies were the "clubwomen who represented respectability without controversy, who took part in the round of women's teas and fund-raisers for worthy causes, or who studied Shakespeare and Milton in discussion groups." Those white-gloved ladies who decided to work for woman suffrage learned that a more active, aggressive posture was called for in this fight. Some responded and joined the "new women" on the front lines, contributing in a more substantial way. Others drew back, and while remaining supportive of the goal, played more traditional "feminine" roles. Rarely did these rise to leadership positions beyond the local level, at least partly because they tended to have more burdensome family responsibilities. By contrast, "new women" tended to be childless or to have the means to free themselves from motherly duties. Finally, Turner found that the WCTU, instead of serving as a training ground for suffragists and supporting the cause, was its adversary, at least in Galveston. The WCTU drew its support mainly from the evangelical churches and from the middle and lower middle classes, while the suffragists came from a wider range of religious affiliations and were more prosperous. She concludes that "the view that Anne Firor Scott and others have painted of an orderly progression from Methodist missionary society to WCTU to suffrage. . . . does not account for the origins of suffrage support among Galvestonians."[15]

Eulalie Salley and Emma Dunovant would seem to represent the "new woman" and the "white-gloved lady," respectively, for South Carolina. But while Salley fits nicely into the new woman mold, a closer look at Emma Dunovant reveals that she does not fit the mold suggested for her as well.

Born in 1883, Eulalie Salley was the daughter of an Augusta entrepreneur and the wife of an attorney and politician. More important, she was an independent businesswoman whose real estate firm catered to the wealthy Northern "winter colony" in Aiken, and thus she had the resources of time and money to devote to the suffrage campaign. Among her friends were Congressman James F. Byrnes and state senator Edgar Brown. She was charming and had a flair for the dramatic. An Episcopalian, she did not find religion an impediment to her secular lifestyle. She would not have gone near a WCTU meeting.[16] She was clearly a "new woman of the new South."[17]

Emma Dunovant, by contrast, would appear to represent Salley's "white-gloved" counterpart. Indeed, if not for their common cause, it is doubtful that either would have initially seen much that was appealing in the other. Born in 1866, Emma was seventeen years Eulalie's senior. She was the oldest of nine children of John Crawford Anderson, a Confederate veteran and a "Redshirt" of 1876, and Emma Buist, whose father was pastor of the First Presbyterian Church of Greenville. The Anderson family, who lived on a plantation named "Plain Dealing," in Spartanburg County, had been prominent in the upper Piedmont since before the Revolution. Emma attended Reidville Female College near her home and Greenville Female College in the next county. Soon after, while working in the Spartanburg post office, where her father was postmaster, Emma met William Lowndes Dunovant of Edgefield, a son of Confederate general Robert Gill Mills Dunovant. They married in 1888 and settled down in the family home on Edgefield's most prominent residential street. The house, "Carroll Hill," had belonged to the Brooks family (Congressman Preston Brooks became Edgefield's most famous son when he caned Senator Charles Sumner in defense of his kinsman Senator Andrew Pickens Butler in 1856) and then to James Parsons Carroll, a chancellor of South Carolina.

But if this suggests wealth and ease, the picture needs correcting, for in the Bourbon era, the Dunovants, like much of South Carolina's population, had fallen on hard times. Though he had a law license, Emma's husband, William, chose not to practice law (family tradition holds that he was repelled by the ethical laxity of the bar) but ran a general store on Edgefield's town square and owned some land that he rented to tenants. The family was far from prosperous, however. Financial reversals plagued them, and parcels of their land were gradually sold to black families to supplement their income. They had four children, one of whom, John, had an undiagnosed mental or emotional condition that left him homebound under the care of Emma throughout her life. Her letters to Eulalie Salley are full of references to her need to stay close to home and "care for my menfolks." She gardened, kept chickens, and painted quite respectably in oil. Her life revolved around her home, her friends and neighbors, and her church, Edgefield Presbyterian. She was made an honorary lifetime member of the Congaree Presbyterial, the women's auxiliary of the district governing body of her church, in recognition of her selfless service to it. She also played the organ and taught Sunday school for many years. A member of the WCTU from 1906 until her death fifty years later, she served as its state secretary and vice president.[18]

Emma Dunovant was truly a product of what Jean Friedman has called the "enclosed garden" of Southern womanhood.[19] Her father-in-law, General Dunovant, in whose home she lived, was a constant reminder of the Lost Cause and its mythology of the Southern lady. Her church, the Southern branch of the Presbyterian Church in the United States, decreed in 1893 that "the session must absolutely enforce the injunction of Scripture forbidding women to speak in churches, or in any way failing to observe that relative subordination to men that is taught in I Corinthians 11:13 and other places."[20] Her adopted hometown, Edgefield, while known for its hot-blooded politicians, was not the cosmopolitan or urban industrial environment that bred most feminists. Yet as we shall see, she belied the psychological confinement that her circumstances seemed to dictate for her.

This odd couple, Salley and Dunovant, with all their differences, complemented each other wonderfully as partners in the cause of woman suffrage. Dunovant, the penny-pinching, pious homebody, was the wordsmith of the movement in South Carolina. Though she did not own a typewriter until years after women got the vote, her weekly column, which ran in the (Columbia) *State* and other papers around the state, was the lifeline of the movement. In it she mobilized the troops, kept them informed, and parried the attacks of the opponents with delicious wit, heavily flavored, not surprisingly, with religious references.[21]

Salley, the free-spending, secular gadabout, was a prominent character in Dunovant's columns. As president of the state Equal Suffrage League (ESL), she paid for the publication of the column, subscribed to several papers, passed "ammunition" to Dunovant, and generally acted as her "legs, eyes and ears." When a large mailing was called for, Emma sent the longhand copy to Eulalie, whose secretary typed it and had the copies printed for distribution.

Throughout their correspondence, they addressed each other with the formality that, while common for that day, may signify a mutually recognized distance. Salley clearly was in awe of Dunovant's intellect and writing talent, and she repeatedly expressed disappointment that Emma could not attend state ESL board meetings and other suffrage events, where other women always asked about her.[22]

Dunovant, whose financial constraints and family obligations kept her at home except on rare occasions, lived the life of the "new woman" suffragist vicariously through Salley, whose panache she enjoyed even though it was not her way. Although too polite to say so, Emma must have felt Eulalie neglected her two children, who were often left in the care of her mother, and whose relationship with her was somewhat distant. To the extent that she was aware of it, Emma was no doubt disappointed in Eulalie's rather cavalier view of religion. Her ties to the Episcopal Church were considerably weaker than Emma's to hers, and her lifestyle was far more secular.[23]

They lived in different worlds but were bound to each other in a common cause. Elizabeth Hayes Turner suggests that "new women," more secular and liberated, came to dominate the movement. Perhaps, but as the contributions of Emma Dunovant show, there was room for a "white-gloved lady" with a progressive social agenda and a ready pen.[24]

Dunovant and Salley probably shared not only the cause but the same "conversion experience." That event was a notorious child custody case involving Senator Benjamin R. Tillman of Edgefield and his daughter-in-law, Lucy Dugas Tillman. When an unhappy marriage to the Senator's son, B. R., effectively ended with their separation in 1912 (South Carolina did not permit divorce at that time), "Pitchfork Ben" refused to concede Lucy's control of the couple's children and convinced his son to deed the children to him under an antiquated state law. The distraught Lucy took the case to court and initially lost, arousing the fury of the state's women in general, and Eulalie Salley in particular. She dated her involvement in woman's rights from that event.[25]

While no record of Emma Dunovant's reaction to the case has been found, the notorious reputation of B. R. Tillman, especially his behavior when drunk, was known throughout Edgefield County, and her mother's heart and temperance convictions were surely offended by this family tragedy.[26] While her suffrage activism was not to develop until several years later, this was probably due to her domesticated life and her isolation from the progressive forces of that day. She was at least warming to the cause by 1917, as she asked for information about the Grimké sisters from Margaret Harvey of Charleston.[27] Whatever the reason, she came in "on the homestretch," as she put it, but did so in a dramatic way when she took charge of the Equal Suffrage League's weekly column in the *State* in July 1919.[28]

Once in, Emma Dunovant was a tiger for the cause. She wrote a column for every Sunday edition of the *State,* continuing on after the vote was won, shifting the focus to issues of special concern to women, and campaigned to have the column run in other papers as well. Eventually twenty-six of them carried her "suff stuff," as she called it. In addition, she wrote letters to editors, sometimes signing her name, sometimes using pseudonyms such as "Grandmother," and sometimes allowing other suffragists to sign her work.[29] Eulalie Salley was her main source of "ammunition," but when she had none, she "made bricks (or maybe mud pies) without straw," creating columns from her own inner resources. Perhaps it was in such situations that her vinegar surfaced most forcefully. An Edgefield acquaintance later recalled that "her pungent paragraphs concocted while she picked strawberries from her garden patch are yet remembered."[30] These articles fairly bubble with the joy their author had in launching them at the enemy, "doing contrary to my raising," as she put it.

But Emma Dunovant was often frustrated with this work. Sometimes the column would not appear, though she had mailed it well in advance. Once she wondered about her next piece: "I suppose it will come out Wed. or Thurs. or Friday or Sat. or Sun. or in three or four weeks or just about any old time." Other times it appeared so severely edited that she despaired of bothering to write. Suspecting that editor W. W. Ball was sabotaging her efforts, she resorted to sending the columns by registered mail, although it cost her fourteen precious cents, telling Salley, "I won't work this hard just to see my stuff lost."[31]

Her immobility due to family obligations—"Two lone men with nothing to eat is a sorry mental picture to me"—and lack of funds—"money just will not grow on trees around here," forced her to focus her zeal on the column. So the weekly pieces kept coming, fueled, it seems, by anger as much as hope.[32] As state after state ratified the amendment and South Carolina's legislature rejected it overwhelmingly, she vented her spleen to Salley: "It will take more than political brooms to clean up the filth and slime—we will have to inaugurate a water system and borrow the fire fighting apparatus. Volumes of water and tons of lye soap, carload lots of Dutch Cleanser and I don't know what all." In calmer moments she wondered if too much of this venom found its way into the columns, and she told Salley, "If I should break loose just ask for my portfolio . . . and put in some less opinionated person."³³ But Salley loved her material, complimenting her almost weekly, and she appreciated the praise: "You make me blush. So glad you were pleased with the article," she wrote in June of 1920.³⁴

It is difficult to date Emma Dunovant's maiden voyage into the sea of suffrage writing, but apparently it came in the spring of 1919. A letter she wrote to the *State* so impressed editor Ball that he wrote to her on March 18: "Dear Madam. . . . Your letter received this morning is good reading. It will be printed as soon as we have a place for it—in a few days. I hope you [*sic*] will write again, and believe me, this invitation is not extended every day." Clearly, Ball did not know the woman he addressed here, but within a few days he had learned that there was a connection between them. He wrote her again: "I have known of your people all my life." (Ball was from Laurens, in the upstate.) "Your brother Ebb and I were friends in College." He added that Professor Josiah Morse of the sociology department at the University of South Carolina had praised her letter and again invited her to write "when you have the inclination."³⁵

Ball must have rued the day he issued this open invitation, for Dunovant took him up on it in spades. Two letters signed "Grandmother" appeared later that spring. The first of these provides a fair sample of her style and her biblical exegesis, as well as her cause: "I was getting things on for dinner the other day and sat down to peel some potatoes. Little 'Brown eyes' stood by to get the 'snakes' [potato skin] as I peeled. I got to ruminating on the different ways many good people look at the same things, and this thought struck me. Some of the very best people serve the devil effectively when they are trying hardest to thwart his purposes." The example she had in mind was an anti-suffrage letter by a "Mr. Burton" that had appeared in the *State* recently. "Good men have made mistakes before today," she noted. "When the Jew turned his back upon the Christ he was as sure he was right as Mr. Burton is. But like Mr. Burton he was guilty of pre-judgement and a failure to interpret the whole scripture." "Did you ever hear a deaf man talk? That is the way some of us sound when we go to quoting scripture." Taking issue with Burton on his biblical male chauvinism, she continued tactfully: "That the husband should be the head has never been a disputed point, whether he is in reality or not is another question, and depends upon him. When a woman can get a worthy mate in whom she can put her trust, joy just bubbles over in her soul and she is ready for any sacrifice or service for him and her children. Her right to citizenship does not conflict with his headship. Let him be head, and hands too, if he will. Let every man measure up to the standards implied in Mr. Burton's quotations and we will soon be on hallelujah ground." Turning to the main point, she added: "If there is anything in the Book that denies to woman the expression of her convictions by ballot, I fail to find it. But I do read in one of Mr. Burton's favorite chapters that the seed of the woman shall bruise the serpent's head and that there is to be a restoration of all things."

Then she turned to a recent editorial on the subject: "The editor says that Adam was no suffragist. He may be right. Anyway, we will concede him that for argument. But the second Adam [Jesus] was very partial to the women folk, and they were very loyal to him for some reason, and still are. You had first choice, Mr. Editor." She continued, "Let him who can, read the signs of the times. . . . The world needs all that both [men and women] can do in a harmonious pull together. . . . Social conditions could hardly be worse, and woman has much to offer." She closed with the admonition, "When you search the Bible for truth, give all phases of your subject due consideration. When you want to prove your pet theories, do like Mr. Burton has done." The letter is signed "Grandmother."[36]

This letter illustrates the dispensationalist bent of Emma Dunovant's theology. In other writings she frequently returns to the theme introduced in this first letter, that Christ, as the Second Adam, canceled the flawed first dispensation and brought a new dispensation under which true human fulfillment is possible. Her feminism was inspired by the hope that women would usher in the full realization of this dispensation, making world peace, the eradication of suffering, and harmony in the lives of individuals possible. Women would differ among themselves politically, she agreed, but there were certain things that "almost all intelligent women want." The accomplishment of this agenda would, she hoped, bring in the new millennium.[37]

When Eulalie Salley read this and other of Emma Dunovant's writings, she knew she had found her literary alter ego. As early as May of 1919, she was writing encouraging letters and sending Dunovant material. If Dunovant needed urging on, Salley provided the push. "Don't spare [Ball]," she wrote. "He surely is a mossback [and] isn't going to vote for us any way."[38] That July, when the press chairman of the Equal Suffrage League, Lottie Hammond, resigned, Salley as president wrote to Dunovant, "I want you to take it." "I know you are a busy woman," she added, "but the fight will soon be over . . .

so for the next few months lets work with all our might so that we and our children and all the rest to come may enjoy the rights and privileges so many noble women have striven so unceasingly for these last eighty years."[39]

Women in towns around the state soon responded to the columns by urging their local editors to run them as well. The result was mixed, but Emma Dunovant's words did reach a larger audience as a result. She called on her family resources to add credibility to her pieces, as when she asked her father's cousin, John Anderson, who was chief justice of the Alabama Supreme Court and a woman suffragist, for material. In an essay he provided, he called the woman suffrage amendment "the most important amendment ever proposed to the federal constitution," and added that legislators who voted for the federal prohibition amendment and who favored women voting, could not logically oppose this amendment on states' rights grounds (as some were).[40] On the same point, Emma noted that Georgia's legislature had rejected the suffrage amendment on states' rights grounds, and added, "Georgia, like our own state, will get a legislature after a while that will ratify, but long before that day the men of other States will have handed us the ballot, just as the men of South Carolina and Georgia settled the liquor question for some of the others. 'Oh, consistency, thou art a jewel.'"[41]

A careful reading of these columns, in juxtaposition with the letters to Emma Dunovant in the South Carolina League of Women Voters files, sharpens our picture of this fascinating woman and her South Carolina compatriots. She, and they, displayed an almost cocky confidence as the list of ratifying states grew and it became clear that victory was only a matter of time. Yet this confidence was tinged with dismay, anger, and a sense of humiliation as it also became clear that South Carolina was not to be on the list. Hindsight suggests that they should not have expected any other outcome, but some South Carolina "suffs" seem to have been genuinely optimistic as late 1919. (South Carolina voted no in February 1920).

While they awaited their legislature's action, their anger was directed at other "fearful" states. The arguments used by the anti's enraged Dunovant and her colleagues, perhaps none more that the racist fear-mongering that was rampant as the climax approached. Yet their own prejudices are evident in their rebuttals of these, as in their correspondence. Jewish women made some of them nervous. Salley wrote to Dunovant, "You are right about Mrs. Pearlstine, she is a Jewess, but thank heaven she was only a temporary chairman in Mrs. Darlington's absence." Although apparently free of blatant and sweeping indictment of all blacks as hopeless inferiors, their racial opinions were essentially those of the better-educated white Southerners. Judge Anderson provided his cousin with sophisticated arguments against the notion that the nineteenth amendment, in combination with the fifteenth, would bring massive numbers of black women to the polls. Evidently feeling good about his effort, he wrote to her, "Since the black cloud has been dispelled, and since it has been demonstrated that the constitutions of the southern states protect us against the negro women as well as the negro men, they [the anti's] are now harping on states' rights, as well as attributing everything from the boll weevil on up, to the agitation of the suffrage question." When the idea of a citizenship course for women, in anticipation of the vote, was circulated, some feared that black women would ask to attend. "I believe it would be wiser," wrote one, "not to publish the Citizenship Course we talked of on account of the negro women." "Radical women" brought the same reaction. Another suffragist wrote to Dunovant, "Some [of the men] object to the ultra methods of some in England and Washington DC, and rightly, you'll admit."[42]

Emma Dunovant herself rarely divulged her racial views in writing. She worked hard to dispel the fear of the black vote, but there is reason to think that her Christianity had compelled her to see blacks with more compassion than was common in that era. On one occasion when she did address the subject, she tried humor to combat the other side's rhetoric. "All this negro talk takes me back to the old days on the plantation when the hands came home at nightfall from the fields singing their weird songs; one of them running like this: 'Dark cloud a-risin',' think it goin' to rain—nothin' but my Sallie Ann come walking up the lane." She continued: "Because there are difficulties is no reason for withholding from more than half of our intelligent citizens the franchise. [South Carolina had a black majority then.] Difficulties are made to surmount. It is not that the negro citizen has a dark skin that makes him undesirable. It is his ignorance and ideals. It is his lack of Christian education. They are not," she added, "seeking social equality. They are quick to recognize justice and are not less grateful and appreciative than we of the white race."

Warming to her subject, she pressed on. It is said that "suffrage speakers avoid the negro question. If all negro men in South Carolina were Democrats, they would have the vote now. With a party, they can organize now, and under some demagogue ignorant blacks and whites could be giving us trouble. . . . Certainly the time is coming when the negro will assert his right to citizenship, and withholding suffrage from [white] women will not put off the day.

We cannot deport the negro and few of us wish to. What can we do? Kill him, oppress him. . . . and keep jamming him back into what we conceive is his place? Verily we are treading on dangerous ground." Such views place Emma Dunovant in the vanguard of white racial moderates, but it should be added that she endorsed Senator Ellison D. "Cotton Ed" Smith, a thorough white supremacist, for re-election in 1926.[43]

A survey of the arguments Emma Dunovant used in her column shows that she employed most, if not all, of the arguing points of the national movement. Among these: women pay taxes; Republican-dominated states are enfranchising their women, so Democratic states had better follow suit or Republicans will reap the electoral rewards nationally; children are better protected in suffrage states; women are ready to bring their experience as social activists to the political process; Christianity is the path to enlightened government everywhere in the world, and it is primarily Christian women who want the vote, for the fruit of the gospel is feminism; women did their part in the war effort and thus deserve the vote; war must be eliminated, and women with the vote will see to it; Europe is enfranchising its women, shaming this "enlightened" and "democratic" nation; that not all women want the ballot is no reason to withhold it from those who do; President Wilson wants us to have it; South Carolina ranks near the bottom of the states in health and education statistics, but women's vote will change this; women are better educated than men and would vote more intelligently; they are also more law-abiding; the race issue has nothing to do with woman suffrage—the fifteenth amendment will have no bearing on the nineteenth; we are not for the social equality of the races; the jury duty issue is irrelevant—compulsory jury service is not universal for men and need not be for women; tradition is too powerful in this state, and its power is holding us back in this, as in other instances; South Carolina's Grimké sisters were pioneers in women's rights whose example we should honor and follow; foreigners who can not read English vote, and women are more worthy than they; scientists have concluded that the female brain is identical to the male, and muscular differences are the result of differences in activity, not biology.[44]

These arguments poured forth for seven months before and seven months after the state legislature spoke negatively on the issue in February 1920, ending only when Tennessee put the amendment in the Constitution in August 1920. After that, the column shifted its focus to issues of concern to women voters. Dunovant could not resist sarcasm when her state issued what she and her colleagues took as a slap in the face. "The general assembly has rejected the equal suffrage amendment," she noted. "This was progress—at least they acknowledged our presence. Heretofore the suffrage movement has been a joking matter, a great gnat on an ox horn." Now "we have gained another trench, despite the gas." Insisting that progress had been made even in South Carolina, she recalled that there was a time when to say you favored woman suffrage was risky. "Tell it not in Gath," she added, ready, as ever, with a biblical metaphor. In a vengeful mood, she continued, "We are by no means discouraged . . . soon they will have to face us as candidates." Following another biblical reference—"Let us go up and possess it, for we are well able to overcome it"—she thanked the twenty-five men who had voted yes and concluded: "The legislature has had its chance. Now let it come from without!"[45]

She was even more outraged in June when the state Democratic party convention rejected women's participation in the upcoming primary despite the virtual inevitability of ratification before the November election. Her anger was especially directed at U.S. Senator Christie Benet, who, though previously encouraging suffragists to believe he was on their side, led the opposition in the convention with "many unjust charges" in his speech. Benet had asserted that the women of the SCESL who campaigned for ratification had been paid by the NAWSA. Dunovant demanded that he offer proof or retract this charge. Later, as women who were present provided her with more details, she added that "the undercurrent of the convention was boiling and turbid with 'nigger' and 'divorce' and they dared not let it come to the surface because they were ashamed of the falseness of it."[46] There are hints in her column during this climactic period that South Carolina women should not remain blindly loyal to the Democratic party, but of course these threats did not materialize. The heat of this moment would pass, and Emma Dunovant would regain her optimism. Letters from Eulalie Salley and others cheered her with the coming victory. Salley told her of a conversation with aspiring office holder James Sheppard of Edgefield County. "He tells me he will run for the legislature, and probably thinks he may need a few of the women's votes to get in. Oh, my dear, our fun is just beginning."

As Emma Dunovant contemplated the prospect before her, she may have shared her friend's anticipation of fun, but her sense of the righteousness of women's political involvement tempered her joy, for there was still work to be done. Thus, she wrote to Salley a few weeks after casting her first vote in November 1920:

"I am ready to go . . . into Macedonia and carry the message while next to me stands the woman deaf to the cry, and not believing I hear any, labeling me a crank and fanatic, pursuing her easy way, gadding, embroidering, dolling up and playing bridge. I stop to wonder why it is all so. We are . . . following the call, following the voice that we hear, full of faith in the final outcome because we have been chosen and have been given a willing mind to do and to sacrifice. There is one verse of scripture that buoys me up every step of the rugged path we are treading and assures me that I will be there to shout when all is done, and that I shall not be a spectator but a participator in the triumphal march; it is 'He that (and she that) goeth forth and weepeth, bearing precious seed, shall doubtless come again with rejoicing, bringing his (and her) sheaves with him.' The longer I live the more sure I am that the great plan of God holds for woman the great privilege of striking a death blow to sin, that since through her sin first entered the world, through her it shall leave it, and the first promise of God was to her, that her seed should bruise the serpent with his heel, that is trample it out, and if we go on in the name of Christ to wipe out sin we shall wipe it out."[47]

The ballot was never an end in itself for Emma Dunovant; and as she exulted in the victory, she contemplated the use of the tool that it had placed in women's hands. For her it was a divine gift and was not to be wasted. So she admonished her column readers, "We have come into the Kingdom for such a time as this . . . [and] we should vote for righteousness." We are making a garment. "Are you rust on the needle, or are you the emery that keeps the needle bright . . . ? Many fear that our civilization is trembling on the brink of disaster. . . . By what right do you withhold your part? What excuse have you for drawing about you your self-righteous skirts and passing by on the other side? . . . We cannot plead that politics is too dirty. That fact is your call to duty."[48]

More victories would come, and more disappointments, as Emma Dunovant would continue her work in the League of Women Voters until the South Carolina chapter declined into inactivity a decade later, and through the Woman's Christian Temperance Union and her church until the end of her life. Scholars for whom the church was an agent of oppression of women, or at best a non-factor in the movement for their liberation, have to contend with women like Emma Dunovant. For her religion was the source from which she drew her hope in this, as in all of the challenging aspects of life.[49] She joked that her suffrage work was "contrary to my raising"; but in truth, it was a natural outgrowth of that pious upbringing that made her who she was. It helps to account both for what was traditional and for what was "new" in her manifestation of Southern womanhood.

NOTES

I wish to thank the University of South Carolina's Institute for Southern Studies for a Summer Fellowship that led to the writing of this essay. I also thank Professor Sidney Bland of James Madison University for his helpful comments on it at the 2000 Citadel Conference on the South.

1. Quoted in Anne Firor Scott, "Historians Construct the Southern Woman," in *Sex, Race, and the Role of Women in the South,* ed. Joanne V. Hawks and Sheila L. Skemp (Jackson: University Press of Mississippi, 1983), 96.

2. Barbara Welter, "The Cult of True Womanhood: 1820–1860," *American Quarterly* 18 (summer 1966): 151–74. The quotation is in Suzanne Lebsock, *The Free Women of Petersburg: Status and Culture in a Southern Town, 1784–1860* (New York: Norton, 1984), 232. The expansion of woman's sphere in the South is treated in Anne Firor Scott, *The Southern Lady: From Pedestal to Politics, 1830–1930* (Chicago: University of Chicago Press, 1970).

3. A. Elizabeth Taylor, "South Carolina and the Enfranchisement of Women: The Early Years," *South Carolina Historical Magazine* 77 (April 1976): 115–26. South Carolina's legislature did endorse the nineteenth amendment in 1969.

4. Marjorie Spruill Wheeler, *New Women of the New South: The Leaders of the Woman Suffrage Movement in the Southern States* (New York: Oxford University Press, 1993), chap. 1, "The Southern Lady: Hostage to 'the Lost Cause.'" An excellent example of the thinking of those opposed to woman suffrage, in this case a woman, is the first letter in the files of the South Carolina League of Women Voters: "I'm entirely . . . opposed to woman leaving the home, where her duties are so plainly laid out for her in the Bible—which is my only guide—and usurping the man's responsibility in the political world" (Rosa Glen Witte to Miss Dolly Kennedy Janny, 31 December 1909).

5. See, for example, Wheeler, *New Women of the New South;* Elna C. Green, *Southern Strategies: Southern Women and the Woman Suffrage Question* (Chapel Hill: University of North Carolina Press, 1997). For aspects of the woman suffrage movement in South Carolina, see A. Elizabeth Taylor's article, cited in note 3; Katherine Smedley, "Martha Schofield and the Rights of Women," *South Carolina Historical Magazine* 85 (July 1984): 195–210; Barbara Bellows (now Ulmer), "Virginia

Durant Young: New South Suffragist" (MA thesis, University of South Carolina, 1979); Emily L. Bull, *Eulalie* (Aiken, S.C.: Kalmia Press, 1973); Sidney R. Bland, "Fighting the Odds: Militant Suffragists in South Carolina," *South Carolina Historical Magazine* 82 (January 1981): 82–91; Bland, *Preserving Charleston's Past, Shaping Its Future: The Life and Times of Susan Pringle Frost* (Westport, Conn.: Greenwood Press, 1994); Amy Thompson McCandless, "Anita Pollitzer: South Carolina Advocate for Equal Rights," *Proceedings of the South Carolina Historical Association, 2000*, 1–10; Mary Bryan, *Proud Heritage: A History of the League of Women Voters of South Carolina* (Columbia, S.C.: R. L. Bryan, 1977).

6. Wheeler, *New Women of the New South*, 58.

7. Lebsock, "Woman Suffrage and White Supremacy: A Virginia Case Study," in *Taking Off the White Gloves: Southern Women and Southern Historians,* ed. Michele Gillespie and Catherine Clinton (Columbia: University of Missouri Press, 1998), 30.

8. Frost led a small dissident faction that split with NAWSA in 1917 and joined Alice Paul's National Women's Party (NWP). See Bland, "Fighting the Odds"; Bland, *Frost;* and McCandless, "Pollitzer." On the attitude of Salley and Dunovant toward the NWP, see Eulalie Salley oral history interview by Constance A. Myers, South Caroliniana Library, University of South Carolina.

9. This group, whose presidents during the mid-to-late nineteen teens were Harriet Lynch of Cheraw and Eulalie Salley of Aiken, was called the South Carolina Equal Suffrage League. It was affiliated with the NAWSA. On at least one occasion Dunovant did publicly warn Democratic party leaders that women could use the vote to settle scores with them. See below.

10. Taylor, "South Carolina and the Enfranchisement of Women," 117.

11. Wheeler, *New Women of the New South*, 70–71. In chapter 3, Wheeler argues that most Southern suffragists took care not to appear radical, but she then shows that some of them did move in that direction, saying that they were "radical for their culture" (79).

12. Wheeler, *New Women of the New South*, title of chapter 3.

13. Mary Bryan, *Proud Heritage*, 3.

14. Among other prominent leaders of the SCESL were Harriet Lynch of Cheraw, Bertha Munsell of Columbia, Lottie Hammond of Charleston, Lena Springs of Lancaster, and Mrs. John Gary Evans of Spartanburg.

15. Elizabeth Hayes Turner, "'White-Gloved Ladies' and New Women in the Texas Woman Suffrage Movement," in *Southern Women: Histories and Identities,* ed. Virginia Bernhard et al. (Columbia: University of Missouri Press, 1992). Quotations are on 137 and 147.

16. Emily Bull, *Eulalie,* passim. Bull's favorite label for Salley is "irrepressible" (84). The Eulalie Salley papers in the South Caroliniana Library are, along with the

papers of the South Carolina League of Women Voters, the richest source documenting the mainstream movement in the state.

17. Ibid., 7 and passim. The characterization is taken from the title of Wheeler's
book.

18. Emma Dunovant to Eulalie Salley, 22 March 1920, Eulalie Chafee Salley
Papers, South Caroliniana Library, University of South Carolina (hereafter, Salley
Papers). Obituary of Emma Anderson Dunovant, *Augusta Chronicle,* 15 June 1956;
interview with Dr. William Dunovant, 20 March 2000. Interview with Bettis Rainsford, 19 March 2000. Obituary of Emma Anderson Dunovant, *Edgefield Advertiser,*
20 June 1956, 1.

19. Jean Friedman, *The Enclosed Garden: Women and Community in the Evangelical South, 1830–1900* (Chapel Hill: University of North Carolina Press, 1985).

20. Wheeler, *New Women of the New South,* 10.

21. Equal Suffrage League (ESL) column, *Columbia State,* Sundays, 1919–1924.
She took over the column from Lottie Hammond in the summer of 1919. It
appeared on the "News of Women's Clubs and Activities" page in the *State,* under
the byline "E.A.D." Both Mrs. Salley as president of the ESL and Mrs. Dunovant as
publicity chair, were identified under the title. At its peak the column was carried in
twenty-six papers, according to Dunovant's obituary in the *Edgefield Advertiser.*

22. Papers of the South Carolina League of Women Voters, South Caroliniana
Library (hereafter LWV Papers).

23. Salley's husband stayed out of her suffrage work; in general their relationship,
though permanent, was rocky. Interview with Julian Salley Jr., 11 March 1998; Bull,
Eulalie, 40–41.

24. Turner, "White-Gloved Ladies," 129.

25. Bull, *Eulalie,* 45

26. Ibid., 44–46; Lucy Tillman eventually regained custody. Francis B. Simkins,
Pitchfork Ben Tillman (Baton Rouge: Louisiana State University Press, 1944),
481–83.

27. Margaret Harvey to Emma Dunovant, 15 October 1917, LWV.

28. Emma Dunovant to Eulalie Salley, 5 July 1921, Salley Papers. (Subsequent letters from Dunovant to Salley are all in the Salley Papers unless otherwise noted.)
Emma's first column was in the August 3, 1919 *State.*

29. She acknowledged being "Grandmother" on the back of a letter to her of 10
June 1919. Several of her letters to Eulalie Salley mention preferring that someone
else sign a particular letter, usually because of her running battle with W. W. Ball,
editor of the *State.* See, for example, Dunovant to Salley, 23 February 1920, where
she says she will send another piece "for you to send to Billie [Ball] and you can sign
it Mrs. Sneezeweek or anything else you please."

30. Dunovant to Salley, 21 July 1921; undated clipping in Bettis Rainsford's "Carrol Hill" file, Edgefield, S.C.

31. Dunovant to Salley, 30 March 1920; 23 February 1920; 17 August 1920.

32. Ibid., 22 March 1920; 1 March 1921.

33. Ibid., 16 February 1920; 1 March 1920.

34. Ibid., 5 June 1920.

35. W. W. Ball to Emma Dunovant, 18 and 23 March 1919, LWV.

36. *Columbia State*, 13 April 1919, 31.

37. Ibid., 13 July 1919, 28.

38. Salley to Dunovant, 29 May 1919, LWV.

39. Ibid., 9 July 1919, LWV.

40. *Columbia State*, 13 August 1919, 31.

41. Ibid.

42. Salley to Dunovant, 14 September 1919; Helen Gilbert to Dunovant, 18 September 1919; Judge John Anderson to Dunovant, 3 December 1919; Bertha Munsell to Dunovant, 26 September 1920; Salley to Dunovant, 14 November 1919; LVV. Another woman wrote Dunovant about her work with the national office and added, "I wonder what would be done with me if they all knew what I think on the negro question and a few other issues" (Mrs. E. C. Cathcart to Dunovant, 5 January 1920).

43. "Grandmother" to *Columbia State*, 16 March 1919, copy in Eulalie Salley papers; E. D. Smith to Dunovant, 16 September 1926, LWV.

44. *Columbia State*, 10 August 1919 (first four statements); 17 August 1919; 7 September 1919; 21 September 1919; 28 September 1919; 2 November 1919; 9 November 1919; 23 November 1919, 30 November 1919; 11 January 1920; 28 March 1920; 16 November 1919; 7 December 1919, 17 December 1919.

45. *Columbia State*, 8 February 1920, 24. The number of legislators who favored ratification was incorrectly given here as 75; she corrected this in the next week's column. Twenty-one House members and four Senators voted in favor. "Tell it not in Gath" was David's admonition upon learning of the death of King Saul (2 Samuel 1:20); thus, it means do not give our enemies information that encourages them to attack us.

46. *Columbia State*, 6 June 1920; 20 June 1920.

47. Salley to Dunovant, 13 March 1920, LWV; Dunovant to Salley, 3 January 1921, Salley papers.

48. Draft of a column, undated, LWV.

49. Nancy Hardesty, *Women Called to Witness: Evangelical Feminism in the Nineteenth Century* (Nashville, Tenn.: Abingdon, 1984).

10

The Shape of the Movement to Come
Women, Religion, Episcopalians, and the
Interracial Movement in 1920s South Carolina

JOAN MARIE JOHNSON

In 1927 the South Carolina Home for Delinquent Black Girls, built by the South Carolina Federation of Colored Women's Clubs (SCFCWC), burned down. SCFCWC president Marion Birnie Wilkinson quickly turned to the Episcopal Woman's Auxiliary of the South Carolina Diocese and Bishop Kirkman G. Finlay for help. Finlay donated a building for temporary use and a plot of land on which to rebuild, and he and Episcopal Woman's Auxiliary president Isabelle Cain helped raise funds and lobby the legislature for financial assistance.[1] This was not the first time Wilkinson, Finlay, and Cain had worked together on matters relating to the welfare of African Americans in South Carolina. In fact, along with fellow Episcopalian Clelia P. McGowan, they took the lead in the interracial movement in the state. What drew these black and white members of the Episcopal Church, especially women, to venture into the dangerous terrain of interracial work in the South in the 1920s?

In South Carolina the role of black and white Episcopal women in the interracial movement, while little known, was crucial. The two most important leaders in the state branch of the Commission on Interracial Cooperation (CIC) were Episcopalian: vice chairman Marion Wilkinson, an African American woman; and chairman Clelia McGowan, a white woman. This significant Episcopal influence has not yet been studied, although historian Jacquelyn Dowd Hall discovered a predominance of Methodists in the Association of Southern Women for the Prevention of Lynching, a group that grew out of the CIC. Hall argued that those white women who dared to challenge Southern racial mores drew strength and experience from working with African American women in the Methodist Home Mission Society and the YWCA.[2] This chapter explores why Episcopalians, especially women, assumed such a crucial role in South Carolina, examining Christian and Episcopal doctrine and history, and the elite status typical of many of members, which appears to have buffered them from criticism and motivated them through a sense of service and "noblesse oblige."

The religious motivation behind participation in the CIC and the strengths and weaknesses of the movement in the 1920s suggest insight into the modern civil rights movement which exploded thirty years later.[3] The inability of the CIC and the church to challenge segregation despite their "liberal" ideals of brotherhood and justice gives some indication of the challenges to come and the necessity of direct action. If African Americans were going to be successful at changing the system with or without white allies, they would have to move beyond the well-meant but limited agenda of the CIC. Moreover, the crucial role of Christian ideals and church leadership among both blacks and whites involved finds its roots in this earlier Christian-centered movement. Understanding why blacks and whites took a risk and worked together during the 1920s can therefore help us understand the motivation and ideals of later participants.

In the Jim Crow South, "interracial cooperation" was understood by even the most liberal whites as simply advocating that members of the races work together to improve conditions for blacks. Frequently, this meant efforts to improve black educational opportunities—to make separate-but-equal facilities more equal. As frustrating as it may have been for African Americans involved in the interracial movement, it did not mean social equality or an end to segregation.

Before 1920, cooperation between black and white women in the South was relatively rare.[4] Although Southern women in secular associations such as women's clubs rarely connected across race, *church* women led early attempts at informal cooperation through the Woman's Christian Temperance Union (WCTU), Methodist Missionary societies, and the YWCA. After World War I, moderate white and black leaders in the South came together in an attempt to improve tense and violent race relations.[5] In 1919 William Alexander, a former Methodist minister, formed the Committee on Interracial Cooperation, or CIC, which had a strong Christian foundation in its leadership and ideals.[6] The Committee on Women's Work of the CIC, known as the Women's Section, and local and state CICs soon followed. The Women's Section began when African American clubwoman and YWCA member Lugenia Burns Hope invited Carrie Parks Johnson and Sara Estell Haskin, white Methodist women, to the 1920 National Association of Colored Women convention. Johnson and Haskin then met with a select group of black clubwomen, including Marion Wilkinson, at the home of Margaret Washington, wife of Booker T. Washington. Finally, in October of 1920, three black women addressed a group of mostly Methodist white women on the subject of women and race relations in Memphis, and the Women's Section was created.[7]

In South Carolina, Marion Wilkinson and Clelia McGowan led the state CIC. A native of Charleston, Wilkinson was born around 1873.[8] Her father, Richard Birnie, was a cotton shipping agent, and her family was part of the black elite in the city.[9] She graduated with high honors in 1888 from Avery Normal Institute in Charleston and then taught for nine years before marrying Robert Shaw Wilkinson.[10] When Robert became president of South Carolina State College, they moved to Orangeburg and Marion worked at the college and led various associations, including the South Carolina Federation of Colored Women's Clubs (SCFCWC). As president of the SCFCWC, Wilkinson led the drive to build a home for delinquent black girls when the state refused to provide such a facility. She appealed to white church members to help fund the home both through donations and through aid in lobbying the state legislature for appropriations.

Wilkinson's religious faith suffused her life's activities. Growing up, Marion and Robert were both members of the prestigious St. Mark's Episcopal Church in Charleston, where her father was a lay leader. Wilkinson was a member of the Woman's Auxiliary and presented a paper on women's work at a national church meeting in 1896.[11] When she and Robert moved to Orangeburg, they discovered that there was not an Episcopal church for blacks in the city. Rather than join a different denomination, they established St. Paul Episcopal Mission in 1912, where Marion served as treasurer for more than forty years, and Robert as Senior Warden and Lay Reader.[12]

Many of the associations Wilkinson involved herself in were Christian-based social welfare organizations. For example, in Charleston, in addition to her work in the Woman's Auxiliary, she was president of the local WCTU.[13] While at State College, she worked with students to found a campus chapter of the YWCA. Even the secular organizations she headed, such as the Sunlight Club of Orangeburg and the SCFCWC, were motivated to serve the community in part through Christian ideals.

Wilkinson's white counterpart in the state CIC was Clelia Peronneau McGowan, born January 30, 1865. Although McGowan did not attend the October 1920 meeting in Memphis, she quickly became a leader in the CIC.[14] She married William C. McGowan of Abbeville, son of Confederate general and judge Samuel McGowan, one of the state's most prominent citizens.[15] McGowan was involved in a myriad of activities, including the suffrage movement. After being appointed to the School Board of Education 1919–22, she was the first woman elected to the Charleston city council in 1923.[16] McGowan was also state president of the United Daughters of the Confederacy in 1898.

McGowan's paternalistic appreciation of the loyalty of blacks in slavery coupled with her travels to Sweden, where she "first realized that color was no bar to opportunity, and that education was the open sesame," interested her in the interracial movement. She joined the CIC through her association with the YWCA and organized the first CIC meeting in Florence and the Charleston chapter under its auspices. McGowan did so without the support of many of her friends and even some family members, which was difficult for her. "In my own case," she wrote in an unpublished autobiography, "all my family are opposed to it, which is a very real and constant trial. I had expected criticism and severe judgment from outsiders." McGowan persisted, however, confident that she had to follow her conscience.[17]

Bishop Kirkman G. Finlay and Isabelle Lindsay Cain, president of the Woman's Auxiliary, strengthened the bonds between the Episcopal Church and the CIC. Finlay was born in Greenville, South Carolina, in 1877 and was educated at Furman University, the University of the South, and the University of South Carolina. He became rector of Trinity Church in Columbia in 1907. From there he became the first bishop of the new Upper South Carolina Diocese, formed when the South Carolina Diocese split in 1923. Finlay was well known for his interest in race relations and social welfare issues.[18] When he became bishop in 1923, he prioritized missionary work for the diocese, including ministries to mill workers, rural dwellers, and African Americans.[19] He also attempted, unsuccessfully, to help black church delegates gain representation in the diocesan council (the two South Carolina dioceses were the only ones in the entire Episcopal Church where blacks were denied a vote). In fact, blacks did not vote until after World War II.[20]

Finlay used his position as bishop to bring attention to race issues. His columns and journals printed in diocesan reports and magazines indicate that he frequently visited black churches in the diocese. Perhaps more important, he also spoke out publicly on the need to improve race relations. According to a newspaper report of a speech given to the Greenville Kiwanis Club, Finlay urged that "parallel development of the negro and whites races was . . . the only practicable solution of the race problem." Finlay exemplified racial moderates or liberals at the time: while liberal in his attention to the plight of blacks and genuine in his desire to improve their lives, he promoted a program that was limited, paternalistic, and in no way directly threatened segregation. According to Finlay, "The races, of course, should be distinct, but the negro should be given opportunity to advance and the door of progress should be open to him." Finlay suggested that whites could help blacks reduce their inefficiency, crime, and disease, while white "discrimination of the negro was mentioned as a point of irritation to the negro race," including such things as "injustice in courts, unfavorable living conditions and surroundings, lack of educational opportunities, and the white man's tendency toward mob violence." Finlay believed that committees of the better classes of whites and blacks, such as the CIC, could work together to solve these problems, and pointed out "the impracticality of deportation, extermination, amalgamation and subordination as solutions for the race problem."[21]

Finlay adhered carefully to his policy of parallel development, noting, for example, that during the Crusade of 1927 parallel services would be held both at the white Trinity Church and the black St. Luke's Church in Columbia. He wrote, "In this I am trying to carry out the general policy that I have adopted in all the colored work, that of bringing to them every privilege and every opportunity that is enjoyed by the white church when it is possible to do so."[22] Finlay was steadfast in his refusal to abandon segregation or promote social equality even as he worked to make conditions equal in a separate world. However, because segregation was predicated on white power and black inequality, even this position ultimately undermined the system.

In one of his most hard-hitting addresses, Finlay argued that Southerners had to recognize that selfishness and prejudice had caused the slave trade and slavery and that "we cannot hope for real progress in racial relations till we have at least a considerable body of men and women who are trying to face the issues involved honestly, fearlessly and unselfishly. If we cannot find such an attitude amongst those who are professed followers of Him who accepted no barriers of race or color and saw in all his brothers, where can we hope to find it?" He accused whites of sanctioning slavery and thus denying democracy to blacks. Such rhetoric was quite blunt for the time.[23]

The attention that Finlay, as bishop, drew to race issues undoubtedly influenced some women in the diocese as they thought about their own duties to blacks. One of these may have been Isabelle Cain, who worked with McGowan to cement the relationship between the Woman's Auxiliary and the CIC.[24] Isabelle Lindsay Cain was born in Columbia in 1877 and graduated from Winthrop College in Rock Hill, South Carolina. Married to James Ravenel Cain, she was a member of the United Daughters of the Confederacy, the National Society of the Colonial Dames in America, the Daughters of the American Revolution, and many other organizations, including several gardening clubs, the American Civic Association, the State Board of Health, and the state Federation of Women's Clubs. Dedicated to her church, Cain served as diocesan and provincial president and member of the national executive board of the Woman's Auxiliary and was one of the first four women elected to the National Council. A member of the CIC and a longtime member of the Board of Trustees of Voorhees Normal School, a school for blacks sponsored by her church, "Mrs. Cain worked for interracial relations long before the Civil Rights Amendment and was threatened by the Ku Klux Klan for her interests."[25]

Under Cain and McGowan, the Woman's Auxiliary became closely involved with the CIC, showing signs of involvement in race relations early on, even before the Memphis meeting in 1920.[26] In 1914, for example, a Miss Ford read a paper entitled, "A Short History of the Church's Work among the Negroes," which was followed by a discussion by Bishop Guerry on the decision to appoint suffragan bishops, a controversial compromise over black leadership in the church. At this time, the Woman's Auxiliary typically was concerned with educating and aiding blacks. At this same meeting, Miss Julia Clarkson and Mrs.Willet were commended for the work they were doing locally with blacks, and the bishop announced that Clarkson was to take charge of establishing a new Negro diocesan branch of the Woman's Auxiliary until they were organized, and then remain advisor to the group. This group was organized in June 1914, and the white and black branches were not integrated until 1965.[27] However, the annual reports offer evidence that there was regular contact between the white and black auxiliaries, which would have allowed for significant relationships to develop between black and white women.[28] Additionally, they suggest that white women were beginning to consider the issue more deeply. For example, some reading groups in 1916 used "Mrs. Roberts new Hand Book on the Colored Woman in the South"; while

Trinity Church in Columbia had a six-weeks study course on the race question. Additionally, the Woman's Auxiliary regularly heard reports regarding the Church Institute for Negroes and the archdeacon for colored work.[29]

According to the 1922 pamphlet "The Church, the Woman's Auxiliary, and the CIC," the Woman's Auxiliary became involved in the CIC when the national executive secretary of the Woman's Auxiliary asked the president of the South Carolina branch to cooperate with the CIC. The Woman's Auxiliary further justified their work in this pamphlet by explaining that both the province and the diocese had endorsed the CIC program before 1922. In October of 1921 the province approved of the efforts of the Southern white-led CIC to promote friendly relations between the races and pledged cooperation. A year earlier, in May of 1920, the South Carolina Diocese had passed a resolution approving and endorsing the principle of the CIC. It simply stated that it "approves of and endorses the principle of the inter-racial committees in the interest of good order and Christian civilization and fellowship."[30] The Woman's Auxiliary became directly involved when seven church members attended the state CIC meeting in January 1922 and passed several resolutions calling for Episcopal women to "co-operate in bringing about a Christian settlement of the problems that overshadow the homes of both races." As women, they believed they were called to "shap[e] the moral issues of our national life."

Time was set aside for the women present from each denomination to meet separately. At their meeting, members of the Episcopal Woman's Auxiliary drew up a memorial resolution of their own, which they presented to the bishops for approval and then to the entire Auxiliary. The pamphlet specifically indicates that the executive council of the Woman's Auxiliary did not report to the general meeting until after approval had been obtained from the bishops. Evidently, such a dangerous topic could be broached only with the approval of higher church powers. The resolution called for blacks and whites to "develop side by side in progress and prosperity," noted that the Episcopal Church was in an advantageous position to foster such a relationship because of the church's relation to the Negro church, and therefore proposed to form a joint committee of five members each from the white and colored women's auxiliaries to conference at least twice a year. According to the 1924 annual report, this committee, which was to be "for conferential purposes," was not acted upon. Yet the committee was described as being "along the lines of 'parallel development' desired by the Bishop." Thus, it appears that in 1924 white women in the Woman's Auxiliary either wanted to acknowledge inspiration from Bishop Finlay or felt compelled to defend their desire to work on race relations as legitimized by his agenda, as well as to emphasize that the committee was not against segregation but was working on parallel development.[31]

The Woman's Auxiliary supported the CIC financially as well as providing its leadership. For example, in 1927–28, the Upper and Lower South Carolina Dioceses' auxiliaries donated $75 to the CIC (and Finlay donated $5). The only other donation from a church was $25 from the Lutheran synod; all other donations came from individuals.[32] Furthermore, the Woman's Auxiliary included "Suggestions for Those Interested in Inter-Racial Cooperation" in its yearbooks for several years in the 1920s and 1930s. These included forming a group of women interested in the subject and reading T. J. Woofter's "Basis of Racial Adjustment." After the group was established, the Woman's Auxiliary further recommended inviting a group of black women to meet with them in order to "work together for betterment of conditions in the community, along lines of schools, or housing, or recreation, justice in the courts, etc., etc." They also recommended personal service, such as helping the sick or starting a Bible class, and noted that McGowan was available to cooperate with any interested groups.[33]

Marion Wilkinson, an African American, and Bishop Finlay, Clelia McGowan, and Isabelle Cain, all white, offered critical leadership in the interracial movement in South Carolina, and led the Episcopal Church to an active role in the state CIC. The remainder of this chapter examines the motivation behind their efforts. Was their Episcopal faith a factor in their action? How can this shed light on the motivation of participants and nonparticipants alike in the civil rights movement of the 1950s and 1960s?

Episcopal women clearly heard a call to action from the Christian doctrine they heard and prayed. Central to this was a belief in the "brotherhood of man," which lends itself to interracial cooperation, perhaps best summarized in this statement from the Federal Council of Churches: "Recognizing one God as the father of all and conceiving mankind as His family, we are convinced that all races are so bound together in an organic unity that only on the basis of brotherhood can satisfactory relations be secured."[34] This belief that blacks and whites were both created by God in his image gave some white Christians pause as they observed the inadequate living conditions and educational opportunities, and the violent discrimination experienced by their black neighbors. One can imagine that Cain and others were moved by the very words they prayed, such as "That They All May Be One," which asked for unity among all Christian people, including, "Give us penitence for our divisions, wisdom to know Thy truth, courage to do Thy will, love which shall break down the barriers of pride and prejudice, and an unswerving loyalty to Thy Holy Name. Suffer us not to shrink from any endeavor, which is in accordance with They will, for the peace and unity of Thy Church."[35]

The CIC, with its emphasis on cooperation and on ameliorating living conditions for blacks, allowed white Christians to feel that they were working to achieve brotherhood without necessarily forcing them to fight segregation directly. Belief in the brotherhood of man did require, however, that white Christians no longer ignore the plight of blacks but work with them. Mrs. Claude Whaley of the South Carolina Diocese Woman's Auxiliary in 1930 focused on women's role in ameliorating "deplorable" living conditions and emphasizing the duty of white Southerners to blacks. She encouraged Woman's Auxiliary members to establish community centers, train black leaders, cooperate with health clinics and the tuberculosis association, improve school equipment, and cooperate with the CIC. Such work was necessary, Whaley concluded, because "racial prejudice must be put aside and we must apply the principles of Christian brotherhood."[36] The interracial movement thus provided an opportunity for Episcopal women to put their faith into practice. Mrs. E. R. Lucas, a proponent of work among Negroes, claimed, "Here is an opportunity 'to show forth our *Faith*—not only with our lips—but *by* our lives.'"[37]

Women in particular were able to take up social service work because of their tradition of benevolence and participation in the social gospel movement of the turn of the century.[38] The social gospel was the belief in the "extension of God's kingdom on earth," or the idea that the practice of Christian religion required service to others in order to "bridge the gap between the spiritual and personal world and the world around you." Historian John Patrick McDowell first drew attention to the Methodist Woman's Home Mission movement as evidence that Southerners, and women in particular, made up much of the work force involved in the social gospel movement. According to Mary Donovan, Episcopal women were well suited for the work because they were less concerned with evangelical preaching than with the educational components of the social gospel.[39]

In its interest in the social gospel, the Woman's Auxiliary was probably influenced by the Department of Social Service, later renamed Christian Social

Services (CSS) of the larger church, which pushed for action on social issues.[40] Both Finlay and Cain worked locally with the CSS, with Cain serving as chair of the department. In South Carolina the CSS began to speak directly about race as early as 1919, for example, when its chair, Rev. O. T. Porcher, reported to the diocesan convention on the "Proper Relations, Economic, Social, Political, Between the Races." His subject was the need following World War I to provide justice and educational opportunities to blacks who had fought in the war. He issued a sweeping call to action that may have spoken dramatically to McGowan, Cain, and others: "It is high time that the Church make her power and influence felt with ever-increasing strength, as a mighty force impelling and compelling men in the direction of social and industrial, political and economic, justice and righteousness, demanding and insisting that the Fatherhood of God and consequent brotherhood of man and of men are not philosophical or doctrinal platitudes, but living, vitalizing, all controlling principles of life and conduct."[41]

Under Finlay and Cain, the CSS focused on interracial relations, child labor, and marriage laws as it sought to interest church members in social justice. The CSS took a direct interest in interracial work and supported Wilkinson's home for black girls. In 1922 it urged "the Church people of this Diocese to make the enlarging [of the school for black girls] a definitive objective for their work during the coming year" by attempting to influence the legislature to provide funding.[42] The CSS suggested that counties could form committees "to take up the negro questions, looking into the condition of the home life from a moral as well as a physical point of view, their churches, denominations, type of ministers, type of religious services, etc." The CSS also extracted a report from members of the Woman's Auxiliary who attended the first national Department of Social Service conference in Milwaukee, where they heard Bishop Gailor of Colorado on the theme of "Love Thy Neighbor as Thyself." "God had made all of us brothers," he said. "Be prayerful, that through no worldliness we draw lines of class or color."[43] This progressive social thinking and willingness to ask Christians to affect social institutions and policy was influential to CIC members.

Those white South Carolinians who responded to church statements on race may have also been influenced by several prominent Christians who wrote on Christianity and race relations, arguing that Christians were called to foster cooperation between the races. Books by Edgar Gardner Murphy, executive secretary of the Southern Education Board, T. J. Woofter of the CIC,

Willis D. Weatherford of the YMCA, and J. H. Oldham, an Anglican, pro-moted the need for a Christian-influenced cooperation between the races. Weatherford, for example, emphasized the brotherhood of man; social respon-sibility; the sacredness of all life, black and white; and the need for Southern whites to get to know blacks, their churches, their families, and their schools, especially those of the higher classes.[44]

But even if Christianity lent itself to interracial cooperation, why was the CIC in South Carolina so tied to the Episcopal Church, especially to the Woman's Auxiliary? A comparison to Methodist women, who were in the fore-front of the CIC regionally, sheds some light on the issue. Historian Alice Knotts argues that Methodist women "came from a religious tradition that, since its earlier roots, understood that spiritual life is related to all aspects of life," and consequently they were active in social issues. Organizationally, the Women's Missionary societies were semi-autonomous and, perhaps more importantly, widely supported the WCTU, where, in the 1880s and 1890s, a tradition of interracial cooperation, though short-lived in the South, was established. She credits black women, some Methodist, for first approaching representatives of the Women's Missionary Society to attend a meeting with black clubwomen. The Methodist Church also has a history of antislavery work. Finally, like Episcopal women, white Methodist women involved believed their interracial work to be cooperation between the better classes of blacks and whites.

In South Carolina, some of these same conditions pointed toward involvement from Episcopalians. First, although the Methodist Church over-all has a stronger tradition of social activism than the Episcopal Church, in South Carolina it is evident that Bishop Finlay and Isabelle Cain did encour-age such activism through the CSS. Second, as chairman of the CSS and presi-dent of the Woman's Auxiliary, Isabelle Cain certainly called on Episcopal women to focus on interracial work. More importantly, the Woman's Auxil-iary had the approval and support of Bishop Finlay, which meant that regard-less of their autonomy within the diocese, he would not have stopped them in their work.

Third, when black clubwomen, under their president, Marion Wilkinson, reached out to whites in the community for aid in building, and later rebuild-ing, a home for delinquent black girls, they turned to the Episcopal Church. Finlay donated land near Columbia, and Cain visited the home regularly. They led the delegation of prominent white citizens to the state legislature to lobby on behalf of the home. Inasmuch as black women themselves determined who they approached for aid, as an Episcopalian, Wilkinson would naturally have turned to McGowan and others in her church rather than to the Methodist leadership. Historian Glenda Gilmore has argued for the importance of such connections, positing that black women served as ambassadors to white society once black men were politically silenced through disenfranchisement because they were too threatening. Marion Wilkinson's role therefore becomes even more crucial. She corresponded regularly with Clelia McGowan, and together they, along with the leaders of the black and white woman's auxiliaries, may have been able to build bridges of communication between black and white Episcopal women.[45] Additionally, black and white Episcopal women had some exposure to each other through the founding of the "colored" Woman's Auxiliary and the continued assistance and interest the white Woman's Auxiliary showed in it. Such a relationship between the two groups was possible because black and white Episcopalians belonged to the same diocese, even if individual churches were segregated. The history of the Episcopal Church's relationship with its black members therefore was also a significant factor shaping the Episcopalian interest in interracial work in South Carolina.

Although the Episcopal Church did not have the same antislavery tradition as the Methodist Church, it was a united (North and South) church in the 1920s, with black churches as part of the larger church although in separate parishes, and it prioritized the idea of the catholicity of the Episcopal Church itself.[46] In the antebellum South, blacks had a strong tradition of attending white churches as slaves with their masters, or, for free blacks such as in Charleston, in white-controlled churches under the aegis of paternalistic ministers.[47] The desire of many blacks to control their own church was evident as early as 1816, when Richard Allen and Absalom Jones withdrew from St. George's Methodist Church in Philadelphia to form their own black church. Jones led the membership in a vote to join the Episcopal Church, while Allen dissented and formed the first African Methodist Episcopal Church in 1816. Thus, the history of black Episcopal churches, beginning with Jones, is one of both a desire to be recognized as a part of the Episcopal Church and to maintain black control over black parishes with black priests.[48] The fact that there was not a black Episcopal church, that the blacks who remained Episcopalian after the Civil War tried to be part of the mainstream church, even if not fully accepted, is crucial to the white church's position on race issues: blacks were in their midst, perhaps harder to ignore. Although the South Carolina Diocese lost 2,698 of 2,960 black members after the Civil War, those several hundred who remained in the church were a constant reminder of the call to catholicity and brotherhood.[49]

After the war, the church maintained its silence on race issues as the South instituted Jim Crow laws and disfranchised blacks; at the same time those blacks who remained in the Episcopal Church were in segregated parishes. In the early twentieth century, when McGowan, Cain, and others were beginning to become interested in race relations, the General Convention did make a statement in 1919 condemning mob violence and lynching, the first acknowledgment of blacks as the victims of injustice rather than as subjects to be converted. However, this was not followed with further statements regarding a proactive stance on race and justice until 1943. South Carolina did not desegregate at the diocesan level until the 1950s; however, it is possible that McGowan, Cain, and Finlay were affected by debates over the place of blacks in the national church.[50]

Episcopalians in South Carolina also certainly shared a belief in the alliance across the better classes, arguably even more so than Methodists. Traditionally, both black and white Episcopalian churches are known for the wealth and prominence of their members. This also engendered a sense of "noblesse oblige" or, at least, a desire to aid those less fortunate than oneself. For example, historian Elizabeth Hayes Turner argues that white activist women in Galveston, Texas, were disproportionately Episcopalian. She attributes this to the lack of a strong WCTU (typically not Episcopal but associated with evangelical churches), the economic status that Episcopal women enjoyed and that propelled them into leadership roles in secular organizations, and a sense of noblesse oblige.[51]

White Episcopal women in South Carolina appear to have shared the same characteristics. This attitude was supported by their church leadership, as Bishop Finlay clearly articulated the belief in the responsibility of those who have to share with those who have not. In an editorial entitled, "Privilege vs. Obligation," he acknowledged that humans all feel superior at times, whether based on heredity, economic status, race, education, or religious affiliation; but he argued that that superiority carries with it responsibility and obligation. Israel, for example, was a people chosen by God, but according to the prophet Amos, this meant "being chosen carries with it not simply privilege, but obligation." Finlay then directly addressed South Carolina Episcopalians. "We too have been chosen, but to what?" he wrote. "To the enjoyment of a sense of superiority over others? To the selfish enjoyment of our special privileges? If the past has a lesson for us, it is that God chooses for service, and that when service is withheld, privilege is withdrawn."[52] Since he stated that race was one of the reasons for superiority, some white Episcopalians may have interpreted his remarks to mean that they had a duty to blacks.

Finlay's sermon was also understood by blacks who were relatively better off, such as Wilkinson, to mean that they also had a duty to less fortunate members of their race. Finlay had argued that the key to racial harmony was an alliance across the better classes of blacks and whites; this appeal was directed to both races. The South Carolina Diocese itself had reported to the General Convention that although they had lost many of their black members after the war, those remaining were "of the better class."[53] It is probable that Cain, McGowan, and Wilkinson were more easily able to work together because Wilkinson was considered by both blacks and whites to be a member of the black elite. As the wife of the president of the state college for blacks and a former member of St. Mark's in Charleston, Wilkinson represented well the better class of blacks. Her elite status also meant that for Wilkinson leadership in the CIC grew naturally from her other leadership roles in women's clubs and the YWCA. In addition, the need to gain support for a specific club project, the home for black girls, seems to have motivated her to reach out to whites for cooperation.

Despite the goals enunciated by the Woman's Auxiliary for interracial cooperation, it is difficult to determine the extent of interracial work done by local chapters. For example, in the early 1930s more than twenty chapters reported doing "interracial work," although most chapters were donating food, clothing, or medicine or were teaching in a black Sunday school. While this work was undoubtedly beneficial, it focused even less than the CIC on questions concerning justice and black socioeconomic conditions in the South, instead treating blacks as the object of charity and benevolence.[54] The CIC was also a paternalistic organization both at the regional and local level and was criticized by some blacks as not achieving any real results.

Yet notwithstanding the paternalistic attitude it created, the elitism of Woman's Auxiliary and CIC members was crucial not only as a motivating factor through a sense of noblesse oblige but also because it helped sanction their work. The best hope for the CIC to be successful was for prominent white Southern citizens to lend their support to the movement. Moreover, the more thoroughly they could convince other white Southerners that they were one of them, the more successful they could be, as white Southerners were particularly leery of interference from Northerners. McGowan could point to her presidency of the United Daughters of the Confederacy, and Isabelle Cain to her membership in the UDC, as proof of their Southern loyalty. When Bishop Finlay gave an address calling for better educational opportunities for blacks, he prefaced his remarks by claiming that he did not think Northerners could tell Southerners what to do and claimed, "I am not an outsider. Born on a Greenville County farm, I played with little negroes. . . . I speak as a Southern man, as a son of South Carolina, who rejoices in her accomplishments, laments her failures, but loves her always and thinks he can best prove his love and loyalty by an honest facing of facts and an earnest effort to bring about change where change in needed." Finlay justified his own refusal to perpetuate the past, despite his devotion to the South, because he was seeking to improve the future. He pointedly reminded those who looked back with longing to the antebellum South, "Let us never forget that the patient toil and mighty brawn of the black man made possible the flowering of that unique phase of our life as a nation."[55]

Although these individuals should legitimately be critiqued for their paternalistic and limited approach to improving race relations, it is notable that they were involved for altruistic reasons coming from their deep faith. This was not necessarily the case with all whites who supported more moderate or liberal racial positions. In his study of white Southerners in the civil rights movement of the 1950s and 1960s, David Chappell argues that most whites who supported integration did so, not because of a moral belief in racial equality, but for more pragmatic reasons, such as sustaining economic development and ending violence.[56] Unlike Chappell's subjects, Episcopal members of the CIC in South Carolina may have desired to maintain peace, but they also clearly connected their Christian faith to their interracial work.

Christian beliefs, Episcopal doctrine, and elitism all created the climate in which women like Marion Wilkinson, Clelia McGowan, and Isabelle Cain could step forward. The movement then grew from these influential leaders. At the least, they helped begin conversations between blacks and whites in the years before the modern civil rights movement began.

The work of Episcopalians in South Carolina in the 1920s points to recent interest in the religious ideals and motivation of white clergy and church leadership in the 1950s and 1960s.[57] Many of those involved in the movement of the 1950s and 1960s were inspired by Christian ideals, including the call to brotherhood and justice; and in fact, many individual Episcopal priests supported the movement throughout the South as Finlay had in the 1920s. More importantly perhaps, the history of the CIC suggests that a working relationship between black and white leaders was crucial and that Marion Wilkinson's role in involving the white church was influential. A specific project such as the home for black girls gave Wilkinson the need to appeal to whites for needed financial assistance and influence at the legislature and gave whites the opportunity to aid a "worthwhile" endeavor. Significantly, respectable women were perhaps viewed as less threatening than men and were thus able to lead the CIC (with Bishop Finlay's support).

Finally, the limited agenda of the interracial committee of the 1920s also presages just how difficult the struggle would be, particularly in the face of white backlash to the Brown decision and other attempts at desegregation. In 1956 the South Carolina Diocese of the Episcopal Church passed a prosegregation resolution, and Woman's Auxiliaries across the state proclaimed integration to be a Communist plot—a far cry from the emphasis on the brotherhood of man emphasized by Wilkinson, McGowan, Finlay, and Cain.[58]

NOTES

The author would like to acknowledge the support of the Frank Sugeno Award from the Episcopal Women's History Project for this research.

1. For more on the home for girls, see Joan Marie Johnson, "The Colors of Social Welfare in the New South: Black and White Clubwomen in South Carolina, 1900–1930," in *Before the New Deal: Social Welfare in the South, 1830–1930,* ed. Elna C. Greene (Athens: University of Georgia Press, 1999), 160–80.

2. Jacquelyn Hall, *Revolt against Chivalry: Jesse Daniel Ames and the Women's Campaign against Lynching* (New York: Columbia University Press, 1979), 66–87. Hall found that Methodists represented 55 percent of a survey of ASPWL members and Episcopalians 16 percent, in comparison to their proportion of all white Southern Protestants, 29 percent Methodist and 5 percent Episcopalian (185).

3. Historically, Southern white churches have generally supported slavery and segregation (Quakers are the exception), although there is variation within denominations, among denominations, and over time. H. Shelton Smith, *In His Image But . . . : Racism in Southern Religion, 1780–1910* (Durham: Duke University Press, 1972). On Christianity and the interracial movement prior to the 1950s/60s, see also Ronald C. White, *Liberty and Justice for All: Racial Reform and the Social Gospel, 1877–1925* (San Francisco: Harper and Row, 1990); Fred Hobson, *But Now I See:*

The White Southern Racial Conversion Narrative (Baton Rouge: Louisiana State University Press, 1999); and Morton Sosna, *In Search of the Silent South: Southern Liberals and the Race Issue* (New York: Columbia University Press, 1977).

4. Most historians of Southern clubwomen argue that black and white women worked separately. See, for example, Mary Martha Thomas, *The New Woman in Alabama: Social Reforms and Suffrage, 1890–1920* (Tuscaloosa: University of Alabama Press, 1992), 7–8. Cynthia Neverdon-Morton cites a CIC document that admitted that the CIC was not "popular with the rank and file of [white] club women in the South in 1920. Many women were indifferent while others were openly antagonistic" (*Afro-American Women of the South and the Advancement of the Race, 1895–1925* [Knoxville: University of Tennessee Press, 1989], 230).

5. This followed the death of Booker T. Washington and his accomodationist program, the Great Migration, the participation of blacks in the World War I, and subsequent race riots nationwide. Paula Giddings also cites the South's need to improve conditions for blacks for overall economic development and the presence of an established black middle class available to work with whites (*When and Where I Enter: The Impact of Black Women on Race and Sex in America* [New York: William and Morrow, 1984], 171).

6. This organization began in 1919 as an "After the War Program" and changed to the CIC in 1920. Originally it was composed of white men only; black men joined in 1920. See Hall, *Revolt against Chivalry,* 62–64.

7. *Southern Workman,* September 1920, 392. Will Alexander's biographers claim that Josiah Morse, a professor at the University of South Carolina and member of the CIC from Columbia, suggested adding women to the CIC in March of 1920. Alexander said that the white women attending the October meeting were members of the United Daughters of the Confederacy and had no idea what was going to happen at the meeting. See Wilma Dykeman and James Stokely, *Seeds of Southern Change: The Life of Will Alexander* (New York: W. W. Norton, 1962), 82, 91.

8. According the 1910 U.S. Census, Marion was 37 years old, although according to the 1920 census, she was 45.

9. Richard and his brother Charles Birnie were cotton shipping agents, and Richard was wealthy enough to own two homes, both worth $2100, in 1880. This class assumed status not only from its wealth but also according to occupation, education, and skin color. See Willard B. Gatewood, *Aristocrats of Color: The Black Elite, 1880–1920* (Bloomington: Indiana University Press, 1990), 9–13.

10. Edmund L. Drago, *Initiative, Paternalism, and Race Relations: Charleston's Avery Normal Institute* (Athens: University of Georgia Press, 1990), 95.

11. *The Church Messenger,* Columbia, S.C., November 1896.

12. They held services at their home, the president's house on State College campus. Ministers from various Episcopal churches served the Mission. Services were later moved to the YWCA building on campus. Finally, in 1950, St. Paul's Mission erected a separate church building, located on the outskirts of campus ("Brief History of Saint Paul's Episcopal Mission, Orangeburg, SC, Nov. 12, 1950," pamphlet, private collection, Mrs. Emma Casselberry, Orangeburg, S.C.).

13. *A History of the Club Movement among the colored women of the United States of America, as contained in the minutes of the conventions, held in Boston, July 29, 30, 31, 1895, and of the National Federation of Afro-American Women held in Washington, D.C., July 20, 21, 22, 1896,* Records of the National Association of Colored Women's Clubs, 1895–1992, part one, ed. Lillian Serece Williams, Bethesda, University Publications of America, microfilm (hereafter referred to as Records of the NACW), reel 1, 106, 121. There is evidence that in North Carolina the black and white branches cooperated to some degree in the 1880s and 1890s. Although little is known about Marion's particular chapter, it is possible that through the WCTU she grew hopeful of someday cooperating with white women, as she eventually did through the CIC. See Glenda Gilmore, *Gender and Jim Crow: Women and the Politics of White Supremacy in North Carolina, 1896–1920* (Chapel Hill: University of North Carolina Press, 1996), 45–59.

14. Five white women from the state attended the October 1920 meeting (four Methodists and one Presbyterian who was representing the YWCA) and, upon their return, organized a state women's division: Mrs. L. E. Brown, Mrs. S. W. Henry, Mrs. R. L. Kirkwood, Mrs. C. D. Stanley, all as representatives of the Methodist Church; and Mrs. Samuel G. Stoney, a Presbyterian, representing the Charleston YWCA ("Southern Women and Race Co-Operation," Records of the NACW, reel 6, 3–4, 12). Although McGowan was chair, it is clear from the minutes that Wilkinson played a major role in the committee, often speaking, and at times leading the meetings. Wilkinson was also on the board of directors of the national CIC (Will Alexander to "Dear Friend," 5 May 1936, Nannie Helen Burroughs Papers, Container 6, Collections of the Manuscript Division, Library of Congress, Washington, D.C.).

15. *Charleston News and Courier* (obituary), n.d., (ca. 1956).

16. *Columbia State,* 25 August 1923.

17. This and all quotations come from an unpublished autobiography, last edited by McGowan in 1949; McGowan Family Papers, William McGowan Matthew, Charleston, S.C. Excerpt in the possession of the author, 43–50. After an initial burst of energy, the committee was almost defunct by 1930. In 1935 Bishop Finlay wrote to Will Alexander informing him that blacks in Columbia were interested in

reviving the committee, which finally occurred in 1938. Both McGowan and Marion Wilkinson remained involved through the 1940s. See minutes, South Carolina Interracial Committee; and K. G. Finlay to Will Alexander, 2 February 1935, CIC, series 7:192–93.

18. In fact, at his funeral five black priests joined the procession. See clipping, n.d. (circa 1938), in Kirkman G. Finlay, "A Collection of Sermons, Notes, and Clippings (Found Dec. 1, 1965)," private papers, Mr. Gayle Averyt, Columbia, S.C., 121; *Diocese of South Carolina Annual Report of the Woman's Auxiliary to the Board of Missions* (title and publisher vary; hereafter referred to as *ECW Annual Report*),14–15.

19. For his address, see *Journal of the Annual Convention of the Protestant Episcopal Church in the Diocese of Upper South Carolina* (Columbia: R. L. Bryan: 1923), 50–51 (hereafter referred to as *USCD Journal*).

20. Thomas, "Episcopate of Bishop Finlay," 468–73; and clipping, 7 September 1938, Archives of the Episcopal Church, Austin, Texas.

21. *Greenville (S.C.) Piedmont,* 6 April 1923, clipping, Episcopal Churchwomen of the Diocese of Upper South Carolina Records, Special Collections, Dacus Library, Winthrop University, Rock Hill, South Carolina (hereafter referred to as ECW Records), box 12, folder 48.

22. *USCD Journal,* 1927, 52.

23. Finlay, "A Collection of Sermans, Notes, and Clippings," 68–76.

24. Finlay and Cain's influence appears to have led the Upper South Carolina Diocese to discuss race issues at its conventions and in its journals to a greater degree than the South Carolina Diocese after the split, although both Wilkinson and McGowan belonged to the South Carolina Diocese. This may have been due to the relationships established before the split and also to the fact that Wilkinson worked with white Episcopalians for aid to the industrial school through the CIC and the SCFCWC rather than through a black branch of the Woman's Auxiliary, perhaps because she did not have a local branch in Orangeburg. Approximately 25 miles south of Columbia, Orangeburg is closer to Columbia than to Charleston.

25. Celina McGregor Vaughan, "Isabelle Lindsay Cain (Mrs. James Ravenel Cain)," typescript, n.d., private collection, Patricia Page, Durham, N.C.

26. The Woman's Auxiliary to the South Carolina Diocese was formed in 1885 when a representative from the national organization came to Charleston. When the diocese split in 1923, a new Woman's Auxiliary was quickly formed in the Upper South Carolina Diocese. See Harriet Linen Goodbody, *A Goodly Heritage: A History of Episcopal Churchwomen in the Diocese of South Carolina* (Charleston: Nelson Printing Corporation, 1984), 2.

27. *ECW Annual Report,* 1914, 10–11; Goodbody, *A Goodly Heritage,* chap. 7.

28. See, for example, *ECW Annual Reports,* 1916, 10, and 1917, 12, in which the white Woman's Auxiliary president and Clarkson both attended meetings of the black Woman's Auxiliary and reported on their progress.

29. *ECW Annual Report,* 1916, 20, and 1919, 10–11, 21.

30. "Resolutions Adopted by the Council of the Episcopal Church of South Carolina, May 11, 1920," CIC papers, reel 3, series 1:38.

31. *ECW (Upper South Carolina Diocese) Annual Report,* 1924, 13.

32. Minutes of the Meeting of the State Interracial Committee of South Carolina, 19 November 1925, CIC papers, reel 53, series 6:191.

33. *ECW (Upper South Carolina Diocese) Annual Report,* 1928, 126.

34. "Action of the Commission on Negro Churches and Race Relations of the Federal Council of Churches of Christ in America," 12 July 1921, CIC papers, reel 3, series 1:38.

35. *ECW Annual Report,* 1919, 2.

36. Ibid., 1930, 42–43.

37. *ECW (Upper South Carolina Diocese) Annual Report,* 1928, 111.

38. Alice Knotts claims that women were in the forefront because they experienced gender discrimination and so could feel some empathy. They also had a tradition of benevolence, and black and white women had crossed paths in the WCTU and YWCA (*Fellowship of Love: Methodist Women Changing American Racial Attitudes, 1920–1968* [Nashville: Kingswood Books, 1996]). Gilmore (*Gender and Jim Crow*) stresses that black women were less threatening to male order before woman suffrage and that after suffrage passed, the links were already forged. Knotts also claims that the Women's Missionary Society kept proposing to the general convention more radical positions than the church as a whole would undertake. For example, they desegregated themselves before the church did.

39. John Patrick McDowell, *The Social Gospel in the South: The Woman's Home Mission Movement in the Methodist Episcopal Church, 1886–1939* (Baton Rouge: Louisiana State University Press, 1982), 4–5, 20–28; Mary Sudman Donovan, *A Different Call: Women's Ministries in the Episcopal Church, 1850–1920* (Wilton, Conn.: Morehouse-Barlow, 1986), 15–16.

40. In 1901 the General Convention created the Joint Commission on the Relations of Capital and Labor, which became the Department of Social Service in 1919 (later named the Christian Social Service or CSS). In 1932, for example, CSS stressed the "elimination of race prejudice and the application of Christ's teaching that 'under the Fatherhood of God all men are brothers.'" A committee appointed to deliberate on an interracial program in the province echoed this teaching and recommended that Southern women cooperate with their CIC and work to improve

living and education conditions for blacks in their area. They also asked women to support the ASWPL and promote its program to church and civic groups. (The committee was led by Jeannie O. M. Cornell of Charleston, who was Woman's Auxiliary president in 1919.) In 1935 the Provincial Woman's Auxiliary also resolved that in its support of Negro work, members would pray "that God may give us His grace and power in enabling us to understanding more sympathetically the souls of Negroes, and the will to serve them in the name of our Lord, and His Church, without condescension" (*Provincial Woman's Auxiliary Yearbook,* 1933, 34–36, and 1935, 11).

41. *Journal of the Protestant Episcopal Church in the Diocese of South Carolina,* 1919, 38–39.

42. "Report, Department of Christian Social Service," January 1922 (Columbia, S.C.: Publicity Department, Diocesan Headquarters), ECW Records. See various minutes, South Carolina CIC; and Woman's Auxiliary to the Protestant Episcopal Church, South Carolina Branch, "The Church, the Woman's Auxiliary, and the CIC," 1922, pamphlet, CIC, reel 53, series 7:192.

43. "Suggested Programme of Christian Social Service for Parish Branches, 1921–22" (Columbia, S.C.: Department of Publicity, Diocesan Headquarters), 4–5.

44. Willis D. Weatherford of the YMCA, "Religion, the Common Basis of Cooperation," in *Battling for Social Betterment,* ed. James E. McCulloch (Nashville, Tenn.: Southern Sociological Congress, 1914), 184–88; and *Negro Life in the South* (New York: Association Press, 1910). J. H. Oldham similarly points to the brotherhood of man, making a strong assertion that Christians cannot ignore injustice but are compelled to fight evil. He dismisses differences among people as related to biological race and calls on Christians to fight for morality and justice (*Christianity and the Race Problem* [New York: George H. Doran Co., circa 1925).

45. Gilmore, *Gender and Jim Crow,* 46–47, 147–49, 178–79.

46. Methodist antislavery sentiment was stronger than in other denominations, although it was limited by disagreement among church leaders. The church was known for strict morality and had several bishops who were strongly antislavery. However, when the church tried unsuccessfully to force members to manumit slaves, tension caused it first to back down before it finally led to the split in 1844–45 between the Southern and Northern churches. See Donald Mathews, *Slavery and Methodism: A Chapter in American Morality, 1780–1848* (Princeton, N.J.: Princeton University Press, 1965). The Episcopal Church reunited almost immediately after the Civil War and then began to discuss segregation in terms of diocesan and national convention participation in the 1880s and 1890s (individual parishes were already segregated in the South). On the Episcopal Church, see Gaines Foster,

"Bishop Cheshire and Black Participation in the Episcopal Church: The Limitations of Religious Paternalism," *North Carolina Historical Review* 54 (January 1977): 49–65; and Harold T. Lewis, *Yet with a Steady Beat: The African-American Struggle for Recognition in the Episcopal Church* (Valley Forge, Pa.: Trinity Press International, 1996). In comparison, Foy D. Valentine found that in the Baptist Church ideas of black inferiority and white paternalism predominated until the 1940s and later, when the reactionary voices grew quieter (though not silenced completely) and rhetoric began to change in tone from paternalistic to advocating justice (*A Historical Study of Southern Baptists and Race Relations, 1917–1947* [New York: Arno Press, 1980]).

47. Erskine Clarke, *Wrestlin' Jacob: A Portrait of Religion in the Old South* (Atlanta, Ga.: John Knox Press, 1979), 87–116; Robert A. Bennett, "Black Episcopalians: A History from the Colonial Period to the Present," *Historical Magazine of the Protestant Episcopal Church* 43 (September 1974): 235–37.

48. Historian Robert A. Bennett argues that the silence of the Episcopal Church during the Civil War and the ease with which Southern bishops returned to the fold (having never formally been separated) led to the mass defection of black Episcopalians after the war into their own AME or CME churches. Northern Episcopalians can therefore be thought of as not having strong enough abolitionist sentiment or interest in African Americans to force a split with their Southern brethren. They condemned secession but not slavery in 1862 ("Black Episcopalians," 238–39). See also, Robert E. Hood, *Social Teachings in the Episcopal Church* (Harrisburg, Pa.: Morehouse Publishing, 1990), 105.

49. Lewis P. Jones, "South Carolina," in *Religion in the Southern States: A Historical Study* (Macon, Ga.: Mercer University Press, 1983), 276.

50. Hood, *Social Teachings*, 111–13; Lewis, *Yet with a Steady Beat*, 67–79. A local controversy in the 1880s took place when, at the end of the Civil War, black Episcopalians in Charleston formed their own independent black church, St. Mark's. The white diocese of South Carolina denied their continued applications for membership—and in fact, a group of white laity and clergy withdrew from the convention in a storm of protest. See various printed reports on the controversy, including, *Report on Admission of St. Mark's*, 1876, at the South Caroliniana Library, University of South Carolina, Columbia. Rather than send a delegate to the alternative Reformed Episcopal Conference, which had many black churches, lay leaders at St. Marks elected to remain independent. This exacerbated claims that St. Mark's was elitist and only allowed wealthy light-skinned blacks to join.

51. Elizabeth Hayes Turner, "Episcopal Women as Community Leaders: Galveston, 1900–1989," in *Episcopal Women: Gender, Spirituality, and Commitment in an*

American Mainline Denomination, ed. Catherine M. Prelinger (New York: Oxford University Press, 1992), 72–110. Some of these factors apply equally well to Wilkinson.

52. Finlay, "A Collection of Sermons, Notes, and Clippings," 40–41.

53. Hood, *Social Teachings,* 108.

54. See, for example, *ECW Annual Report,* 1932, 67–68; 1933, 67.

55. Finlay, "A Collection of Sermons, Notes, and Clippings," 77–78. Others also had to defend their pedigree. Jessie Daniel Ames, head of the ASWPL, was accused of being a "damnyankee" and having black blood, and David Chappell argues that white dissenting voices at the turn of the century had to establish themselves as true Southerners, citing Lewis Harvie Blair and George Washington Cable (*Inside Agitators: White Southerners in the Civil Rights Movement* [Baltimore: Johns Hopkins University Press, 1994], 12–13).

56. Chappell, *Inside Agitators.*

57. See James F. Findlay, *Church People in the Struggle: The National Council of Churches and the Black Freedom Movement, 1950–1970* (New York: Oxford University Press, 1993) and Michael B. Friedland, *Lift Up Your Voice like a Trumpet: White Clergy and the Civil Rights and Antiwar Movements, 1954–1973* (Chapel Hill: University of North Carolina Press, 1998) as well as, for example, David Garrow's work on Martin Luther King Jr.

58. Howard Quint, *Profile in Black and White: A Frank Portrait of South Carolina* (Washington, D.C.: Public Affairs Press, 1958), 61–62.

11

Reconciliation and Regionalism

Reunion among Southern Methodists and Presbyterians, 1920–1955

WILLIAM R. GLASS

In 1938 B. W. Crouch, a judge from Saluda, South Carolina, appeared before the General Conference of the Methodist Episcopal Church, South (MECS). He represented the Layman's Organization for the Preservation of the Southern Methodist Church and was there to ask the General Conference to reject the plan that would reunite the members of the MECS with Northerners in the Methodist Episcopal Church (MEC) and the Methodist Protestant Church. He argued that the plan would be "destructive to Methodism in much of the South," suggesting that the 18,000 people he claimed had sent protests against reunion to his organization would leave a reunited Methodist denomination.[1] His plea went unheeded as the General Conference overwhelmingly endorsed the plan by a vote of 434 to 26.

In 1941 Crouch made good his threat and led more than fifty members out of the Methodist Church in Saluda to form a new congregation. Interestingly, they joined, not the Southern Methodist Church, a small splinter group that formed a new denomination after reunion, but rather the Presbyterian Church in the United States (PCUS, or the southern Presbyterian Church).[2] In just a few years, Crouch found himself in the same battle but in a different denomination, and he joined the ranks of those trying to stop Presbyterian reunion. He contributed two articles to the *Southern Presbyterian Journal,* the main forum of antiunion opinion. One suggested that reunion would mean the loss of congregational control over its property, and the other affirmed the biblical basis of segregation.[3]

As one of the few direct connections between these two episodes, Crouch was not a typical example of southern Methodism or Presbyterianism, but he is representative of several important aspects of the battles waged in these two traditions over reunion. As a layperson, he illustrates both the Methodist laypeople who felt they were betrayed by their clerical leaders who sought reunion at the expense of southern traditions, and the Presbyterian laypeople who played a key role in stalling reunion for almost forty years. The subject of his two *Southern Presbyterian Journal* articles exemplifies important ways that Methodist and Presbyterian opponents of reunion reveal their identification with southern traditions and their defense of southern culture that they felt was threatened by reunion. Indeed, while the effort to reunite Methodists and Presbyterians could be studied profitably from many angles, one of the more intriguing perspectives is the way this persistent regionalism undercut the efforts to bring reconciliation to the antebellum religious schisms.[4]

The starting point for this investigation is C. C. Goen's analysis of the antebellum divisions in America's Protestant denominations in *Broken Churches, Broken Nation.*[5] Goen saw the 1840s split of Baptists and Methodists into sectional churches as foreshadowing the division of the nation. Mitchel Snay in the *Gospel of Disunion* called the antebellum schisms "harbingers of disunion" and demonstrated precisely how religion contributed to growth of southern sectionalism.[6] If these separations provide such good insight into the *development* of southern regional identity, then the possibility exists that the examination of the efforts to reunite the broken churches will yield some understanding of the *continuance or decline* of southern regionalism. This chapter suggests that the fight over reunion among southern Methodists and Presbyterians reveals the persistence of sectional identity. It shows how some Southerners continued to put their faith to the defense of southern culture.

Several limitations of this particular study must be noted, however. First is that Southern Baptists never seriously engaged in the same kind of prolonged and serious negotiations to rejoin northern Baptists that Methodists and Presbyterians did. Consequently, using opposition to reunion as a marker for the endurance of southern regionalism misses how the members of the largest denomination would have responded to reunion. Also this chapter focuses on those opposed to reunion, not those who supported the endeavor. A similar study of the rhetoric and arguments of reunion's southern advocates would yield interesting insights into a differing vision of southern identity. Indeed, a case could be made that the battle over reunion reflected a struggle for defining what it meant to be southern in the middle of the twentieth century.

Serious discussion of reunion among southern Methodists began in 1910 when the General Conference expressed approval of the idea of reunion and encouraged the start of negotiations with northern Methodists to develop a plan to achieve that end.[7] The two denominations formed a joint commission that produced its first plan in 1919, which was rejected by the MEC. The commission went back to work and offered a second plan in 1922. Northern Methodists overwhelmingly approved the plan, but after a long and bitter battle, southern Methodists rejected it in 1925. A new commission sent a third plan that both denominations approved in 1937.

Several changes occurred in the intervening twelve years to produce this result. First, a new generation of leaders emerged. In the 1920s, an older generation of bishops, typified by Warren Candler, effectively used their position to rally opposition to reunion. By the late 1930s, they had retired and no leaders of their stature took their place. Second, the plan itself changed. The 1920s plan left ambiguous the status of the northern denomination's African American members and bishops, and southern opponents of reunion used this circumstance to raise fears that approving this plan was a step toward undoing Jim Crow and establishing racial equality. The 1930s plan provided for a separate "jurisdiction" for African Americans, thus easing Southerners' concerns. Third, southern proponents of reunion were better tacticians the second time around. In the 1920s, the plan was before the denomination for two-and-a-half to three years, allowing the opposition time to mobilize a formidable campaign; whereas in the 1930s, about half that time was allowed for debate. The speed with which the plan was pushed through the denomination did not allow an effective opposition to organize.[8]

About the time that Methodists concluded their reunion, Presbyterians began intensive negotiations, and almost two decades later, southern Presbyterians rejected a plan for merging the two denominations.[9] In the fall of 1954 and the winter of 1955, after seventeen years of negotiation, the presbyteries of the PCUS rejected a plan that would have united this denomination with the Presbyterian Church in the United States of America (PCUSA, or the northern Presbyterian Church) and another, smaller northern church. Each of the southern church's eighty-six presbyteries had one vote, and how that vote was cast was determined by a majority of the ministers and elders attending the presbytery's meeting. At first glance, the vote of forty-two for and forty-three against the plan (the vote in one presbytery tied) suggests a fairly evenly divided church, but in addition to revealing deep divisions, the vote was decisive because the PCUS's Book of Church Order required the approval of three-quarters of the presbyteries. Negotiations resumed, and the patience and persistence of those favoring reunion were rewarded in 1983 when the United Presbyterian Church held its first General Assembly in Atlanta. However, the success came only after a substantial number of the conservatives opposed to reunion left the southern church to form the Presbyterian Church in America in 1973.

This analysis of the issues and rhetoric that surfaced in the debates among southern Methodists and Presbyterians does not ignore real differences between the two denominations in terms of polity, nor does it fail to recognize the changing cultural context in which the debates occurred. The episcopal structure of the Methodist Church diminished the representation of laypeople and increased the influence of the clergy, particularly the bishops, in its decision-making process. This impact can be seen in several ways. First, in the 1920s vote, the decision in the district conference coincided with the supervising bishop's position.[10] In both the 1920s and 1930s debates, some laypeople loudly complained that the leadership forced the plan on the church without giving sufficient attention to their concerns or the opportunity to participate in the decision. These kinds of grievances were missing among Presbyterians because laypeople had the opportunity to participate in significant ways in the deliberations through their representation at all levels of the denomination's structure. For example, at the crucial presbytery meetings where the votes on reunion were cast, elders outnumbered clergy.[11] Moreover, a greater support for the principle of reunion was evident among Methodists. A fair number of 1920s opponents claimed they objected to the specific plan but not to the principle of reunion.[12] Such comments were much rarer among anti-reunion Presbyterians in the 1940s and 1950s. Furthermore, Methodists in the 1930s did not debate unification under the same cultural pressures to maintain distinct southern institutions as in the previous decade or as Presbyterians would in the 1950s. The first denomination-wide debate on reunion among Methodists occurred in the turbulent first half of the 1920s as the debate over evolution climaxed in the Scopes Trial and Southerners heard H. L. Mencken deride their region as the "Sahara of the Bozart." While the years of the Great Depression were not free of cultural conflict, the South as a region did not come under the same kind of attack as in the 1920s and 1950s. In fact, Southerners saw their experiences in the Civil War and Reconstruction as told by Margaret Mitchell and filmed by Darryl Zanuck become an allegory for the nation's experiences in the Depression.[13]

An analysis of the themes in southern Methodist and Presbyterian newspapers reveals how opponents of reunion appealed to regional identity to stop the efforts to join the northern and southern branches of these denominations. Among Methodists, two independent newspapers were the main voices of opposition. In the 1920s, *The Southern Methodist* was edited by Rev. Robert A. Meek in Memphis; while in the 1930s, *The Southern Methodist Layman,* edited by John Magnet of Atlanta, took over the fight. Both made only the barest pretense of presenting opposing views. Editors of official Methodist denominational papers in the 1920s and 1930s made an effort to include all perspectives on reunion, while their editorial columns committed a paper to a particular position. Among Presbyterians, the main expression of anti-union opinion was the independent *Southern Presbyterian* founded by L. Nelson Bell, a former medical missionary to China, who recruited for its editor Henry B. Dendy, a pastor in western North Carolina.

Opponents made the case for rejecting reunion in a variety of ways, but a significant element in most arguments involved either an explicit appeal to regional identity or carried an implicit one. For example, the argument based on the danger of reunion to the orthodoxy of the southern denominations began with an analysis of the state of those churches. The editors and contributors to the independent papers, the *Southern Methodist* and the *Southern Presbyterian Journal,* were intensely critical of the indications that suggested their denominations were straying from their tradition's doctrinal standards. For example, in the 1920s, Robert Meek, editor of the *Southern Methodist,* made the case that theological liberalism had infected almost every aspect of the MECS, from its pulpits, to its schools, to its publications and literature, to the missionaries in foreign countries, to its leaders.[14] S. A. Steel, a lay contributor to the *Southern Methodist* explained that should this trend continue, the result would be the end of southern "Methodism as an evangelical agency."[15] The source of this infection was not hard to trace, according to an unnamed Mississippi contributor: the liberalism in the MECS resulted from the fact that teachers in Methodist schools had been educated in the North "where rationalism is unblushingly propagated."[16] Meek and his contributors detailed the extent of liberalism among northern Methodists and argued that thus a grave danger threatened southern Methodism.[17] In apocalyptic terms, Meek challenged his readers with these questions:

> Southern Methodists, are you willing to commit the superintendence of the affairs of our beloved Church to such a body of men—a body in which the Rationalists would be in complete control? . . . Will you thus pave the way for the wrecking of the faith

of the Southern people, the ruin of our noble denomination, and the destruction of all the ideals and traditions of the South? *We do not believe that any greater calamity could befall the Christianity of America and the World.*[18]

One circumstance regarding the northern church deserves special notice because it provoked some of the most interesting and emotionally charged rhetoric in the 1920s Methodist debates. This discussion specifically played on the southern experience of the Civil War and summoned images of marauding Yankees despoiling the MECS. One of the most common justifications for reunion was that it would end the problem of "altar versus altar," or the competition between the two denominations in which each church had congregations in the same community. The MEC had several hundred thousand members in congregations scattered across the South. Opponents of reunion charged this circumstance resulted from the MEC's violation of the antebellum agreements concerning the division of church's resources and territory. Furthermore, they alleged that this plan of reunion should be rejected because it did nothing to stop northern annual conferences from continuing to establish congregations where southern conferences already had churches. Opponents of reunion most frequently described the presence of MEC churches in the South as a result of an "invasion." According to Bishop Candler, this plan "legalizes and legitimizes the invasion of our territory by the Northern Church."[19]

Furthermore, Candler saw an antisouthern bias at work in the MEC's actions: "It is pertinent to note that the Northern Church invades no other Church but ours, and invades ours nowhere but in the South."[20] Similarly, Bishop W. N. Ainsworth argued that the plan left in place all the northern conferences and congregations, thus they "will penetrate the heart" of the South and "will perpetuate the Northern Church in the South and legalize their occupancy of territory where they are now trespassers."[21] In this regard, J. N. Peacock noted that, while northern Methodists claimed to be brothers in Christ with Southerners, some of these "brothers" should "get to acting more like it and stop Brother Sherman's ecclesiastical 'march through Georgia.'"[22] The final result of this invasion, according to W. A. Patterson, would be northern mastery over southern religion just as in other areas: "Since the Civil War, the North has dominated the politics of the United States. They dominate our finances. They dominate our publications of all kinds, and just so sure as we unite with the Northern Methodist Church they will dominate our religion so far as the Methodist Church is concerned."[23]

In the 1930s, the *Southern Methodist Layman* made similar arguments about heterodoxy in the MEC in its campaign to stop reunion.[24] Various articles attacked the modernism of the northern Methodist Church and suggested that reunion would encourage the liberal tendencies already present in southern Methodist seminaries and publications.[25] One correspondent to the *Layman* believed the consequences of reunion had significance beyond its impact on the MECS. This letter to the editor warned that if reunion occurred, "it will be a hopeless surrender of the evangelical Christianity in the Southern states to the counterfeit Christianity called modernism."[26]

Not only was the northern church theologically suspect, but the politics of some of its leaders cast doubt on the wisdom of reunion. Contributors to the *Southern Methodist Layman* believed they saw communist leanings in some of the northern Methodist leaders. Articles charged E. Stanley Jones, G. Bromley Oxam, and Ivan Lee Holt with endorsing communism.[27] Thus "the burning question" was will southern Methodists "allow themselves to be dragooned in to supporting . . . [an] assault upon the constitution and free institutions of our republic in order that a collectivist, communistic social order may be set up on their ruins?"[28] Couched in these terms, the only answer was for southern Methodist laypeople to awaken to the dangers and resist reunion.

In the 1940s, as the writers for the *Southern Presbyterian Journal* surveyed the condition of their denomination, they believed that the most serious threat to its doctrinal integrity was liberalism in its seminaries and colleges. They attacked schools for inviting noted liberals to address their students because these lectures gave the impression that the schools endorsed the speakers' views.[29] More dangerous than an occasional lecture, though, was the presentation of liberalism in the classrooms by the schools' professors, particularly in the seminaries. Theological education from a liberal perspective meant liberal ministers for the pulpits. One editorial explained, "A low view of inspiration on the part of the professor will inevitably bring many of his students to the same position. This, in turn, must affect the ministers of the Church."[30]

While a similar concern over doctrinal compromise was an important element in the *Journal*'s criticism of the Federal Council of Churches (FCC),[31] equally disturbing was the FCC's social, economic, and political pronouncements. And though couching its criticisms of these statements in a traditional southern Presbyterian analysis of the church's mission, the *Journal*'s contributors displayed a traditional southern understanding of the church's primary purpose as a base for attacking their denomination's membership in the FCC.

According to editorials and articles in the *Journal,* membership in the FCC meant that the organization spoke for southern Presbyterians when it took positions on various issues facing America, positions few southern Presbyterians supported.[32] For example, Robert Vining described the FCC as a "foe of capitalism" and, if not a friend of communism, sympathetic to its defense of the rights of workers.[33] According to other writers, its pacifism in the early 1940s was out of step with America's battle to defend democracy.[34] Its support of racial integration showed the shallowness of its analysis of southern racial problems and its ignorance of southern race relations.[35] Furthermore, such efforts contradicted the traditional southern Presbyterian understanding the relationship of their church to the world. The FCC's activities misdirected the denomination's energy by representing a social gospel understanding of the church's mission in society. For writers in the *Journal,* the church had first and foremost a spiritual mission to evangelize the world and nurture its members, not one of influencing politics or reforming society.[36] According to Tom Glasgow, in words most Methodist anti-unionists would heartily approve, "The *primary objectives* of the church are *neither moral nor social uplift nor the improvement of individual or community ethics and economic standards* . . . The *primary objective* of the Church is *SALVATION*!"[37]

At the same time, the discussion of the church's spiritual mission had a distinctly southern accent. For example, J. J. Hill reminded readers that the northern denomination had not repudiated the Springs Resolutions of 1861 that demanded loyalty to the federal government as a condition of membership. This meddling in political affairs, according to Hill, provoked the split that established the southern church on the principle of the spirituality of the church's mission.[38] Some thirty years earlier, as evidence that "the Northern Church constantly meddles with political matters," Bishop Candler pointed out that at the 1924 northern Methodist General Conference a variety of resolutions touching on political issues, like offering support for an antilynching bill, won the approval of the delegates. Candler therefore concluded that "the two Churches are not 'one in spirit'" and should not reunite.[39]

Underlying this concern for doctrine was a series of objections that reflected these Southerners' desire to maintain their church as a central part of their region's identity. Consider the issue of liberalism in the southern Methodist and Presbyterian schools. From the discussions of the necessity to reject reunion because of the northern church's liberalism and the complaints concerning liberal professors in southern seminaries, a perceptive reader might conclude that southern seminaries were being run by a group of theological scalawags whose teachings undermined the distinctive character of the southern church. For example, one Presbyterian layman blamed the turmoil over reunion on these seminary professors. Writing to the moderator of the General Assembly after the plan had been defeated, he claimed, "Those in our ranks . . . [who] started this idea were *not of us,* they came in to us in the Trojan horse. They had the idea instilled in them in our USA dominated Seminaries. Why can't these preachers go North, if they dislike the South so much and let the US [Church] alone. You would see God prosper the Southern Church as never before."[40]

One theme frequently mentioned was that reunion would mean the loss of the southern church's distinctive mission and the disappearance of the southern church altogether. In an editorial, Presbyterian R. Wilbur Cousar feared the result of reunion would be that "our Southern Church would not really be merged, but absorbed, since it is less than one third the size of the Northern body."[41] Randolph E. Lee, an elder, charged that a "vote for this plan of Union means a vote for the destruction of our Southern Presbyterian Church."[42] Cousar also appealed to pride in the southern church's work. "We do not like comparison," wrote Cousar, "but the Southern Presbyterian Church is already one of the leading churches in the world in Stewardship, Women's Work, Home Missions, and in other phases. We see no reason for abandoning these programs that have proven themselves so highly efficient and useful in the Master's service."[43]

Finally, reunion not only threatened the southern church's theological traditions but also its broader mission as a voice of evangelical Protestantism crying in the Babel of theological liberalism. Randolph Lee believed that the southern Presbyterian "testimony for the Lord Jesus Christ would never be heard in the concerted din of Modernism and the Social Gospel which is so loudly preached by those two Northern churches."[44]

Southern Presbyterian Journal contributors also argued that the structure of the new denomination would give Northerners control over its policies and property. For example, articles and editorials pointed out the actual consolidation of church institutions would be left up to a committee in which southern representatives had only one third of the votes. Thus the fate of southern seminaries, mission boards, publishing houses, and the rest would be determined by Northerners. Some comments almost sounded as though the authors believed reunion would unleash predatory theological carpetbaggers to pillage the southern church's institutions and property. William Child Robinson pointed out:

> The adoption of the Plan of Union means that our home missions will be directed from New York, not conducted by each local Presbytery. It means that our world missions will be directed also from New York by consultation with other New York denomination boards but with little left to the discretion of the missions that are on the foreign field. It means that our educational institutions will be supported by gifts to a National Board of Education rather than by local interested constituencies. Whether all of these institutions will survive such a program only time can tell.[45]

But the most emotional issue was church property, particularly control of congregational buildings and land. *Journal* contributors suggested that the Plan of Union prevented local congregations from selling property without approval of the presbytery. Significantly, they argued that such a policy imposed a northern practice on Southerners. Furthermore, the purpose of this provision, according to Randolph E. Lee, was to "secure denominational control of the physical property of an individual church, in order to make it easier to whip the church in line."[46] A decade earlier, the issue of property arose in a different context among Methodists. In the 1930s, Methodist opponents to reunion linked the threat to their denomination's property to their sense of betrayal by the MECS leaders. This attitude emerged most clearly in the *Layman*'s efforts to explain why more clergy did not oppose reunion. Contributors alleged that the lopsided vote favoring reunion at the 1938 General Conference resulted from the power the bishops had over the denomination's ministers. Bishops determined which church a pastor served, and all but one of the bishops supported reunion. According to opponents, the roll call vote on the proposition required each minister to declare his position on the plan, whereas a secret ballot would have allowed the clergy to vote their consciences without fear of reprisal from the bishops. The latter method, opponents confidently claimed, would have resulted in the defeat of reunion.[47] Thus, according to one editorial, many ministers were nothing more than "political 'yesmen' of the bishops used by them in maintaining the machinery over which they rule with Czaristic power."[48] Articles also emphasized that the procedure for approving reunion denied southern laypeople a voice in the decision, that the movement for union was a plot by the "czars" of the MECS, and that their leaders deliberately withheld information from the laity and misled them as to consequences of reunion.[49]

One frequently cited result involved the fate of the denomination's property at both the local and regional level. Significantly, it yoked the sense of betrayal by their leaders among Methodist laypeople to regional pride and fears of northern influence. Editorials and articles asserted that because Northerners would have numerical superiority in the new church, southern Methodists effectively lost control of their denomination's property to Yankees, even the buildings housing local congregations and constructed with funds raised by those congregations.[50] One contributor tied these objections together in a burst of frustration with the MECS's leadership:

> The attitude of the machine, composed of Bishops and other Czars, toward laymen . . . appears about like this: YOU pay the money IN, WE pay it OUT. YOU build churches and establish loan funds for the MEC, S, WE manipulate the machinery so that your property is placed under the absolute control of the Church, North; in addition to that we will drive you like dumb animals into an organization under absolute control of said Northern Church, without permitting you to be informed much less express yourself.[51]

Perhaps the most important link between regionalism and rejection of reconciliation was the discussion of reunion's implication for southern race relations. The general argument in all three decades was similar in outline. The northern denominations were integrated; therefore, the united denomination would be racially mixed. This kind of change in such an important institution of southern society would undermine Jim Crow, the foundation of the South's racial arrangement. Almost all opponents of reunion who played this race card professed the best intentions for, and "friendship" with, African Americans and claimed concern for them as Christian brothers and sisters. But the Bible, according to these opponents, and longstanding social customs required separation of the races. What varied from decade to decade was the specific circumstances in the denominations, the details of the particular plan under consideration, and the intensity of the rhetoric used to denounce reunion because of its potential for promoting an end to segregation.

Southern Methodists in the 1920s faced the prospect of uniting with a northern church that had two African American bishops and about 300,000

black members, most in congregations in the South. The plan would not permit any bishop to preside over a district or annual conference without the
conference's invitation, nor could a church transfer membership from one
conference to another without both conference's permission. Moreover, each
congregation remained free to accept or reject a person's application for membership, whether by profession of faith or transfer of letter. The assumption
was that no southern conference would invite an African American bishop to
preside, that no southern white district would approve the transfer of a black
congregation to its conference, and that southern white churches would continue their practice of excluding African Americans from membership.

These guarantees were not enough for those opposed to reunion. They
seemed to prefer an explicit statement that the reunited denomination would
maintain a policy of racial separation. In the *Wesleyan Christian Advocate,* Reverend J. N. Peacock of Albany, Georgia, noted that the MEC has "two Negro
Bishops who sit on perfect equality with the white bishops. To be sure, they
preside at present only over conferences of their own color, but how long this
will last no one can tell, and the plan fails to specify."[52] David Barbee in the
Southern Methodist pointed out that while the plan did not require southern
white congregations to accept African American members, nothing prevented
African Americans from applying for membership, thus "constantly annoying
and vexing the Southern people who are members of this great Church."[53]
Reverend W. C. Lovett noted that African Americans would remain in separate churches and then asked, "Suppose a colored member of the united
church desire to be in the Southern Jurisdiction and in a church of white
members. Could any pastor under the present plan refuse him membership?"[54]

But even if no violation of the South's racial code occurred, the mere symbolism of an integrated denomination demanded rejection of the plan. While
MECS Bishop W. N. Ainsworth pointed out that African American bishops
would continue to preside at sessions of the college of bishops and General
Conference,[55] Colonel E. C. Reeves described what he believed was the logical
consequences, even to the point of invoking the need to protect southern
white women from association with African American men:

> The plan not only does not provide against the tendency to social
> equality, but on the contrary encourages it by providing for equal-
> ity in the Church. The Negro member is just as eligible to any
> position in the proposed Church as is the white member. . . . He
> is eligible to the Episcopacy. He is eligible to a seat on the Judicial

Council . . . which will have finally determined the church rights of white members of the Church. He is eligible to be elected, or appointed, to the head of any bureau, or organization of the Church where the whites will have to serve as equals, or as inferiors by appointment of a Negro, and if our Southern daughters are under the necessity to work in some department of the Church they would have to work beside a Negro, or under one as the head of a department.[56]

Methodist opponents in the 1920s affirmed that they wished no disrespect to African Americans. They confessed that they had grown up with African Americans, that African Americans could enjoy all the privileges appropriate to their place in southern society including education, opportunity, and protection from lawlessness. But a fundamental principle of southern society was at stake, the violation of which would lead to its destruction with serious consequences for the entire nation. Therefore, reunion had to be rejected. Contributors to the *Southern Methodist* seemed to press this point with more force than those who wrote for official MECS publications, though a writer for the latter did argue that reunion with an integrated church violated a basic tendency of human nature:

> No power or authority, civil or ecclesiastical, can sweep aside or nullify the instinct for racial integrity implanted into the warp and woof of the heart and character of the Anglo Saxon people of our section of our great republic. It would be an appalling disaster to civilization, to Christianity and to our country's welfare if this instinct could be suppressed or strangled.[57]

Furthermore, it was argued, the Bible mandated racial separation. "Because Christ died for all men, it does not follow that it is the Divine Will that all barriers of every kind should be broken down and that they should all be gathered promiscuously into one ecclesiasticism," the editor of the *Southern Methodist* argued. Meek was quite blunt about the nature of the MECS: "It is a white man's church, and is going to continue as such."[58] And since the plan under construction to reunite Methodists threatened that purity, it must be rejected. Colonel Reeves went further. He saw the plan as a "scheme to revolutionize the social relations of the Southland" and believed that it was "conceived in iniquity and born in sin."[59]

In the 1930s Methodist debate, similar themes were voiced, though the harsher racial comments came from contributors to the *Southern Methodist Layman*. The mainstream Methodist press carried little in the way of overt comments on reunion's impact on race relations. While capitalizing on the disaffection of the laity with their leaders, the *Layman* exploited as its most potent reason for stopping reunion the fear that these plans meant a racially integrated denomination. Unlike Presbyterian and Baptist congregations, which chose their own ministers, Methodists had theirs assigned to them by bishops. Therefore, the possibility existed that a black minister could be assigned to a white church and a black bishop have oversight of southern white churches. One contributor bluntly pointed out that "white Southerners do not wish Negro Bishops over them and will not stand for it."[60]

Readers of the *Layman* heard many stories about activities among northern Methodists that indicated support for "race mixing." For example, the *Layman* reported that northern Conferences encouraged interracial youth group meetings, that a northern white bishop took a minister into his home because no hotel would rent a room to an African American, and that plans for a reunion celebration included seating black and white bishops at the same table.[61] Moreover, the *Layman* claimed that plans for restructuring the denomination included eliminating the Central Jurisdiction of the MECS for its black members. Finally, the *Layman* linked these actions and policies to the theologically suspect character of the northern church by pointing out that modernists among northern Methodists promoted integration of the races.[62] The message to southern Methodists was clear: reunion would be "a driving force toward the social equality" of the races and would undermine the southern system of race relations.[63] *Layman* authors denied that racial prejudice motivated their opposition to reunion and affirmed that they lived "in peace" and had "friendly relations" with their "colored brethren."[64] Nevertheless, the attitude that undergirded most of the *Layman*'s commentary linking reunion with southern race relations was encapsulated in a remark by T. Hicks Fort at a meeting to establish a local committee of the Layman's Organization. He told his audience, "I love darkies in their place, but their place is not with a man or woman who wears white skin."[65]

As in the Methodist debates, the objection to reunion because it would create a racially integrated denomination most clearly reveals the *Southern Presbyterian Journal*'s defense of southern traditions. Rarely mentioned, and in some ways significant for this reticence, the disturbing prospect of uniting with a racially integrated denomination hovered in the background of the other objections. In 1940 southern Presbyterians maintained a separate synod embracing the entire South with four presbyteries for its black members and separate presbyteries for its Mexican American members in Texas and Native American members in Oklahoma.[66] The negotiations on reunion considered eliminating this synod, incorporating its churches into white presbyteries and including black northern Presbyterian churches in southern presbyteries along the border between the two regions. Only one article addressed this suggestion, condemning it because, according to the author, the Bible required racial segregation and because the consequence of allowing black churches in white presbyteries eventually would mean allowing black members in white churches.[67] Though no other contributor quite so directly rejected reunion because it might lead to racial integration, the *Journal* consistently carried articles commenting on southern race relations. It is worth noting explicitly that these articles and editorials commenting on race began in mid-1945, at the height of the changes being wrought by World War II in the region and in race relations. Thus, they may also be read more broadly as part of conservative southern reaction to these developments.[68]

The *Journal* reassured readers that segregation was scriptural.[69] It attacked the FCC for supporting a permanent Fair Employment Practices Committee (FEPC) and the elimination of poll taxes, for declaring segregation contrary to the gospel, and for promoting interracial brotherhood.[70] It criticized their denomination for permitting black and white young people to mix at summer camps and apocalyptically warned that this practice might lead to intermarriage and "racial amalgamation."[71] Along with acknowledging that the South had racial problems, it offered several recommendations for solving them. Most prominent among them were conversion, Christian charity, and a kinder, gentler system of Jim Crow that maintained the separation of the races while ending lynching and providing education and jobs for blacks.[72] On one other point, the *Journal*'s contributors were clear: the South should not have solutions for its racial problems imposed upon it by northern outsiders.[73] Race was not exploited as a reason for opposing reunion. Nevertheless, this line of commentary kept the issue before *Journal* subscribers, and when read in conjunction with articles on the liberalism of the northern denomination and about the northern dominated FCC, it became, perhaps only subliminally, part of the mosaic of factors that demanded resistance to reunion and the continuation of a separate southern Presbyterian denomination.

Two actions taken by the General Assembly in the early 1950s kept the issue of race relations within the denomination on the minds of southern Presbyterians and heightened concerns over how reunion would affect the PCUS's racial policies. First, the General Assembly took a step toward integration by approving a plan to consolidate the African American presbyteries into three, to eliminate the separate synod, and to incorporate the presbyteries into existing white synods. The presbyteries ratified the plan.[74] Then in 1954, the same General Assembly that approved the plan for Union also endorsed a report from the General Assembly's Council of Christian Relations that urged the desegregation of southern Presbyterian churches and recommended that local churches receive people into membership "on the Scriptural basis of faith in the Lord Jesus Christ without reference to race."[75] The Council made these recommendations out of the conviction that "enforced segregation of the races is discrimination which is out of harmony with Christian theology and ethics and that the Church, in its relationship to cultural patterns, should lead rather than follow."[76] Contributors to the *Journal* reaffirmed their beliefs that segregation of the races was scriptural and natural, that separation benefited African Americans, that desegregation would lead to intermarriage and racial amalgamation, and that this "agitation" disturbed the peaceful pattern of southern race relations.[77]

For L. Nelson Bell, the key to good race relations was to apply the Golden Rule and to see each person regardless of race as "a person for whom Christ died and who is loved by Him." This belief led Bell to modify slightly his views on segregation. He argued that insofar as Jim Crow laws denied black citizens their rights as Americans they should be struck down. But he continued to believe that mandated integration "un-Christian, unrealistic, and utterly foolish" because it denied a person "the inherent right to choose his or her own intimate friends."[78] J. S. Robinson perhaps best summarized the *Journal*'s post-*Brown* view of race relations: "Certainly we should be kind and gracious to all races of people, seeking to give them the Gospel that they might be saved. But evidently the Lord never intended a union of the races in domestic life. 'Physical separation and spiritual union' is the best formula for race relations."[79]

But this commentary was made while the presbyteries debated the Plan for Union. Though the anti-union forces rarely mentioned race as a reason for rejecting reunion, the connection was nonetheless apparent in a variety of ways.[80] For example, when it voted to reject the plan, the Tuscaloosa Presbytery also approved a resolution rejecting the General Assembly's 1954 action on race relations as being "ill-advised and thus in error."[81] F. A. Mathes, pastor of Birmingham's South Highland Church, told his congregation that he supported the principle of reunion but opposed this plan, citing, among other reasons, its centralization of church government, its limitations on congregational control of church property, and its failure to address "social questions, and in particular the racial problem."[82]

The *Journal* reminded its readers of both the social activism of the northern church and its views on race relations by pointing out that the PCUSA's stated clerk testified before a congressional committee in favor of the FEPC.[83] The most extreme comment from a contributor to the *Journal* came from the pen of J. E. Flow, a retired minister in North Carolina. Flow mentioned several reasons why the PCUS had a right to maintain a separate existence but his final reason was that "our church stands for the purity and integrity of the white man of North America upon whose shoulders are laid the burdens of the world. He cannot fulfill his destiny nor meet the fearful responsibilities except by remaining white as God made him and intended him to be."[84]

Comments such as these were quite rare, but they do indicate that for some southern Presbyterians reunion not only meant the loss of a distinctive southern institution but also represented a threat to the South's racial arrangements.

In 1948 D. Maurice Allan, a liberal elder in the Hamden-Sydney Presbyterian Church, perceptively analyzed the underlying factors to explain opposition to reunion:

> This alarm at the passing of the old South is transforming itself
> into a desperate determination to find in the church a stronghold
> of purity and fidelity to the old order in which to take refuge. The
> reasoning, whether conscious or unconscious, seems to be as
> follows: We are in the midst of a shifting population, confused
> standards, changing school curricula, radical universities, unpre-
> dictable politics, headstrong young people, a declining Sabbath, a
> menacing Negro problem, a rising crime rate, a mounting divorce
> rate, vanishing loyalties. Here is one institution—the Southern
> Presbyterian Church—which we may hope to keep pure, un-
> changing, and loyal to the faith of our fathers.[85]

His words seem to apply equally well to the Methodists of the 1920s and 1930s. Opponents of reunion used a variety of arguments to make the case that reunion should not occur, but two in particular are worthy of special notice in the way in which they express the anti-unionists' regionalism. The first concerns the doctrinal character of the northern church, and the second involves the meaning of reunion for southern race relations. With the first, anti-unionists shaped their defense of southern religious traditions in opposition to a negative evaluation of those in the North. In varying degrees, they saw the northern churches as having strayed from traditional Methodist and Presbyterian teachings. Reunion would encourage the same tendency to heterodoxy already present in the southern churches and thus sap the vigorous testimony to evangelical Protestantism that was the hallmark of southern Christianity. On the other hand, in the second, they contended that reunion with the racially integrated northern denominations would undermine Jim Crow with disastrous consequences not just for their churches but for all of southern society. Thus, they came to making a positive defense the South's racial settlement. That opponents ultimately were not successful in stopping reunion reveals something of the changing nature of the southern regionalism. That they stalled it for as long as they did suggests the persistence of the pattern of southern pastors coming to the defense of southern culture.

NOTES

1. *Daily Christian Advocate*, 30 April 1938, 5.

2. Minutes of the Congaree Presbytery (PCUS), July 1941, 11–12. The various statistical reports in the Minutes of the South Carolina Conference of the Southern Methodist Church do record a congregation of that denomination in Saluda. Membership of this denomination remained small and largely concentrated in South Carolina. In 1945, the Southern Methodist Church had 44 congregations and 3,811 members. By 1950, the figures stood at 53 and 4,634; for most of the 1950s they hovered around 50 and 4,500. Figures taken from Joan Stanley, "A Brief History of Southern Methodist Missions," December 1972, Term Paper File, Southern Methodist College, Orangeburg, S.C. Administratively, the denomination had two conferences, the South Carolina Conference, with approximately two-thirds of its members in small towns of rural eastern South Carolina, and the Mid-South Conference, with small church in urban areas like Nashville and Memphis, Tennessee, and Birmingham and Montgomery, Alabama. See the statistical reports contained in the *Annual Journal of the South Carolina Conference of the Southern Methodist Church* and the *Annual Journal of the Mid-South Conference of the Southern Methodist Church*.

3. B. W. Crouch, "The Proposed Plan of Union," *Southern Presbyterian Journal* (*SPJ*), September 1944, 9; and "Dr. Palmer on Racial Barriers," *SPJ*, 2 December 1946, 5–6. Crouch did not appear as a member of the Board of Directors of the *SPJ* nor as leader in the Presbyterian lay organizations that developed in the 1940s. In general, the editors and authors of the *SPJ* did not acknowledge any debt to the Methodists. For example, not one article used the Methodist situation as an warning to southern Presbyterians of what might happen to their church unless reunion was stopped.

4. For example, in *Strangers in Zion: Fundamentalists in the South, 1900–1950* (Macon, Ga.: Mercer University Press, 2001), 68–73, 153–84, 260–73, I have looked at how these controversies over reunion played a role in the development of fundamental factions in these denominations. I am grateful to Mercer University Press for permission to use material from this book in this chapter.

5. C. C. Goen, *Broken Churches, Broken Nation: Denominational Schisms and the Coming of the American Civil War* (Macon, Ga.: Mercer University Press, 1985).

6. Mitchell Snay, *Gospel of Disunion: Religion and Separatism in the Antebellum South* (New York: Cambridge University Press, 1993; reprint, Chapel Hill: University of North Carolina Press, 1997).

7. General discussions of Methodist efforts at reunion can be found in Frederick E. Maser, "The Story of Unification, 1874–1939," in *The History of American Methodism*, 3 vols. (New York: Abingdon Press, 1964), 3:407–78; and in Robert Watson Sledge, "A History of the Methodist Episcopal Church, South, 1914–1939" (Ph.D. diss., University of Texas at Austin, 1972), 97–132, 261–73. The role of race has been considered by Paul Carter in "The Negro and Methodist Union," *Church History* 21 (March 1952): 55–70; and by Kirk Mariner in "The Negro's Place: Virginia Methodists Debate Unification, 1924–1925," *Methodist History* 18 (April 1980): 155–70. For regionalism in the Methodist story, see William R. Glass, "Religion in Southern Culture: Southern Methodists and Reunion, 1920–1940" (paper presented at the Popular Culture Association, New Orleans, 22 April 2000).

8. Organized opposition developed after the decision had been made to reunite; in other words, the 1930s opponents to reunion waged a different battle—to reverse a decision already made in the district conferences rather than the 1920s effort to stop it from being approved in those conferences. The opposition took institutional form as various groups of laypeople met across the South in 1938 in an effort to mobilize opposition to reunion. Though antiunion sentiment found some support in most parts of the South, it was the strongest in Georgia and South Carolina. From this region eventually emerged the Layman's Organization for the Preservation of the Methodist Episcopal Church, South, and a newspaper, the *Southern Methodist Layman,* edited by John A. Manget of Atlanta. Glass, "Strangers," 260–63.

9. The most comprehensive discussion of Presbyterian reunion is in Ernest Trice Thompson's *Presbyterians in the South,* vol. 3, *1890–1972* (Richmond: John Knox Press, 1973), 558–55. The role of race has been covered in Sanford M. Dornbusch and Roger D. Irle, "The Failure of Presbyterian Union," *American Journal of Sociology* 64 (January 1959), 353–54; David M. Reimers, "The Race Problem and Presbyterian Union," *Church History* 31 (June 1962): 213; and Joel L. Alvis, *Religion and Race: Southern Presbyterians, 1946 to 1983* (Tuscaloosa: University of Alabama Press, 1994). For a consideration of regionalism in the Presbyterian story, see William R. Glass, "Regional Identity, the Rise of a Fundamentalist Faction, and the Failure of Reunion in the Southern Presbyterian Church, 1940–1955" (paper presented at the Southern Historical Association, Louisville, Ky., 10 November 1994).

10. This conclusion was reaching by studying the minutes of each district conference meeting where the vote on reunion was taken and comparing it to the position of the bishop as indicated in his publications in Methodist newspapers. Out of 45 conferences, 6 defied their bishops, 4 voted in favor of reunion against their antiunion bishops, while 2 rejected reunion over the wishes of their pro-union bishops.

11. This conclusion was reached by inspecting all the available minutes of the presbytery meetings and counting the number of elders and clergy present. Elders outnumbered clergy in 56 meetings, an equal number attended 3, more clergy than elders attended 18, and the minutes of 9 meetings were either missing or did not record attendance. In part, this circumstance results from the fact that each church may send an elder, while pastors may serve several churches.

12. This theme of approving the principle of reunion but not a particular plan was expressed more commonly in the MECS-sponsored newspapers than in the independent papers like the *Southern Methodist* or the *Southern Methodist Layman.*

13. Thomas H. Pauly, "*Gone with The Wind* and *The Grapes of Wrath* as Hollywood Histories of the Great Depression," *Journal of Popular Film* 3 (1974) as reprinted in Steven Mintz and Randy Roberts, *Hollywood's America: United States History through Its Films* (St. James, N.Y.: Brandywine Press, 1993), 103–11.

14. A comprehensive article detailing the evidence is Robert A. Meek, "Can Southern Methodism Be Saved from the Menace of Rationalism?" *Southern Methodist* (*SM*), August 1922, 1–5. The following is a sampling of articles on specific issues. Pulpit: Ruby Burgess, "A Plea for Doctrinal Preaching," *SM,* 5 December 1923, 2; "Some Sputterings of a North Carolina Preacher," *SM,* 30 January 1924, 6. Schools: "A Brave Texan Protests," *SM,* August 1922, 7; Bob Shuler, "The Wrong Way," *SM,* 16 January 1924, 6; "A Protest against Dr. Rall as Lecturer and Teacher," *SM,* 17 December 1924, 8. Methodist literature: Robert A. Meek, "There Are Things Worse Than Failure," *SM,* April 1922, 6; Maurice Johnson, "Henry Hunting in the S.S. Literature," *SM,* 13 February 1924, 6–7. Missions: J. F. Corbin,

"Modernism in the Foreign Field," *SM,* April 1922, 1; "The China Christian Advocate, the Official Organ of Our Church in the Orient, Is Boldly Advocating Modernism," *SM,* 9 January 1924, 6–7. Leadership: Bob Shuler, "Mouzon and Channing," *SM,* 12 March 1924, 1.

15. S. A. Steel, "From the Pelican Pines," *SM,* April 1922, 8.

16. "Why the Surprise," *SM,* April 1922, 10.

17. See, for example, "The Address of the Bishops on the Unification Commissions," *SM,* 28 November 1923, 4; "Southern Methodists, Are You Ready for This?" *SM,* 7 May 1924; L. W. Munhall, "Conditions in the Methodist Episcopal Church (North)," from *Breakers: Methodism Adrift,* reprinted in *SM,* 18 May 1924, 8; "Against Union with Modernism," *SM,* 8 October 1924, 7; and "Bishop Berry Declares Modernism Dominant in the Methodist Episcopal Church," *SM,* 31 December 1924, 1.

18. Robert A. Meek, editorial comment on Munhall, "Conditions," 1.

19. Warren A. Candler, "Some Objections to the Proposed Plan of Reunion," *Wesleyan Christian Advocate* (*WCA*), 6 June 1924, 3.

20. Warren A. Candler, "At One with My Church," *WCA,* 13 June 1924, 6.

21. W. N. Ainsworth, "Methodist Union-Which Way?" *WCA,* 13 June 1924, 4.

22. J. N. Peacock, "Unification, Some Things to Consider," *WCA,* 27 June 1924, 5.

23. W. A. Patterson, "Unification Dangerous," *WCA,* 12 September 1924, 3.

24. For general articles opposing reunion combining many of the objections, see "Mississippi Had Gone to Work," *Southern Methodist Layman* (*SML*), 11 November 1938; and C. E. Weddington, "Laymen Warned," *SML,* 17 February 1939, 9. See also the eleven points from a declaration published by the Layman's Organization quoted in John C. Smith, "Organizational History of the Southern Methodist Church," *SM,* January 1971, 6.

25. On modernism in the northern Methodist church, see "From a Brilliant Mississippi Woman," *SML,* 2 September 1938, 6; and J. F. Yarbrough, "Criticized and Condemned," *SML,* 25 November 1938, 6–7. For complaints about liberal theological trends among southern Methodists, see L. M. Beacham, "Quo Vadis," *SML,* 5 August 1938, 5; Allen L. Rogers, "Why I Resigned as General Superintendent of the Sunday School of the Bethel MEC-S," *SML,* 21 October 1938, 7–8; and "A Revealing and Ominous Memorial," *SML,* 13 January 1939, 4–5.

26. Anonymous letter, *SML,* 8 July 1938, 2; cf., "Excerpts from the Laymen," *SML,* 29 July 1938, 2.

27. "More about Communism," *SML,* 2 September 1938, 2; Rembert Gilmore Smith, "Redism Rushes on in American Methodism," *Tomorrow,* n.d., reprinted in *SML,* 14 October 1938, 5; "Communism," *SML,* 2 December 1938, 12; and James

W. Lipscomb, "Is the 'New' Methodist Church to Help Pave the Way for a Communistic Government in Our Country," *SML*, 24 February 1939, 9.

28. James W. Lipscomb, "Is the 'New' Methodist Church to Help Pave the Way for a Communistic Government in our Country," *SML*, 3 March 1939, 7.

29. See, for example, R. William Cousar, "Van Dusen at Union Seminar," *Southern Presbyterian Journal* (*SPJ*), February 1945, 5; and H. B. Dendy, editorial, "Anent Dr. Buttrick," *SPJ*, 1 June 1950, 2–3.

30. Editorial, "Needed—A Clear Distinction," *SPJ*, August 1943, 2; cf., editorial, "A Sacred Trust," *SPJ*, September 1943, 2–3; and R. E. Hough, "The Heresy of Silence," *SPJ*, February 1945, 11–12.

31. The main complaint was that the FCC was dominated by liberals. See comments in Daniel Iverson, "The Aims and Purposes of the Federal Council," *SPJ*, May 1942, 21–23; Robert L. Vining, "Is the Federal Council Evangelical?" *SPJ*, May 1945, 22–25; Vernon W. Patterson, "The Federal Council Speaks for the Churches," *SPJ*, 1 July 1946, 6–8; and L. Nelson Bell, editorial, "Come Let Us Reason Together," *SPJ*, 15 May 1947, 4–6.

32. This point is central to the criticisms in Patterson, "Federal Council Speaks," 6–8; and L. E. Faulkner, "The Voice of the Federal Council of Churches of Christ in America Speaks for Your Church and for You," *SPJ*, 15 October 1946, 7–8.

33. Robert L. Vining, "The Federal Council: Foe of Capitalism," *SPJ*, August 1943, 5–7; idem., "The Federal Council and Communism," *SPJ*, September 1943, 21–23

34. Iverson, "Aims and Purposes," 21–23; and Vernon W. Patterson, "The Principles and Objectives of the Federal Council," *SPJ*, October 1944, 15–18.

35. L. Nelson Bell, editorial, "Race Relations: Whither?" *SPJ*, March 1944, 4–5; Patterson, "Principles," 16; idem., "Federal Council," 7; and L. E. Faulkner, "The Federal Council of Christ in America," *SPJ*, 15 April 1947, 13.

36. On the widespread belief in the church's spiritual mission among southern Presbyterians, see Ernest Trice Thompson, *The Spirituality of the Church* (Richmond: John Knox Press, 1961).

37. Tom Glasgow, "Lest We Forget," *SPJ*, October 1943, 10; cf., L. Nelson Bell, editorial, "The Mission of the Church, *SPJ*, June 1945, 5–6; and D. S. George, "Characteristics of the Presbyterian Church in the United States," *SPJ*, 1 March 1948, 11–12.

38. J. J. Hill, "Some Things to Think about As We Face Reunion with the U.S.A. Church," *SPJ*, 1 July 1947, 14–15.

39. Warren A. Candler, "Some Objections to the Proposed Plan of Unification," *WCA*, 6 June 1924, 3.

40. W. P. Dickson to Wade H. Boggs, 27 April 1955, in Wade H. Boggs Papers, Department of History, Presbyterian Church (USA), Montreat, North Carolina.

41. R. Wilbur Cousar, "Beamed at Our Northern Brethren," *SPJ,* 4 March 1953, 4.

42. Randolph E. Lee, "Analysis of the Concurrent Declarations," *SPJ,* 27 May 1953, 8.

43. Cousar, "Beamed," 4.

44. Lee, "Analysis," 8.

45. William Childs Robinson, "The Plan of Union Lacks Those Tokens Which Have Evidenced God's Presence with and Favor upon Our Church," *SPJ,* 7 October 1953, 9.

46. Ibid., 7. See also Henry E. Davis, "The Ownership of Local Church Property," *SPJ,* 29 July 1953, 4–8; William Childs Robinson, editorial: "Denominational Ownership of Local Presbyteries—But Doctrinal Soundness Measured Exclusively by Presbyteries," *SPJ,* 17 February 1954, 3–4; and W. C. Tenney, "The Plan of Union," *SPJ,* 3 March 1954, 7–8.

47. "A Significant Omission," *SML,* 2 September 1938, 7.

48. Editorial, "Where Are We?" *SML,* 24 February 1939, 2; cf., a similar attitude expressed by one minister who confessed, "We are doing little more than running a corrupt political institution in the interest of the 'plums'" ("Unification by a Methodist Preacher," *SML,* 4 November 1938, 4).

49. "General Conference Observations," *SML,* 8 July 1938, 5; "Special Notice," *SML,* 22 July 1938, 2; G. G. Pike to J. Marvin Post, reprinted in *SML,* 22 July 1938, 3; "The Same Old Story," *SML,* 30 September 1938, 3; J. F. Yarborough, "Money vs. Christianity," *SML,* 21 October 1938, 2.

50. "General Conference Observations," *SML,* 8 July 1938, 5; "Union Propaganda: Slandering the Nation's Courts," *SML,* 19 August 1938, 1; and "From a Florida 'Loyalist,'" *SML,* 11 November 1938, 8.

51. "Benevolences Again," *SML,* 14 October 1938, 4.

52. J. N. Peacock, "Unification, Some Things to Consider," *WCA,* 27 June 1924, 5.

53. David Rankin Barbee, "The Status of the Negro in the Proposed New Church," *SM,* 16 July 1924, 6.

54. W. C. Lovett, "Unification," *WCA,* 4 July 1924, 7.

55. W. N. Ainsworth, "Methodist Reunion—Which Way?" *WCA,* 13 June 1924, 4.

56. C. E. Reeves, "A Negro Equality Church," *SM,* 3 September 1924, 2.

57. James W. Austin, "Divided We Stand, United We Fall," *WCA,* 6 July 1924, 14.

58. R. A. Meek, "A CME Editor Attacks Bishops Candler and Ainsworth," *SM,* 6 August 1924, 7; idem, "A Group of Six Matters," *SM,* 10 December 1924, 8.

59. Reeves, "Negro Equality Church," 4.

60. "Correction for Memphis Papers Regarding Bishop's Estate," *SML,* 3 March 1939, 10. In "An Open Letter to Bishop Charles Edward Locke of the M. E. C., Santa Monica, Cal.," (*SML,* 27 January 1939, 5–6), T. C. Keeling warned that schism would result when African Americans began applying for membership to southern Methodist churches.

61. Untitled article, *SML,* 16 September 1938, 7; Editorial, "Why Not Tell the Plain Truth, Bishops?" *SML,* 9 December 1938, 2; and "Northern Bishops Practice Social Equality," *SML,* 24 February 1939, 10.

62. "More about the Race Question," *SML,* 23 September 1938, 6. One contributor blamed the increase of racially mixed marriages in the North on the presence of communist teachers in schools ("Northern White Woman and Southern Negro Marry in Staid, Aristocratic 'Hub,'" *SML,* 7 December 1938, 11).

63. Editorial, "Race Discrimination," *SML,* 23 September 1938, 6. Another contributor suggested that southern Methodist colleges would be controlled by a board dominated by Northerners who would force the colleges to integrate ("Methodist Leaders Form Single Board to Handle Schools," *SML,* 16 December 1938, 4).

64. "Excerpts from the Laymen," *SML,* 29 July 1938, 2; untitled article, *SML,* 16 September 1938, 7; "Negroes and Crime," *SML,* 14 October 1938, 9; and Editorial, "Racial Problems," *SML,* 21 October 1938, 6.

65. "Report of South Carolina Meeting," *SML,* 5 August 1938, 3.

66. In 1948 the synod of Snedecor Memorial had 47 churches with only 2,410 members, slightly more than a third (958) in the presbytery of North and South Carolina. The Indian Presbytery had 13 churches with 534 members, while the Texas Mexican had 29 churches with 2,798 members. PCUS, *Minutes of the General Assembly,* 1948, 336.

67. William Childs Robinson, "Are the U.S.A. Liberals to Determine the Terms of Union?" *SPJ,* 15 March 1946, 5–6.

68. Some liberal southern Presbyterians also were troubled by developments in postwar race relations. In "The Real Issues, Part II," D. Maurice Allan commented, "In the deep South the feeling is intense on this issue. The conviction has been growing that the Negro is being encouraged to aspirations and demands that *we* [emphasis added] are not yet ready to grant. Many feel that the liberals in our church are hardly less guilty than Mrs. Roosevelt and the protagonists of the F.E.P.C. in fomenting Negro ambition and rushing this impressionable race headlong towards total equality. Many others who feel that we have not yet rendered Christian justice to the Negro are nevertheless honest in thinking that in this realm so full of hidden explosives we must hasten slowly" (*Presbyterian Outlook,* 1 March 1948, 5).

69. The argument was primarily on the basis of Acts 17:26, which says that God has set "the bounds of habitation for the nations." Also mentioned was Noah's curse on Canaan to explain the inferior status of blacks and God's commands to the Jews to maintain their racial separation. B. W. Crouch, "Dr. Palmer on Racial Barriers," *SPJ*, 2 December 1946, 5–6; W. A . Plecker, "'Interracial Brotherhood Movement,' Is It Scriptural?" *SPJ*, 1 January 1947, 9–10; J. David Simpson, "Non-Segregation Means Eventual Inter-Marriage," *SPJ*, 15 March 1948, 6–7; William H. Frazer, "The Social Separation of the Races," *SPJ*, 15 July 1950, 6–7; and J. E. Flow, editorial, "Is Segregation Unchristian?" *SPJ*, 29 August 1951, 4–5.

70. William Childs Robinson, "Christ Our Peace in Race Relations," *SPJ*, July, 1945, 7–8; J. E. Flow, "The Federal Council and 'Race Relations,'" *SPJ*, 15 May 1946, 9–10; and Plecker, "Interracial Brotherhood Movement," 9–10.

71. William Childs Robinson, editorial, "Distinguishing Things That Differ," *SPJ*, 15 January 1947, 3–4; and L. Nelson Bell, "Race Relations: Whither?" *SPJ*, 15 November 1947, 4–5. In 1950, Bell served on a committee to establish policies for meetings at Montreat, the Presbyterian campground in the North Carolina mountains. It recommended the integration of all adult meetings, including the General Assembly, but the continuation of segregated youth meetings. As an aside in this editorial, Bell suggested establishing the black synod as a separate Presbyterian denomination (Editorial, "Race Relations and Montreat," *SPJ*, 15 June 1950, 2–3).

72. William C. Robinson, editorial, "Georgia and the Slain Negroes," *SPJ*, 15 August 1946, 2–3; L. Nelson Bell, editorial, "Racial Tension, Let Us Decrease—Not Increase Them!" *SPJ*, 15 February 1947, 2–3; idem., editorial, "Some Little Things Which Help," *SPJ*, 2 June 1947, 3–4; idem., editorial, "Murder," *SPJ*, 16 June 1947, 2; Simpson, "Non-Segregation," 6; and W. G. Foster, Young People's Department, "The White Faction," *SPJ*, 1 July 1948, 14–15.

73. Crouch, "Dr. Palmer," 6; Bell, "Murder," 2; and Simpson, "Non-Segregation," 6. In "Real Issues," pp. 5–6, Allan noted that this kind of "holier-than-thou meddling in Southern affairs by Northern and Western politicians" had sparked a "rebirth of southern sectionalism" among conservative opponents to reunion.

74. Reimers, "The Race Problem," 208–9. During these years, the Oklahoma Synod reorganized and eliminated the separate Indian presbytery; and at the end of 1954, the Mexican-American presbytery was dissolved with its churches incorporated in Anglo presbyteries.

75. PCUS, *Minutes of the General Assembly,* 1954, 194; the entire report can be found on 187–97.

76. Ibid., 193.

77. L. Nelson Bell, "Montreat and Desegregation," *SPJ*, 15 September 1954, 3; "Segregation," *SPJ*, 7 July 1954, 7; William Childs Robinson, "Pluralism," *SPJ*, 7 July 1954, 6–7; "They Don't Want It," *SPJ*, 7 July 1954; 8; and J. S. Robinson, "Determining the Bounds of Their Habitation," *SPJ*, 6 October 1954.

78. L. Nelson Bell, "Christian Race Relations Must Be Natural, Not Forced," *SPJ*, 17 August 1955, 4–5. Bell offered only slim concessions that these ideas might create circumstances where African Americans might join white churches.

79. Robinson, "Determining the Bounds," 4.

80. Dornbusch and Irle, "Failure," 353; Reimers, "The Race Problem," 212–13; and Thompson, *Presbyterians*, 3:570–17 all note the thin commentary on race in anti-union propaganda.

81. Tuscaloosa Presbytery, *Minutes*, 20 July 1954, 465.

82. F. A. Mathes, "Church Union," church bulletin, South Highland Presbyterian Church, 12 September 1954, in Robert McFeran Crowe Papers, Department of History, Presbyterian Church (USA), Montreat, North Carolina.

83. "Disturbing," *SPJ*, 10 March 1954, 1.

84. J. E. Flow, "Positive or Negative?" *SPJ*, 29 September 1954, 9.

85. Allan, "Real Issues," 6.

PART V

Along the Color Line

The four essays in this section explore ways in which the legal walls of racial separation were built and eventually disassembled during the age of Jim Crow. Collectively, they remind us that the interaction between black and white Southerners has always been as complex as it has been volatile and central to any attempt to understand the region.

In "*State v. William Darnell:* The Battle over De Jure Housing Segregation in Progressive Era Winson-Salem," Michael E. Daly and his coauthors examine the events surrounding the adoption of a municipal ordinance mandating racially segregated housing in Winston-Salem, North Carolina, in 1912. The next year, a black man, William Darnell, bought a house in a predominately white neighborhood and was prosecuted for the offense. In the litigation that followed, Darnell's advocates included a group of white property owners who wanted unfettered right to sell, two aristocratic Democratic attorneys who felt a paternalistic obligation to defend his rights, and the "Progressive" chief justice of the North Carolina Supreme Court who ultimately nullified the ordinance as an "unauthorized" municipal violation of the sole right of the state government to legislate on such matters. This unorthodox alliance across racial and class lines and the invocation of "the language of states' rights to nullify a white supremacy measure," the authors suggest, ought not only to challenge preconceptions but also encourage new looks into how the main forces in Southern life could shift according to local circumstances to produce unexpected outcomes.

The relatively moderate course that North Carolina charted in race relations continued into the 1950s and is the subject of Peter Wallenstein's "Higher Education and the Civil Rights Movement: Desegregating the University of North Carolina." While tracing the convoluted route through which the first African Americans were admitted to North Carolina's three state universities, Wallenstein makes it clear that it was the students themselves who were the prime movers in gaining admission. Afterward, as the handful of black pioneers who first performed with whites in marching bands, intercollegiate athletic teams, and other extracurricular activities, they established beachheads that "left a legacy from which others benefited" and "blazed a trail that others followed."

The trail, however, had been and continued to be more difficult to follow in the region's military colleges. In "Training for Partial Citizenship: Black

Military Schools in the Age of Jim Crow," Rod Andrew Jr. surveys racial trends in this little-studied aspect of Southern education. A rich military tradition, the Confederate experience, and the terms of the Morrill Act combined to launch "a wave of military education" across the South during the late nineteenth century, and with it, a strong tendency among white Southerners to believe that civic virtues such as courage, integrity, self-discipline, and moral rectitude were best cultivated in a martial environment. Many African American leaders shared that belief and tried to implement it in the region's all-black colleges as a means to accelerate their people's rise from slavery. Governing white officials acquiesced in formal regimentation designed to improve personal conduct but, Andrew demonstrates, drew the line at authorizing drill with rifles or preparing blacks for any sort of military career. "White Southerners," the author explains, "understood that an unhindered black military tradition implied full citizenship for blacks and thus . . . the end of white supremacy."

The persistence of that belief made the desegregation of South Carolina's state-supported military college a particularly noteworthy event and is the subject of Alexander S. Macaulay Jr.'s "Black, White, and Gray: The Desegregation of The Citadel, 1963–1973." It was 1966 before The Citadel admitted its first black cadet, Charles Foster, and over the next seven years the total number of black undergraduates rose to only one percent of the Corps of Cadets. Those African American pioneers, Macaulay discovers, encountered a paradox. On the one hand, the military environment and the rigors of cadet life increased the threat (and the reality) of physical and psychological abuse. But on the other, those same conditions forced black and white cadets into closer contact than at most colleges and thus, in many cases, more rapidly eroded racial barriers and prompted quicker reevaluation of racial attitudes that had been founded on stereotype and unfamiliarity. Meanwhile, Citadel faculty and administrators "plodded forward, doing the minimum" to comply with federal guidelines, diminish racial tensions, and address legitimate black concerns—including the playing of "Dixie" and the display of the Confederate flag. "A handful of Citadel cadets, both black and white," the author argues, "were the driving force behind the school's desegregation as they strove to overcome a recalcitrant and often hostile administration in an attempt to change their alma mater" and, in a small way, their region, for the better.

12

State v. William Darnell

The Battle over De Jure Housing Segregation in Progressive Era Winston-Salem

MICHAEL E. DALY AND JOHN WERTHEIMER with the assistance of
R. Stanley Baker, John Bell, Wilson Buntin, Scott Herr,
Andrew Holbrook, Sarah House, J. Matthew Strader

At the corner of Eleventh Street and Highland Avenue in Winston-Salem, North Carolina, a swing set now stands sentinel over land that was once the center of an important legal controversy. In 1913, a tobacco worker named William Darnell attempted to move into a house on this site. For this act, and this act alone, he was arrested. A 1912 city ordinance forbade people from moving onto blocks where they would be in the racial minority. The other residents of Highland Avenue's east side between Eleventh Street and Twelfth Street were white; William Darnell was black. Darnell's arrest initiated a chain of legal events that, given the time and place, had a surprising result: the North Carolina Supreme Court overturned his conviction and invalidated the segregation ordinance.

Other than the case that bears his name, William Darnell left but a scant paper trail. He was born in 1859 in Guilford County (not far from Winston-Salem), making him in all likelihood a slave at birth. As a middle-aged man, he moved to Winston-Salem to take up tobacco work. He died of stomach problems in his ninetieth year and was buried in an unmarked grave in Winston-Salem's Evergreen Cemetery. We know little else about him.[1]

Darnell's lawsuit has generally been relegated to footnote status in historical writing. It deserves better. That a Progressive Era Southern court invalidated a Jim Crow measure in itself justifies greater attention. In addition, the case opens the curtains onto a fascinating New South drama played by an unlikely cast against a backdrop of social change, political conflict, and racial tension.

Because *State v. Darnell* resulted in a rare defeat for de jure segregation, it raises an important historical question: What prevented Jim Crow's "strange career"[2] from advancing even further than it did? Some scholars have credited "the powerful American commitment to economic *laissez-faire*" with setting outer limits on legalized racial segregation, especially when private property was at issue, as it was in *Darnell* and other cases involving residential segregation ordinances.[3] Other scholars, mindful of the NAACP's dramatic victory in *Brown v. Board of Education,* have emphasized the important role played by African Americans in resisting—and ultimately reversing—the segregationist tide.[4] In this light, *State v. Darnell* has been portrayed as a case in which the city's African American community "challenged Winston-Salem's housing segregation ordinance and won."[5]

Both the "laissez-faire ideology" model and the "African American resistance" model have merit. Neither approach, however, accurately describes *State v. Darnell.* Although William Darnell, an African American, clearly played a role in his lawsuit, he was but one member of a diverse ensemble. A small-time white realtor and two prominent, elderly, paternalistic lawyers also played crucial (and heretofore unappreciated) roles. So too did a judge who, far from being a conservative proponent of laissez-faire, advocated greater governmental activism and marched in the progressive vanguard of his day.[6] In *State v. Darnell,* the efforts of this varied group combined to set an outer limit to Jim Crow's distressing reach.

JIM CROW IN THE PIEDMONT

In 1910, Baltimore, Maryland, became the nation's first city to adopt a residential segregation ordinance. Two years later, Winston-Salem followed suit.[7] Winston-Salem was then a booming New South city—North Carolina's largest and fastest growing.[8] Its rise reflected the growth of its tobacco industry.

By no mere happenstance did North Carolina's first residential segregation ordinance appear in a tobacco town. Like textiles—the region's other major industrial employer—tobacco work attracted thousands of rural migrants. But unlike textile mills, which tended to have their own villages and employ mostly whites, Winston-Salem's tobacco factories clustered downtown and employed mostly African Americans.[9] R. J. Reynolds, Winston-Salem's leading tobacco mogul, was particularly dependent on black labor. Reynolds sent special trains to South Carolina and eastern North Carolina to recruit African American workers.[10] The new arrivals settled primarily in East Winston, near the tobacco factories that clustered around the railway lines on that side of town.[11] It was in East Winston that pressure for a residential segregation ordinance would build.

The push toward de jure housing segregation had three sources. First, Winston-Salem's breakneck growth created an extremely volatile real estate market.[12] Concerned whites initially sought racial stability through "restrictive covenants"—clauses written into property deeds prohibiting buyers from selling or renting to African Americans for specified periods of time, usually five or ten years.[13] By around 1910, however, these private contractual devices had clearly failed to prevent the movement of African Americans into neighborhoods where whites did not want them. Disgruntled whites searched for stronger alternatives.

Second, the general impulse to segregate was on the rise. Although Jim Crow came relatively late to the Tarheel State—railroad segregation and African American disenfranchisement, for instance, both arrived around 1900, a decade after their implementation in Mississippi—segregation soon swept through North Carolina's public and private life.[14] In Winston-Salem, separate annual fairs appeared, as did separate YMCAs, separate Women's Civic Leagues, separate insurance firms, and separate hospitals, to name but a few examples.[15] Separation of residential neighborhoods—by government decree, if necessary—might well have seemed a logical next step.

Third, Winston-Salem's city government, in step with "Progressive Era" trends elsewhere, grew more active by the year. At the time of the debate over residential segregation, the city was busily building regulatory muscle. It adopted a new traffic ordinance; it imposed speed limits; it hired a milk and meat inspector.[16] In 1912, a supportive local editor effectively captured the Progressive spirit that underlay such initiatives: "The citizens of Winston . . . now have an opportunity of taking a long step forward that will put their city in the forefront of Progressive cities of the South. . . . If we fail to provide for municipal improvements . . . to make life pleasant and living convenient . . . it cannot but mean that our growth will be stopped."[17]

In 1912, the racially volatile housing market, the general urge to segregate, and the Progressive trend toward governmental solutions to perceived social problems converged in a proposal for a residential segregation ordinance. The initial push came from white residents living on or around East Fourth Street, a major east-west corridor onto which some African Americans had recently moved.[18] Fourth Street ran from the overwhelmingly white residential districts on the west side of town, through the city center, to a "stable white residential area" in the east.[19] In between these two white residential areas, and just to the east of downtown, was a low-lying, north-south strip of soggy creek-beds and noisy rail lines, where African Americans traditionally lived. The influx of tobacco workers swelled this African American strip in an arc to the northeast and southeast. By 1912, African American residences surrounded white East Winston on three sides (the remaining side was the city's uninhabited eastern edge).

Increasingly cut off from whites elsewhere in the city and threatened by what they saw as black encroachment, East Fourth Street whites grew desperate enough to petition the Board of Aldermen for relief. The Board convened a special session on June 13, 1912. More than two hundred citizens packed the meeting to express their concerns. Not a single African American was among them.[20]

The petitioners' arguments revealed their anxieties. Some criticized realtors for "robbing the white people" of East Winston by "selling them land at exorbitant prices, all the time holding over [them] the threat that they will sell it to the negroes." Others complained about East Fourth Street whites who breached their restrictive covenants by selling to African Americans. Still others contended, more progressively, that a segregation ordinance would reduce "friction of the races."[21]

The Board of Aldermen responded on July 1, 1912, by passing a residential segregation ordinance.[22] Henceforth, it would be illegal in Winston for any black to occupy a residence on a majority-white block and for any white to occupy a residence on a majority-black block. Violators faced up to fifty dollars in fines and thirty days in prison for each offence, with each day in violation constituting a separate offense.[23]

The African American response appears to have been subdued.[24] After the Fourth Street ordinance's adoption, a local white newspaper reported that "there was no opposition . . . and it is understood that many of the better class of colored people look with favor upon the ordinance."[25] While it is reasonable to be skeptical of the white press during this era,[26] this particular assertion may not have been groundless. The city's most prominent black leader, Simon G. Atkins—president of the all-black Slater Industrial Academy (today's Winston-Salem State University) and founder of Columbia Heights, a fashionable all-black Winston suburb—did endorse voluntary segregation.[27] To Atkins and others who shared his perspective, legally mandated segregation, while surely not a preferred policy, was apparently not intolerable. Other African Americans objected more strongly to the ordinance but appear to have held their tongues at the time of its enactment.[28]

The ordinance had a relatively uneventful first year.[29] In the spring of 1913, however, some whites began to grumble about lax enforcement. One of the incidents that prompted this concern involved an African American grocer, George W. Penn, who sought a building permit for a lot on a majority-white stretch of Twelfth Street in East Winston. The lot was between North Liberty and Highland—about a block from Darnell's lot. Board of Aldermen secretary William Holcolmb, under pressure from white Twelfth Street residents, refused Penn's request, citing the ordinance. Penn secured the services of a prominent white attorney and appealed. His lawyer admitted that the particular block in question was mostly white but noted that the surrounding area was predominantly black. The Board agreed to a compromise: Penn could build on the lot, but he could not move in. He would have to sell or rent to a white.[30]

Although this result does not seem like much of a victory for Penn, segregationists viewed it as a setback for their side. They urged stiffer enforcement of the ordinance. In response, city leaders affirmed their support for segregation and warned transgressors that the police would soon act against them.[31] Indeed, the police soon acted. On June 13, 1913, they made their first arrest—of William Darnell.

THE *DARNELL* CASE

In 1906, forty-seven-year-old William Darnell came to East Winston to work, like most black men in town, in a tobacco factory.[32] At first, he and his wife Lillie lived in Southeast Winston, in an inexpensive Johnson Avenue home that was too often irrigated by nearby creeks and rattled by nearby railroad yards. By 1913 the Darnells had saved enough money to move to a more expensive home. They sold their Johnson Avenue house for $450 and presumably looked forward to a more comfortable life in a Northeast Winston home on Highland Avenue worth more than twice that amount.[33]

Northeast Winston was a neighborhood in flux. Above Seventh Street, it was predominantly black.[34] Highland Avenue, however, was something of an anomaly. It retained a substantial white presence well north of Seventh. Prior to the Darnells' arrival, the east side of Highland between Eleventh and Twelfth was exclusively white.

The Darnells purchased "lot 169" on Highland Avenue from a white man named Francis M. Sledge.[35] Sledge was a small-time real estate broker who rented and sold properties in all parts of the city to customers white and black.[36] Sledge's actions in the Darnell case betray a strong dislike for the housing ordinance, perhaps because it reduced the market for any given property by at least 40 percent (Winston-Salem being about 40 percent African American).

After buying lot 169 just one month earlier, Sledge took three steps to defy and defeat the ordinance. First, he approached the block's other property owners, all of whom were white, with a striking proposal—call it an "*un-restrictive covenant.*" "We, the undersigned citizens owning property on the East side of Highland Avenue between Eleventh and Twelfth streets," the document read, "do hereby agree to sell our property to colored people." Only one inhabitant of the all-white block failed to sign.[37]

Second, Sledge moved quickly to flout city law by selling lot 169 to William Darnell, an African American. By June 10, 1913, just five days after Sledge signed his covenant, Darnell had purchased the property and had been arrested. A municipal court judge found that Darnell had violated the ordinance and fined him five dollars plus court costs. Darnell announced his intent to appeal to the Superior Court.[38]

Third, pending the Superior Court retrial, Sledge paid Darnell's twenty-five dollar bail bond. He then appeared in court with Darnell in August, November, and December of 1913 to confirm that Darnell would be present for his Superior Court retrial.[39] Sledge's continued involvement with Darnell after "flipping" the property to him reinforces the suspicion that this was a test case engineered to challenge the segregation ordinance.

At the time of Darnell's search for legal counsel, according to the 1913 Winston-Salem Directory, Winston-Salem had three practicing African American attorneys. None of them worked on Darnell's case. We do not know why. In this racist era, however, even the city's leading black attorney, John Fitts, made it a point to appear in Superior Court only as the associate of a white lawyer, to avoid damaging his clients' fortunes with potentially racist jurors and judges.[40] Prudence suggested the use of white counsel.

Even so, the firm that represented Darnell—Watson, Buxton, and Watson —catches the eye. It was "one of the very strongest in the state."[41] Cyrus B. Watson was one of Winston-Salem's most distinguished citizens. After fighting for the Confederate Army, Watson served terms in both houses of the North Carolina legislature. He was the Democratic nominee for governor in

1896.[42] In court, he had few peers. Some considered him the greatest criminal lawyer in his state's history. When Watson died in 1916, the chief justice of the North Carolina Supreme Court would proclaim him "the uncrowned king of the North Carolina bar."[43]

Watson's law partner, John C. Buxton, also had an impressive résumé. He had served as mayor of Winston. He had been a state senator. For twenty-six years, he chaired the city's school board. Like Watson, Buxton had a "splendid" courtroom reputation.[44]

What motivated these two prominent Democrats to represent a black tobacco worker in a petty criminal appeal? Paternalism may have played a part. Watson and Buxton represented a class of elderly, elite Southern whites whose sense of noblesse oblige drove them to seek at least some justice for African Americans. Both lawyers were in their sixties, members of a pre–Civil War generation of whites that was less captivated by Jim Crow than younger generations were.[45] Both lawyers were privileged enough to be immune to status anxiety; both lived in Winston's West End, far from tobacco factories and their workers. Both had histories of paternalistic concern. In 1893, Watson drafted and fought for an anti-lynching bill in the state legislature.[46] Buxton, for his part, frequently provided legal services to African Americans, especially those charged with crimes. (It was he who represented George W. Penn, the black grocer who sought permission to build on a street with a white majority in May 1913.)[47]

The two lawyers may also have had financial incentives to oppose the Winston ordinance. Both had longstanding real estate interests in the city.[48] They often served as "trustees" on deeds securing mortgage loans.[49] It was they, in fact, who secured the loan that Sledge took out on lot 169 prior to selling it to Darnell. The mortgage itself came from the Winston-Salem Building and Loan Association, whose president was none other than J. C. Buxton.[50]

The opposing counsel was Winston-Salem solicitor Gilbert T. Stephenson. He was of a different generation—just twenty-nine at the time of the trial. Besides being a respected lawyer, Stephenson was "perhaps the country's foremost" scholar of racial segregation law.[51] In an important 1910 treatise, Stephenson separated race *distinctions* ("separate but equal" measures) from race *discriminations* (measures affording blacks inferior legal treatment). "The welfare of both races," he argued, "requires the recognition of race distinctions and the obliteration of race discriminations."[52] Stephenson considered Winston's "separate but equal" housing ordinance to be a legitimate race "distinction."[53]

In the Superior Court retrial of *State v. Darnell,* in January 1914,[54] Stephenson's case for the prosecution was straightforward. He offered testimony from a white man named V. E. Barnes, who lived just around the corner from lot 169. Prior to Darnell's arrest, he had petitioned the Board of Aldermen for stiffer enforcement of the segregation ordinance. Barnes testified that there were "four white families and no colored ones living there at the time Darnell bought." J. D. Welch, the man who sold lot 169 to Sledge in May 1913, confirmed the existence of a white majority on the block in question.[55] The state rested.

Watson and Buxton were more creative. (They had to be—the facts and the law were both against them.) First, they raised the sorts of technical objections to the ordinance that lawyers routinely raise and judges routinely reject.[56]

Second, they argued that the ordinance was unconstitutional because it "deprive[d] the defendant of his property without the due process of law."[57]

Third, they sought to demonstrate that African Americans dominated surrounding blocks, albeit not Darnell's immediate block, at the time of the purchase. The state objected to all defense questions regarding the racial composition of surrounding blocks. The court sustained the state's objections.

Fourth, they offered testimony from F. M. Sledge. Sledge sought to introduce the "unrestrictive covenant" whereby he and the block's other white property owners had agreed to sell to African Americans. The judge ruled this evidence inadmissible.

After deliberating for thirty minutes, the jury returned a verdict of guilty.[58] Perhaps hoping to discourage an appeal, the court lowered Darnell's fine from five dollars to one dollar and costs. Nonetheless, Watson and Buxton promptly announced their intent to appeal to the state Supreme Court. Pending that appeal, Sledge again posted Darnell's bond, this time for forty dollars.

The local press loudly applauded the verdict.[59] The *Winston-Salem Journal* wrote that the *Darnell* jurors, like most jurors, had "decide[d] things right, because they are on the ground." The editors worried, however, that the North Carolina Supreme Court might use Darnell's appeal to strike down the ordinance. They warned Darnell: "The best thing this colored citizen can do is to abide by the law of the city without getting the Supreme Court mixed up in the affair at all."[60]

But Darnell and his backers would not drop their appeal. Nor would the social forces that underlay the dispute await the case's resolution. As the lawyers prepared their Supreme Court briefs, two additional African Americans—

Dr. Edward Smith and George Crews—were arrested under the segregation ordinance.[61] Strikingly, both cases arose in the 1100 block of Highland Avenue—Darnell's block. Dr. Smith's new house was one lot to the south of Darnell's; Crews' new house was two lots to the north. The vendors of both properties were signatories of Sledge's "unrestrictive covenant."[62]

THE SUPREME COURT DECISION

In April 1914, *State v. Darnell*—a case "awaited with interest from every section of the state"[63]—came up for oral argument. The Supreme Court pressed Solicitor Stephenson about Winston's authority to adopt the ordinance. Stephenson pointed to the "general welfare" clause in the city's charter and insisted that the ordinance provided for the welfare of blacks as well as whites: "Wherever there is indiscriminate residence there is irritation, constant irritation, and it always works hardship upon the negro. He gets the worst of every clash. It [the ordinance] will be a protector to him. It will help the weaker race."[64]

The author of the North Carolina Supreme Court's unanimous ruling in *State v. Darnell*, Chief Justice Walter Clark, was no civil rights crusader. He grew up on a large Virginia plantation with many slaves. After the Civil War, in which he fought for the Confederacy, he advocated *white* labor for the South on the grounds that freedmen could not "live among us in the present state of things."[65] Later, Clark employed the language of white supremacy in championing women's suffrage. North Carolina's fifty thousand white women, he noted enthusiastically, outnumbered—and thus could outvote—the state's black women and black men, combined.[66]

Clark's long judicial record—he served from 1889 until his death in 1924—offered the Darnell camp additional cause for pessimism. Clark was a Progressive judge.[67] In classic Progressive fashion, he favored measures—an *elected* federal judiciary, the direct election of U.S. senators—that would amplify the popular voice in government. He also favored measures—labor laws, railroad regulation—that would enhance the role of government in society.[68] These views underlay his outspoken opposition to judicial review, the practice whereby judges nullified legislation on constitutional grounds. "If a legislature should not observe the Constitution," he argued, "the supervision lies with the people in electing another legislature."[69] Clark's respect for the popular will, his preference for active government, and his hostility to judicial review did not bode well for Darnell and his lawyers, who challenged the constitutionality of a popularly enacted governmental regulation.

At the same time, however, Chief Justice Clark was an elite and elderly (upper sixties) paternalist. Like Darnell's attorney, C. B. Watson, who happened to be one of Clark's "closest friends,"[70] Clark saw himself as a benevolent guardian of African Americans.[71] During the Civil War, when Clark's slave Neverson sought to accompany his master to the front, Clark reputedly insisted that he stay back, out of danger. Throughout Clark's thirty-five years on the state bench, a former slave named Alston attended him daily at work and at home.[72] Given this background of close (though clearly hierarchical) relationships with African Americans, Clark may have believed that residential segregation was undesirable and unwarranted. In short, while Clark's Progressivism inclined him to the state's arguments, his paternalism favored Darnell's.

Clark resolved this dilemma by distinguishing between acts of the state legislature and acts of a *city* government. This distinction enabled him to side with Darnell and strike down the segregation ordinance without violating his long-stated opposition to judicial review. Bypassing the constitutional claims upon which Darnell's lawyers principally relied, Clark held the Winston-Salem measure *unauthorized*, not unconstitutional. The city's charter simply did not empower its Board of Aldermen to pass the ordinance in question, he ruled. Admittedly, the charter authorized Winston to provide for the "general welfare" of its inhabitants. But to uphold the ordinance under this provision, he ruled, "would give the words 'general welfare' an extended and wholly unrestricted scope," far beyond the state legislature's intent.[73]

Clark presented his nullification of the ordinance as a defense of state legislative prerogatives. In so doing, he put an intriguing twist on two bedrock concepts of Southern history: states' rights and white supremacy. From slavery through civil rights, white Southerners steadily beat the drum of "states' rights" against federal "intrusion."[74] In *Darnell*, however, the North Carolina Supreme Court invoked the language of states' rights to *nullify* a white supremacy measure, not to defend it. By enacting a residential segregation ordinance, Clark ruled, Winston had encroached on the policy-making prerogative of the North Carolina state legislature. The city had threatened states' rights, as it were, from below.

Clark bolstered his unorthodox "states' rights" argument by citing North Carolina legislation concerning out-of-state "labor agents." In the late nineteenth century, Northern labor agents had traveled south to recruit cheap black labor. Fearing an exodus of black agricultural workers—and a threat to the local racial caste system—North Carolina had adopted statutes requiring labor agents to pay steep licensing fees. By enacting these measures, Clark noted, the state had made clear its interest in preventing black workers from leaving the state. Clark then invoked some European history. "In Ireland there were years ago limits prescribed beyond which the native Irish or Celtic population could not reside," he wrote. One of the results of this unhappy "Irish Pale" policy was the departure of more than half of the Irish population. Similarly, in Russia "to this day, there are certain districts to which the Jews are restricted, with the result that vast numbers of them are emigrating." Reasoning that Winston's ordinance would have similar demographic effects—that is, it would encourage productive African American workers to leave the state—Clark concluded that the Winston measure was contrary to the state's legislative will as expressed in the "labor agent" laws.[75] Based on this reasoning, Clark nullified the ordinance and overturned Darnell's conviction.

The Winston-Salem *Journal* received Clark's "anxiously awaited" decision with immense disappointment.[76] "We lament, of course, along with most of the best citizens of this city, that the court could not . . . uphold the Winston-Salem segregation ordinance," the paper editorialized. "There is no doubt in our minds but that segregation of the races in the cities is the best policy. In fact, we believe that experience will prove that it is the only way to maintain peace in the community." The editors noted happily, however, that segregation was proceeding steadily throughout the region "without a law requiring it."[77]

The reaction was scarcely more positive in the nation's law reviews. The *University of Pennsylvania Law Review* objected to Clark's "time worn sophistry" about segregation's dangers and criticized him for ignoring *Plessy v. Ferguson.* Similar complaints about Clark's "rather obscurely reasoned opinion" appeared in the *Virginia Law Review.*[78]

In contrast, the National Association for the Advancement of Colored People (NAACP) applauded *Darnell* and printed "gratifying comment" on the decision from select Northern newspapers.[79]

SIGNIFICANCE OF *DARNELL*

State v. Darnell probably prevented other North Carolina cities from adopting residential segregation ordinances. It may also have discouraged the state legislature from adopting a like measure on a statewide basis, although nothing in the ruling expressly barred statewide legislative action.

Darnell did not, however, end housing segregation in Winston-Salem. Indeed, because the ordinance had sought to freeze residential patterns as of

1912, a relatively *integrated* year by twentieth-century standards, Chief Justice Clark's decision had the practical effect of clearing the way for greater housing *segregation*.[80] In subsequent years, blacks flowed into East Winston, and whites flowed out.[81] By 1960, East Winston was 84 percent African American. By 1970, Winston-Salem was the second most segregated city in the United States.[82]

≫

At first blush, it is tempting to view *State v. Darnell* as a straightforward African American triumph, a case in which Winston-Salem blacks "directly initiated reform."[83] Deeper investigation forces a different conclusion. In *Darnell,* we submit, three groups crossed racial and class lines to oppose Jim Crow: (1) black property owners, both professionals (Dr. Smith) and workers (Darnell), who sought the right to live where they chose; (2) small businessmen, both black (Penn) and white (Sledge), who had at least one eye on the bottom line; and (3) elite, elderly whites (Watson, Buxton, Clark), who mixed paternalistic and economic motivations. In the courts, if not on the streets, their combined efforts prevailed over the nervous white homeowners and "Progressive" city leaders who favored de jure housing segregation.

State v. Darnell challenges preconceptions. Here, a Southern court during Jim Crow's heyday voided a segregation measure. A "Progressive" judge, an outspoken champion of majority rule and active government, nullified a popularly enacted social regulation. The language of states' rights, forged in racist state capitals as a shield against federal attack, was recast as a sword for attacking a racist local measure. Former slave-owners and former slaves collaborated on the segregation ordinance's demise. The perverse result of their triumph, however, was increased, not decreased, segregation.

There was one final result. Following his Supreme Court victory, William Darnell moved back into his house at 1105 Highland Avenue. This time, he was not arrested.

NOTES

The authors acknowledge the generous support of an Abernethy Research Grant from Davidson College. They also thank the following good people: David Bernstein, Carolyn and Edward Daly, Bobby Donaldson, Ann Douglass, Earl Edmondson, the Forsyth County Public Library staff, Beverly Gabard, Pam Grundy and Peter Wong, Joe Gutekanst, Brian Luskey, Sally McMillen, James Miller, Gregory

Mixon, Langdon Oppermann, Malcolm Partin, Patricia Perkins, Janet Shannon, and Loretta and Richard Wertheimer.

1. Even Darnell's last name remains something of a mystery. During the law case, legal papers and press accounts consistently referred to him as "Darnell." His death certificate, however, calls him "Donnell." Winston-Salem's annual directories list him variously as "Darnell," "Donnell," "Donald," and "Daniel." (In each case, consistency of wife's name—Lillie—street address, and occupation assure that the same person is being described.) See "William H. Donnell," Certificate of Death, no. 34–95/285, North Carolina State Board of Health, Bureau of Vital Statistics, Office of the Register of Deeds of Forsyth County, N.C.; and Winston-Salem City Directories, Forsyth County Public Library.

2. C. Vann Woodward, *The Strange Career of Jim Crow*, 3d rev. ed. (New York: Oxford University Press, 1974).

3. Quotation from George Fredrickson, *White Supremacy: A Comparative Study in American and South African History* (New York: Oxford, 1981), 236, 254. See also David E. Bernstein, "Philip Sober Controlling Philip Drunk: *Buchanan v. Warley* in Historical Perspective," *Vanderbilt Law Review* 51 (May 1998): 802–20, 873; and Alan F. Westin, "John Marshall Harlan and the Constitutional Rights of Negroes: The Transformation of a Southerner," *Yale Law Review* 66 (April 1957): 695–96.

4. One scholar has attributed "nearly every major [pre-*Brown*] courtroom triumph" over Jim Crow to the efforts of African American civil-rights crusaders. Richard Bardolph, ed., *The Civil Rights Record: Black Americans and the Law, 1849–1970* (New York: Thomas A. Cromwell, 1970), 168. Although C. Vann Woodward's *The Strange Career of Jim Crow* acknowledges that the mix of forces that ultimately turned the tide against Jim Crow was "bewilderingly complex," it places prominent emphasis on the role played by "the Negro himself" (124). See also Catherine A. Barnes, *Journey from Jim Crow: The Desegregation of Southern Transit* (New York: Columbia University Press, 1983) 11; John Hope Franklin and Alfred A. Moss Jr., *From Slavery to Freedom: A History of African Americans,* 7th ed. (1947; New York: McGraw-Hill, 1994), 352, 461; Gunnar Myrdal, *An American Dilemma: The Negro Problem and Modern Democracy,* 2 vols. (New York: Harper Brothers, 1944), 2:1005.

5. Bertha Hampton Miller, "Blacks in Winston-Salem, North Carolina: Community Development in an Era of Benevolent Paternalism" (Ph.D. diss., Duke University, 1981), 147.

6. C. Vann Woodward, *Origins of the New South, 1877–1913* (Baton Rouge: Louisiana State University Press, 1971), 469.

7. Winston and Salem merged in 1913, one year after Winston passed the segregation ordinance. Towns in Virginia, Kentucky, South Carolina, Georgia, Oklahoma, Missouri, and Louisiana also passed residential segregation ordinances. See Gilbert T. Stephenson, "The Segregation of White and Negro Races in Cities," *South Atlantic Quarterly* 8 (January 1914): 1–8; Garrett Power, "Apartheid Baltimore Style: The Residential Segregation Ordinances of 1910–1913," *Maryland Law Review* 42 (1983): 289; Bernstein, "Philip Sober Controlling Philip Drunk," 835–36; Roger L. Rice, "Residential Segregation by Law, 1910–1917," *Journal of Southern History* 34 (May 1968): 179–99; A. Leon Higginbotham Jr., F. Michael Higginbotham, and S. Sandile Ngcobo, "De Jure Housing Segregation in the United States and South Africa: The Difficult Pursuit for Racial Justice," *University of Illinois Law Review* 1990 (1990): 763–877.

8. See Mary Plegar Smith, "Municipal Development in North Carolina, 1665–1930: A History of Urbanization" (Ph.D. diss., University of North Carolina–Chapel Hill, 1930); National Urban League, *A Study of the Economic and Cultural Activities of the Negro People of Winston-Salem (and Forsyth County), North Carolina*, Book One, 10; Davyd Foard Hood, "Winston-Salem's Suburbs: West End to Reynolda Park," in *Early Twentieth-Century Suburbs in North Carolina*, ed. Catherine W. Bishir and Lawrence S. Earley (Raleigh: Division of Archives and History, 1985), 64.

9. Nannie M. Tilley, *The R. J. Reynolds Tobacco Company* (Chapel Hill: University of North Carolina Press, 1985), 38; Miller, "Blacks in Winston-Salem," 9, 78. Thanks to Pamela Grundy on this point.

10. Langdon E. Oppermann, "Historic and Architectural Resources of African-American Neighborhoods in Northeastern Winston-Salem, North Carolina (ca. 1900–1947)," Multiple Property Documentation Form, National Register of Historic Places, Forsyth County Joint Historic Properties Commission [no date], E8.

11. In 1880, over 75 percent of the city's African American population lived within a 21-square-block area in which a majority of Winston-Salem tobacco factories were located. Michael Shirley, *From Congregation Town to Industrial City: Culture and Change in a Southern Community* (New York: New York University Press, 1994), 202. The area was bounded by Main, Seventh, Depot, and Bellews Creek. See also Alan Willis, "Blacks in Winston—A History Emerging from Obscurity," *Winston-Salem, Sentinel,* 10 February 1983, A13; Oppermann, "Historic and Architectural Resources," E9–E12 and E27–E30; and Langdon E. Oppermann, "Winston-Salem's African American Neighborhoods: 1870–1950," Architectural and Planning Report, 1994, Forsyth County Joint Historic Properties Commission, 43–44.

12. In 1890, the city had only three real estate agents; by 1910, it had twenty-four. Similar booms occurred in contractors and building and loan associations.

Winston-Salem Directories, 1890 and 1910, North Carolina Room, Forsyth County Public Library, Winston-Salem.

13. Restrictive covenants appeared in Winston-Salem deeds at least as early as 1890. For a representative sampling of such covenants, see Deed Book 35, pp. 281 and 395; and Deed Book 38, pp. 46, 83, and 325, Register of Deeds, Winston-Salem. On restrictive covenants generally, see Herman H. Long and Charles S. Johnson, *People vs. Property: Restrictive Covenants in Housing* (Nashville, Tenn.: Fisk University Press, 1947); and Thomas W. Hanchett, *Sorting Out the New South City: Race, Class, and Urban Development in Charlotte, 1875–1975* (Chapel Hill: University of North Carolina Press, 1998), 116.

14. See Glenda Elizabeth Gilmore, *Gender and Jim Crow: Women and the Politics of White Supremacy in North Carolina, 1896–1920* (Chapel Hill: University of North Carolina Press, 1996); Woodward, *Origins of the New South;* David S. Cecelski, *Along Freedom Road* (Chapel Hill: University of North Carolina Press, 1994). Jim Crow would linger at least through the early 1960s.

15. "Colored Fair to Be Held at Rural Hall," *Winston-Salem Twin-City Daily Sentinel,* 29 August 1912, 2; "Erection of a Colored Y.M.C.A. Building Proposed," *Twin-City Daily Sentinel,* 22 March 1913, 4; "Colored Women's Civic League Organized Here," *Twin-City Daily Sentinel,* 8 March 1913, 7; for marriage notices, see *Twin-City Daily Sentinel,* circa October 1912; for hospitals, see Miller, "Blacks in Winston-Salem," 139–141.

16. Newspapers from this period are saturated with reports of these reforms. A good example is the *Winston-Salem Journal,* 16 July 1912, which has front-page articles on the traffic ordinance, public parks, and milk and meat inspection. See also *Twin-City Daily Sentinel,* 31 July 1912, 5.

17. "Winston Faces a Crisis," *Journal,* 17 July 1912, 4.

18. By 1911, C. H. Jones, the African American president of the Forsyth Savings and Trust Company, had moved onto East Fourth Street; a handful of other African Americans would soon join him there (Winston-Salem Directories, 1911–1913).

19. Oppermann, "Historic and Architectural Resources," E11.

20. "Segregate Negroes in East Winston," *Journal,* 14 June 1912, 1. See also "Race Segregation Ordinance Is Enacted by Aldermen," *Twin-City Daily Sentinel,* 14 June 1912, 5; "Race Segregation," *Winston-Salem Union Republican,* 20 June 1912, 6.

21. "Segregate Negroes in East Winston," *Journal,* 14 June 1912, 1. On the very day that petitioners appealed to the Board of Aldermen, a white plaintiff initiated a suit to recover an East Fourth Street house that had been sold to an African American in breach of the restrictive covenant in the original deed. If this plaintiff won, others were expected to follow, causing "scores of lots in this section [to] change hands" ("Movement to Oust Negroes," *Journal,* 14 June 1912, 1).

22. The July 1 ordinance replaced a short-lived June 13 ordinance. The earlier measure, which was narrowly tailored to meet the East Fourth Street neighborhood's concerns, prohibited "any colored person to own or occupy any dwelling fronting on East Fourth Street, between Depot Street [near downtown] and the city limits on the east." The measure also banned white people from residing on specified sections of Third and Depot streets—sections already wholly settled by African Americans. This earlier ordinance called for separate and *un*equal treatment of whites and blacks. It forbade African Americans from *owning or occupying* certain residences, but forbade whites only from *occupying* specified residences. This distinction benefited white landlords by allowing them to maintain houses in "colored" sections as long as they rented to "colored" tenants. In the age of "separate but equal," however, this disparity exposed the ordinance to constitutional challenge. Recognizing the ordinance's legal vulnerability, proponents of segregation urged revision. The July 1 ordinance was the result. The June 13 measure is reproduced in Miller, "Blacks in Winston-Salem," 273; and "Race Segregation," *Union Republican,* 20 June 1912, 6. For an account of discussion that led to the replacement of the first ordinance, see "Mass Meeting of Citizens," *Journal,* 19 June 1912, 1; "Mass Meeting to Be Held in East Winston," *Twin-City Daily Sentinel,* 19 June 1912, 1.

23. The ordinance was not retroactive; it applied only to residences occupied after July 1, 1912. The measure made an exception for "servants or employees" who occupied residences on blocks where they worked. Builders of new residences on previously uninhabited blocks had to state in their building permit applications whether future occupants were to be "white" or "colored." See "Segregation in Whole City," *Journal,* 6 July 1912, 1; "General Segregation," *Union Republican,* 11 July 1912, 6; Miller, "Blacks in Winston-Salem," 273–74.

24. The immediate African American response to the housing ordinances appears especially muted when contrasted with the uproar one year later when the Board of Aldermen sought to move an established black school to a less desirable location. Irate African Americans then sent a caustic letter to the Board of Aldermen, opposing the move and expressing mock gratitude for the $20,000 that the city spent annually on black schools (as opposed to the $150,000 spent on white schools): "We thank you for the crumbs from the table." African Americans also published a letter of protest in a local newspaper and secured legal representation to make their case before the Board of Aldermen. See "Against Removal Depot Street School," *Twin-City Daily Sentinel,* 11 Nov.1913, 6; "Colored Man Writes on Removal of School," *Journal,* 15 Nov. 1913, 6; "Removal Colored Graded School Discussed," *Twin-City Daily Sentinel,* 8 Nov. 1913, 3; "Removal of Depot Street School Is Abandoned," *Twin-City Daily Sentinel,* 17 Nov. 1913, 1.

25. "Segregate Negroes in East Winston," *Journal,* 14 June 1912, 1.

26. Although at least one local black paper may have existed, we failed to find any copies.

27. Oppermann, "Historic and Architectural Resources," E13–E15; "Atkins Outlines Negroes Progress," *Winston-Salem Journal and Sentinel,* 10 February 1929, 7b.

28. African American displeasure with the segregation measures surfaced months after passage. In November 1912, S. J. Bennett, a leader of the segregation drive, ran for the state legislature. A group of blacks passed a resolution opposing Bennett's candidacy. They cited Bennett's efforts "on behalf of the white people of East Winston" to secure the segregation ordinance. African Americans worried that Bennett, if elected, might try to pass a statewide residential segregation law. (Bennett won.) "Negroes Fight Mr. Bennett," *Journal,* 5 November 1912, 1; "Colored Voters Hold Meeting Here Tonight," *Journal,* 1 November 1912, 1.

29. An unsuccessful drive for *business* segregation temporarily diverted the city's attention during the ordinance's first year. See "Oppose Negro's [*sic*] on Third Street," *Journal,* 24 November 1912, 1.

30. "Segregation Discussed by Aldermen," *Winston-Salem Western Sentinel,* 20 May 1913, 3; "Favor Strict Enforcement of Segregation Law," *Journal,* 17 May 1913, 1; "Segregation Law Discussed by Alderman," *Twin-City Daily Sentinel,* 17 May 1913, 8.

31. "Thinks City Should Provide Good Streets for Negroes," *Twin-City Daily Sentinel,* 9 June 1913, 8.

32. Bertha H. Miller estimates that between 50 and 75 percent of African Americans in Winston-Salem around the turn of the twentieth century worked as "tobacco jobbers" ("Blacks in Winston-Salem," 264).

33. Deed Book 121, p. 167; Deed Book 108, p. 374.

34. See 1912 and 1913 maps. Because the city directories on which we relied when composing our maps are neither complete nor perfectly reliable, our maps may not reflect housing patterns precisely. They should be viewed as general guides, not precise reconstructions.

35. Unfortunately, the Registrar of Deeds Office contains no record of the transaction. Based on subsequent court testimony, it would appear that Darnell bought the house about a month after Sledge himself did. Sledge acquired the house on 2 May 1913 for $1100. Deed Book 108, p. 374.

36. *Journal,* 12 May 1912, 4. Sledge's previous jobs included selling groceries and selling sewing machines. In 1916, he became a farmer (Winston-Salem City Directories, 1902–1913, 1916). A sampling of Sledge's advertisements appear in the *Journal* (usually on page 6 or 7) in 1912 on 7 January, 17 February, 22 March, and 21 June; and in the *Twin-City Daily Sentinel* in 1912 on 23 March, 30 March, 30 April,

and 18 May. See also the *Twin-City Daily Sentinel* in 1913 on 24 May, 9 June, 28 June, and 18 September. Sledge even advertised at least one property specifically "For Colored People," revealing both an interest in attracting an African American clientele and an awareness of what, in the standards of the day, constituted a "colored" property (*Twin-City Daily Sentinel*, 23 June 1913, 7). The practice of advertising specifically to blacks was not widespread, but Sledge was not the only realtor to do so. See, for instance, the Foltz and Spaugh ad in the *Journal*, 1 May 1912, 11.

37. A photocopy of this document, written on the letterhead of Sledge's real estate office, appears at page 1030 of the Superior Court Record of the *Darnell* case. The document is also introduced into the record on page 1043. The Superior Court records can be found in *Criminal Cases Docket*, vol. 14, in room 216 of the Winston-Salem Hall of Justice. This brief entry leads to the fuller court record on microfilm 1066, pp. 1021–55 (hereafter cited as "Superior Court Record").

38. "Segregation Ordinance to Be Tested in Courts," *Twin-City Daily Sentinel*, 9 July 1913, 5. Only about one in twenty Winston-Salem municipal court cases was appealed in 1913. See "Municipal Court Did a Rushing Business," *Winston-Salem Union Republican*, 8 January 1914.

39. Sledge's bond payment is reported in the Superior Court Record, pp. 1027–29. A typewritten copy of this Superior Court record, which was sent to Raleigh for the Supreme Court hearing, lacks some of the more exciting details available in Winston-Salem but is more accessible. See North Carolina Supreme Court Original Cases, 1909–1929, February Term, 1914, Case 337, North Carolina State Archives, Raleigh.

40. "The African-American Lawyer in Forsyth County, North Carolina: 1895–1960," 1996 calendar (Winston-Salem: Society for the Study of African-American History in Winston-Salem). This source can be found in the North Carolina Room, Forsyth County Public Library, Winston-Salem.

41. R. B. Glenn, "John Cameron Buxton," in *Biographical History of North Carolina: From Colonial Times to the Present*, ed. Samuel A. Ashe, 8 vols. (Greensboro, N.C.: Charles L. Van Noppen, 1906), 5:49.

42. Many Democrats would blame his 8,500-vote gubernatorial loss in 1896 on African Americans, who cast over 30,000 votes for his Republican-Populist "fusion" rival. See Jeffrey J. Crow, "'Fusion, Confusion, and Negroism': Schisms among Negro Republicans in the North Carolina Election of 1896," *North Carolina Historical Review* 53 (October 1976): 381–83.

43. Annie Lee Singletary, "Cy Watson: Builder of Winston-Salem," *Journal*, 9 November 1941, 39; Thomas H. Johnson Jr., "Watson, Cyrus Barksdale," in *Dictionary of North Carolina Biography*, ed. Wm. S. Powell, 6 vols. (Chapel Hill: University of North Carolina Press, 1996), 6:131; W. A. Blair and S. A. Ashe, "Cyrus

Barksdale Watson," in *Biographical History of North Carolina: From Colonial Times to the Present,* ed. Samuel A. Ashe (Greensboro, N.C.: Charles L. Van Noppen, 1906), 6:460–68.

44. Buxton also was a Democratic candidate for the United States House of Representatives in 1900. Some would attribute Buxton's loss, like Watson's four years earlier, to African American opposition (*Winston-Salem Union Republican,* 15 November 1900, 2). See "In Memoriam: John Cameron Buxton, 1852–1917" [1917], North Carolina Collection, University of North Carolina Library, Chapel Hill, 12; R. B. Glenn, "John Cameron Buxton," in *Biographical History of North Carolina: From Colonial Times to the Present,* ed. Samuel A. Ashe (Greensboro, N.C.: Charles L. Van Noppen, 1906), 5:47–49.

45. Guion Griffis Johnson, "Southern Paternalism toward Negroes after Emancipation," *Journal of Southern History* 23 (November 1957): 490. See Glenda Gilmore's discussion of the "New White Man" in *Gender and Jim Crow,* 61–89.

46. Annie Lee Singletary, "Cy Watson: Builder of Winston-Salem," 39.

47. *Western Sentinel,* 22 March 1910; *Twin-City Daily Sentinel,* 23 July 1912, 8. When Buxton died in 1917, many African Americans reportedly grieved "the loss of a true friend . . . one who had always shown an interest in things that were for the advancement of the negro race" ("In Memoriam: John Cameron Buxton," 12–13).

48. In 1890, Watson and Buxton and two others formed a partnership to sell real estate on the north side of the city. They continued selling from their tract of approximately 50 lots until 1905. See Deed Book 35, p. 367, for a plat of the Watson-Buxton-Allen-Allspaugh lots. A record of their sales can be traced in the General Index to Real Estate Conveyances, under "Grantor 'W,'" for Watson.

49. The law firm served as Trustee for 129 Deeds of Trust in 1913. See General Index of Real Estate Conveyances under "Grantee 'W.'" Service as a trustee was not in itself lucrative, but it could lead to payment in the event of foreclosure and auction, in which case trustees would likely receive a commission.

50. Deed of Trust Book 73, p. 258. Buxton had been president since 1908. See Power, "Apartheid Baltimore Style," 293.

51. Clarence Poe, "Rural Land Segregation between Whites and Negroes: A Reply to Mr. Stephenson," *South Atlantic Quarterly* 8 (July 1914): 208. Poe, the major proponent of a rural segregation scheme for North Carolina (roughly contemporary with Winston-Salem's experiment with urban segregation), bestowed this compliment on Stephenson in an article in which he disagreed with Stephenson's critique of rural segregation.

52. Gilbert T. Stephenson, *Race Distinctions in American Law* (New York: D. Appleton and Co., 1910), 361. For a rephrasing of the same argument, see Gilbert T. Stephenson, "Colored People and Law Enforcement," *Journal,* 10 May 1913, 2.

53. Gilbert T. Stephenson, "The Segregation of the White and Negro Races in Cities," *South Atlantic Quarterly* 8 (January 1914): 1–17. The quoted passage appears on p. 1. So close chronologically were Stephenson's argumentation in the *Darnell* case and his drafting of this article that the outlines for both appear in his office journal sequentially, with the outline for the article sandwiched between his outlined legal brief and a newspaper clipping that praises C. B. Watson, calling him the "dean of the legal profession" in North Carolina. See Gilbert T. Stephenson Papers, PCMS 160, box 11, folder 126, Office Journal no. 1, pp. 213–31, Special Collections, Z. Smith Reynolds Library, Wake Forest University. It merits noting, however, that just three months later—and perhaps as a result of his experiences in the *Darnell* case—Stephenson published an article that *opposed* a rural segregation proposal. While still insisting that segregation was lawful, Stephenson now intimated that it was immoral. Citing the story of the Good Samaritan, and invoking noblesse oblige, he argued that physical separation of the races would lead to white neglect of the "weaker" race ("The Segregation of the White and Negro Races in Rural Communities of North Carolina," *South Atlantic Quarterly* 8 [April 1914]: 107–17).

54. "Appeal to Supreme Court in the Segregation Case," *Journal*, 18 January 1914, 8. Darnell's Superior Court retrial was originally scheduled for October 3, 1913. The trial was postponed, however, pending the outcome of a Maryland case involving similar issues. The delay reveals that the residential segregation debate was a national one—and North Carolina's judges knew it. See "Segregation Case in the Superior Court," *Twin-City Daily Sentinel*, 3 October 1913, 1. In *State v. Gurry*, 88 A. 546 (Md. 1913), the Maryland Supreme Court struck down Baltimore's path-breaking segregation ordinance on constitutional grounds because of its retroactivity. Winston's ordinance was not retroactive.

55. Superior Court Record, 1036–40.

56. Ibid., 1034–35. They argued, for instance, that the ordinance was not submitted in writing to the Board of Aldermen before it was passed, in violation of city rules.

57. Ibid., 1035–36. Unimpressed, Judge W. A. Devin would instruct the jury to consider the ordinance "to have been duly passed and in force" at the time of Darnell's alleged violation.

58. "Appeal to the Supreme Court in the Segregation Case," *Journal*, 18 January 1914, 8.

59. The local press had followed the case closely. "Perhaps no case tried" in Superior Court at that time "was of greater local interest than that of William Darnell" ("Verdict of Guilty in Segregation Case Here," *Twin-City Daily Sentinel*, 19 January 1914, 5).

60. Editorial, *Journal,* 20 January 1914, 4. "Verdict of Guilty in Segregation Case Here," *Twin-City Daily Sentinel,* 19 January 1914, 5.

61. Final disposition of their cases would await the *Darnell* outcome. "Verdict of Guilty in Segregation Case Here," *Twin-City Daily Sentinel,* 19 January 1914, 5.

62. The precise chronology of these cases is somewhat muddled. From the newspapers, it appears that Smith was found guilty on August 11, 1913, and Crews on September 3, 1913. See "Colored Doctor Appeals Case," *Journal,* 12 August 1913, 5; and "In Municipal Court," *Journal,* 4 September 1913, 8. The records in the Deeds Office, however, complicate matters. Smith is recorded as purchasing his lot on February 18, 1914 from the Winston Development Company for $1500 (Deed Book 122, p. 207). Crews' purchase was on July 18, 1913, for $850 (Deed Book 127, p. 136). He bought from J. B. Phillips.

63. "Mr. Stephenson's Contentions as to Segregation of Races," *Twin-City Daily Sentinel,* 4 April 1914, 9.

64. "City Segregation," *Union Republican,* 9 April 1914, 3. Stephenson understood the significance of the court's questions about Winston-Salem's authority to legislate. After oral argument, he perceptively told the press that "the apparent question [would be] the right of the city to act without permission from the legislature." Although hopeful that the principle of segregation would be upheld, Stephenson worried that the court might "divide upon this technical point" (*Twin-City Daily Sentinel,* 4 April 1914, 9).

65. Aubrey Lee Brooks, *Walter Clark Fighting Judge* (Chapel Hill: University of North Carolina Press, 1944), 28–31 and 253–54. See also Willis P. Wichard, "A Place for Walter Clark in the American Judicial Tradition" (masters thesis, University of Virginia, 1984), 19–23. The Civil War experience appears to have had a greater impact on Clark's later life than on Watson's. Clark was a dedicated writer and reader of Civil War history; he also advocated the use of federal money to fund pensions for Confederate war veterans. Chief Justice Clark was the last Civil War veteran to hold public office in North Carolina. See David Blackwell, "Walter Clark—North Carolina's Foremost Liberal," in Walter Clark vertical file, North Carolina Supreme Court Library. Quote in Wichard, 23–24. During these same early postwar years, Clark, like Watson and Buxton, was defeated for elective office "on account of the Negro vote" (Brooks, 42).

66. Clark, "Ballots for Both," 10; Clark, "Votes for Women," 2–3; Wichard, "A Place for Walter Clark," 28–29.

67. Legal historian David E. Bernstein has explored how differing attitudes toward active government during the years under study tended to affect judicial attitudes toward de jure segregation. According to Bernstein, "traditional" jurisprudes—those who opposed active government on constitutional grounds—were predisposed to

frown on segregation laws. In contrast, "Progressive jurisprudes"—those who supported active government—were predisposed look kindly on segregation laws. Bernstein, "Philip Sober," 804–20. Walter Clark was a Progressive jurisprude.

68. Platform of Walter Clark, Candidate for U.S. Senate, North Carolina Collection, Wilson Library, University of North Carolina. This platform is also reprinted in *Twin-City Daily Sentinel,* 21 June 1912, 3.

69. Walter Clark, "Address on Reform in Law and Legal Procedure," 30 June 1914 (Wilmington, N.C.: Wilmington Stamp and Printing Co.), 15. See also Walter Clark, "Centennial of the Supreme Court of North Carolina: Response to Addresses," 4 January 1919, 4–5; Walter Clark, "Address by Chief Justice Walter Clark, of North Carolina Supreme Court, at Cooper Union, New York City, 27 January 1914" (Raleigh, N.C., 1914), 1–24.

70. Both Watson and Clark were veterans of the Confederate army and the two occasionally corresponded about the war. But their mutual regard surpassed mere nostalgia. In 1912, Watson ("one of the judge's closest friends") "warmly" endorsed Clark's failed bid for the Democratic Party's nomination for United States Senate. Likewise, Clark held Watson in high esteem. Clark dubbed Watson the "uncrowned king" of the North Carolina bar; he also commissioned a portrait of Watson for display in the Supreme Court House in Raleigh. This personal association assured Watson's client, at the very least, a careful hearing. See C. B. Watson to Walter Clark, 4 and 6 September, 4 November, and 9 December 1901; and 19 June 1913; Walter Clark Papers; Brooks, *Walter Clark,* 72; "Chief Justice Clark To Speak Here October 26," *Twin-City Daily Sentinel,* 16 October 1912, 1; "Judge Clark Is Confident," *Journal,* 27 October 1912, 1; "Cyrus B. Watson for Judge Clark: Distinguished Democrat Warmly Endorses Him for United States Senate" ([Raleigh, N.C.?], 1912); "Cyrus B. Watson," *Raleigh News and Observer,* November 1916, in North Carolina Clipping File through 1975, University of North Carolina Library, Chapel Hill, reel 39, 116–17.

71. For instance, in *State v. Michner,* 172 *N.C.* 895 (1916), Clark argued that the race (black) of a flogged prisoner was immaterial, saying it "matters not what color an African sun has printed upon him. He was a human being and entitled to the elementary rights of man." In 1920, Clark said the following: "A colored man may have differences with a white man, as will happen between any two men, but when they go into the court house to have it settled every man knows that colored men are at no disadvantage" ("The Negro in North Carolina and the South," Speech, 26 May 1920, in Daniel Harvey Hill Jr. Papers, North Carolina Archives, Raleigh). In addition, African Americans apparently held favorable impressions of Clark. In 1919, James E. Shepard, an African American who headed the National Training

School in Durham, wrote Clark to thank him "for the words of fairness, truth, and soberness which [Clark] expressed in behalf of [Shepard's] race" (James E. Shepard to Walter Clark, 7 February 1919, Walter Clark Papers, North Carolina State Archives, Raleigh [hereafter Walter Clark Papers]). For a further discussion of Clark and African Americans, see Wichard, "A Place for Walter Clark," 20–22.

72. Brooks, *Walter Clark*, 175.

73. *State v. Darnell*, 166 N.C. 300 (1914). Prior to *Darnell*, the North Carolina Supreme Court had generally accorded wide latitude to local governments on local matters. As Clark wrote in a typical pre-*Darnell* opinion, "Local matters are properly left to the people of a self-governing community, to be decided and determined by them for themselves, and not by a judge or court for them" (*Small v. Edenton*, 146 N.C. 527 [1908]). This case involved an ordinance mandating the removal of street awnings. Similarly, in a previous decision involving a city's authority to cut down a resident's shade trees to assure the free flow of traffic, the court had stated that it would interfere with such exercises of municipal discretion "only in cases of fraud and oppression, constituting manifest abuse" (*Tate v. Greensboro*, 114 N.C. 392 at 401 [1894], quoting from *Chase v. City*, 81 Wis. 313 [1892]). However, the court had previously invalidated some broadly drafted sin ordinances. In *State v. Webber*, 107 N.C. 962 (1890), the court struck down an Asheville bawdy house ordinance that imposed fines on the owner of any house in which unmarried men and women cohabited, with or without the owner's knowledge; in *State v. Thomas*, 118 N.C. 1221 (1896), the court struck down a Marion town drinking ordinance that prohibited any person, even the owner of a barroom, from remaining in the barroom between ten o'clock in the evening and four o'clock in the morning; and in *State v. Dannenberg*, 150 N.C. 799 (1909), the court struck down a Morehead City liquor ordinance barring the sale of any drink for which a federal license was required, an ordinance that was at variance with county and state liquor laws. In *Darnell*, Clark may well have been influenced by the recent reasoning in *State v. Gurry*, 88 A. 546 (Md., 1913).

74. See Richard E. Ellis, *The Union at Risk* (New York: Oxford University Press, 1987), ix, 1; Arthur Schlesinger, "The State Rights Fetish," in *New Viewpoints in American History* (New York: Macmillan, 1926), 220–44; Jesse T. Carpenter, *The South as a Conscious Minority, 1789–1861* (New York: New York University Press, 1930; reprint, Columbia: University of South Carolina Press, 1990), 245–54; Harold Mixon, "The Rhetoric of States' Rights and White Supremacy," in *A New Diversity in Contemporary Southern Rhetoric*, ed. Calvin M. Logue and Howard Dorgan, (Baton Rouge: Louisiana State University Press, 1987) 166–87; Bruce Nelson, "Black Equality in Mobile during World War II," *Journal of Southern History* 80

(December 1993): 984; Howard W. Allen, A. R. Clausen, and Jerome M. Clubb, "Political Reform and Negro Rights in the Senate, 1909–1915," *Journal of Southern History* 37 (May 1971): 191–212; Kenneth R. Johnson, "Kate Gordon and the Woman's Suffrage Movement in the South," *Journal of Southern History* 38 (August 1972): 365; and Adrienne Koch and Harry Ammon, "The Virginia and Kentucky Resolutions: An Episode in Jefferson's and Madison's Defense of Civil Liberties," *William and Mary Quarterly* 5 (April 1948): 145.

75. *State v. Darnell,* 166 N.C. 300 at 304 (1914). Clark also found that residential segregation interfered with the basic right of property owners to sell to whomever they pleased (302–3). Was the segregation ordinance unconstitutional, as Watson and Buxton had insisted? Clark, an outspoken critic of judicial review, sidestepped the question. "Whether if the General Assembly had passed a statute conferring on town or county commissioners the authority to make such an ordinance as this, it would have been constitutional," he wrote, "is not now before us" (305).

76. "Segregation Not Constitutional Declares Court," *Journal,* 9 April 1914, 1. For additional reaction from the Winston-Salem press, see "Segregation Law," *Union Republican,* 16 April 1914, 1; "Winston Segregation Ordinance Cannot Be Enforced Says Court," *Twin-City Daily Sentinel,* 9 April 1914, 5; and "Segregation," *Union Republican,* 9 April 1914, 2. Reporting on the *Darnell* ruling extended well beyond Winston-Salem. "There is a general interest throughout the state in the disposal of the race segregation ordinance of Winston," a Raleigh paper wrote before running Clark's opinion in its entirety. "Segregation Not Allowed by Law," *Raleigh News and Observer,* 12 April 1914, 11. The *Charlotte Observer* considered *Darnell* a case "of special note," for Charlotte had been contemplating a segregation ordinance of its own ("Cannot Enforce Segregation Law," 9 April 1914, 3).

77. "Segregation Not Constitutional Declares Court," *Journal,* 9 April 1914, 1. They also were "confident" that the fight for residential segregation would be carried to the General Assembly in Raleigh and would be "waged successfully." Should any resulting state law then be declared unconstitutional, the editors called for "changing the constitution, whether that constitution be Federal or State or both" ("Segregation Up to the Legislature," editorial, *Journal,* 10 April 1914, 12). In 1913, "a bill to provide for the segregation of races" had been introduced in the North Carolina Senate. The bill was tabled and died. See Stephenson, "Segregation in the Cities," 4; *Journal of the Senate of the General Assembly of the State of North Carolina,* Extra Session, 1913 (Raleigh, N.C.: Edwards and Broughton Co., State Printers, 1913), 17, 210, 219.

In subsequent weeks the *Journal's* language softened somewhat as its focus shifted to ways of reinforcing segregation "without any law on the subject." The editors suggested improving conditions in African American neighborhoods in order to discourage out-migration. They championed Columbia Heights, the "most respectable negro community in the city," as an "ideal negro district," an "example of what the colored people can do when they are segregated." The editors warned, however, that without modern conveniences (little details like city sewers, sidewalks, and paved streets, none of which existed in Columbia Heights), voluntarily segregated residents would never "stay segregated." See "Segregation by Common Consent," *Journal,* 19 April 1914, 12; "Columbia Heights," *Journal,* 24 April 1914, 4; "How to Insure Segregation," editorial, *Journal,* 22 April 1914, 4.

78. *University of Pennsylvania Law Review* 63 (1914–1915): 895–98; *Virginia Law Review* 3 (January 1916): 305–6. The *Michigan Law Review* 13 (May 1915): 59, simply (and incorrectly) noted that the North Carolina Supreme Court had "argue[d] against the constitutionality of the act." In fact, Clark carefully avoided ruling on the ordinance's constitutionality.

79. "Segregation," *Crisis* (June 1914): 69–70. Specifically, this article focused on the Cleveland *Plaindealer's* assertion that the North Carolina Supreme Court "has decided against the un-American policy of segregating whites and Negroes." Also listed as supporting the *Darnell* decision was an article in the *New York Evening Post.* Within weeks of the ordinance's original passage, the NAACP's *Crisis* had reported on it. *Crisis* 4 (August 1912): 177; 4 (October 1912): 273; 5 (January 1913): 118. NAACP attorney J. Chapin Brinsmade followed the case keenly (Memo for Miss Henery from Mr. Brinsmade, 11 June 1914, Papers of the NAACP, Part Five, "The Campaign against Residential Segregation," ed. August Meier and John Bracey, reel one, frame 0462–0463).

80. In a counterintuitive comment from 1929, Simon G. Atkins, Winston-Salem's most prominent African American, paradoxically stated that *Darnell* had prepared African Americans "more readily to accept . . . voluntary segregation" because it "reassured the negroes as to the spirit of our city in regards to their rights under the law" ("Atkins Outlines Negroes Progress," *Journal and Sentinel,* 10 February 1929, 7B).

81. Troubled by these trends, the Winston-Salem Board of Aldermen passed a new residential segregation measure in 1930. Although this ordinance flew in the face of both *Darnell* and *Buchanan v. Warley,* 245 U.S. 60 (1917), in which the U.S. Supreme Court declared de jure residential segregation to be unconstitutional, it went unchallenged for nearly a decade. Finally, in 1939, a group of white landlords challenged the measure in court. In *Clinard v. Winston-Salem,* 219 N.C. 119 (1940), the state Supreme Court, citing *Darnell,* once again nullified de jure housing segregation in Winston-Salem.

82. Ed Campbell, "East Winston: New Day Dawns on a Shadowed Scene" *Twin City Sentinel,* 16 April 1962, 7; Hanchett, *Sorting Out the New South City,* 262.

83. Miller, "Blacks in Winston-Salem," (1981), 147.

13

Higher Education and the Civil Rights Movement
Desegregating the University of North Carolina

PETER WALLENSTEIN

As late as 1950, no black citizen of North Carolina studied at the University of North Carolina in Chapel Hill. Nor could a solitary African American enroll at North Carolina State College of Agriculture and Engineering (now North Carolina State University) in Raleigh or, for that matter, at what was then Woman's College and is now the University of North Carolina at Greensboro (UNCG). By 1960 a sprinkling of black students took classes at each of those three schools, and in fact, black students were earning degrees at each school. In the intervening decade, the 1950s, desegregation occurred—or at least began—at all three schools. Before that time a number of black North Carolinians had sought to enroll but had been turned way because of their racial identity.

Historians of the civil rights movement have told much about the efforts of the 1940s through the 1960s to achieve racial desegregation and political empowerment. In that literature, however, the story of desegregating higher education tends to end at 1950 with a vague gesture toward a future in which the process somehow gets completed, typically with the dramatic encounter of Ole Miss and James Meredith in 1962 supplied as an afterthought.[1] Not until the historiography of higher education catches up with that of the civil rights movement will it be possible to bring the two areas of inquiry together. Only then will it be possible to develop in full the role of higher education in the flowering of the civil rights movement or the role of the civil rights movement in fostering new social and political patterns in higher education.

This chapter supplies some groundwork, in one Southern state, pointing toward a merger of these two literatures. It does not emphasize the literature but seeks to develop the story of desegregation in North Carolina. It highlights the challengers of the 1950s—graduate students at midcentury, undergraduates a few years later—and the changes they helped bring about.

For these purposes, North Carolina is as representative as any state—not among the first states to begin to desegregate their public institutions of higher education (in the 1930s and 1940s) nor among the last to do so (in the 1960s). Located in neither the Border South nor the Deep South, North Carolina moved more slowly, on the one hand, than did Delaware, Maryland, or Oklahoma, and more quickly and easily, on the other hand, than did Georgia, South Carolina, or Mississippi. Unlike West Virginia or even Virginia, North Carolina forced black citizens to go the distance in the federal courts before it conceded defeat and changed its policies. Yet in contrast to Georgia, Mississippi, and Alabama, no violence accompanied the resistance to change in the Tarheel State. North Carolina charted a middle course.[2]

Nonblack Applicants, Higher Education, and "Separate but Equal" before 1950

At midcentury, the greater University of North Carolina had three campuses, each with its own chancellor. The flagship campus at Chapel Hill had graduate and professional programs—in particular, law and medicine—as well as undergraduate programs. North Carolina State emphasized technical fields. Woman's College, formerly a teachers' college, offered a liberal arts curriculum for white women.

These were historically *nonblack* institutions—they admitted no African American students before midcentury. They were not, however, exclusively white schools. At each of these schools, some nonwhite students could attend without apparent difficulty. It is clear that they could, because they did. Before the first African American enrolled at Woman's College, that school graduated a young woman from China. The university at Chapel Hill, by the early 1950s, awarded various students from China undergraduate degrees as well as master's degrees and even a doctorate. At NC State, the numbers were larger, with nineteen undergraduates and twenty-two graduate students from China earning degrees by the early 1950s. Tsong-Cheu Chang earned a bachelor's degree in agriculture in 1923; Ji Jih Woo earned his in textile management in 1950; both came from Shanghai, China.[3] Students also came from Korea and other countries in Asia. Yet African Americans were categorically excluded.

Chapel Hill, in particular, did not remain nonblack simply because no black student applied or because none met the academic qualifications imposed on nonblack applicants—as Thomas Raymond Hocutt demonstrated when he applied in 1933 to study pharmacy. Rejected on the basis of race, he took his case to the Durham County Superior Court.[4] Hocutt's attorneys included local lawyer Conrad Pearson, who earned his law degree at Howard University in 1932 in the class before Thurgood Marshall's, and NAACP attorney William Hastie, who earned a Harvard University law degree in 1930 and then began teaching at Howard, where Hocutt was studying at the time. Pearson and Hastie argued that the state was violating the Fourteenth Amendment's equal protection clause in offering a curriculum in pharmacy to some state residents but, solely on the basis of race, denying access to that program to other state residents at the only campus at which it was offered. Whatever might be the subsequent fate of "separate but equal" as regarded public education at one level or another, North Carolina—like the other Southern states at the time—was not even going through the motions of satisfying anything but the "separate" part of that formula.[5]

Hocutt lost on a technicality. He had graduated from North Carolina College for Negroes (now North Carolina Central University), but its president refused to supply a transcript, so Hocutt could not meet all the nonracial qualifications for admission.[6] The crisis passed and segregation persisted, but that event and others prodded the state to inaugurate changes that might ensure successful deflection of future efforts by black Tarheels to gain entrance to nonblack institutions.

Those other events included a successful suit in state court in 1935–36 by Donald Murray to gain admission to law school at the University of Maryland as well as a victory at the U.S. Supreme Court in 1938 regarding Lloyd Gaines's application to enter the law school at the University of Missouri.[7] They also included an application by Pauli Murray in 1939 to do graduate work in sociology at Chapel Hill. Murray had graduated from Hillside High School in Durham in 1926, a year before Hocutt.[8] Rejected, as Hocutt had been, Murray wanted to carry a lawsuit to federal court, but the NAACP declined to assist her. She was living in New York at the time, and if the court chose to treat her as no longer a North Carolina resident, she might lose on that basis without the merits of her case ever being considered. It was not sufficiently clear that she had a claim on North Carolina—that just because she had been rejected on racial grounds, equal protection under North Carolina state law had been denied her.[9]

In response to these various developments, North Carolina educators and officials inaugurated several new programs for black Tarheels. By the early 1940s, black North Carolinians might enroll in law school in Durham at North Carolina College for Negroes, and there were master's programs in agriculture and technology at the black land-grant school, North Carolina Agricultural and Technical College, in Greensboro. Not equal opportunity, but more of a hint of it than had existed before, emerged within segregation.[10]

There matters stood in the late 1940s when various black North Carolinians challenged the new status quo as inadequate and unconstitutional. On the eve of the 1950s, it was no longer true that the state was supplying black Tarheels no opportunities for graduate and professional study at one North Carolina school or another. Yet whether the programs were truly equal was open to dispute, and in many fields no separate courses were available. Moreover, the Supreme Court was on the move again, redefining equality in professional education in ways that would make it even more difficult for the state, if challenged, to satisfy the Fourteenth Amendment within the framework of "separate but equal." Among the higher education cases that built on the 1938 *Gaines* case from Missouri, the most important was *Sweatt* v. *Painter,* a 1950 decision regarding access to law school at the University of Texas.[11]

Further Litigation Proves Successful

A number of black Tarheels brought just such challenges. In 1948, several black North Carolinians applied to UNC. Two law students at North Carolina College, Harold Thomas Epps and James R. Walker, wished to transfer to Chapel Hill. James Edward Thomas and James H. Henderson applied to the medical school.[12]

While the school dithered over the applications, Harold Epps and fourteen other NCC law students took their argument directly to the legislature, which was in session at the time. There, though to no immediate effect, they demanded a new law building, for they understood that, by upgrading the library and other facilities, the school might finally gain accreditation from the American Bar Association. Two months later Epps directed his transfer application to the UNC board of trustees. "I am certain," he wrote the board, "that I am not receiving and cannot receive equal educational advantages at North Carolina College."[13]

Nothing happened. In October 1949, Harold Epps and Robert Davis Glass filed suit in federal court to obtain admission to the UNC law school. By the time their case was heard between August and October 1950, the U.S. Supreme Court had handed down a decision in June 1950 in *Sweatt v. Painter,* the case from Texas that raised the standard that a segregated black law school had to meet in order for the state to forestall integration at its white law school. In October 1950, District Judge Johnson Jay Hayes nonetheless ruled in the state's favor, arguing that North Carolina's story differed from Texas's in that the law school at North Carolina College was a going concern and adequate to meet the constitutional challenge.[14]

The plaintiffs appealed the district court decision—or at least some of them did. Harold Epps had graduated, and Floyd McKissick's name led the new list of plaintiffs, a list that also included Solomon Revis, James Lassiter, and J. Kenneth Lee. Years later, McKissick explained his group's motivation partly in terms of the lack of law books at the unaccredited North Carolina College law school. More than that, though, he said about his fellow veterans of World War II that, after they returned to civilian life, they were determined to do what they could to end segregation in North Carolina. In particular, McKissick said, they targeted the law school.[15]

In March 1951, the appeals panel sent the case back to district court, which it directed to order the university to stop employing race as a criterion for admission. With Judge Morris Soper speaking for the panel, the court ruled that the NCC law school could not measure up against its UNC counterpart. The state decided to admit qualified black applicants to the medical school, for which NCC had no counterpart, but regarding the law school, it appealed the decision of the court of appeals to the U.S. Supreme Court. But that court, on June 4, let the appeals ruling stand.[16] North Carolina had won the case in October, then lost it in March. When it lost again in June, it ran out of courts to which it might appeal.

The state had conceded as to the medical school and had lost its fight as to the law school. Four days after the Supreme Court dashed the state's hopes, five black students enrolled at the UNC law school—Floyd McKissick, James Lassiter, Kenneth Lee, and James Walker, as well as a new name, Harvey Elliott Beech. McKissick had just graduated from NCC law school and took additional courses only that summer. Not only did he wish to participate in the actual desegregation, but, as he later explained, he wanted to help demonstrate that his cohort really did have the ability to succeed at UNC. In addition to the first five students at the law school, Edward Oscar Diggs desegregated the medical school, and William Andrew Marsh Jr. entered the law program in September.[17]

Other questions remained, or rather new questions arose. For example, UNC figures showed 89 black North Carolinians currently studying outside the state, with financial assistance from the state, during the regular school year 1949–50—and another 218 receiving state aid to do graduate work during the summer.[18] How many of those students, school officials worried, would qualify for admission under the university's new regulations, and how many might wish to act on the new policy? In fact, what policies and practices should the university follow?

Gwendolyn L. Harrison applied to do doctoral work in Spanish and was admitted to the university and assigned a room on campus. When she showed up to register and claim her room, school officials discovered that she was black, not white. A scramble ensued as officials sought to rescind her acceptance and refund her room deposit. She put the matter in the hands of her lawyer, the omnipresent Conrad Pearson, who filed suit in federal district court. Unless the university discontinued its doctoral program in Spanish—an option that had some support, but not a lot—the school and the state were bound to lose the case. The board of trustees conceded yet another defeat and voted to admit her.[19]

Resolved in the months after March 1951 were various questions regarding segregation—like housing on campus and seating arrangements at football games—as black applicants and black students continued to push the school and the process of desegregation along.[20] Yet it would be a number of years before the three schools that constituted the University of North Carolina system came to grips with other implications of the March 1951 decision. Black North Carolinians kept pushing those implications to the surface so that white North Carolinians had to deal with them, and access to the federal courts gave black Tarheels a tool that, in time, helped topple one barrier after another.

Litigation regarding access to the law school led to the enrollment, beginning in 1951, of small numbers of black students in the law school and the medical school at Chapel Hill. Two years later, in 1953, North Carolina State enrolled two black graduate students. Hardy Liston Jr. enrolled to study mechanical engineering, but finding himself burdened by a weak background in mathematics and, on top of that, carrying a full teaching load at NC A&T in Greensboro, he successfully completed only one of two courses and withdrew after a term. Robert Lee Clemons studied electrical engineering and, a bit more prepared as well as less encumbered than Liston, became NC State's first African American alumnus when he earned his professional certificate in 1957.[21]

DILEMMAS OF UNDERGRADUATE SCHOOLING

At the graduate level, desegregation had begun at both UNC and NC State, yet all *undergraduate* programs at those two schools, as well as at Woman's College, remained closed to black applicants. Just as various African Americans had attempted to enroll in Chapel Hill's graduate and professional programs before the change in policy and practice in 1951, African Americans tried to enroll as undergraduates in the next few years but were uniformly rebuffed. Nor did North Carolina's post-*Hocutt* program of helping pay the extra costs of out-of-state tuition necessarily supply any benefits.

In August 1953, the Rev. S. F. Daly of Shady Hill Baptist Church in Roxboro wrote Chancellor Harrelson concerning his son, Algernon, who had been told by the school, as Daly put it, that "because the supreme court had not ruled on the undergraduate level he could not be admitted" to NC State. Daly expressed his dissatisfaction that his son could neither enroll at NC State nor abide the poor quality of instruction in mechanical engineering that he experienced at North Carolina A&T, which he had attended his first year. Nor could he obtain state assistance to go out of state to Howard University, where he had transferred. Daly asserted that he would be satisfied with state aid to attend Howard, "even though the boy was born in North Carolina and the NAACP desired of me that I permit them to make a case of it."[22]

Expressing a combination of grievances that many black North Carolinians must have felt, he appealed to the chancellor's sense of fatherhood, fairness, and state pride. "Maybe I feel a bit keenly about the whole matter, and I think you would and justly so were you in my [situation]. For you must know," Daly went on, describing the school of mechanical engineering at Greensboro, "that to many it is a sham, a disgrace and a deception, as compared with State College. I am sure also that you can see that for the boy . . . [to be] graduated from a college that has neither the faculty nor the equipment to teach what it purports to teach, and that in a field that is already highly technical and competitive, to say nothing about the additional restrictions which race imposes, would be to place on him handicaps which I do not think he should bear."[23]

Chancellor Harrelson, in one of the last letters he wrote before his successor moved into the office, offered Daly very little. Black undergraduates could not be admitted, insisted Harrison: "The College is permitted to admit qualified Negro college graduates to our Graduate School and we have admitted two for the term which opens in September." Regarding state aid, Daly should consult the Department of Public Instruction, which handled that responsibility.[24]

A year later, school officials were still advising African American prospective students that their racial identity barred their admission. In November 1954, six months after the Supreme Court's decision in *Brown v. Board of Education,* Chancellor Carey H. Bostian had to write a North Carolinian serving in the military, Sgt. William J. Dixon, that there was no way the man could enroll at NC State: "Regulations of our Board of Trustees prohibiting the admission of Negroes except in graduate programs of study are still in effect and will probably remain so throughout the 1954–55 school year. It, therefore, will not be possible for us to consider your application at this time."[25]

In May 1955, the chancellor at NC State formulated a letter that he suggested be sent to all black applicants for undergraduate study at any of the three schools in the UNC system. A first version of the letter opened by acknowledging receipt of the application and closed with best wishes: "We trust you will be able to pursue your education at another college." In between came the explanation for the blanket rejection: "The Board of Trustees of the Consolidated University of North Carolina has decided that applications of Negroes to the undergraduate schools at the three branches of the Consolidated University not be accepted." Several iterations later, after a meeting that included the governor and the attorney general, the second paragraph was modified to state: "Under the policy of the Board of Trustees of the University of North Carolina relating to admissions at this institution, we can not accept your application."[26]

Though the form letter was in place, Chancellor Bostian could not use it when writing to a third party who had inquired on behalf of state assistance to Walter J. Davis Jr., an engineering student at Ohio State University. Bostian outlined the situation still in effect on the eve of the 1955–56 school year. "If he is taking a course of study available at A&T College in Greensboro, he is not eligible for any aid to study outside the state. If he is following a course of study not available at A&T College but which is given at North Carolina State College, he is eligible for assistance to the extent of the additional costs over and above what they would be in North Carolina."[27] As a black North Carolinian, in short, Davis had three options if he wanted to study engineering: attend North Carolina's black land-grant school; obtain a modicum of state aid to attend Ohio's multiracial land-grant school and pursue a curriculum available at North Carolina's white land-grant institution but not its black one; or pay his own way to whatever institution would accept him.

The routine rejection of prospective black undergraduates remained in effect into the summer of 1955. At that point, just as it was black applicants who forced the change in policy at the graduate level, black applicants forced the question at the undergraduate level.

BLACK UNDERGRADUATES AT CHAPEL HILL

Three seniors at all-black Hillside High School in Durham—the same school from which Thomas Hocutt and Pauli Murray had graduated three decades earlier—applied to UNC for admission as freshmen entering fall term 1955. The three were Leroy Benjamin Frasier Jr.; his brother, Ralph Kennedy Frasier; and John Lewis Brandon. They were summarily rejected on the basis that, though the university had changed its policy of black exclusion at the graduate level, nothing had changed at the undergraduate level.[28]

The three requested that the institution change its policy. The school declined to do so, and the three went to federal district court. Their attorneys included Conrad Pearson, who had been involved in such cases since Hocutt's challenge to segregation back in 1933; Floyd McKissick, one of the plaintiffs who brought the case that led to his own admission to the law school in 1951; and William A. Marsh Jr., who had entered the UNC law school in September 1951.[29]

The state argued that *Brown v. Board of Education* applied only to "the lower public schools and did not decide that the separation of the races in schools on the college and university level is unlawful." But the federal court was having none of that. The three students and their lawyers—and indeed all black North Carolinians who might wish, then or at some time in the future, to apply for admission to the state's nonblack schools—gained a victory on September 16, 1955, when the court interpreted the 1954 decision in *Brown* as applying to public higher education as well as elementary and secondary schooling.[30]

Writing for a three-judge panel as he had five years earlier in the *McKissick* case, Judge Morris Soper rejected the state's position that *Brown* had no bearing on the case at hand. "We think that the contention is without merit," he declared. "That the decision of the Supreme Court was limited to the facts before it is true, but the reasoning on which the decision was based is as applicable to schools for higher education as to schools on the lower level."[31]

Among those for whom it must have been a particularly sweet victory were Floyd McKissick and, above all, Conrad Pearson.

UNC enrolled the trio in September 1955. But the school and the state did not give up their fight to stay white—or at least nonblack—and took the case to the U.S. Supreme Court. Would the decision stick? Only time would tell. In the meantime, new applications from black North Carolinians fostered uncertainty and then bewilderment. Communications between school officials and the state attorney general twisted and turned.

The U.S. Supreme Court had yet to rule on the *Frasier* case when Walter Van Buren Holmes and Charles James Dewanna Thorpe applied to NC State in mid-February 1956. The admissions office, following what was thought to be the appropriate line in view of the district court decision in *Frasier*, sent each of them a letter indicating that all was well. The one to Holmes, a high school senior, said in part: "This will acknowledge your application for admission together with your partial high school record which indicate that we will be able to approve your admission if you maintain your present scholastic average . . . and are graduated. A tentative dormitory reservation will be made as of this date." The letter to Thorpe, who was seeking to transfer to NC State from NC College, said much the same: "We have received your general application and your high school record. We will give you a statement concerning your admission as soon as we have received a complete official transcript of the work which you have completed from North Carolina College at Durham."[32]

Then the wrinkles developed. In February 1956, the chancellor—in what he appears to have thought was a routine message—advised the attorney general that two applications from black North Carolinians had been received, and the attorney general surprised the chancellor by urging that no action be taken on them. To be sure, the state had felt compelled to admit the three freshmen who brought the court case, but until the Supreme Court ruled on the state's appeal, the attorney general was unconvinced that any other black undergraduates ought to be admitted. Chancellor Bostian observed that "Mr. Rodman's reply leaves me greatly confused." Bostian had believed that "the judgment of the Court did apply to State College" and that black applicants were to be treated "exactly" like other candidates for admission.[33]

Within days, William C. Friday, acting president of the entire state university system, distributed a memorandum declaring that the attorney general's "attitude right now is that all we should do is merely to acknowledge the application received from a Negro who is a resident of the state." Such applicants

should receive only a terse, noncommittal note that "This letter is to acknowledge receipt of your application dated _____, which I received in my
office today."[34]

Later in March, another black high school senior, Irwin Richard Holmes
Jr., applied to NC State. By no means clear as to how to respond to the latest
black applicant, particularly in view of the earlier application from Walter Van
Buren Holmes, the NC State admissions director sought clarification from the
school's chancellor: "Since these two applicants are in the same class [at Hillside High School in Durham] and, we believe, related [though living at different addresses], the difference in the acknowledgement is quite likely to be
noticed and cause considerable publicity and embarrassment."[35]

THE SUPREME COURT DECISION IN *FRASIER*

Meanwhile, events had overtaken the "attitude right now" of the attorney general as characterized on March 1. On March 5, 1956, the U.S. Supreme Court
upheld the lower court's decision, much as it had five years earlier.[36] The state
was rebuffed again. The February language was appropriate after all; the judgment in *Brown* should be understood as applying to higher education as well
as to elementary and secondary schools. Black applicants could be admitted to
NC State. And both Irwin Richard Holmes Jr. and Walter Van Buren Holmes
were admitted.

A handful of black Tarheels had taken on the state establishment and,
through their recourse to the federal judiciary, had ended the policy of racial
exclusion. Hocutt had lost his bid in 1933; Epps and others had lost in 1950;
but McKissick and his colleagues had carried a successful appeal to higher
courts in 1951. In 1955 another case challenged black exclusion, this time
from undergraduate schools. This time the plaintiffs won in the first round,
and the state and the school were unsuccessful in their appeal to higher
authority.

The three students continued their studies, and henceforth their challenge
was entirely in the classroom, not in the courtroom. All three returned for a
second year, and a third, but none of the three completed a degree at UNC.
Their class graduated in 1959 without them. Leroy Frasier transferred to a
black school, NC College. "All three of us had scholastic difficulties," he
explained. His brother Ralph entered the army, and John Brandon went to
work at the Duke Medical Center.[37]

Though all three had left UNC, other black undergraduates had followed
them into the school, so it did not revert to nonblack. Lawrence Zollicoffer

enrolled in 1956 as an upperclassman and by 1962 had graduated from the UNC medical school. David Mozart Dansby Jr. enrolled at UNC as a freshman in 1957, graduated in 1961, and earned a law degree there in 1964.

The pioneers left a legacy from which others benefited, blazed a trail that others followed. To borrow a phrase from Martin Luther King Jr., they may not have gotten to the promised land; they may not have graduated. But they did get to the *un*promised land—and converted it into something of a promised land. After their pioneering efforts, the promise of higher education at any of North Carolina's public institutions extended to black Tarheels. The UNC trio's victory at the U.S. Supreme Court affected admissions practices at Raleigh and Greensboro, not just at Chapel Hill. All three schools in the UNC system changed their exclusionist policies and began to treat black applicants more like they treated other prospective students.

BLACK UNDERGRADUATES AT NC STATE

At North Carolina's nonblack land-grant school, Manuel Houston Crockett Jr. and Edward Carson began classes in summer 1956 in electrical engineering. Both were from Raleigh and lived at home. When they returned in the fall, they were joined by at least three other black undergraduates, among them Irwin Richard Holmes Jr. and Walter Van Buren Holmes, both of them from Durham and sharing a dorm room. All four graduated from NC State in engineering—Manuel Crockett and Irwin Holmes in 1960, Edward Carson and Walter Holmes in 1962.[38]

What began among graduate students at NC State in 1953, and among undergraduates in 1956, continued to build in the years that followed. In September 1958, the African American students at North Carolina State numbered ten, including three for whom it was their first term. Hazel Virginia Clarke, for one, was continuing work toward a graduate degree, and Irwin Holmes, starting his third year, was maintaining just above a B average in electrical engineering.[39]

Walter Holmes joined the band his freshman year. In view of his playing at football games, his participation called attention to his presence at NC State and raised hackles in North Carolina and South Carolina alike. Chancellor Bostian wrote an unhappy citizen: "We are fully aware of the attitude of the people of North Carolina [as Bostian put it] about the admission of Negroes and their participation in activities." Yet the five black freshmen each had a right to try out for student activities, or the school would be in "violation of the decree from the Federal courts." Two of the five had tried out. One was rejected because, it was said, he was an indifferent musician, but the other was "an excellent musician and there was no way the Director of the band could eliminate him."[40]

The next fall, Walter Holmes traveled to Clemson College, neighboring South Carolina's nonblack land-grant school, which was very similar to NC State except that desegregation had not yet begun there. Not only did Holmes march right out onto the football field with his fellow band members, but he ate with the rest of the band in Clemson's dining hall. Such affronts to South Carolina's laws and customs led Clemson College's president and South Carolina's attorney general to issue a policy statement designed to prevent such infractions in the future. They determined that, whatever a school might do on its own turf, it would have to respect the home team's laws and customs when it went on the road. South Carolina attorney general T. C. Callison was said to have explained that "the entire segregation structure of state supported schools and colleges presupposes that any integration on school grounds is untenable."[41]

Irwin Holmes, a classmate of Walter Holmes at NC State just as he had been at Durham's Hillside High School, graduated in 1960 in electrical engineering and went to work for IBM. Not only did he graduate, but he joined the student electrical engineering honor society. Not only did he play tennis for his school—all four years, one on the freshman squad and three on the varsity—but he served as team captain his senior year. In view of the fact that on most Southern campuses black students could not play varsity sports before at least 1967, Holmes's wielding a tennis racket for his school was only slightly less significant than his presence and performance in the classroom.[42]

Irwin Holmes's presence led his classmates and teammates to face questions of equal access in the Jim Crow South. That might mean that the tennis team looked for a place to eat until they found a place where *all* team members could eat. It might mean that the honor society, seeking a place to hold its annual banquet, refused all establishments that would not permit Holmes and his date to accompany them.[43] White and black students alike learned from their time together at NC State. The enrollment of even one black student, followed by his inclusion in school activities outside the classroom, had ripple effects across the campus and beyond it.

BLACK STUDENTS AT GREENSBORO

On the evening of August 13, 1956, a long-distance phone call came for a young lady in Raleigh named JoAnne Smart. A stranger at the other end, a news reporter, asked her: "How does it feel to be one of the first two Negro girls accepted to attend the Woman's College in Greensboro?" A letter from the school, confirming the news, soon arrived. A month later, JoAnne Smart headed west to Greensboro. Proud yet apprehensive, her parents drove her to college in the family's '38 Buick.[44]

Many white campuses, when they first accepted black students, offered no dormitory accommodations or on-campus eating arrangements, but Woman's College found another way to deal with the beginnings of racial change. When JoAnne Smart found her way to her dormitory room, she found her new roommate, Bettye Tillman, already settling in. Bettye Tillman was the other African American the reporter had had in mind in that phone call the month before. Smart and Tillman shared a room. In fact, that year they shared an entire wing of Shaw Residence Hall.[45]

Each year, more African American students followed the two pioneers. When JoAnne Smart and Bettye Tillman returned for their sophomore year, they were joined by Margaret Anne Patterson, Zelma Elizabeth Amey, and Claudette Treva Graves. Claudette Graves, who lived in Greensboro, came as a day student. She had originally wanted to go to Howard University, but could not afford the expense. While still in high school, she worked as a switchboard operator at North Carolina A&T, and she might well have gone to college there. But a class project at her high school during her senior year led her elsewhere. Years later, Graves recalled: "We had decided that many of us would try to enter the greater University of North Carolina," and the Dudley High School class of 1957 "selected someone to go to Chapel Hill, to [North Carolina] State, [and] to Woman's College." Her best friend, nominated to apply to Woman's College, did not want to go alone to take the mandatory entrance exam, so Graves accompanied her, and "I was accepted and she wasn't."[46]

Internal documents during the first couple of years of desegregation sometimes referred to one or another black applicant as a "Supreme Court Model." For example, when the admissions director reported that Claudette Graves and Zelma Amey had been accepted, she headed the memo "Admission of two Supreme Court Models."[47] Indeed, the Supreme Court, by responding favorably to those three young men who wanted to attend the University of North Carolina at Chapel Hill, fostered black enrollment at Greensboro. There is no doubt as to how the opportunity came about. But the court decision resulted in desegregation at Woman's College only because black high school students followed through and took advantage of the opening—and not just the two pioneers, but others each year afterwards. Every year, a few more black students enrolled at the school, and in 1960 the two pioneers completed their studies there, earned their degrees, and left the school a very different place than it had been four years before.

Thirty-plus years later, in 1992, Robin Edwards, the president of a black student group at UNCG, came to a realization that the school could and should do something to commemorate the first two black students on the campus. It "would be nice to have the parlor" in Shaw Hall, she said, "dedicated" in honor of Smart and Tillman. As she later explained her sense of the two pioneers' significance for the school and for herself: "Had these two ladies not had the courage to come here," black students "wouldn't have been here today."[48]

The idea gained approval, and dedication of the Tillman-Smart Parlor in Shaw Residence Hall took place in front of the dormitory on April 20, 1992. Bettye Tillman had died a number of years before, but JoAnne Smart, now JoAnne Smart Drane, attended the ceremony and in fact was the main speaker. "I only wish Bettye was here to share it," she told her audience—which included the university chancellor, the student government president, and representation from the board of visitors.[49] Drane reflected on how much had changed since her time as an undergraduate. "Who in my class, the class of 1960," she asked, "would have believed that there would be black faculty and black administrators teaching and overseeing programs and policies at this university? And who in my class would have envisioned that this university would name any place on this campus in honor of persons of African descent?"[50]

Four years later, in 1996—forty years after that drive from Raleigh to Greensboro so that JoAnne Smart could go to college and help end the school's long and absolute exclusion of African Americans—she was elected to the UNCG board of trustees. The very next year, Claudette Graves, class of 1961, now Claudette Graves Burroughs-White, joined her on the board.[51] Their terms on the board of trustees, like their time as undergraduates at the school, overlapped. Members of the first two integrated classes, distinguished graduates of the university, they became members of its board of trustees. Indeed, who would have thought?

BLACK TARHEELS, HIGHER EDUCATION, AND THE CIVIL RIGHTS MOVEMENT

During the 1950s, pioneers cracked the Jim Crow barrier to admission at historically nonblack institutions of higher education in North Carolina. The persistence of three seniors at a black high school in seeking admission to

UNC led to the enrollment of the first black undergraduates not only at Chapel Hill but also at North Carolina State and the first African American students at Woman's College as well, within months of the Supreme Court decision in March 1956 that the logic of *Brown v. Board of Education* should be understood as applying to undergraduate education.

In February 1960, several black students, including two at Woman's College in Greensboro, were just a few months away from becoming the first African Americans to earn undergraduate degrees from historically nonblack campuses in North Carolina. That month sit-ins began to take place in that city, protest actions from which the civil rights decade of the 1960s is often dated. A few black students at Woman's College—and a few white students there too—participated in those sit-ins. They found themselves caught up in the civil rights movement.

Claudette Graves Burroughs-White has fascinating recollections of the 1960 sit-ins that took place in her hometown while she was studying at Woman's College and commuting to school from home. In 1990 she participated in the thirtieth anniversary celebration—in fact, she chaired it: "And that gave me an opportunity to finally be a part of that, because I was a part of it in '60, but unnoticed"—unnoticed, she says, "because I was in the community, . . . but Woman's College didn't get noticed until the third day after the sit-ins started because that's when the white students came." She wanted the white students from the college "to be recognized," she said, because she felt it significant that they "would take the risk to come and be a part of the sit-ins." Moreover, they wore their class jackets from the college, so there could be little doubt regarding their institutional as well as their racial identities. Yet "nobody ever thought about the black students [from Woman's College] who may have been there already. But that's because we . . . looked like everybody else there." Edith Mayfield Wiggins, too, reports (apparently referring to black students at Woman's College): "We participated in the picketing."[52]

So some students from Woman's College participated in the civil rights movement in early 1960. Indeed, even before that, black North Carolinians had become part of the movement. They did so when they applied to non-black institutions of higher education. They did so when they went to court if necessary, as in the litigation at midcentury and again in 1955. They did so when they gained admission and took classes as black students on historically nonblack campuses—when they did what had never been done until their time at Chapel Hill, Raleigh, or Greensboro.

Floyd McKissick and others refused to let their racial identity keep them from attending the best law school in the state. Leroy Benjamin Frasier Jr. and two classmates at Durham's all-black Hillside High School refused to let their racial identity keep them out of UNC, and their victory in court led directly to the desegregation of undergraduate education at NC State and Woman's College as well as Chapel Hill. At NC State, Irwin Holmes played tennis for a school that had never until the 1950s enrolled an African American, and he graduated with honors in 1960.

JoAnne Smart and Bettye Tillman refused to be deterred by the thought that they would be the first of their race to take a class at Woman's College. Claudette Graves was part of a senior class project at Greensboro's all-black Dudley High School to propel North Carolina's public nonblack institutions of higher education farther along the process of desegregation, a process only just beginning at that time. What's more, having enrolled at Woman's College, she and some classmates, white and black alike, went downtown to participate in the Greensboro sit-ins.

At black and white schools alike, higher education and the civil rights movement were continuing to merge, to flow together. Studies of the two phenomena should also converge. Histories of the civil rights movement routinely tell the dramatic story of James Meredith at the University of Mississippi in 1962, but other pioneers, including the Frasier brothers, have remained invisible. The dominant visual image of the civil rights movement from 1960, a photograph of four North Carolina A&T freshmen at a Greensboro lunch counter, captures the significance of black students at black schools. Yet the graduation that year of black students from historically nonblack schools—Manuel Crockett and Irwin Holmes at NC State in Raleigh, JoAnne Smart and Bettye Tillman at Woman's College in Greensboro—displays another facet of the civil rights movement: the desegregation of higher education, at both the graduate and undergraduate levels, in state after state and at school after school.

NOTES

1. Richard Kluger, *Simple Justice: The History of Brown v. Board of Education and Black America's Struggle for Equality* (New York: Random House, 1974), presents the 1950 Supreme Court cases as stepping stones on the road to *Brown v. Board of Education*. Representative of the prevailing approach is a statement regarding the *Sweatt* decision that "once separate but equal fell in the realm of higher education, it was

only a matter of time before it fell in secondary and elementary education"—as though nothing more needed to be said about higher education once the Supreme Court had spoken in *Sweatt* (Donald G. Nieman, *Promises to Keep: African-Americans and the Constitutional Order, 1776 to the Present* [New York: Oxford University Press, 1991], 147). Robin D. G. Kelley and Earl Lewis, eds., *To Make Our World Anew: A History of African Americans* (New York: Oxford University Press, 2000), does not explore the desegregation of higher education in the 1950s.

2. I place the North Carolina events of the 1930s through the 1960s in a regional context, in Peter Wallenstein, "Black Southerners and Non-Black Universities: Desegregating Higher Education, 1935–1967," *History of Higher Education Annual* 19 (1999): 121–48.

3. *A Survey of Chinese Students in American Universities and Colleges in the Past One Hundred Years* (New York: China Institute in America, 1954), 46; *Agromeck* (1923), 64, and (1950), 137. A Chinese-American from Hawaii, Harold Chow, enrolled as a freshman in mechanical engineering in 1953. NCSU *Student Directory* (1953–54), 16.

4. Augustus M. Burns III, "Graduate Education for Blacks in North Carolina, 1930–1951," *Journal of Southern History* 46 (May 1980): 195–96.

5. Burns, "Graduate Education," 196; Gilbert Ware, *William Hastie: Grace under Pressure* (New York: Oxford University Press, 1984), 46–54; Neal King Cheek, "An Historical Study of the Administrative Actions in the Racial Desegregation of the University of North Carolina at Chapel Hill, 1930–1955" (Ph.D. diss., University of North Carolina at Chapel Hill, 1973), 35–39; Walter B. Weare, *Black Business in the New South: A Social History of the North Carolina Mutual Life Insurance Company* (Urbana: University of Illinois Press, 1973), 232–36; Walter White, *A Man Called White: The Autobiography of Walter White* (New York: Viking Press, 1948), 156–60.

6. Burns, "Graduate Education," 196.

7. *University v. Murray,* 169 Md. 478 (1936); *Missouri ex rel. Gaines v. Canada,* 305 U.S. 337 (1938).

8. Pauli Murray, *Song in a Weary Throat: An American Pilgrimage* (New York: Harper and Row, 1987), 64, 110; Burns, "Graduate Education," 207–8.

9. Ibid., 108–29.

10. Burns, "Graduate Education," 196–207; Cheek, "An Historical Study," 39–42, 59–105.

11. *Sweatt v. Painter,* 339 U.S. 629 (1950). Mark V. Tushnet, *The NAACP's Legal Strategy against Segregated Education, 1925–1950* (Chapel Hill: University of North Carolina Press, 1987), 120–37.

12. Burns, "Graduate Education," 209–11.

13. Ibid., 211–12.

14. Ibid., 212–15; *Epps v. Carmichael,* 93 F. Supp. 327 (M.D.N.C., 1950); Cheek, "An Historical Study," 118–32.

15. Unpaginated transcript of a taped interview with Floyd McKissick, 31 May 1989, in the Southern Oral History Program, Wilson Library, UNC.

16. *McKissick v. Carmichael,* 187 F.2d 949 (1951); *Carmichael v. McKissick,* 341 U.S. 951 (1951); Burns, "Graduate Education," 215–17; William D. Snider, *Light on the Hill: A History of the University of North Carolina at Chapel Hill* (Chapel Hill: University of North Carolina Press, 1992), 246–48; Cheek, "An Historical Study," 133–44; Jean L. Preer, *Lawyers v. Educators: Black Colleges and Desegregation in Public Higher Education* (Westport, Conn.: Greenwood Press, 1982), 114–15.

17. Burns, "Graduate Education," 217; Cheek, "An Historical Study," 145; Floyd McKissick interview. Further characterizing the pioneer black law students at UNC and their experiences is James H. Vaughan Jr., "The Integration of Negroes into the Law School of the University of North Carolina" (master's thesis, University of North Carolina at Chapel Hill, 1952), esp. 54–58. As for Diggs, see the *Durham Morning Herald,* 29 April 1951.

18. Cheek, "An Historical Study," 151–52.

19. Ibid., 153–60.

20. Ibid., 160–81.

21. Donald B. Anderson, associate dean of the graduate school, NC State, to Gordon Gray, president, UNC, 26 January 1954, University Archives, NC State; Alice Elizabeth Reagan, *North Carolina State University: A Narrative History* (Ann Arbor, Mich.: Edwards Brothers, 1987), 255.

22. Rev. S. F. Daly to J. W. Harrelson, chancellor, 27 August 1953, in Chancellor C. H. Bostian Papers, "Students, Negro, 1954" file, University Archives, NCSU.

23. Ibid.

24. Harrelson to Daly, 31 Aug. 1953.

25. Bostian to Dixon, 4 Nov. 1954.

26. Carey H. Bostian, chancellor NC State, to Gordon Gray, president, UNC, 31 May 1955; draft 7 July 1955; Gordon Gray, president, memorandum, 8 July 1955.

27. Bostian to Irving E. Carlyle, 22 Aug. 1955.

28. *Frasier v. Board of Trustees,* 134 F. Supp. 589, 590–91 (1955).

29. Ibid., 590.

30. Ibid., 592; William A. Link, *William Friday: Power, Purpose, and American Higher Education* (Chapel Hill: University of North Carolina Press, 1995), 82–84; Richard Paul Chait, "The Desegregation of Higher Education: A Legal History" (Ph.D. diss., University of Wisconsin, 1972), 139–41.

31. *Frasier v. Board of Trustees,* 592. Snider, *Light on the Hill,* fails to mention undergraduate desegregation in 1955. Jeffrey J. Crow, Paul D. Escott, and Flora J. Hatley, *A History of African Americans in North Carolina* (Raleigh: Division of Archives and History, 1992), 173–74, contains a brief account (not entirely consistent with the version presented here). For a fuller account, see Cheek, "An Historical Study," 182–201.

32. K. D. Rabb, director of admission and registration, to Dr. C. H. Bostian, chancellor, 4 April 1956; F. H. Spain, assistant director of admission and registration, to Thorpe, 17 Feb. 1956.

33. Bostian to Friday, 29 Feb. 1956.

34. William C. Friday, memorandum, 1 March 1956.

35. Rabb to Bostian, 4 April 1956.

36. *Board of Trustees v. Frasier,* 350 U.S. 979 (1956). The trio's lawyers at the U.S. Supreme Court included Thurgood Marshall as well as Conrad Pearson and Floyd McKissick.

37. "3 Negroes in South Quit College Class," *New York Times,* 24 May 1959, 113.

38. "'Same Basis' Planned for Housing Negroes at N.C. State," *Raleigh Times,* 19 June 1956; "Former Students Eligible to Return," undated list from summer 1957 in "Negro Students" vertical file; NCSU *Alumni Directory* (1997).

39. "Here at Present," typed list dated 29 Sept. 1958, "Negro Students" vertical file, University Archives, NCSU.

40. Bostian to A. W. Boswell, 5 Oct. 1956.

41. Del Booth, "S.C. Racial Policy Is 'Clear,'" *Raleigh News and Observer,* 17 Oct. 1957, 18.

42. *Agromeck* (1960), 169; Todd McGee, "Remembering the Pioneers," *Wolfpacker,* 15 March 1997, 8–9.

43. McGee, "Remembering the Pioneers," 8–9.

44. Joanne Smart Drane, "The Way It Was . . . ," UNCG *Alumni News* 68 (spring 1980), 9–10.

45. Ibid. Drane's recollections are incorporated in Amy Thompson McCandless, *The Past in the Present: Women's Higher Education in the Twentieth-Century American South* (Tuscaloosa: University of Alabama Press, 1999), 224, 226–27, in a chapter that tells of people who participated in comparable developments on other Southern campuses. For a sociological study of black female students—most of them Northern—attending predominantly white institutions of higher education in a city in the North in the 1960s, see Elizabeth Higginbotham, *Too Much to Ask: Black Women in the Era of Integration* (Chapel Hill: University of North Carolina Press, 2001), xi, 163–203.

46. Claudette Graves Burroughs-White, interviewed by Cheryl Junk, 25 Feb. 1991, unpaginated transcript, UNCG Centennial Oral History Project, University Archives, University of North Carolina at Greensboro. David Mozart Dansby Jr. was her classmate who went to Chapel Hill, and Richard H. Bowling was the one who went to NC State. Each of the three students in the Dudley High School senior class project went on to graduate—Bowling in electrical engineering in 1964. For a first-person exploration of the beginnings of desegregation in Greensboro's public schools—with occasional comments about segregation in the city's colleges—see Josephine Ophelia Boyd Bradley, "Wearing My Name: School Desegregation, Greensboro, North Carolina, 1954–1958" (Ph.D. diss., Emory University, 1995), 285, 351.

47. Mildred P. Newton to Mrs. Yoder, 9 May 1957, in "Segregation," Box 4, Pierson Records; Mildred P. Newton to Mrs. Yoder, 25 May 1957, ibid.; Mildred P. Newton to Dr. Blackwell, 29 June 1957, Chancellor Gordon Williams Blackswell Records, 1957–1960, University Archives, UNCG.

48. Anubha Anand, "Parlor Re-named to Honor Alumni," *Carolinian,* 27 April 1992, 1.

49. Ibid.; dedication program, 20 April 1992, in "Tillman-Smart Parlor" file, University Archives, UNCG.

50. "Remarks—Dedication Tillman-Smart Parlor," in "Tillman-Smart Parlor" file.

51. Press release, "JoAnne Smart Drane of Raleigh Named to UNCG Board of Trustees"; and *Alumni News* (fall 1997): 21.

52. Claudette Graves Burroughs-White and Edith Mayfield Wiggins, unpaginated transcripts. Reference to the three white students from Woman's College, though without any names, is made in Miles Wolff, *Lunch at the 5 & 10* (1970; rev. ed., Chicago: Ivan R. Dee, 1990), and in William H. Chafe, *Civilities and Civil Rights: Greensboro, North Carolina, and the Black Struggle for Freedom* (New York: Oxford University Press, 1980). One of the three writes briefly of her experience, includes some sketches she drew at the time (an artist, she was studying fine arts at Woman's College), and names the other two, Marilyn Lott and Jeanie Seaman, in Ann Dearsley-Vernon, "A White at the Woolworth Sit-In," *Alumni News* 68 (spring 1980): 7–8, 29.

14

Training for Partial Citizenship
Black Military Schools in the Age of Jim Crow

ROD ANDREW JR.

In the decades immediately following the Civil War, a wave of military education swept the South. The rebirth of Virginia Military Institute and The Citadel reinvigorated the Southern tradition of state-supported military colleges. Scores of private military academies sprouted across the region; and most importantly, every white Southern land-grant college founded under the terms of the Morrill Act of 1862 operated as a full-fledged military school, mimicking the military features of Virginia Military Institute and The Citadel. Mississippi State, Louisiana State, Texas A & M, Arkansas, Auburn, North Georgia, Virginia Tech, Tennessee, Clemson, and North Carolina State all required their male students to join a corps of cadets, wear uniforms on a daily basis, and submit to a system of military regulations, demerits, promotions, and court-martials.

The Southern obsession with military training in higher education for young men grew out of the region's rich military tradition, further strengthened by the Confederate experience. The legend of the "Lost Cause," by which white Southerners interpreted and glorified their Confederate experience, strengthened the philosophical ties in Southerners' minds between martial valor and moral and civic virtue. There was a broad consensus among Southern whites that military life and training would instill in future generations the very virtues on which the safety and health of the Republic depended— courage, patriotism, integrity, self-discipline, respect for the law, and moral rectitude.[1]

The fact that is usually overlooked is that this pro-military philosophy profoundly influenced higher education for black Southerners as well. Educators at black colleges pursued goals similar, though not identical, to leaders of white schools when they incorporated military training. Conditions unique to black schools, however, stunted the growth of military traditions at those institutions before World War I. Black normal schools and land-grant schools found it practically impossible to obtain arms, inhibiting student interest in the military program, dampening esprit de corps in student military companies, and limiting the perceived benefits of military drill. Leaders of black schools faced other difficulties stemming from the fact that a military tradition among African Americans as a whole was still only partially developed. Perhaps most important, though, was the fact that white Victorian America, at heart, desired neither full citizenship nor soldiership for African Americans. In the South especially, the very idea of black youth fortified with a combination of arms and military discipline was repugnant and threatening to white citizens. The black military tradition, therefore, along with black citizenship, was only precariously established in the age of Jim Crow.[2]

The first black school to introduce elements of military life to its male students was Hampton Normal and Agricultural Institute, founded by Samuel Chapman Armstrong in Hampton, Virginia, in 1868 and initially supported by the Northern-based American Missionary Association. Armstrong was a former Union army officer who had commanded black troops in the Civil War. He was heavily influenced by many of the racist attitudes of his day. While he praised the abilities of black men as soldiers, Armstrong believed that slavery had instilled strong tendencies toward laziness in the black race. Through strict discipline (provided in part through the military program at Hampton) and steady, routine work, Armstrong hoped to train a corps of self-disciplined black teachers in the industrial arts who would transmit the Puritan work ethic to the black working class. Hampton male students therefore drilled in military formations, wore uniforms, and were subject to daily personnel and room inspections. In 1878 Hampton began admitting Native American students as well.[3] Hampton continued as one of the few black "military" colleges until the 1890s.

Congress passed a second Morrill Act in 1890, largely to ensure that the states provided higher education for black as well as for white youth. Under the 1890 law, states either had to admit blacks to existing land-grant colleges or establish separate institutions for them. The Southern states, of course, all chose the latter course. The second Morrill Act, unlike the first, did not explicitly call for military education. Its stated purpose was "the more complete endowment and maintenance of colleges" established under the original Morrill Act, but it omitted any reference to military instruction, mandating that land-grant funds "be applied only to instruction in agriculture, the mechanic arts, the English language and the various branches of mathematical, physical, natural, and economic science, with special reference to their applications in the industries of life."[4]

The passage of the second Morrill Act led to the opening of several black institutions that followed Hampton's lead in concentrating on teacher training and industrial education. Some of them instituted the military system as well. Georgia State Industrial College (now Savannah State) opened in Savannah in 1891 and had organized its students into a corps of cadets by 1898. The South Carolina legislature formed the Colored Normal, Industrial, Agricultural, and Mechanical College of South Carolina (now South Carolina State) out of an earlier institution in 1896, and this school immediately established a military program. The Florida legislature reorganized the school now known as Florida A & M as a land-grant institution in 1890–91, and the faculty had instituted a military system for the young men—possibly by 1903, and certainly by 1908.[5]

Inasmuch as Armstrong was interested in the role of military discipline in the formation of character, his goals at Hampton were similar to those of the leaders of white military colleges. The main difference was that racial stereotypes influenced Armstrong's objectives. He saw military drill and routine as a means to correct the perceived flaws of the Negro (and Native American) races. Whereas military discipline supposedly tamed the high-spirited, rebellious nature of Southern white boys, Armstrong intended for it to correct the perceived sloth, licentiousness, lack of self-discipline, and improper bearing of blacks and Indians. "Military drill," he wrote, "makes possible a training in self-discipline . . . and does much to promote that esprit de corps in which the Negro is markedly lacking."[6] Daily drill and inspections of rooms and persons would "create ideas of neatness, order, system, obedience, and produce a better manhood."[7] It would also contribute to the students' physical bearing, self-control, and sense of personal responsibility. As in the case of white military schools, Armstrong also thought military discipline complemented his school's emphasis on piety, regular church attendance, and mandatory daily chapel.[8]

Skeptics argued that Armstrong's policy of allowing coeducation at Hampton was unwise, as they saw Negro character as both "passionate and indolent." Armstrong's reply was that "there is little mischief done when there is no time for it. Activity is a purifier . . . I have little fear of the abuse of co-education at Hampton. My boys are rung up at 5 o'clock in the morning, called to military parade before breakfast, kept busy all day until 8 P.M., always under military discipline, and after that hour I will risk all the harm they will do to anybody."[9] Thus, according to Armstrong, the military system could reform the behavior, if not the inborn character, of the Negro race. Northerners who supported Hampton agreed that blacks lacked discipline. Lyman Abbot, Congregational minister and executive secretary of the American Freedman's Union Commission, lauded the system of work and drill at Hampton, saying, "This is just the discipline the Negro race needs to fit it for manhood."[10]

Armstrong and those who commanded his cadets also instituted a system of student courts-martial, or "officers' court," in which cadet officers (older students) tried and punished their fellow students for breaches of conduct. Thus, Hampton leaders claimed they could use the military system to teach their students lessons in "self-government." Armstrong's successor as principal, Hollis Burke Frissell, reported to the trustees in 1890 that "discipline has more and more been administered by the cadets themselves, through their own court martial. Self-government is as important a lesson as self-help."[11] This self-government, though, always meant black oversight and supervision over the behavior of members of their own race, and the standards of behavior corresponded with those of the Northern white, middle-class Protestants who ran the school. It never implied the possibility of black control over whites or full participation in American democracy.[12]

Remarkably, some of Armstrong's black graduates and faculty members repeated these racial stereotypes when they praised the usefulness of military education. One of the most prominent black educators of the early twentieth century, Robert R. Moton, echoed these claims. Moton was a Hampton graduate and served as commandant of cadets there from 1891 to 1916, when he succeeded Booker T. Washington as president of Tuskegee. In his 1893 report to Principal Frissell, which was forwarded to the Board of Trustees and printed in the *Southern Workman,* Moton wrote:

> The physical training which military drill makes imperative . . . is of great value, securing the best physical culture, a firm and elastic step, erect form, graceful carriage, and vigorous bodily powers.
>
> The habit of attention and mental concentration, which the Negro and Indian sadly lack, is developed in a large measure. The habits of neatness, good order, and promptness form a part of his

daily routine, while the constant necessity of quick, responsive, and decided physical and mental action results in habitual decision of manner, movement, and speech. Further than this, he receives training in self-government, self-restraint, in prompt obedience, in submission to law and authority, and in the exercise of authority.[13]

Black colleges in the late nineteenth and early twentieth centuries mimicked Hampton's focus on strict discipline, hard work, and piety. In this sense, they were quite similar to white land-grant schools. Yet only a handful turned to the military system before World War I and the advent of the Reserve Officers Training Corps program. The biases of their white supporters and sponsors were partially responsible for that. A large number of the black schools founded between 1865 and 1890 (including Hampton, Claflin, Fisk, LeMoyne, Talladega, Tuskegee, Meharry Medical, Wiley, Morgan State, Rust, Howard, and what became Atlanta University) grew from the initiative and oversight of Northern philanthropy and missionary efforts. Most of these, except Talladega and Claflin, never seriously contemplated instituting a full-fledged military system. Their Northern missionary sponsors were certainly interested in imparting middle-class Victorian virtues of punctuality, neatness, order, and self-discipline but probably did not see military discipline as a means of instilling them. Subsequently, the second Morrill Act virtually forced Southern states after 1890 to provide land-grant schools for blacks. Though the states satisfied black demands by usually allowing the schools to hire black principals and faculty, the illusion of black control was just that. In reality, white administrators were determined to exercise firm control over the black colleges' organization, policies, curriculum, and finances. These Southern white state officials were indifferent if not hostile to the idea of establishing military programs at those schools. Southern land-grant schools that did not incorporate the military feature until after World War I included North Carolina A & M, Prairie View A & M (in Texas), Southern (in Louisiana), and Tennessee A & I.[14]

Those black land-grant schools that did organize a corps of cadets justified the move for reasons similar to those of Hampton. South Carolina State catalogs claimed that the military organization taught obedience to law and order, and promoted healthful habits and physical vigor. Florida A & M said it complemented study, taught manly bearing, instilled respect for law and order, and contributed to the overall "physical, mental, and moral development of the boys."[15]

Often, though, the military feature at black colleges evolved slowly. In the schools' earliest years, it had little influence on student life. While most white land-grant schools, for example, required students to wear uniforms on a daily basis soon after their opening, black schools were slow to adopt this requirement. Florida A & M did not require uniforms or military drill until 1902, twelve years after its reorganization as a land-grant school. The first mention of uniforms at Savannah State appeared in the 1899–1900 catalog, which advised male students that it "would be wise" to purchase a uniform from the school's department of tailoring, since it was cheaper than a civilian suit.[16]

Another indicator of how much prominence educators gave the military system is whether or not they appointed a faculty member whose full-time job was teaching military science courses and overseeing the discipline of cadets. White schools designated this instructor "Professor of Military Science and Tactics" and usually referred to him as the "commandant." Usually they were able to obtain the services of a Regular Army officer sent by the War Department to help them comply with the provisions of the Morrill Act in regard to military instruction. When the War Department neglected to send such an officer, they hired retired officers or former cadets at their own expense.

It was some time before the black colleges gave military instruction enough attention to designate a faculty member officially as the commandant. Florida A & M did not appoint anyone to serve as commandant of cadets until it hired William A. Howard in 1908. Howard took his military duties seriously, but even he was not a full-time commandant, since he was also professor of mathematics and painting. Savannah State was even slower to take this step.[17]

There was another area in which black colleges steered their curricula away from a military orientation—they neglected the study of military tactics. Hampton students occasionally received such instruction, especially during years when the commandant was a Regular Army officer or when the school was able to get an officer from nearby Fortress Monroe to visit the campus a few times a week. But Armstrong carefully tried to calm white fears that he was training a black soldiery. He made it clear that "it is not intended to make soldiers out of our students, or to create a warlike spirit. Such a course would be most unwelcome to our friends and supporters."[18]

South Carolina State was exceptional among black schools in that it provided its students instruction in military science and tactics. That school was uniquely fortunate in its early years to have two of the very few black men who had attended West Point, Robert Shaw Wilkinson and Johnson C. Whittaker, as faculty members. The school dropped its military science courses in 1910. It continued, though, to retain a corps of cadets for purposes of discipline.[19]

South Carolina State was unique in this regard, however. At Savannah State and Florida A & M there was probably no official instruction in military tactics. Despite the fact that Savannah State's original "Plan of Organization" stipulated that the students would take military science courses, there is no evidence from college catalogs and course schedules that they did. Savannah State allowed students to form a military company in 1892 as an extracurricular activity and provided them with a tactics manual, but this training never became a part of the official curriculum. Lack of official white encouragement was probably a reason for this, as Savannah State received no federal or state funds for military equipment. Savannah State and Florida A & M quickly gave up all pretensions of being training grounds for professional soldiers or even citizen-soldiers.[20]

Even more significant is the fact that cadets at black schools rarely, if ever, were allowed to carry rifles. Federal law provided for the War Department to supply 150 Springfield rifles and other ordnance items to land-grant schools who enrolled at least 150 male students. Despite easily meeting that criterion, Georgia State and Florida A & M cadets never drilled with weapons. The South Carolina State 1896–97 catalog contains a picture that appears to show some of the cadets carrying a rifle, a stick, or a short lance, and the text indicates that the military instruction included "the manual of arms and bayonet exercise."[21] Talladega cadets drilled with lances during that school's brief experiment with military training from 1877 to 1879, and Hampton cadets in some years had the opportunity to drill with wooden sticks or pikes. Yet the remarkable fact remains that at most black "military" schools, male students awoke every morning to a bell or bugle, wore military uniforms, formed into companies, marched and drilled, and yet rarely, if ever, touched a rifle.[22]

The correspondence of black college presidents that is still extant does not explicitly indicate whether it was college officials, War Department officers, or white men in state and local government who most objected to black cadets drilling with rifles. There is, however, a small collection of reports and letters written by Hampton commandants and faculty members that indicates that although a few Hampton officials and Regular Army officers connected with Hampton desired weapons for their cadets, it was an extremely sensitive issue.

In 1872 Hampton cadets drilled with wooden sticks. From 1874 through 1879, however, Armstrong reported to the Board of Trustees that his cadets were not supplied with, and did not drill with, weapons. Possibly, then, Hampton cadets had stopped drilling even with wooden sticks after 1872. In 1882 the commandant, First Lieutenant George Leroy Brown of the United States Army, reported the same thing. Brown went on to recommend that the school acquire a stand of arms so that he could instruct the senior class "in the manual and the use of the rifle." This, he said, would "do much towards increasing the spirit of the battalion."[23] Probably in response to white fears of a large black armed force, however, Brown carefully advocated arming only the seniors, not "the entire battalion."[24]

Lieutenant Brown did not give up. In 1883 he repeated his argument that arms were needed to aid in the drill exercises and in increasing the "spirit of the drill," although the "foot-lance or pike [recently] approved by the principal" would help.[25] By 1887, the cadets once again used a "sword-stick" at drill.[26] In 1895 another officer made a long, determined argument in favor of Hampton cadets being allowed to train with rifles. By this time, Hampton had its first black commandant, Robert R. Moton. However, the request came, not from Moton, but from First Lieutenant E. W. Hubbard, an officer stationed at Fortress Monroe who aided Moton in drilling the cadets. After discussing the situation with Principal Frissell, Hubbard wrote a letter to Frissell so that the latter could pass it on to the Trustees. Hubbard anticipated the objections of local white citizens and the concern, perhaps of the trustees, that arming young black men would lead to violence and other "improper use" of the weapons:

> Sir—
>
> In accordance with my verbal agreement with you, I have the honor to submit for your consideration and that of the Trustees at their approaching annual meeting, the following considerations relative to the procuring of arms and equipments for the use and instruction of the cadets of the Institute.
>
> This question is, I am aware, somewhat complicated by considerations which do not obtain elsewhere, and I write solely from the standpoint of Military Instructor, and with a view of bringing the cadets to as high a standard of drill, soldierly bearing and conduct as the necessarily limited time devoted to military matters will permit.
>
> Without entering into any argument as to the value of military drills at a school such as this, it may be said that the highest

benefits of such instruction can only be obtained by the use of arms at drill. The bearing of arms is the natural aim of all military instruction. Although at this school the incidental advantages of discipline, soldierly bearing etc. must properly outweigh mere proficiency in the use of arms, still it must be acknowledged that the prospect of bearing arms would operate powerfully towards securing the incidental advantages mentioned. A prime requisite of successful instruction is to get and keep the pupil's interest. Applying this to the case in hand nothing would do more among the cadets to foster an interest in drill than the prospect of having arms put into their hands on their attaining a proper degree of proficiency. . . .

Without arms the drill is limited almost entirely to the gymnastic or "setting up" drills and marching manoeuvres. This naturally becomes somewhat monotonous. With arms a greater variety could be introduced, the appearance of the battalion made more effective and an opportunity given for acquiring a degree of exactness and steadiness at drill which can scarcely be obtained without their use.

In case arms are issued to the School the time now devoted to military instruction need not be increased. The drill session would begin at the bottom as now, without arms, and arms taken up later on. Arms and equipments are issued to institutions of learning by the Government under conditions set forth in circular from the Chief of Ordnance, U.S. Army, herewith enclosed. It is suggested that the arms be not actually put into the hands of the cadets except during drills. At other times they could be securely stored in a suitable room fitted up as an arsenal. If any additional precaution is needed against improper use the firing pins can be removed from the arms and placed securely elsewhere as without them the arms are useless.

Very respectfully,
E. W. Hubbard
1st Lieut.
3rd Artillery, U. S. A.
Military Instructor[27]

Lieutenant Hubbard clearly understood that the question of arming black and Indian youths at Hampton was "complicated by considerations which do not apply elsewhere." Probably those considerations included local white hostility to the idea of hundreds of black and Indian youth being trained to arms at a school founded by an ex-Union army officer. They may also have included the fears of the Northern white men who led Hampton's board that arming what they believed to be inferior, undisciplined races was improper if not dangerous. The lieutenant therefore made several assurances to reassure the trustees that Hampton would not become a training ground for black warriors, nor would serious incidents occur that would give the school negative publicity. The amount of time devoted to military instruction would remain the same, the cadets would not handle the weapons except during drill, the school would secure the arms in an armory, and the firing pins would be removed.[28]

Hubbard's diplomatic appeal failed to secure arms for the cadets. In the following year, 1896, the young black commandant Robert R. Moton repeated Hubbard's request, and Principal Frissell officially endorsed it. Moton avoided the issue in 1897, but he returned to it in 1898, saying: "I think the time has come when the school could reasonably adopt guns to be used in the squad, company, and battalion drills, though not necessarily for other ceremonies."[29] By "other ceremonies," Moton probably meant parades, commencements, and other occasions in which the public was invited. That spring saw Hampton ex-cadets enlisting, becoming noncommissioned officers (NCOs) in the Regular Army, and deploying to fight against Spain; thus, Moton could reasonably argue that "the time had come" to trust blacks with rifles. Yet his argument failed to convince the authorities, and he dropped it in later reports. There is no evidence that Hampton cadets ever drilled with rifles before World War I, and pictures from the period continue to show the young men of the school standing in formation in blue uniforms without weapons.[30]

The details of this story are, of course, sketchy. It is unclear whether the leaders of Savannah State and Florida A & M, preoccupied with more pressing issues, even sought rifles. The black principal of Savannah State, Richard R. Wright Sr., found himself constantly trying to persuade white trustees and administrators to give him more control over the organization, curriculum, and finances of the school. Savannah State fell under administrative control of the Board of Trustees of the University of Georgia, and the trustees believed that the black college required the "oversight of competent white [men]."[31] White trustees and local administrators denied Wright the privilege of appealing directly to the state legislature for funds or attending meetings of the trustees —privileges enjoyed by the leaders of white colleges of the state. With these handicaps, Wright waged an ongoing and mostly unsuccessful campaign to acquire adequate funding for his school. Probably, then, he regarded securing arms and a professor of military science as the least of his problems. He had to pick his battles, and meeting the more basic needs of his impoverished institution came first.[32]

Besides the absence of weapons, several factors may have inhibited the growth of a military tradition at some black schools, especially those who had no military program at all. Many, like Florida A & M, Savannah State, and South Carolina State, maintained a policy of having an all-black faculty, and there was a severe shortage of trained military and ex-military officers who were black. This is not to say that there was no black military tradition. Blacks were justifiably proud of their service in the Civil War. More than 178,000 had served in the Union Army, helping to secure their own freedom. But while white military schools could draw from a vast reservoir of experienced and senior Confederate officers, very few black men had received wartime commissions even as junior officers. By the time South Carolina State, Savannah State, and Florida A & M opened three decades later, even these black veterans would have been quite old. During the Spanish-American War, the War Department decided that blacks could serve as officers in the four regiments of the United States Colored Troops, but that none would be commissioned above the rank of lieutenant.[33]

For a time the tradition of black military service survived in the many black militia companies organized in the South during and after Reconstruction. These units had been quite important to black communities, offering their members social status and self-respect. The War Department, however, seldom sent Regular Army officers to assist in their training. It did send Inspectors General, who wrote critical evaluations of these units' readiness. It is questionable whether these units produced many officers capable of teaching drill at the battalion level, much less those familiar with the West Point system of adapting military discipline to an educational environment. In any case, the black militia and National Guard units were already beginning to decline by the time of the Spanish-American War. One by one, Southern states (and some Northern states) took legislative action to restrict and finally eliminate black units. By 1905 the black contingent of the National Guard had virtually disappeared.[34]

White schools, additionally, could and did draw from a large pool of white men educated in the dozens of antebellum Southern military schools. Besides Hampton, of course, there were few black military schools, nor were there many black men educated under the military system. Between 1872 and 1889 only twenty-two blacks received appointments to West Point. Twelve passed the entrance examination, and only three survived the ostracism and demanding coursework to graduate, only to struggle against severe discrimination in their Regular Army careers. The record of the Naval Academy at Annapolis was even more dismal. African American military experience, then, largely resided in the enlisted and NCO ranks. The black military man was typically an enlisted figure—trained, disciplined, and supervised by white officers. The cadre of black officers who had been allowed the opportunity to command large bodies of troops or who had experience with the system of military education was small indeed.[35]

While it was some time before Savannah State and Florida A & M hired anyone truly qualified to teach military science and tactics, South Carolina State was unusually fortunate. In 1896 the school applied to the Secretary of War for an army officer to teach military science and tactics and specified that he be "colored."[36] The War Department replied, probably quite truthfully, that no colored officer was available. The school was eventually fortunate enough, however, to secure one of the few African Americans who had ever attended West Point, Robert Shaw Wilkinson, as its professor of mathematics, and he assumed the additional duties of commandant. Wilkinson had attended West Point from 1884 to 1885, when he had resigned due to "insufficient physical strength."[37] In 1900 another black ex-cadet of West Point, Johnson C. Whittaker, assumed Wilkinson's duties. Whittaker had been the victim of a brutal hazing incident inflicted by white cadets in his final year at West Point and was court-martialed before graduation for allegedly inflicting his own injuries. After his dismissal from West Point, he became a teacher and lawyer in Camden, South Carolina. Thomas E. Miller, Whittaker's good friend and former classmate at the University of South Carolina, was then president of South Carolina State and asked Whittaker to join the faculty there as professor of mathematics and commandant.[38]

The lack of opportunity for a career in the military surely dampened the military enthusiasm of many black cadets. While the white land-grant schools never aimed specifically to train professional soldiers, some of their cadets did win commissions to West Point. Others who distinguished themselves in the military department had their names published in War Department reports so that the army would have a pool of potential officers to call upon in case of war. Some college catalogs advertised this fact. A large number of white ex-cadets, in addition, became militia officers. Black men, however, had little chance to become militia officers in Southern states, especially after the abolition of black militia units around the turn of the century. Their opportunities in the Regular Army also were slim. In 1917, the total number of black line officers in the Regular Army was three; in 1939, five. Even if a black college student wanted a military career in the enlisted ranks, opportunities were few. Between 1869 and 1939 Congress and the War Department limited the number of black regiments in the Regular Army to four. When these regiments were filled, which was often, the army allowed no blacks to enlist until vacancies appeared.[39]

There were, then, several reasons why a black military school tradition remained only partially developed. The ambivalence or hostility of white Southerners, the shortage of trained black commandants, and the lack of opportunity for a military career for black cadets all played a role. Yet the most fundamental factor, and the one that underlay all the others, was the recognition that soldiership implied full citizenship, and whites were unprepared to concede the latter to blacks.

Historians today recognize that, like other white educators of his day, Samuel Chapman Armstrong of Hampton had limited goals for black education. Armstrong did not believe blacks should engage in politics or push for equal civil rights. Instead, he sought to instill social discipline and good work habits so they could properly fill "subordinate roles in the southern economy."[40] Armstrong even favored black disfranchisement. As James D. Anderson has noted, Armstrong insisted on a "second-class education" for blacks, to prepare them for "second-class citizenship."[41] Thus, he probably never endorsed the recommendations of white army officers from Fortress Monroe that his cadets should have rifles. Instead, he assured local white citizens that his cadets were not a threat and that he was not preparing them to challenge white hegemony. Military training, then, was useful for imparting habits of discipline, obedience, and industry to a subordinate race; but when it included the bearing of arms, it became a dangerous recognition of full citizenship.[42]

The story was similar for Southern land-grant schools. Occasionally, both white and black educators recognized the usefulness of, or at least tolerated, military training for black youth in the belief that it contributed to an orderly, industrious, and responsible black community. White leaders conceded that as long as military training aimed only to foster discipline and lawful subordination, it was acceptable, if not beneficial, for black youth. But black military education was a double-edged sword. White leaders balked when it included the bearing of arms, for this implied "first-class" or "full" citizenship in which the citizen was encouraged to defend his rights in a bold, assertive way. A group of armed citizen-soldiers, imbued with a sense of martial pride along with the belief that it was an aggrieved minority, reminded white Southerners too much of themselves in 1861.

Whether consciously or subconsciously, then, white Southerners understood that an unhindered black military tradition implied full citizenship for blacks and thus racial equality and the end of white supremacy. It was no accident, therefore, that the disfranchisement of blacks in the Southern states occurred during the same period in which the states disbanded their black militia or National Guard units. Joel Williamson has identified the period between 1889 and 1915 as the time in which the "Radical" mentality most governed white thinking on race. Racial radicals, he says, believed that the Negro was "retrogressing rapidly into his natural state of savagery" and that there was "no place for the Negro in the future American society."[43] This was also the same period in which black land-grant schools were opening, trying to establish military traditions, and possibly contemplating the likelihood of being able to obtain arms for their young cadets. Their timing could not have been worse.

Black military education got off to a difficult start. It began at Hampton, where a Union ex-general introduced the concept in an attempt to create a disciplined, industrious, and subordinate black working class. A few black land-grant schools followed. When they instituted military programs, some of their reasons for doing so were similar to those of the white schools—to instill discipline and mold character.

The postbellum white schools, however, had a far deeper tradition of military education from which to draw than did the black schools. The South had a long tradition of educating its white youth to be soldiers as well as citizens. The myth of the Lost Cause perpetuated the Southern military tradition and served to strengthen the connection between martial and moral virtues in the minds of white Southerners. This, in turn, had an effect on how educators at white land-grant schools ran their institutions.[44]

The South also had a long tradition of keeping weapons out of the hands of black men as well as denying them access to higher education. Thus, black colleges had no antebellum tradition of black military schools to sustain them. The federal government, too, was ambivalent if not hostile to the idea of black men serving as U.S. soldiers and took little interest in developing a black officer corps. Most important of all, whites recognized the political implications of granting blacks the status of armed soldiers and therefore of full citizens. Thus, while black Southerners did have a proud tradition of military service drawn from their militia, Civil War, and earlier experiences, there were serious obstacles to black military achievement in the age of Jim Crow. Consequently, black military education as a whole was slow to develop.

Perhaps this chapter will provoke further study and more detailed answers concerning the extent of black military education. But the information presented here indicates that in late-nineteenth- and early-twentieth-century America, especially the South, citizenship implied soldiership and vice-versa. The society that granted only nominal citizen status to blacks was also hesitant to honor them or train them as soldiers. While blacks struggled unsuccessfully for full citizenship during this period, their military traditions—their claims to status as citizen-soldiers—foundered as well.

NOTES

1. Rod Andrew Jr., *Long Gray Lines: The Southern Military School Tradition, 1839–1915* (Chapel Hill: University of North Carolina Press, 2001).

2. This essay focuses on Hampton Institute, Florida A & M, Georgia (now Savannah) State, South Carolina State, and, to a lesser degree, Talladega. The records of these schools, especially in regard to military training, are generally sparser, more scattered, and more difficult to locate than white land-grant and military colleges (Hampton is an exception). Often there is enough evidence to offer speculations and educated guesses but not enough to prove them. I hope this essay will be the springboard to more conclusive studies of this topic. Special thanks go to the librarians and archivists of the five schools mentioned above.

3. James D. Anderson, "The Historical Development of Black Vocational Education," in *Work, Youth, and Schooling: Historical Perspectives on Vocationalism in American Education* (Stanford: Stanford University Press, 1982), 185–87; Anderson and Vincent P. Franklin, *New Perspectives on Black Educational History* (Boston: G. K. Hall, 1978), 70–71; "Hampton Institute Military Drill," collection of reports concerning military matters by Hampton officials found in Military Science Collection,

Hampton University Archives; Samuel Chapman Armstrong, *Twenty-two Years' Work of Hampton Normal and Agricultural Institute* (Hampton, Va.: Normal School Press, 1893), 2–3, 6, 8, 9.

4. *U.S. Laws, Statutes, Session Laws, 1889–90,* 51st Congress, 1st sess. (Washington, D.C.,: Government Printing Office, 1890), 417–18. Though Hampton originally relied exclusively on private funding, it secured one-third of Virginia's land-grant funds for several years beginning in 1872, making it less dependent on private Northern funding (Robert Francis Engs, *Freedom's First Generation: Black Hampton, Virginia, 1861–1890* [Philadelphia: University of Pennsylvania Press, 1979], 148).

5. *Announcement and Catalogue of the Georgia State Industrial College* (1898–99) [hereafter, *GSIC Catalog*], 25; *GSIC Catalog* (1899–1900), 64; John F. Potts Sr., *A History of South Carolina State College, 1896–1978* (Columbia, S.C.: R. L. Bryan Company, 1978), 20, 28, 31. Anecdotal evidence suggests Florida A & M boys were marched to breakfast in military formations by 1903; certainly by 1908 the school had a well-organized corps of cadets with a commandant and cadet officers appointed (Leedell W. Neyland and John W. Riley, *The History of Florida Agricultural and Mechanical University* (Gainesville: University of Florida Press, 1963), 146–47; *The Florida State Normal and Industrial School Twenty-first Annual Catalogue* (hereafter, *FAMC Catalog*), [1908], 14–15).

6. *Southern Workman* 15 (April 1886): 47.

7. *Hampton Normal and Agricultural Institute Annual Reports* (1878) [hereafter, *Hampton Reports*].

8. *Southern Workman* 14 (June 1885): 74; *Southern Workman* 9 (June 1880): 65; Francis Greenwood Peabody, *Education for Life: The Story of Hampton Institute* (Garden City, N.Y.: Doubleday, Page, 1926), 135, 220–23; *Hampton Catalog* (1872–73), 21; Mrs. M. F. Armstrong and Helen W. Ludlow, *Hampton and Its Students, by Two of Its Teachers* (New York: G. P. Putnam's Sons, 1874), 23–24; "Hampton Institute Military Drill," collection of reports concerning military matters by Hampton officials, found in Hampton University Archives.

9. Peabody, *Education for Life,* 175; Armstrong, *Twenty-two Years' Work,* 6.

10. Ralph E. Luker, *The Social Gospel in Black and White: American Racial Reform, 1885–1912* (Chapel Hill: University of North Carolina Press, 1991), 126. Other Northern educators and reformers agreed that African Americans needed discipline. See "Report of President Hopkins, Williams College, Massachusetts, Mr. Hyde, of the Board of Agriculture, Massachusetts, Secretary Northrup, of the Board of Education, Connecticut, and General Garfield, M. C. upon the Hampton Normal and Agricultural Institute," written in 1869: "Emotional in their nature, unaccustomed

to self-control, and improvident by habit, Freedmen need discipline and training even more than teaching" (*Hampton Reports* [1868–78], 3).

11. *Hampton Reports* (1890). For other references to cadet "self-government," see, for example, *Southern Workman* 10 (June 1881): 66.

12. Engs, *Freedom's First Generation,* 154–55, 202–3.

13. *Southern Workman* 22 (June 1893).

14. June O. Patton, "Major Richard Robert Wright Sr. and Black Higher Education in Georgia" (Ph.D. diss., University of Chicago, 1990); Willard Range, *The Rise and Progress of Negro Colleges in Georgia, 1865–1949* (Athens: University of Georgia Press, 1951), 116, 136–45; Maxine D. Jones and Joe M. Richardson, *Talladega College: The First Century* (Tuscaloosa: University of Alabama Press, 1990), 56–58; Addie Louise Joyner Butler, *The Distinctive Black College: Talladega, Tuskegee, and Morehouse* (Meutchen, N.J.: Scarecrow Press, 1970). Besides Hampton and the three land-grant school schools studied here, Tuskegee made limited moves toward the military system by adopting regular inspections and military drill; Talladega experimented with organizing the male students into a corps of cadets between 1877 and 1879, when Principal Edward P. Lord was fired and replaced with Henry DeForest; and the original curriculum of Claflin University included instruction in military tactics. See Butler, 58, 69; Jones and Richardson, 37, 40; *Southern Sentinel* 1 (Sept. 1877); *Southern Sentinel* 1 (March 1878); E. Horace Fitchett, "The Role of Claflin College in Negro Life in South Carolina," *Journal of Negro Education* 12 (winter 1943), 48; Edward M. Pollard, *Military Training in the Land-Grant Colleges and Universities* (Columbus: Ohio State University, n.d.), 11–12; Arnold H. Taylor, *Travail and Triumph: Black Life and Culture in the South since the Civil War* (Westport, Conn.: Greenwood Press, 1976), 128; George Rable Woolfolk, *Prairie View: A Study in Public Conscience, 1878–1946* (New York: Pageant, 1962); Joe M. Richardson, *A History of Fisk University, 1865–1946* (University: Univeristy of Alabama Press, 1980); R. Grann Lloyd, *Tennessee Agricultural and Industrial State University, 1912–1962* (Nashville, Tenn.: n.p., 1962).

15. *Bulletin of the Florida Agricultural and Mechanical College* (1923–24), 11–12; *FAMC Catalog* (1908), 14; *State Agricultural and Mechanical College of South Carolina Extension Work Bulletin: Twenty-first Year Catalogue* (1915–1916–1917), 77–78.

16. *GSIC Catalog* (1899–1900), 64; *FAMC Catalog* (1908), 14; Neyland and Riley, *History of Florida A & M,* 52. Savannah State is the modern name for Georgia State Industrial College.

17. *FAMC Catalog* (1908), 7; *GSIC Catalog* (1898–99), 25; (1899–1900); (1905–06); (1915–16); (1922–23), 15; (1923–24), 6.

18. *Hampton Reports* (1878); *Southern Workman* 16, no. 6 (June 1887): 72; *Hampton Reports* (1884), 72; (1885), (1893). A course of study from 1913 shows that Hampton students still participated in drill but had no regular courses in military tactics (Mae Barbee Boone Pleasant, *Hampton University: Our Home by the Sea* [Virginia Beach, Va.: Donning, 1992], 67).

19. Dean N. C. Nix, "Tentative History of South Carolina State College," unpublished manuscript, 32; Potts, *History of South Carolina State College,* 20, 23, 43, 55; *Catalogue and Special Announcements of the Colored Normal, Industrial, Agricultural, and Mechanical College of South Carolina* (1896–97) [hereafter, *SCS Catalog*], 3, 34–35.

20. Patton, "Major Richard Robert Wright Sr.," 314, 348, 371 n, 287 n. See also Savannah State and Florida A & M catalogs, especially *GSIC Catalog* (1898–99), 25; Neyland and Riley, *History of Florida A & M,* 52, 62.

21. *SCS Catalog* (1896–97), 34–35.

22. General Orders no. 74, Headquarters of the Army, Adjutant General's Office, 19 July 1884; *Southern Sentinel* 1, no. 6 (Feb. 1878), Savery Library, Talladega College; "Hampton Institute Military Drill," 1; *Hampton Reports* (1883).

23. *Hampton Reports* (1882); *Hampton Reports* 1874, 1876, 1878, 1879; "Hampton Institute Military Drill," 1.

24. *Hampton Reports* (1882).

25. *Hampton Reports* (1883).

26. *Southern Workman* 16, no. 6 (June 1887): 72.

27. First Lieutenant E. W. Hubbard to H. B. Frissell, 20 May 1895, Military Science Collection.

28. Ibid. The same collection also includes a document written in pencil, apparently written by a faculty committee to the Board of Trustees. The letter specifically supported Lieutenant Hubbard's recommendation. The committee said the use of arms would encourage "worthy ideals" and that the argument that the use of weapons in school instills a "barbaric view of duty and ambition . . . seems without force, especially in the case of young men, who may at any time be called on to defend their country, & who know what their country has suffered for the sake of the negro race" (undated letter with heading "Discipline and Military Instruction," Military Science Collection).

29. *Hampton Reports* (1898).

30. *Hampton Reports* (1896). See also Moton's reports to Frissell in 1900 and on 1 March 1909, Military Science Collection; *Southern Workman* 30, no. 9 (Sept. 1901): 494. A picture of the cadet battalion without arms appears in *Hampton Catalog* (1912), 33.

31. Patton, "Major Richard Robert Wright Sr." 287.

32. Ibid., 349–51, 381–82.

33. Glatthar, *Forged in Battle: The Civil War Alliance of Black Soldiers and White Officers* (New York: Free Press, 1990) 182, 250–51, 264; James L. McPherson, *The Negro's Civil War* (Urbana: Univeristy of Illinois Press, 1982), 237–39; Hondon B. Hargrove, *Black Union Soldiers in the Civil War* (Jefferson, N.C.: McFarland, 1988), 67–68; 95. For further evidence of black men's pride in their Civil War military service, see Joel Williamson, *After Slavery: The Negro in South Carolina during Reconstruction* (Hanover, N.H.: Wesleyan University Press, 1965), 26; and Willard B. Gatewood Jr., *Black Americans and the White Man's Burden, 1898–1903* (Urbana: University of Illinois Press, 1975), 88.

34. Charles Johnson Jr., *African-American Soldiers in the National Guard* (Westport, Conn.: Greenwood Press, 1992), 19–26, 34–42, 55; Alwyn Barr, "The Black Militia of the New South: Texas as a Case Study," *Journal of Negro History* 63 (July 1978): 214–16; Beth Taylor Muskat, "The Last March: The Demise of the Black Militia in Alabama," *Alabama Review* 43 (January 1990): 18–34; Gatewood, "North Carolina's Negro Regiment in the Spanish-American War," *North Carolina Historical Review* 48 (October 1971): 385; Frances Smith, "Black Militia in Savannah, Georgia, 1872–1905" (master's thesis, Georgia Southern College, 1981), 16, 80–81.

35. Jack D. Foner, *Blacks and the Military in American History: A New Perspective* (New York: Praeger, 1974), 64, 68; Joel Williamson argues for the existence of a significant black military tradition in South Carolina during Reconstruction, vestiges of which were still present at the turn of the century (Williamson, *After Slavery*, 25–31).

36. Potts, *History of South Carolina State College*, 20.

37. Nix, "Tentative History of South Carolina State College," 32.

38. Potts, *History of South Carolina State College*, 23, 26. For a detailed account of Whittaker's court-martial and subsequent career, see John F. Marszalek Jr., *Court-Martial: A Black Man in America* (New York: Scribner's, 1972).

39. *NGAC Catalog* (1897–98), 19; *Texas A & M Bulletin* (1914), 164; *Texas A & M Biennial Report, 1909–1910;* Foner, *Blacks and the Military*, 107, 131; Warren L. Young, *Minorities and the Military: A Cross-National Study in World Perspective* (Westport, Conn.: Greenwood Press, 1982), 208.

40. James D. Anderson, *The Education of Blacks in the South, 1860–1935* (Chapel Hill: University of North Carolina Press, 1988), 92.

41. Ibid., 92, 1.

42. Engs, *Freedom's First Generation*, 154.

43. Joel Williamson, *The Crucible of Race: Black-White Relations in the American South since Emancipation* (New York: Oxford University Press, 1984), 6.

44. See Andrew, *Long Gray Lines*, especially chaps. 2 and 3.

15

Black, White, and Gray
The Desegregation of The Citadel, 1963–1973

ALEXANDER S. MACAULAY JR.

With its 1954 decision in *Brown vs. Board of Education of Topeka, Kansas,* the United States Supreme Court established public education as "the yardstick by which racial progress would be judged."[1] In addition to broadening African Americans' economic and social opportunities, the Court hoped its ruling would establish a foundation on which young whites "would come to see blacks as classmates, as peers, and as friends. And blacks in turn would learn not to bow the head and doff the hat, but to compete in terms of equality and respect."[2] The idea of black and white children attending the same schools "moved desegregation into the most sensitive zone of white fears," and as Reed Sarratt notes, the Court's decision "changed the law, but it did not change the thoughts and feelings of vast numbers of white Southerners."[3]

Nine years later, Alabama governor George Wallace ushered in 1963 by pledging to maintain "segregation now, segregation tomorrow, and segregation forever." That year brought the vivid image of Wallace standing in the doorway at the University of Alabama. Americans watched police officers turn fire hoses and attack dogs on student protestors, and listened in horror at the news that a bomb blast had killed four young girls at the Sixteenth Street Baptist Church in Birmingham, Alabama. These acts sparked a "national revulsion against southern segregation," and in the center of the storm, the debate raged over the desegregation of public schools. From the riots at the University of Mississippi to Clemson University's "integration with dignity," Americans witnessed Southerners' reactions to federally enforced social change.[4]

In September of 1966, Charles Foster enrolled as the first African American cadet at The Citadel, The Military College of South Carolina amid little fanfare. The number of black cadets increased over the next seven years, but by 1973, they constituted scarcely more than one percent of the student body.

With the college's unique traditions and military structure, the first African American cadets faced challenges far different from their peers at other schools. Unlike other state institutions such as Clemson and the University of South Carolina, the course of The Citadel's integration depended more on students than on powerful political or civic leaders.[5] A handful of Citadel cadets, both black and white, were the driving force behind the school's desegregation as they strove to overcome a recalcitrant and often hostile administration in an attempt to change their alma mater.

The years 1963 through 1973 marked a transitional period in The Citadel's history in many ways. General Mark W. Clark had served as the school's president since 1954, and under his guidance the college prospered. Enrollment reached its maximum, and Clark's national prestige helped obtain funding for a new library, a new student activities building, and a new military science building. Clark raised teachers' salaries and made it easier for them to further their education. In return, he expected little opposition to his views. He disagreed with the Supreme Court's attempts to "force indiscriminate racial integration upon the South," and he informed potential faculty members, "If you've got any ideas on—private ideas—on integration and all that stuff that you want to publish and identify The Citadel [with], we don't want you."[6]

While school officials hoped to delay integrating for as long as possible, they opposed segregationist extremism. In 1956 the rising chairman of The Citadel's Board of Visitors urged General Clark to speak against a "drastic proposal" before the South Carolina legislature that would close any college or university required to admit pupils by court order. Months before the passage of the 1964 Civil Rights Act, The Citadel received its first application request from an African American student. The Board of Visitors declared that the student's application would "be processed exactly as all applications received from residents of South Carolina regardless of race." On November 11, 1964, General Clark addressed the board concerning the "application of the Civil Rights Act on ROTC programs," and four months later he signed a certificate of compliance.[7]

Citadel cadets viewed integration with a mixture of resentment, resignation, and racism. In the wake of Harvey Gantt's enrollment at Clemson, the student newspaper, the *Brigadier*, asked cadets their opinions on the desegregation of South Carolina's public schools. A freshman conceded the inevitability of integration but asserted that a "peaceful, gradual settlement with time for adjustment is the only answer." One student disapproved of the Supreme

Court's efforts to "force" social change, while a Charleston native believed segregation should continue "until the Negroe [*sic*] race has improved its moral standards and its living standards."[8]

Three years later, The Citadel received six applications from African Americans, and it approved three of them. Of these three, only Charles Foster enrolled for the upcoming school year. The imminent enrollment of an African American cadet sparked the student body's interest. Many cadets doubted whether African Americans could withstand the rigors of the plebe system and worried about the consequences should they quit.[9]

School administrators remained ambivalent in their attitude toward desegregation. General Hugh P. Harris had succeeded General Clark as president of The Citadel in 1965, and Harris worked hard to enhance the school's reputation. He wished to avoid any situations that reflected poorly on the college, and his emphasis on public opinion and expediency determined his administration's commitment to integration.[10]

When Charles Foster entered The Citadel's gates in September 1966, his brother sensed an undercurrent of resentment on campus. "People didn't want him there . . . but they treated him as any other plebe coming into the system." The G Company commander, cadet William Riggs, and the cadre platoon leader, cadet Michael Bozeman, placed Foster in a room adjacent to theirs, and throughout that year, they tried to watch over Foster without setting him apart from the other plebes. A few times they pulled an overly aggressive junior or sophomore away from Foster, but as one of Foster's classmates recalls, "for the entire freshman year Charlie was one of us and he caught it just the same as we did."[11]

Even with the efforts of cadet officers, the success or failure of The Citadel's integration rested on the shoulders of Charles Foster. In addition to Foster's impressive physical stature, his classmates describe him as good natured and easy to get along with. His personality and the school's demanding lifestyle helped Foster establish interracial loyalties and friendships. A telling incident occurred after the first week on campus. Henry Kennedy was a G Company freshman from Charleston who decided to go home for the day. Charles Foster opted to spend the day at his parent's house also. However, some upperclassmen refused to allow the two men to leave without proper shirt tucks. Administering a shirt tuck according to Citadel standards requires two people, and it took several attempts before Kennedy and Foster met the upperclassmen's approval. This type of trivial harassment forms an integral part of freshman year at The Citadel, but in this instance it forced a black man and a white man to rely on each other in a way not found at other institutions. As Foster and his classmates sweated in formation, did push-ups in the barracks, and struggled during long training runs, white cadets viewed Foster more as another plebe trying to survive the year than as the man who broke The Citadel's color barrier.[12]

This acceptance was not universal. As Foster walked to and from class, cadets hurled racial epithets out their windows. One day as Foster and the other freshmen stood in formation, some cadets from another company dressed in white sheets and ran towards him screaming and yelling. Foster's roommate, Dave Hooper, remembers that early in the year a group of freshmen called him into a room and announced their intention to run Foster off. Hooper noticed a homemade noose looped over an exposed pipe in the ceiling and left the room immediately. He never told Foster about the incident, and the cadets never carried out their threat. While the cadets I interviewed agree that the physical abuse Foster endured stayed within the limits of The Citadel's plebe system as it then existed, it did exceed the treatment suffered by his peers in both intensity and duration.[13]

Foster persevered, and he emerged from his first year with a great deal of confidence and little resentment. He refuted claims that he received extra attention, and when asked about returning as a sophomore, Foster replied, "I feel like I'm lucky and I'm part of the school and the military. Sure I'm going back, I wouldn't miss it." General Harris congratulated Riggs for the successful completion of Foster's indoctrination and acknowledged, "The Citadel is much in your debt for the effective manner in which you handled all the details associated with this matter."[14]

As an upperclassman, Foster developed close friendships with a few of his peers. He attended Citadel parties and on one occasion literally carried a drunken classmate into the barracks. A former roommate recalls several occasions when he went home with Foster or the two socialized in Charleston. Philip Hoffmann participated in a field training exercise with Foster, and the two men shared a foxhole for three days. Hoffmann had not known Foster personally prior to this exercise, but afterwards he spoke to Foster on a regular basis. According to Hoffmann, "We had camped together. We had peed on the same bush. Now we were buddies."[15]

Foster graduated in May of 1970, and his cadet career parallels that of numerous past, present, and future cadets. He survived plebe year, put on weight, harassed freshmen, and went to bars. However, Foster's Citadel career differed vastly from that of other cadets. He entered an incredibly harsh environment where many people believed he did not belong. Every night he lay in bed in a room without locks, knowing that some men hated the very idea of a black man in a Citadel uniform. The anxiety he must have felt when he heard footsteps or voices outside his door cannot be measured in push-ups or demerits. William Foster called The Citadel his brother's "toughest challenge. He never got the prize or recognition. But he's still a Citadel man."[16]

In September 1967, Joseph Shine reported to Kilo Company as The Citadel's second African American cadet. Shine lived in Charleston and respected The Citadel's academic reputation. With the Vietnam War in full swing, he knew that "if I had to go in the military, then I wanted to be an officer." Shine does not recall much racial animosity his first few days on campus, but he admits that as a freshman "you're treated lower than dirt anyway." However, the bigoted attitudes of some cadets resulted in extra physical and psychological badgering. Men in other battalions urged freshmen to alienate Shine and force him to leave. Others yelled racial slurs out their windows as Shine walked by. On several occasions, Shine returned from mess with shins bloodied where an upperclassman had been kicking him underneath the table. One classmate claims that Shine "went through ten times more than we ever went through, both physically and emotionally."[17]

At five foot eight and a hundred and eighteen pounds, Shine struggled physically as a freshman. When his physical shortcomings resulted in longer runs or extra "training" sessions, some freshmen complained. However, rather than abandoning him to concentrate on their own survival, the K Company freshmen helped him meet the upperclassmen's demands. Shine continued to struggle, but as his classmate Larry Gantt claimed, "Whether you were black or white, you both had the same goal; trying to get through there."[18]

Shine's energy, sense of humor, and intellect overshadowed his physical shortcomings. He earned academic honors, achieved the rank of cadet captain, served on regimental staff, received an Air Force scholarship, and gained recognition as an exemplary Air Force ROTC student. In his senior year an incident at a local bar solidified Shine's standing in the class of 1971. Under the headline "Rights Denied," the editor of the *Brigadier* informed the corps that a Charleston tavern refused to serve Shine because of his race. When the administration failed to respond, many members of the corps carried out an informal boycott of the establishment. The strong show of support by white cadets won over a few men who still harbored prejudices against Shine. Even his "chief antagonist" joined the cadets' boycott.[19]

The supposed smoothness of the school's initial integration lulled Citadel officials into a sense of complacency. In September 1968, General Harris alerted the Board of Visitors to a pending civil rights inspection by the federal government. Rather than use the investigation as an opportunity to address and correct flawed policies, Harris concluded that The Citadel had fulfilled the federal government's basic requirements concerning integration. This thoughtless assessment of the college's obligations to its students resulted in turmoil and controversy with the increased enrollment of black cadets. Moderate and necessary efforts to raise the school's awareness faced resistance from various forces within The Citadel, and the black members of the class of 1973 bore the brunt of the backlash.[20]

I was able to interview four of the six African American members of the class of 1973: Herbert Legare, Norman Seabrooks, George Graham, and Larry Ferguson. Legare grew up in Charleston and entertained thoughts of a military career. The Citadel's academic and military reputation appealed to him, and in the summer of 1969, he reported to first battalion, D Company. Seabrooks arrived from Florida as The Citadel's first African American scholarship athlete. Graham was a self-described "hot-headed kid" from South Carolina who sought the discipline of a Citadel education. Ferguson was a Charleston native who earned a full academic scholarship to the college. When he reported to Regimental Band Company, he fulfilled his father's wish of having a son integrate The Citadel.[21]

All four men survived The Citadel's plebe system, and in many cases the experience eroded the stereotypes of both black and white cadets. As a freshman, Legare experienced limited racial animosity from other cadets, and he says that their attitudes ranged from acceptance to avoidance. Seabrooks says he never encountered any overt racial hostility, but as The Citadel's first African American scholarship athlete, he admits that even the most rabid racists thought twice about angering an all-state defensive tackle.[22]

When George Graham arrived on campus, he "understood one thing early on, a lot of people . . . did not want me there." He endured repeated racial slurs, and one sophomore required Graham to sleep with a Confederate battle flag to prove he belonged at The Citadel. Graham grew up in a predominantly black environment, and his limited exposure to white people and the racism he encountered hindered his willingness to trust upperclassmen as well as his classmates. Eventually he understood that his classmates "were just like me, they were having a unique experience." When Graham saw another freshman faint from exhaustion, he broke ranks to help his classmate. While this outraged the training cadre, other freshmen noticed and appreciated it. Through experiences such as these, Graham and his classmates formed friendships based on character and ability, not on skin color. Reminiscent of Shine's experience, when a local bar refused Graham service, his white companions walked out.[23]

With increased awareness and knowledge, black and white cadets learned to judge others based on personal qualities and strengths rather than racial stereotypes. This shift came gradually, however, and throughout the 1960s and into the 1970s, black students suffered racial affronts. For example, in 1968 a *Brigadier* article blamed the unrest following the assassination of Martin Luther King Jr. on the opportunist "seeking revenge on 'whitey' to whom he owed money and to get his supply of 'booze' restocked."[24]

Offensive articles such as these faded with the increased enrollment of African American cadets and a heightened activism within the student body. The antimilitarism of the 1960s crept into the corps of cadets in the 1970s, and many cadets openly questioned some of the school's policies. Students accused school officials of ignoring the changing needs of the corps, and they appealed for longer furloughs, less stringent uniform polices, and new haircut regulations.[25] Unhappy with the administration and benefiting from the increased interaction between white and black cadets, the corps worked to improve campus race relations through education and communication. Declaring that "now is the time to search our own campus for a way to eradicate interracial misunderstandings which thrive on prejudicial ignorance," the student newspaper volunteered to gauge the corps' interest in instituting a black studies group and to see whether the school possessed enough resources to support the endeavor. An article in the March 7, 1970, edition of the *Brigadier* asked black cadets, "Is The Citadel Biased?" When asked how African Americans adjusted to life on an overwhelmingly white campus, the interviewees credited The Citadel's military environment and small student body for facilitating the formation of relationships across racial lines.[26]

Meanwhile, Citadel officials plodded forward with a stated goal of "conservative progress" and "change where change is desirable and has been proven necessary." In April 1970, a federal civil rights inspection found that black cadets at The Citadel enjoyed many of the same privileges and opportunities as their white peers, but that the school failed to foster among African American cadets "a feeling of belonging or being a part of the college." The inspectors noted that the absence of black faculty members and administrators offered black cadets few opportunities to discuss sensitive racial matters with a sympathetic older person. Furthermore, they recommended that the school compensate for the extreme numerical discrepancy between black and white students by enacting "an affirmative action program to begin to disestablish past patterns of racial segregation." The inspectors noticed that few pictures of black students appeared in Citadel films, brochures, or other publications, and they suggested addressing this oversight to remedy the enrollment disparities.[27]

General Harris concurred with many of the inspectors' proposals and pointed out that the school had either already implemented the changes or planned to do so in the near future. He claimed the institution awarded financial assistance on a nondiscriminatory basis and that school-sponsored activities remained open to all cadets. When outlining his reply to the Board of Visitors, however, Harris concluded: "We should not turn The Citadel into a HEW . . . instrument of social reform." He opposed any measure "to build up the population of any specific ethnic group" and decided that "no issue is made of black studies so we should not announce our intent on this at this time." Despite the cadets' calls for an increased focus on African American history, the administration refused to go beyond the federal government's requirements.[28]

Tea dances offer another obvious and particularly hurtful reminder that the school failed to integrate socially. During the school year, the administration orchestrated tea dances and made attendance mandatory for freshmen. College officials arranged for female students from nearby schools to provide companionship for the awkward and unrefined cadets. As the freshmen in the class of 1973 ambled in, they realized the school had only invited white women. This oversight left a lasting impression on these cadets. Norman Seabrooks asserts: "You can't take a young black man in 1969, force him to go to a tea dance, and then not have anyone for him to dance with."[29]

The African American cadets who entered The Citadel in 1970 and 1971 outnumbered those of the class of 1973, but not by much. The class of 1974 had five black cadets, while the class of 1975 had nine. Out of a student body of 1,817, about one percent were black. A few of these cadets came from Charleston, and almost all grew up in South Carolina. Hometown alumni and the prestige and challenge of a Citadel education attracted many, while others received scholarships.[30]

As with all cadets, their experiences differed. Ken Feaster played baseball and would later become the first African American Citadel graduate to attain the rank of colonel. He says that he encountered little overt racism but concedes the difficulty of distinguishing racial hatred from freshman abuse.[31] John McDowell recalls a couple of isolated racial confrontations but says that for the most part, "we got our company assignments, got our room assignments, and we continued to march at that point."[32]

Reginald Sealey was the first African American in Hotel Company, and even though he felt isolated at times, he depended upon his classmates and they relied on him.[33] Keith Jones followed Sealey as the second black member of Hotel Company, and he recalls a few times when upperclassmen singled him out due to his race. One Friday afternoon, a sophomore entered Jones's room and ordered him to perform a variety of arduous physical activities. The cadet claimed that he was trying to overcome his animosities towards African Americans, but he blamed Sealey and Jones for reinforcing his prejudices. This confusing monologue ended after an hour, and Jones reported the incident to Sealey. Cadet officers handled the situation within the company, and the offenders received light punishments.[34]

In his first year, Patrick Gilliard faced a frightening and dangerous situation in Alpha Company. One night, a group of cadets pulled Gilliard from his bed and led him to an upperclassman's room. They blindfolded him, put him on top of a chair, and tied a noose around his neck. While screaming threats and racial slurs, they looped the noose over an exposed pipe in the ceiling, but left the end unsecured. When they pulled the chair out from under Gilliard, he suffered "the longest second of my life." Rather than report the incident to school authorities, Gilliard told his cousin, a junior cadet in an adjacent company, who contacted other African American cadets. These men visited the A Company commander and the cadets involved to make sure this incident would not be repeated. Gilliard's assailants were punished, but details of the incident never reached beyond the battalion tactical officer. By keeping the news of this abuse of the fourth class system at the company and battalion level, Gilliard earned the respect of the cadets in his company, including a few of his tormentors. As his freshmen year progressed, Gilliard formed close bonds with his classmates. As with Graham and Shine, a group of cadets left a bar in protest after the proprietor refused to serve Gilliard.[35]

The challenges faced by African American cadets required them to work closely with one another. Knowing that the entire school monitored their actions, black cadets pushed each other to excel. In addition to earning South Carolina Football Player of the Year honors, Norman Seabrooks served as captain of the football team and attained the rank of cadet officer. Reginald Sealey helped train incoming freshman, and as a senior, he commanded a platoon. George Graham was third battalion adjutant and twice made the Commandant's Distinguished Service List. Two of Graham's more impressive and revealing accomplishments were his election to The Citadel's Honor Committee and his selection as a Summerall Guard, both peer-elected groups steeped in Citadel tradition.[36]

In 1971 a controversy erupted that tested the strength of African American cadets collectively and individually. During that time, "Dixie" served as The Citadel's unofficial fight song, and the waving of the Confederate flag and the playing of "Dixie" figured prominently at sporting events. As freshmen, many African Americans sang the song out of fear. As they grew more accustomed to Citadel life and their relationships with other cadets, they refused to sing.[37]

Each cadet encountered resistance for his decision not to sing or play the song, but Larry Ferguson's refusal drew the most severe backlash. As a sophomore in the band, Ferguson's protest infuriated cadets and school officials. The band director threatened to kick him out of the company, and some school officials warned him that he could lose his scholarship. Ferguson's duties as president of The Citadel's newly formed Afro-American Society, combined with his stance against the school's fight song, solidified his reputation as a "militant radical" and "troublemaker." Facing constant criticism and harassment, he contemplated leaving, but his family and friends convinced him to stay.[38]

Before the "Dixie" controversy died out, the black cadets found themselves embroiled in another, more intense struggle over the Confederate battle flag. On numerous occasions, the Afro-American Society requested that school officials ban the waving of the flag at Citadel football games. When these pleas went unheeded, the cadets took matters into their own hands.[39] Before the Illinois State football game, black cadets constructed a banner featuring a black fist crushing a Confederate flag. When the white cadets began waving the battle flag, the black cadets hoisted their banner. With a remarkable penchant for understatement, Graham admits that their flag "excited some problems."[40]

Most white cadets disagreed with the African American students' aggressive form of protest. A few tried to sympathize with the black cadets' plight, but others reacted vindictively. Ferguson and his roommate returned one night to find their room trashed, racial threats painted on the walls, their books shredded, and a doll hung from the ceiling by a noose. An inquiry failed to uncover the culprits, and the incident drew the black cadets closer. This controversy passed, but the African American cadets' struggles with the administration continued.[41]

In 1972 Citadel faculty and administrators conducted a comprehensive examination of the college and found that blacks took issue with many aspects of Citadel life. Their grievances included the college's preoccupation with the "Confederate Legend," its reluctance to recruit black students, the absence of black speakers at Citadel functions, the belief that many racial incidents went unpunished, and the faculty's tendency to overlook African Americans' contributions to American history. These problems contributed to a sense of neglect and a lack of belonging among African American cadets.[42]

The examiners dealt cavalierly with these concerns. Regarding the complaint about the "Confederate Legend," the panel claimed that society's "current preoccupation with the influence of slavery is responsible for the extreme unpopularity of anything associated with the Confederacy." They questioned the Confederate flag's use as a "football standard" but ended the discussion with the statement that "neither the black nor white cadet can presume to sit in judgement upon the past, nor can he expect the school to repudiate its heritage." The study dismissed the indictment of the school's recruiting policies quickly and with no elaboration. School officials conceded the need for more African American guest lecturers but advised that the speaker's expertise should not be limited to the "narrow, however important, field" of civil rights. They recommended that professors emphasize the social and cultural contributions of African Americans without "distorting their subject."[43]

School officials treated the black students' requests as pleas for special treatment, particularly the cadets' proposal that an African American serve on The Citadel's Presidential Advisory Committee. The panel rejected this idea with the argument that "special favors should be granted neither to blacks nor whites." This argument seems especially harsh and shortsighted. Placing an African American on the committee would have provided the school with a new and much-needed perspective on the feelings and ideas of black cadets. These young men did not ask for special treatment, merely a voice.[44]

By taking a reactive rather than proactive approach to integration, Citadel authorities reinforced the black students' sense of isolation. Years later, many of the African American alumni agree that they never felt welcome or a part of The Citadel. This lack of connection lessened their loyalty to their alma mater. When other exuberant cadets threw their hats in the air following graduation, Larry Ferguson quietly placed his on his chair.[45]

As part of *Brown v. Board of Education,* the U.S. Supreme Court hoped to lessen racial prejudice by bringing blacks and whites into closer contact.[46] In this sense, The Citadel provided an interesting testing ground. While the military environment and physical rigors of Citadel life increased the threat of violent confrontations, these conditions helped erode racial barriers and prompted the reevaluation of racial attitudes founded on stereotypes and unfamiliarity. The endless number of shirt tucks, inspections, and training runs provided the cadets with common experiences on which relationships based on trust and ability, not skin color, could be built. Benefiting from this interaction, and faced with a stagnant and indifferent administration, the cadets stepped to the forefront and displayed the leadership lacking among Citadel officials.

As the years progressed, each group of African American cadets broke new barriers and built on the accomplishments of the previous ones. Charles Foster proved that an African American could graduate from The Citadel. Joseph Shine showed that an African American could excel. The progression continued as members of the classes of 1973, 1974, and 1975 performed on the Summerall Guards, won accolades on the athletic fields, and served as cadet officers.

Observing current conditions on The Citadel's campus, the black alumni realize more fully how future cadets benefited from their trials and hardships. When George Graham saw a black man serving as the cadet regimental commander in 1994, he viewed his own hopes of leading a company as a "dream deferred." The sense of belonging, missing from the cadet experience of many African American alumni, arrived over twenty years later, as black graduates return to campus and see black cadets in high-ranking positions, hear of The Citadel participating in black history month, and see the administration supporting the Afro-American Society. While some of the conflicts they faced still endure, many African American alumni witness these changes and take added pride in what they accomplished at The Citadel.[47]

NOTES

1. Numan Bartley, *The New South, 1945–1980* (Baton Rouge: Louisiana State University Press, 1995), 159.

2. J. Harvie Wilkinson III, *From Brown to Bakke: The Supreme Court and School Integration, 1954–1978* (New York: Oxford University Press, 1979), 42.

3. C. Vann Woodward, *The Burden of Southern History,* 3rd ed. (Baton Rouge: Louisiana State University Press, 1993), 251; Reed Sarratt, *The Ordeal of Desegregation: The First Decade* (New York: Harper and Row, 1966), viii.

4. C. Vann Woodward, *The Strange Career of Jim Crow,* 2nd rev. ed. (Oxford: Oxford University Press, 1966), 174–76; Bartley, *New South,* 335–38; George McMillan, "Integration with Dignity," in *Perspectives in South Carolina History: The First 300 Years,* ed. Ernest M. Lander and Robert K. Ackerman (Columbia: University of South Carolina Press, 1973), 385.

5. For informative studies of the integration of South Carolina's public schools, see Walter Edgar, *South Carolina: A History* (Columbia: University of South Carolina Press, 1998), 538–40; John G. Sproat, "Firm Flexibility: Perspectives on Desegregation in South Carolina," in *New Perspectives on Race and Slavery in America,* ed. Robert H. Abzug and Stephen E. Maizlish (Lexington: University of Kentucky Press, 1986), 164–84; Marcia G. Synnott, "Desegregation in South Carolina, 1950–1963: Sometime between Now and Never," in *Looking South: Chapters in the Story of an American Region,* ed. Winfred B. Moore Jr. and Joseph F. Tripp (Westport, Conn.: Greenwood Press, 1989), 51–64; Maxie M. Cox, "1963—The Year of Decision: Desegregation in South Carolina" (Ph.D. diss., University of South Carolina, 1996).

6. *Charleston News and Courier,* 12 March 1968; W. Gary Nichols, "The General as President: Charles P. Summerall and Mark W. Clark as Presidents of The Citadel," *South Carolina Historical Magazine* 95 (October 1994): 315, 326–27, 331, 332–33; Mark W. Clark to Dink R. Rigsby, 13 June 1956, General Mark W. Clark Papers, The Citadel Archives and Museum, Charleston, S.C.; Clark to Eric F. Goldman, 24 April 1956, Clark Papers.

7. *Charleston News and Courier,* 15 February 1956; J. M. Moorer to Clark, 17 February 1956, Clark Papers; Dennis Dewitt Nicholson Jr., *A History of The Citadel: The Years of Summerall and Clark* (Charleston, S.C.: The Citadel Print Shop, 1994), 348; The Citadel's Board of Visitors, "Minutes," 1 April 1964, document 668; 13 November 1964, document 793; 19 March 1965, document 797, all in The Citadel Archives and Museum, Charleston, S.C.

8. Nichols, "The General as President," 332; *The Brigadier: The Newspaper of the Military College of South Carolina,* 2 March 1963, The Citadel Archives and Museum, Charleston, S.C. Attitudes remained relatively unchanged a year later when a student's editorial condemned the 1964 Civil Rights Act for destroying an American society based on "private property and self-determination" (*Brigadier,* 18 April 1964).

9. During those three years, several African American students requested Citadel application forms, a few completed the initial steps toward applying, and one was

rejected for scoring below the school's minimum requirements on the college entrance exam. See Nicholson, *Summerall and Clark*, 348–49; *Charleston News and Courier,* 6 September 1964 and 13 July 1966; *Charleston Evening Post,* 12 July 1966; Michael Barrett, interview by author, 14 January 1998; Philip Hoffmann, interview by author, 29 October 1997; Adolphus Varner, interview by author, 20 November 1997; William Jenkinson, interview by author, 5 October 1997; Charles Funderburk, interview by author, 15 January 1998; Scott Madding, interview by author, 10 October 1997; Philip Clarkson, interview by author, 10 October 1997; Paul Short, interview by author, 6 October 1997 (unless otherwise noted, all interviews were tape recorded and are in the author's possession).

10. Board of Visitors, "Minutes," 1 October 1965, documents 177–80; Hugh Harris to Reuben Tucker, 19 November 1965, box 50, folder 2, General Hugh P. Harris Papers, The Citadel Archives and Museum, Charleston, S.C.; Memo to Tucker from Harris, 27 September 1965, box 50, file T, Harris Papers; Memo to Tucker from Harris, 11 November 1965, box 50, file T, Harris Papers; Board of Visitors, "Minutes," 1 January 1967, documents 468–76; Memo to Tucker from Harris, 27 September 1967, box 50, folder 2, Harris Papers; Board of Visitors, "Minutes," 22 March 1968, documents 736–41; Board of Visitors, "Minutes," 25 November 1969, documents 213, 219, 220; *Charleston News and Courier,* 12 March 1968; J. Palmer Gaillard to Harris, 12 April 1968, box 44, folder 7, Harris Papers; Memo to Harris from Dennis D. Nicholson, n.d., box 50, bolder 1, Harris Papers; Memo to Harris from Dennis D. Nicholson, 14 July 1966, box 44, file F, Harris Papers; Alderman Duncan to Harris, 9 January 1967, box 44, folder 1, Harris Papers; Harris to Alderman Duncan, 16 January 1967, box 44, folder 1, Harris Papers; Board of Visitors, "Minutes," 1 June 1967, documents 571–72.

11. Charles Foster died in 1986, and his cadet career must be pieced together from interviews with his classmates and other people who knew him. The author spoke with many of Foster's friend and roommates as well as cadet officers from his freshman year. See *Charleston News and Courier,* 1 December 1996; Michael Bozeman, interview by author, 19 October 1997; Dave Banner, interview by author, 22 January 1998; William Riggs, interview by author, 7 December 1997; George Gray, interview by author, 25 November 1997; Leon Yonce, interview by author, 14 January 1998; Jenkinson interview; Dave Hooper, interview by author, 14 October 1997; David Dawson, interview by author, 27 January 1998; David McGinnis, interview by author, 20 January 1998; Henry Kennedy, interview by author, 24 October 1997 (all tape recorded interviews in the author's possession).

12. Riggs interview; Jenkinson interview; Dawson interview; Hoffmann interview; Gray interview; Ira Stern, interview by author, 30 January 1998; Varner interview; Short interview; Alan Hughes, interview by author, 10 October 1997; Richard

Bagnal, interview by author, 13 January 1998; Thomas Byrd, interview by author, 13 January 1998, no tape; Barrett interview; Madding interview; Kennedy interview 1997 (all tape recorded interviews in the author's possession).

13. Barrett interview; Hoffmann interview; Hughes interview; Hooper interview; Dawson interview; Madding interview; Kennedy interview; Lieutenant Colonel T. Nugent Courvoisie, interview by author, 4 October 1997; McGinnis interview; Yonce interview; Laurence Moreland, interview by author, 22 October 1997, no tape; *Charleston News and Courier,* 1 December 1996.

14. *Rockland County Journal-News,* 16 October 1967, box 44, file G, Harris Papers; *Charleston Evening Post,* 8 June 1967; Letter to Riggs from Harris, 1 June 1967, box 49, folder 7, Harris Papers.

15. Short interview; Bagnal interview; Barrett interview; Kennedy interview; Dawson interview; Hughes interview; Hoffmann interview.

16. *Charleston News and Courier,* 1 December 1996.

17. Joseph Shine, interview by author, 20 December 1997; *Brigadier,* 23 September 1967; James Cassidy, interview by author, 23 January 1998; Funderburk interview; Robert Vogel, interview by author, 17 November 1997; Douglas Rich, interview by author, 21 January 1998; John Reid, interview by author, 30 October 1997; Barrett interview; Stern interview; James Lockridge, interview by author, 26 January 1998; Samuel Jones, interview by author, 16 November 1997 (all tape recorded interviews in the author's possession).

18. Shine interview; Hoffmann interview; Lockridge interview; Albert Fitzgerald, interview by author, 21 December 1997; Claude Moore Jr., interview by author, 20 January 1998, tape in Moore's possession; Vogel interview; Funderburk interview; Stern interview; Cassidy interview; Reid interview; Rich interview; Larry Gantt, interview by author, 5 February 1998 (all tape recorded interviews in the author's possession).

19. *The Citadel Official Register for the Period September 1968–September 1969,* The Citadel Archives and Museum, Charleston, S.C.; 1971 *Sphinx,* 134, 143, The Citadel Archives and Museum, Charleston, S.C.; Lockridge interview; Fitzgerald interview; Shine interview; Vogel interview; *Brigadier,* 2 October 1970.

20. Board of Visitors, "Minutes," 27 September 1968, documents 14 and 15. No African American students graduated in the class of 1972. An African American cadet named Nathaniel Addison entered with the class of 1972, but he resigned before graduating. The Citadel does not keep records on nongraduates, and the author was unable to unable to contact him.

21. Herbert Legare, interview by author, 15 January 1998, tape in Legare's possession; Norman Seabrooks, interview by author, 17 October 1997; George Graham, interview by author, 28 January 1998; Larry Ferguson, interview by author, 23

January 1998. The author was unable to contact one member of the class of 1973, and another declined to participate.

22. Legare interview; Seabrooks interview; Ferguson interview.

23. Graham interview.

24. Legare interview; Seabrooks interview; Barrett interview; *Brigadier*, 11 May 1968.

25. *Brigadier*, 11 October 1969, 14 February 1970, 7 March 1970, 1 May 1970, 8 May 1970; Lockridge interview; Shine interview.

26. Ibid.

27. Board of Visitors, "Minutes," 26 September 1970, document 503; "A Self Study: The Citadel, 1972," I-7, documents in possession of author; Board of Visitors, "Minutes," 29 May 1970, letter from Dewey E. Dodds to Hugh Harris, 22 April 1970, documents 335–40.

28. Board of Visitors, "Minutes," 29 May 1970, Harris's "Comments for Board of Visitors on Civil Rights Report," 2 May 1970, documents 341–42.

29. Legare interview; Ferguson interview; Seabrooks interview.

30. "Self Study," III-84; Ken Feaster, interview by author, 9 January 1998; John McDowell, interview by author, 21 January 1998; Reginald Sealey, interview by author, 18 October 1997, hereafter cited as "Sealey interview"; Keith Jones, interview by author, 9 January 1998; Patrick Gilliard, interview by author, 13 December 1997.

31. Feaster interview.

32. McDowell interview.

33. Sealey interview.

34. Sealey interview; Keith Jones interview.

35. Keith Jones interview; Gilliard interview.

36. Seabrooks interview; Ferguson interview; Reginald Sealey, interview by author, 2 February 1998; McDowell interview; Gilliard interview; Legare interview; Keith Jones interview; Feaster interview; 1973 *Sphinx*, 285, 300; 1974 *Sphinx*, 323.

37. Seabrooks interview; Gilliard interview; Graham interview; McDowell interview; Ferguson interview.

38. Ferguson interview; Graham interview; Seabrooks interview; Kennedy interview.

39. Keith Jones interview; Graham interview; Feaster interview; Ferguson interview.

40. Graham interview; Ferguson interview; Feaster interview; Keith Jones interview; *Brigadier*, 19 November 1971.

41. *Brigadier*, 19 November 1971, 8 December 1972, 5 October 1973; Graham interview; Legare interview; Ferguson interview.

42. "Self Study," VII-29, VII-30, VII-31.

43. "Self Study," VII-30, VII-31.

44. Ibid.

45. Legare interview; Keith Jones interview; Graham interview; Seabrooks interview; Feaster interview; Ferguson interview.

46. Bartley, *The New South,* 159; Wilkinson, *From Brown to Bakke,* 42, 44.

47. Graham interview.

PART VI

Of Memory and Memorials

"Nothing," Harry Crews once wrote, "is allowed to die in a society of story-telling people. It is all—the good and the bad—carted up and brought along from one generation to the next. And everything that is brought along is colored and shaped by those who bring it."[1] The following essays examine aspects of how public memory was formed in the South and the impact it had and continues to have on Southern life.

In "Whispering Consolation to Generations Unborn: Black Memory in the Era of Jim Crow," W. Fitzhugh Brundage demonstrates that a widespread tradition of black memory emerged to compete with the quite different and better-known tradition of white memory that arose out of the ashes of the Civil War. During the late nineteenth century, African Americans adopted at least a half-dozen major holidays and countless lesser ones as appropriate occasions to stage elaborate public processions and ceremonies. Those affairs often challenged the racial segregation of public places. The order of march within the processionals (military veterans, firemen, union members, entrepreneurs) provided symbols of black achievement. And the orations at the climax of the celebrations often directly challenged conventional white views of Africa, the Civil War, Reconstruction, and current affairs. Thus, Brundage writes, "even as whites used history as a tool with which to erase blacks from annals of civilization, blacks fashioned an alternative past that gave meaning to their sufferings and could sustain their ambitions." In the process, "the contest over the meaning of Southern history" quickly became not just one "between the North and the South, but also between white and black Southerners."

The contest over the meaning of the death of the Jim Crow era is the subject of Glenn Eskew's "Memorializing the Movement: The Struggle to Build Civil Rights Museums in the South." Focusing on museums that were built in Atlanta, Selma, Birmingham, and Albany, the author shows how all such efforts had to overcome financial and political wrangling among supporters as well as detractors. Although each memorial began as a spontaneous and independent enterprise, they all produced similar outcomes. Heritage tourism ultimately emerged as the driving force behind the operation of the centers. And their honoring of past civil rights victories often, ironically, seemed to retard acknowledgment, much less discussion, of current racial problems. "Certainly," Eskew concludes, "the dynamics of heritage tourism have elicited a public support that few people would have dreamed of thirty years ago when Coretta Scott King initiated the process of memorializing the movement."

NOTE

1. Harry Crews, *Classic Crews: A Harry Crews Reader* (New York: Simon and Schuster, 1995), 21.

16

Whispering Consolation to Generations Unborn
Black Memory in the Era of Jim Crow

W. Fitzhugh Brundage

On January 1, 1864, 15,000 blacks packed the streets of Norfolk, Virginia, to observe the first anniversary of the Emancipation Proclamation. The high-point of the celebration was a huge parade that, even at a time when the outcome of the Civil War remained in doubt, attested to the resolve of blacks to embrace freedom and citizenship. The splendid marching of four regiments of black troops, the gusto of the brass bands, the obvious pride of the volunteer black fire companies, and the respect accorded the procession of black clergymen were all facets of a cathartic, communal celebration of freedom.[1]

Seventy-two years after the Emancipation celebration in Norfolk, tens of thousands of blacks flocked to Dallas to commemorate both the Lone Star State's centennial and the seventy-first anniversary of Juneteenth (the date in 1865 when General Gordon Granger arrived in Galveston and informed Texans that the United States government intended to enforce the Emancipation Proclamation throughout the region). Excited crowds followed a gigantic parade to the centennial fair grounds where they thronged the Negro Hall of Culture. The festivities were intended to underscore, for generations of blacks born long after slavery, the continuity between their present circumstances and their race's past. Certainly, the Juneteenth ceremonies in Fort Worth, Texas, three years later did so. Beyond reminding the gathered crowd about past traumas and accomplishments, the presence of fifty-five former slaves as guests of honor at the local Prince Hall Masonic Mosque made the reality of bondage a living history, if only temporarily and symbolically.[2]

The celebrations in Norfolk, Dallas, Fort Worth, and elsewhere attested to the dedication of blacks to acknowledge and ennoble what James Weldon Johnson called their gloomy past.[3] These events are reminders of the existence of a powerful alternative to white historical memory in the New South. Scholars have done much to expose the labors of whites elites and others to define the meaning of the Civil War and the past in the postbellum South. But historians have devoted virtually no attention to the simultaneous expressions of black historical self-representation and dissent. Isn't it curious that we know more about Election Day and Pinkster Day parades in the antebellum North than we do about the complex tradition of ceremonial citizenship enacted in Norfolk, Dallas, and across the hinterland of the South?[4]

Any attempt to reconstruct black historical memory should begin with these festivals of memory. Despite the oppressive conditions that Southern blacks faced, the public sphere remained sufficiently porous and open to voluntary, collective action that they could not be entirely excluded from it. They made creative use of the resources at their command and defiantly gave public expression to their collective memory, thereby offering a counter-memory to that of Southern whites.[5] Diverse public ceremonies, which became the preeminent forum in which African Americans displayed their recalled past, enabled vast numbers of blacks to learn, invent, and practice a common language of memory. By providing blacks with highly visible platforms for the expression of black collective memory, celebrations ensured that their sense of the past was something more than a rhetorical discourse accessible principally to literate, elite African Americans. Instead, black memory existed as recurring events that could be joined in and appreciated collectively. Such celebrations had a unique capacity to celebrate the recalled past before an audience that incorporated the breadth of the black community, from the college-trained preacher to the illiterate day laborer and the impressionable school child.

The conventions of nineteenth-century public life encouraged blacks to develop such spectacles of memory. Public festivals of all kinds proliferated in the Gilded Age until the collective display of patriotism and community spirit became a competitive process with a dizzying array of groups vying to exhibit their civic enthusiasm. Blacks understood the importance of interrupting their individual, day-to-day routines in order to enter into public space and perform coordinated roles in pageants of representation. By insinuating celebrations of black history into the region's civic life, Southern blacks strove to break down their historical exclusion from a ceremonial citizenship. And by providing blacks with an opportunity to stage complex self-portraits of their communities, commemorative celebrations represented a bold act of both communal self-definition and cultural resistance.[6]

Within a decade of Appomattox, African Americans had adopted at least a half-dozen major holidays and countless lesser occasions during which they staged elaborate processions and ceremonies. New Year's Day, previously the most bitter day of the year because of its associations with slave auctions, now provided an occasion to commemorate, with acclamations of the wildest joy and expressions of ecstasy, Lincoln's 1863 Emancipation Proclamation and the abolition of slavery. Southern blacks joined in the February commemoration of Washington's birthday, using it to highlight the cruel irony that their ancestors had fought beside Washington to found a nation that subsequently had rejected them. To the extent that Lincoln's birthday was celebrated in the South, it was by African Americans, who understandably were eager to link their history with that of their martyred liberator. They added February 18, Frederick Douglass's purported birthday, to their calendar of holidays after the beloved abolitionist's death in 1895. In 1865 the eager participation of blacks in Charleston, South Carolina, and elsewhere helped to establish Memorial Day in late May as the fitting commemoration of military valor and sacrifice. They also gave new meaning to Independence Day. Only at the end of the nineteenth century, when the patriotic fervor aroused by the Spanish-American War swept the region, did most white Southerners resume celebrating the nation's founding. Blacks understood that if the Declaration of Independence was to be a resounding appeal to liberty and equality, the Fourth of July, its anniversary, was the appropriate occasion to present their unfulfilled claims to freedom.[7]

The black commemorative calendar also included a panoply of celebrations of hallowed religious events. Perhaps the most widely observed denominational holiday was the birthday of Richard Allen, the founder of the African Methodist Episcopal (AME) Church. Initially adopted by the AME Church in 1876 as a way to arouse black interest in the nation's centennial, Allen Day became, by the late 1880s, an enduring region-wide celebration.[8] Admittedly an affair exclusive to black Methodists, it and other religious anniversaries were conceived of as celebrations of collective black achievement and as important milestones in the day-to-day lives of black communities. Thus, even members of competing churches and organizations were encouraged to take pride in ceremonies honoring their rivals' history and accomplishments.

Blacks likewise set aside dates to commemorate anniversaries associated with the benevolent organizations that multiplied across the South. Although the principal objectives of these societies were benevolent and social, they also invariably cultivated an awareness of their own histories through meetings, parades, fairs, and anniversary celebrations.[9] The nineteenth anniversary of the founding of the Covington, Virginia, chapter of the Order of Good Samaritans in July 1896 typified the public ceremonies that such groups staged. The men and women of the order, dressed in elaborate regalia, gathered at their hall and then, following behind a local cornet band, marched through the main streets of the small western Virginia mining town. Eventually the paraders reached the Covington Baptist Church, where officers of the order recounted the Good Samaritan's history and ministers blessed the occasion. Then the celebrants enjoyed a ceremonial feast and an evening of fellowship. Similar extravaganzas were commonplace in the region's larger cities, where month after month, year after year, the rhythms of everyday life were interrupted by spectacular parades of flamboyantly garbed black marchers honoring their respective benevolent and fraternal societies.[10]

Seemingly, no black community was too small to nourish a commemorative tradition. In Purcellville and Hamilton, two neighboring rural villages in northern Virginia, for instance, blacks organized the Loudoun County Emancipation Association, which in turn planned and hosted an annual celebration every September 22. The fact that the association had its own printed letterhead stationery was only one indication of its ambitions. Although both poor and obscure, the association nonetheless enlisted prominent figures, including W. Calvin Chase, the editor of the Washington *Bee,* to deliver the annual orations. So audacious were the association's directors that in 1922 they displayed no insecurity when they wrote, in labored and ungrammatical prose, to Mary Church Terrell, one of the most respected black clubwomen of the era, requesting her to deliver an address at the upcoming Emancipation Day celebrations. Although Terrell eventually begged off and the association had to make alternative plans, the organization's request itself revealed the initiative of even the most humble black organizations.[11]

The size and spectacle of black ceremonies testified to the significance that blacks attached to them. In Norfolk, Virginia, for instance, Emancipation Day on each January 1 routinely attracted tens of thousands of onlookers eager to watch parades that stretched for miles through the principal streets of the city. In Beaufort, South Carolina, Memorial Day evolved into a similar region-wide celebration that enticed visitors and black military units from the Carolinas and Georgia. In Vicksburg, Mississippi, Fourth of July festivities included grand parades of several hundred marchers and brass bands through the main thoroughfares of the city before celebrants gathered at the city's imposing courthouse and to listen to long slates of speakers. Similarly, the combination of pageantry and festive atmosphere in Charleston, South Carolina, each Independence Day attracted black excursionists from as far away as Columbia, Savannah, and Augusta.[12]

The festivities staged by blacks were boisterous affairs that often challenged the racialized segregation of public spaces, including spaces that were especially hallowed to whites. Blacks in Richmond, for instance, pointedly included the grounds of the Virginia capitol in their July Fourth celebrations. That the former capitol of the Confederacy would be the site for large crowds of blacks to celebrate the founding of the republic by parading, carousing, and selling lemonade, watermelons, and other holiday foods was abhorrent to white sensibilities. Even after conservative whites regained control of the state's government in the 1870s, black paraders continued to conduct imposing ceremonies that tweaked white sensibilities. After 1890, black militia units incorporated the imposing Robert E. Lee statue on Monument Avenue into their ceremonial musters. By parading at the foot of the monument, they associated themselves with the memory of the city's most renowned military figure. As black men in uniform, they simultaneously reminded Richmond's whites of Lee's defeat at the hands of an army that included former slaves.[13]

If blacks demonstrated the primacy of their racial identity by marching collectively, they made manifest their multiple affiliations by choosing to march as members of distinct social organizations. The organization evidenced much about the accelerating social and class differentiation among blacks during the late nineteenth century. As black communities separated themselves out into discrete groups on the basis of religion, class, occupation, education, and ancestry, they staged celebrations that reflected and acknowledged these same divisions. Driven by the vigorous competition for public prestige among black organizations, they understandably grasped opportunities, such as public ceremonies and parades, to establish their claims for public recognition and influence. Thus, the order of the procession revealed not just the organizational infrastructure of the black community but also what social attributes blacks valued and wanted to display before the larger world.

Unmistakable conventions emerged for ordering parades. The social and political symbolism of black military service suffused black commemorative celebrations. The privilege and prestige of occupying the front ranks of processions often went to black veterans of the Civil War, and later of the Spanish American and First World Wars. Joining the veterans at the front of many black parades were black militia.[14] Parading black veterans were a reminder of the blacks who, by fighting at Port Hudson, Milliken's Bend, Ft. Wagner, San Juan Hill, and in the trenches in Europe, had proved that battle-field heroics knew no color line. Lines of Civil War veterans, in particular, con-nected the agency of ordinary men with great deeds, including the destruction of slavery and the eventual achievement of political rights.[15]

The prestige attached to black men in uniform went beyond respect con-ferred upon them for their willingness to take up arms in times of crisis. The representation of blacks as soldiers took on particular significance at a time of flowering nationalism and shifting attitudes toward the commemoration of military valor. After the Civil War, whites in North and South alike engaged in a frenzy of monument building to celebrate the common (white) soldier. As historian Kirk Savage has observed, "this proliferation of soldier monuments militarized the landscape of civic patriotism." Black soldiers, however, were virtually invisible in the commemoration of war and soldiering.[16] Because blacks were excluded from monumental representations of military valor, dis-plays of military prowess by black militia during commemorative pageants were charged with symbolic significance. Black militia, consequently, seized any pretext to muster and parade. These drills, especially on July Fourth, were intended to demonstrate black military competence and to rebut white criti-cism that black soldiers were little more than overdressed and undertrained poseurs. Well-dressed and well-ordered black troops came to symbolize the ideal of black masculine leadership. News accounts regularly praised the young men's "excellent marching," "neat appearance and splendid soldiery," and "very soldier-like appearance." A company's stylish and correct showing on the parade ground reflected equally on the troops and on their community. As the Savannah *Tribune* observed in 1897, the local black militia had "for over twenty years" borne the burden of representing their people."[17]

In black communities without militia companies, black fire companies often occupied the front ranks of civic festivities. Volunteer fire companies offered another avenue for displays of public service while also contribut-ing pomp and spectacle to civic ceremonies. Perpetuating a tradition that extended back to the earliest years of the republic, black firemen, like their white counterparts, used holidays, especially Independence Day, as a pretext for tournaments during which rival companies vied to see which was fastest in getting to and putting out mock fires. Sometimes the displays of firefighting skills were intended as pure farce. But more often the fire companies strove to demonstrate that black communities possessed courageous men dedicated to selfless public service. Like the militia, the fire companies helped to give meaning to commemorative celebrations by linking them with voluntarism, private association, and civic obligation.[18]

Following behind the militia units, veterans, and fire companies, were labor organizations and trade groups. The 1888 Emancipation Day cavalcade in Washington D.C., for instance, included two floats of whitewashers and plasters who advertised their trades "with yells which would do credit to Comanche Indians." During Emancipation Day in Jacksonville in 1892, the longshoremen's association, the printer's union, the carpenter's union, and a "Trade display" float joined the procession through the city's streets. A quarter-century later, approximately one thousand longshoremen paraded the streets of Savannah in honor of Emancipation Day. These street dramas linked outward displays of occupational pride with both the honored past and contemporary concerns. They announced the workers' determination to be part of the body politic, appearing for all to see on important civic occasions, marching in orderly formation under their various banners. A few even perpetuated ancient traditions associated with European celebrations by performing de facto craft pageants in mock workshops. An enterprising black butcher in Jacksonville, for example, used the July Fourth parade in 1887 as an opportunity to sell literally "his fine fresh meats" from the back of his "well arranged float." When black workers affiliated their collective identity with the commemoration of American independence and emancipation, they linked the blessings of democracy and freedom with their own economic opportunities. And to insist upon the variety and dignity of their labor at a time of systematic discrimination against black tradesmen and workers was to liberate blacks of the stigma of being mere hewers of wood and drawers of water. However much these demonstrations of craft pride and organization by blacks borrowed from older labor iconography, they achieved particular symbolic power because they were staged by former slaves and their descendants whose labor previously had been denied either social status or recompense.[19]

At century's end, the parade lines were joined by business floats that advertised the wares and skills of black entrepreneurs. To some extent, the business floats reflected the commercialism that crept into all manner of public commemoration during the late nineteenth century. In an age when monument companies pandered to white veterans' groups and women's organizations by adopting the latest marketing and advertising techniques, black businessmen could hardly have been expected to forgo similar tactics. Funeral home operators in Charleston, for example, used the 1917 Emancipation Day parade to introduce automobile hearses to the public. The increasing prominence of business floats after the turn of the century also testified to the efforts of black business organizations such as the National Negro Business League to stimulate local black enterprise, inform the public of advances made by black businesses, and inspire community pride. Although black business organizations sometimes were ridiculed for their tub-thumping bluster, their advertising campaigns meshed well with the traditions of communal uplift that were central to black celebrations. Moreover, each business float offered further symbolic confirmation of the black progress that the ceremonies were intended to demonstrate and celebrate.[20]

Just as the processions provided an opportunity for black communities to engage in ceremonial collective representation, commemorative festivities provided black orators with a platform from which to transform the discordant and tragic reality of the black past into something grand and ennobling. At a time when famous speeches were still printed, bound, and sold in editions numbering in the tens of thousands, and in a region where the more ordinary productions of high culture were seldom found and little encouraged, oratory enjoyed continuing prestige and therefore figured prominently in black commemorative celebrations. With eloquent learnedness, stately gestures, studied solemnity, and expertly moderated delivery, black orators shaped the meaning of black celebrations. During orations that commonly lasted two, three, or even four hours, they turned the parade grounds and parks into open-air schools where they informed and inspired as well as entertained.

Black commemorative orators turned the era's civilizationist ideology on its head by insisting that blacks not only had contributed to humankind's progress but were, indeed, the inventors of civilization. This claim demanded a profound revision of ideas about the history of Africa's peoples. Africa, for whites, was a metaphor for barbarism, and Africa's purported lack of civilization was a stigma borne by black people everywhere. Rejecting this dominant vision of African history, black orators responded that Africa had been the cradle of much that the world had come to define and salute as Western. Black celebrations disseminated the distinctive translation of the civilizationist ideology deep into the Southern hinterland so that black lumbermen in East

Texas; mill workers in Birmingham, Alabama; and self-sufficient farmers in Glynn County, Georgia, who almost certainly never read the learned writings of Alexander Crummell and other black intellectuals, encountered interpretations of the black past that meshed seamlessly with the more erudite renderings of distant black intellectuals. At the very least, audiences heard a narrative of ancient black accomplishments that contrasted sharply with white accounts of African savagery.

Black orators differed no less sharply with whites over the meaning of the Civil War. Southern whites, of course, strenuously defended secession and were acutely sensitive to any suggestion that the defense of slavery had motivated their failed rebellion. The black counter-narrative was equally unambiguous. Over and over again, black orators insisted that the Civil War had been God's punishment for slavery and that the plight of African Americans had been the catalyst for the nation's Armageddon. Rather than a tactical sleight of hand dictated by wartime exigencies (as many white Southerners claimed), the Emancipation Proclamation was a redemptive act through which God wrought national regeneration. By so explaining the mystery of slavery and the jubilee of freedom, black orators insisted that the divine providence of history had worked (and might work again in the future) to elevate the African peoples. Emancipation anticipated some profound, imminent, and millennial transformation in the status of black people. At the very least, it held out to blacks the promise of social justice and suggested that the ascendancy of the white race was only temporary.[21]

That the United States was a nation with a millennial destiny and that blacks had an important role to play in that future was apparent to most commemorative orators. The future of civilization in general and the black race in particular would be played out on this continent where black orators already discerned ample evidence of their race's rapid ascent of the ladder of civilization. They viewed the history of Southern blacks paradigmatically, as a parable of racial elevation. Whereas most whites presumed that centuries would be required to elevate blacks above abject barbarism, black orators dwelled on the exceptional, indeed unparalleled strides that blacks had made since slavery.

Although blacks had to watch as the promise of Reconstruction receded, they refused to join in the increasingly shrill denunciation of the postbellum experiment. At the same time that whites, ranging from the playwright Thomas Dixon and filmmaker D. W. Griffith to the historian William Dunning, compiled the dark record of Reconstruction, black commemorative orators recalled with reverence the courage and integrity with which blacks had conducted themselves then. The defense of the legitimacy of Reconstruction in commemorative orations was an important political exercise because blacks had few other venues to challenge the ascendant interpretation of the postwar period. The audience who listened to J. C. Lindsay of Savannah in 1917 lament that the old wail is still heard that the period that followed emancipation was filled with mistakes did not need to wait for W. E. B. DuBois's revisionist account of Reconstruction in order to discover a correction to the virulently critical white commentaries on the postbellum years. Lindsay, like many orators, conceded that black suffrage may have been improperly used and the right abused, but he insisted that even then it severed to check political outrages and political impositions.[22] By defending the legitimacy of Reconstruction, black orators dismissed white claims that the black fortunes had been raised by the redemption of the region and return of white rule.

Reflecting their refusal to promote the appearance of a passive, deferential black populace, orators gave voice to enduring political aspirations. Rev. W. H. Styles, for instance, strongly condemned lynching as barbaric in his address during the anniversary of the ratification of the 15th Amendment in Blackshear, Georgia. He stressed that the political rights guaranteed by the Constitution provided the only protection against white violence. Rev. J. J. Durham warned his Savannah audience in 1900 that any attempts to deal with the Negro as something less than a citizen would cost this country more blood and treasure than it took to establish its independence. Through speeches and resolutions, orators and celebrants made strenuous demands for black political rights, denounced racism, and defended black aspirations on the grounds that they have surpassed all reasonable tests of education, culture, morality, and patriotism they had faced. And when the gathered audiences at celebrations adopted resolutions of protest, they gave voice to concerns and opinions that were otherwise too seldom acknowledged in Southern public life.[23]

By fusing protests, jeremiads, and memorials, black commemorative orations occupied a crucial role in black collective memory in the postbellum South. If black orators at times seemed to parrot the dominant strains of the American faith in a progressive unfolding historical drama, they did so in order to promote an African American collective identity, not because they necessarily identified with white values. This strategy of reversal—of appropriating purportedly American ideals and turning them back on their professors —was fundamental to expressions of black public memory after the Civil War.

Such inversions of white presumptions about the past understandably had especially strong purchase at a time when blacks struggled to establish that the large and central themes of the black experience were only traceable in history's processes. Commemorative addresses did so by serving as an oral archive of both black strivings and African American claims for justice. They historicized the black past for the broad expanse of Southern blacks who otherwise had few occasions to recall and ponder their shared history by situating the particular and individual lived experience of black audiences in larger historical events, revealing to them the political and cultural forces that influenced their lives. Speaking for a generation in transition from the folk memory to a broader historical consciousness, orators contributed mightily to turning the atomized memories of individuals into a collective past, one that could sustain black civic culture throughout the era of Jim Crow.

Taken together, the commemorative processions, orations, and festivities posed an unmistakable challenge to white understandings of the past. Indeed, the contest over the meaning of Southern history was not just between the North and the South, but also between white and black Southerners. White southerners, after all, had argued with their Northern counterparts for decades. But they had no previous experience with a challenge to their interpretative authority over the past from within the South. When white Southerners systematically set about codifying their heroic narrative and filling the civic landscape with monuments to it, they were conscious not only of a challenge from Northern counter-narratives, but also from Southern blacks. The resentment that Southern whites vented every Fourth of July, the mocking derision that they showered on black commemorative spectacles, and the frequency of legal and extralegal harassment directed against black revelers leave little doubt that whites understood that the rituals of black memory represented a form of cultural resistance. For all of the efforts of Southern whites to enshrine their historical understanding of slavery, the Civil War, and black failings, black commemorative celebrations made manifest a forceful and enduring black counter-narrative.

Of course, poverty and oppression sharply circumscribed the expression of this black counter-memory. As Southern whites strengthened their grip over the public realm in the late nineteenth century, some expressions of black memory eventually were marginalized or altogether suppressed. This competition between white and black Southerners over the meaning of the past was never equal: whereas white Southerners created a landscape dense with totemic relics, Southern blacks could never fix their memory in public spaces in the same manner or to the same extent. Not only did whites enjoy an advantage in establishing the materiality of their memory, but they also possessed the power to silence parts of past; for instance, they reverently erected monuments to faithful slaves but raised no statues of black Civil War soldiers. Over the course of the late nineteenth century, Southern whites, with the complicity of white Northerners, secured the cultural resources necessary to make their memories authoritative while rendering those of blacks illegitimate or imperceptible to whites.[24]

Yet even as whites used history as a tool with which to erase blacks from annals of civilization, blacks fashioned an alternative past that gave meaning to their sufferings and could sustain their ambitions. Charles Carroll, the orator at the 1896 Juneteenth celebrations in Waco, Texas, brilliantly expressed the desperate need blacks had to fashion a useable historical memory. We must not sink in despair, he entreated his audience. We must not give up the high hope of our race, for who could determine our existence today had our forefathers ignored the hope of this generation. He refused to believe that the sacrifice of brave Negro heroes during the Civil War, Frederick Douglass, and other redeeming fathers had not eased the way for their successors. Yes, blacks had been defrauded of the full meaning of citizenship by every means human ingenuity can devise. But, Carroll concluded, "as this race unfolds the canvas of time and recollection which represents it from bondage to freedom, it whispers consolation to generations unborn."[25] To find consolation in the black experience in America was an act of extraordinary social imagination. We might well wonder how Southern African Americans would have survived the disappointments and hardships of this age had they not done so.

NOTES

1. *Christian Recorder,* 16 January 1864.

2. *Dallas Morning News,* 20 June 1936; William H. Wiggins Jr. and Douglas DeNatale, *Jubilation! African American Celebration in the Southeast* (Columbia, S.C.: McKissick Museum, 1993), 62; David A. Williams, *Juneteenth: The Unique Heritage* (Austin, Tex.: n.p., 1992), 38.

3. James Weldon Johnson, *Along This Way: The Autobiography of James Weldon Johnson* (1933; reprint, New York: Penguin, 1990), 154.

4. Only in recent years have black commemorative traditions begun to attract scholarly attention. See David W. Blight, *Race and Reunion: The Civil War in American Memory, 1863–1915* (Cambridge, Mass.: Harvard University Press, 2001),

chap. 9; W. Fitzhugh Brundage, "Race, Memory, and Masculinity: Black Veterans Recall the Civil War," in *The War Was You and Me: Civilians in the American Civil War*, ed. Joan Cashin (Princeton: Princeton University Press, 2002), 136–56; Kathleen Clark, "Celebrating Freedom: Emancipation Day Celebrations and African American Memory in the Reconstruction South," in *Where These Memories Grow: History, Memory, and Southern Identity*, ed. W. Fitzhugh Brundage (Chapel Hill: University of North Carolina Press, 2000); Mitchell A. Kachun, "The Faith That the Dark Past Has Taught Us: African-American Commemorations in the North and West and the Construction of a Useable Past, 1808–1915" (Ph.D. diss., Cornell University, 1997), chaps. 5–7;. Wiggins and DeNatale, *Jubilation;* Williams, *Juneteenth.*

5. Of course, the harsh realities that blacks confronted in the New South imposed unmistakable limits on such expression. While of undoubted significance for black elites, publications by black authors failed to reach the vast majority of blacks in Southern hinterland. William Still, the self-educated son of slaves and a prominent abolitionist, confronted these obstacles when he marketed his stirring account of slave escapes, *The Underground Rail Road,* in 1872. Despite soliciting the support of black leaders and organizing Southern canvassers who sold his book for generous commissions, Still failed to garner even modest sales for his book. His experience demonstrated that among an impoverished people in a poor region, the community of black book buyers and newspaper readers was small. And although the percentage of blacks who were literate did rise rapidly, as late as the dawn of the twentieth century, more than 40 percent remained illiterate. See Elizabeth Rauh Bethel, *The Roots of African-American Identity: Memory and History in Free Antebellum Communities* (New York: St. Martin's Press, 1997), 188–91.

6. The idea of "ceremonial citizenship" is elaborated in Mary P. Ryan, *Civic Wars: Democracy and Public Life in the American City during the Nineteenth Century* (Berkeley: University of California Press, 1997), especially chapter 2.

7. *Augusta (Ga.) Colored American,* 13 January 1866; Benjamin Quarles, "Historic Afro-American Holidays," *Negro Digest* 16 (February 1967): 18; Blight, *Race and Reunion,* chap. 9.

8. For descriptions of Allen Day, see *Indianapolis Freeman,* 21 February 1891. See also Mitchell A. Kachun, "The Faith That the Dark Past Has Taught Us," chap. 5.

9. Although some reflected avowedly elitist impulses of their free black founders, the groups nevertheless performed the important function of transmitting the cultural heritage and social traditions of one portion of black Southerners to succeeding generations. For instance, the studiously compiled membership ledgers and precise rituals of the Brown Fellowship Society of Charleston, South Carolina,

founded in 1790, cultivated a refined sense of class privilege and historical distinction among its elite black membership. Elsewhere, black literary societies and fraternal organizations attracted a more diverse membership. Ira Berlin, *Slaves without Masters: The Free Negro in the Antebellum South* (New York: Oxford University Press, 1974), 310–14; Bernard E. Powers Jr., *Black Charlestonians: A Social History, 1822–1885* (Fayetteville: University of Arkansas Press, 1994), 179–81. See John Blassingame, *Black New Orleans, 1860–1880* (Chicago: University of Chicago Press, 1973), 146–47; Howard N. Rabinowitz, *Race Relations in the Urban South, 1865–1890* (New York: Oxford University Press, 1978), 238–39, 292–93.

10. *Richmond Planet,* 14 April 1900. See also *Richmond Planet,* 2 April 1904; *Indianapolis Freeman,* 18 June 1890, *Savannah Tribune,* 30 June 1894, 4 March 1911.

11. *Washington Bee,* 21 September 1901; H. W. Clark to Mary Church Terrell, 1 August and 11 September 1922. Mary Church Terrell Papers, Library of Congress; *Richmond Planet,* 14 April 1906. Such rural celebrations could evolve into imposing affairs. "June Day," a local celebration of emancipation in Gifford, South Carolina, for instance, began in 1869 as a family picnic. Eventually, the festivities attracted large numbers of celebrants from across the state. Likewise, Brenham, Texas, a small county seat located west of Houston, earned the reputation as the site of perhaps the state's biggest Juneteenth celebration. So popular and so eagerly anticipated were the town's festivities that its population doubled, tripled, and even quadrupled with excursionists from as far away as Dallas and San Antonio each Juneteenth (Wiggins and DeNatale, *Jubilation!* 31; *Ebony* 6 [June 1951]: 27).

12. *New York Age,* 19 January 1889; *Indianapolis Freeman,* 19 July 1890; George Brown Tindall, *South Carolina Negroes, 1877–1900* (Columbia: University of South Carolina Press, 1970), 288–90.

13. *Richmond Whig,* 2 January 1867. See also *Richmond Whig,* 6 July 1868; *Richmond Dispatch,* 5 July 1867, 5 July 1883, and 6 July 1886; and Elsa Barkley Brown and Gregg B. Kimball, "Mapping the Terrain of Black Richmond," *Journal of Urban History* 21 (March 1995): 296–346.

14. For discussions of black militias in the various states, see Donald L. Grant, *The Way It Was in the South: The Black Experience in Georgia* (New York: Birch Lane Press, 1993), 299–300; Bobby L. Lovett, *The African-American History of Nashville, Tennessee, 1780–1930* (Fayetteville: University of Arkansas Press, 1999), 101; John M. Matthews, "Studies in Race Relations in Georgia, 1890–1930," (Ph.D. diss., Duke University, 1970), 335–37; Rabinowitz, *Race Relations in the Urban South,* 227–30; Robert E. Perdue, *The Negro in Savannah, 1865 to 1900* (New York: Exposition Press, 1973), 100–101; Lawrence D. Rice, *The Negro in Texas, 1874–1900* (Baton Rouge: Louisiana State University Press, 1971), 270–71; Otis A. Singletary,

Negro Militia and Reconstruction (New York: McGraw-Hill, 1963); Tindall, *South Carolina Negroes,* 286–88.

15. *Richmond Planet,* 2 June 1906, 27 May 1915; *Savannah Tribune,* 13 February 1909, 31 May, 7 June 1913, 30 May, 6 June 1914, 17 February 1917, 24 May 1919. On Civil War veterans and their role in parades, see Brundage, "Black Veterans and the Historical Memory of the Civil War," 136–56.

16. Kirk Savage, *Standing Soldier, Kneeling Slaves: Race, War, and Monument in Nineteenth-Century America* (Princeton: Princeton University Press, 1997), 178.

17. *Savannah Tribune,* 8 January 1876, 3 August 1889, 26 May 1894, 15 May 1897; *Jacksonville Times-Union,* 6 July 1886; *Petersburg Index,* 6 July 1880; *Petersburg Lancet,* 7 July 1883; *Charlotte Observer,* 2 January 1895. The eventual abolition of black militia companies in the South threatened to rob black men of the opportunity to display their military and civic valor. Long-established black secret orders, however, quickly transformed themselves into quasi-military organizations complete with precision drill squads and elaborate faux-military uniforms. For discussions of the role of fraternal societies in post-militia celebrations, see *Richmond Planet,* 8 January 1898; *Savannah Tribune,* 6 January 1906; *Augusta (Ga.) Georgia Baptist,* 7 January 1909.

18. For examples of the ceremonial roles of fire companies, see *Charleston News and Courier,* 2 January 1875; *Huntsville Gazette,* 7 July 1883; *Columbia State,* 1 January 1892; *Natchez Democrat,* 10 July 1892; *Wilmington Morning Star,* 2 January 1895, 2 January 1896; *Greenville (N.C.) Reflector,* 6 January 1896; *Norfolk Virginian-Pilot,* 3 January 1898, 2 January 1902. For scholarly descriptions of black fire companies, see Tindall, *South Carolina Negroes,* 23.

19. *New York Age,* 28 April 1888; *Jacksonville Evening Telegram,* 31 December 1891; *Savannah Tribune,* 6 January 1917; *Jacksonville News Herald,* 5 July 1887. For other examples of conspicuous union participation in celebrations, see *Charleston News and Courier,* 2 January 1874; *New Orleans Pelican,* 9 July 1888; *Huntsville Gazette,* 12 July 1888; *Norfolk Landmark,* 2 January 1889; *Norfolk Virginian,* 2 January 1890; *Birmingham Age-Herald,* 2 January 1899; *Norfolk Virginian-Pilot,* 2 January 1910. In at least one instance, labor unions enjoyed the honor of leading an Emancipation Day parade; see *Twenty-Two Years of Freedom* (Norfolk, Va.: Thomas F. Paige, 1885), 29.

20. *Richmond Planet,* 1 April 1916; *Savannah Tribune,* 13 January 1917; *Charlotte Observer,* 2 January 1915.

21. *Richmond Dispatch,* 2 January 1866; *Savannah Tribune,* 5 January 1889; *Columbia State,* 1 1892; *Richmond Planet,* 11 December 1897; *Savannah Tribune,* 24 February 1917. See also *New Orleans Louisianian,* 9 July 1881; *Petersburg Lancet,*

13 January 1883, 17 January 1885; *Nashville Banner,* 2 January 1891; *Ocala Evening Star,* 2 January 1901; Emancipation Day Resolutions, p. 2, 2 January 1899, Charles N. Hunter Papers. For a cogent discussion of black millennialism, see Timothy E. Fulop, "The Future Golden Day of the Race: Millennialism and Black Americans in the Nadir, 1877–1901," *Harvard Theological Review* 84 (1991): 75–99.

22. *Richmond Planet,* 28 October 1899; *Savannah Tribune,* 24 February 1917.

23. *Savannah Tribune,* 27 May 1893, 6 January 1900. See, for instance, *Savannah Morning News,* 2 January 1900; *Atlanta Constitution,* 2 January 1904; *Raleigh Post,* 3 January 1905; *Raleigh Liberator,* 7 January 1905; *Raleigh Times,* 1 January 1907; *Savannah Tribune,* 5 January 1907; *Raleigh News and Observer,* 2 January 1917. A few orators, contrary to the general pattern described here, were so pessimistic that they advocated emigration to Africa or virtual black autonomy in the United States. See *Savannah Morning News,* 2 January 1890, 6 January 1917; *Indianapolis Freeman,* 13 January 1894; and *Savannah Tribune,* 7 January 1898.

24. This process is traced in Catherine W. Bishir, "Landmarks of Power: Building a Southern Past, 1855–1915," *Southern Cultures* Inaugural Issue (1994): 5–46; Foster, *Ghosts of the Confederacy;* Savage, *Standing Soldiers, Kneeling Slaves,* chap. 5; and Nina Silber, *The Romance of Reunion: Northerners and the South, 1865–1900* (Chapel Hill: University of North Carolina Press, 1993), chaps. 4–5. On the importance of physical manifestations of memory, see Michel-Rolph Trouillot, *Silencing the Past: Power and the Production of History* (Boston: Beacon Press, 1995), esp. 28–30.

25. *Indianapolis Freeman,* 18 July 1896.

17

Memorializing the Movement
The Struggle to Build Civil Rights Museums in the South

GLENN T. ESKEW

Across the South, city and county governments are joining hands with movement veterans and scholars to construct monuments to the civil rights struggle. In Atlanta and Albany, Georgia, and in Selma and Birmingham, Alabama, more and more pilgrims are visiting the celebrated sites of postwar racial strife. The heritage tourism that is being created and the message delivered by the museum exhibitory localizes the life of Dr. Martin Luther King Jr. within the context of particular events. In an effort to be relevant, the message is bifurcated between the cataloging of the past and the reforming of the present. While tensions have resulted from this exercise in collective memory, the process of memorializing the civil rights movement has promoted a new civic ideology for the South—and indeed, for America.

Historical analysis suggests that the initial push to memorialize the movement began only weeks after the assassination of the Reverend Dr. Martin Luther King Jr., when his widow envisioned a living museum within a historical district established in his honor. This Atlanta memorial sat alone until 1989, when Maya Lin installed Morris Dees' somber Civil Rights Memorial in Montgomery, inaugurating a decade of monument building. In Memphis, memorialists bought at foreclosure the Lorraine Motel in 1982 and invested nearly ten million in tax dollars to create the National Civil Rights Museum, which opened in 1991. A year later, civic leaders and movement veterans cut ribbons inaugurating the Birmingham Civil Rights Institute, which cost $12 million and combined a museum with an archive. In 1993 movement veterans in the Southern Christian Leadership Conference (SCLC) opened the National Voting Rights Museum in Selma. When the Woolworth's closed in Greensboro, North Carolina, in 1994, memorialists launched plans to turn the facility into a multimedia International Civil Rights Center and Museum.

Just in time for the Olympics, Congress approved an $11 million expansion and renovation to the U.S. Park Service's Martin Luther King, Jr., National Historic Site in Atlanta. Also in 1996 a less-ambitious facility opened in Savannah, Georgia. In 1998 the old Mount Zion Baptist Church again rebounded with the sounds of freedom songs as it began a new life as the home of the Albany Civil Rights Museum. Other memorials are planned for Little Rock, Arkansas, and Oxford, Mississippi. An analysis of the King Center in Atlanta, the National Voting Rights Museum in Selma, the Birmingham Civil Rights Institute, and the Albany Civil Rights Museum affords an opportunity to draw some conclusions regarding this recent exercise in historical memory.[1]

Within two months of King's assassination in 1968, his widow and the City of Atlanta had outlined the "living, permanent" memorial and historical district to the martyred civil rights leader that has since evolved as the Martin Luther King, Jr., National Historic Site and Preservation District. From the outset, memorialists envisioned a complex containing the King Birth Home, Ebenezer Baptist Church, a library containing King's personal papers, and a permanent "entombment" for King's remains—all located in a "King shrine area" along Auburn Avenue in the heart of the old black business district. To achieve this goal, Coretta Scott King established the Martin Luther King, Jr., Center for Nonviolent Social Change, Inc., and set as its task the memorialization of the man. The King Center petitioned the Johnson Administration to build a monument to King in Atlanta, and Congress to declare King's January 15 birthday a national holiday. Although the Nixon Administration proved unfriendly when asked to designate the area as "Freedom Memorial Park," the King Center attracted funding from corporate America, receiving $100,000 in 1969 from the Ford Foundation to process King's papers. Yet the complex planned by Coretta Scott King cost millions. The King Center acquired the Birth Home and property adjacent to Ebenezer Baptist, relocated King's body to a marble sarcophagus on the land, and announced a $10 million fundraising campaign; but in the short term, it housed its activities in the Interdenominational Theological Center at Atlanta University.[2]

The building of a community center by the city of Atlanta in 1975 furthered the King Center complex but revealed deep fissures among movement veterans as critics assailed the memorialization. Reflecting the importance of black empowerment, Atlanta's new mayor, Maynard Jackson, an African American, allocated $2.8 million to build the Martin Luther King Community Center opposite Ebenezer Baptist Church as the city's contribution. It housed several social agencies, including a child-care facility managed by the King Center. Yet two more years passed before any construction began on the Center's actual complex. In 1977 Coretta Scott King dedicated the Inter-Faith Peace Chapel, which enveloped the tomb with a brick backdrop, but little else showed for the nearly $6 million she had raised since 1968 when she left the movement and devoted herself full time to memorializing her martyred husband. Angry at her departure, members of the SCLC organized protests at the groundbreaking of the community center and at wreath-laying ceremonies at the King gravesite. They demanded an end to hunger and unemployment and saw the memorialization as a waste of money. Coretta Scott King graciously responded by commending their concerns and then organizing a Summer Institute on Non-Violence and Social Change headed by Voter Education Project Director John Lewis. The King Center set full employment as its social agenda and, with a Georgia Democrat in the White House, found a friendly audience.[3]

The final push to complete the King Center complex occurred during the Carter Administration. In 1978 President and Mrs. Jimmy Carter kicked off an $8 million fundraising campaign headed by Henry Ford II to build the offices, archive, gift shop, classrooms, and auditorium planned as Freedom Hall. They raised the money in a year, with a previous donation of $600,000 by the United Auto Workers being topped by a $1 million gift from the Ford Motor Company and support from the U.S. Department of Commerce. A retrospective on the King Center in the *Atlanta Constitution* published at the groundbreaking for the buildings revealed Coretta Scott King's success in creating the memorial. With resources in real estate and other investments valued at $1.8 million, annual mailed donations in excess of a quarter million, and souvenir sales of $175,000, the King Center posted strong receipts; yet its operating budget of $750,000 ate away at its finances. To solve a perennial money shortage, Coretta Scott King returned to her original plan and sought the intervention of the federal government.[4]

On the eve of Carter's failed re-election bid, Congress authorized in October 1980 the Martin Luther King Jr. National Historic Site and Preservation District, initiating direct federal intervention over parts of the "King shrine area" that has evolved into almost complete control of the King memorial. In 1974 the King Center had restored the Birth Home to its appearance when King lived there from 1929 to 1941, but it did not have the resources to stabilize the neighborhood that the government described as a "stricken area." The

legislation authorized the National Park Service to develop historic preservation plans, address resource management, and purchase property to preserve
its appearance. Once on the site, the Park Service expanded its mission in
response to visitor needs. Yet the initial agreement had made clear that the
King Center, "which carries on the work of Dr. King, will continue to memorialize him and explain his philosophies and legacy to visitors. The National
Park Service will not establish a major visitor center in the national historic
site." In a 1986 report, the Park Service recommended expanding its activities,
noting that 350,000 tourists visited the site in 1983 but that "visitors currently
are limited in what they can see and learn about Dr. King and the Sweet
Auburn community. Visitor services and facilities are lacking. In addition, current visitor use places a severe strain on the limited resources of the King Center." The report recommended nearly $5 million worth of improvements
through the restoration of a row of shotgun houses and other key buildings
near the Birth Home, the landscaping of the community center plaza, visitor
parking, and expansion of staff to man an information kiosk. Nowhere did the
report suggest that the Park Service envisioned a "major visitor center."[5]

The King Center dedicated the Freedom Hall complex in January 1982
but spent the balance of the decade searching for money to finance an expanding staff and growing budget. The Center retired the $10 million debt on the
buildings in 1984, using donations from IBM, Coca-Cola, Disney, Southern
Bell, Xerox, and Ford, but also labor unions, the National Education Association, and the kingdoms of Kuwait and Saudi Arabia. The United States government awarded a $4 million grant for the facility. Yet Coretta Scott King
asked for an additional $7 to $9 million for equipment and decorations. The
King Center's annual budget had doubled since 1978 to $1.5 million in 1984,
a third of which paid maintenance and security expenses.

While internal reports decried "a serious cash flow problem" and "severe
financial crisis," the treasurer, King's sister, Christine King Farris, claimed,
"One of our strong points is our ability to manage." Yet the King Center
proved unable to conduct regular tours of the King Birth Home, upsetting the
civil rights pilgrims who traveled to Atlanta. Although the Center had charged
a dollar a head to tour the home, earning from $5,000 in 1978 to $20,000 in
1983, it negotiated a lease with the National Park Service whereby rangers
conducted tours. The agreement provided $100,000 in rents and services to
the King Center complex in 1984. Within ten years the federal government
had paid nearly $4.5 million to manage just the Birth Home.

In 1986 the King Center turned to the Georgia Department of Natural Resources, which manages the state's historic sites, and appealed to it for three tour guides and operating expenses for other areas of the complex. That year the General Assembly failed to approve Governor Joe Frank Harris's budgeted $104,000 for the King Center despite its reputation as Georgia's number one tourist attraction, drawing a half-million people in 1985. Meanwhile, expenses increased as the King Center budget grew from $1.5 to 2 million over two years and the staff expanded from 50 to 63 people between 1985 and 1986. Searching for permanent funding, Coretta Scott King announced the goal of a $13.5 million endowment for the King Center. The campaign was kicked off by Bill Cosby at a 1985 fundraiser that attracted 1,200 people at $250 a plate for a total contribution of $300,000. Although IBM and Coca-Cola loaned staff support, other corporations were less enthusiastic. An executive explained that Atlanta's Citizens and Southern Bank failed to contribute because "they really don't have a tangible program coming out of there." By 1988 the King Center had turned to local government to request full-time security for the facility. Fulton County Commissioner Martin Luther King III, who served on the Center's board, saw no conflict of interest in asking the sheriff to provide a full-time deputy to protect the King family and to patrol the complex. Using creative financing, the King Center struggled to control expenditures.[6]

The Park Service struggled with problems of a different sort—no bathrooms, inadequate parking, poor interpretation of the site—all legacies of the decade-long arrangement with the King Center. But the September 1990 announcement that Atlanta would host the 1996 Olympics offered an opportunity to change everything. Within months, Park Service officials had proposed a visitor center with restroom facilities and interactive exhibits, the restoration of an 1896 fire station and other significant buildings, off-street parking for buses, and a new landscape for a total bill of $11 million. More than two million tourists visited the site in 1991, and the Park Service estimated 100,000 a day would attend during the Olympics for a total of five million in 1996. Local rangers recognized an "unprecedented opportunity to provide additional facilities for visitors" and held to "a tenacious belief that it was now or never for the site to be developed." Site Superintendent Troy Lissimore explained: "The Olympics were not the reason that improvements were needed . . . but the Olympics were the reason it had to be done now." The proposal involved swapping land among the Park Service, Ebenezer Baptist Church, and the City of Atlanta. It called for demolishing the city-owned

Martin Luther King Community Center and building on that site a visitor center and a new sanctuary for Ebenezer Baptist Church that would then turn its old sanctuary over to rangers for regular tours. The Park Service won the support of Ebenezer's clergy, Mayor Maynard Jackson, City Councilman Bill Campbell, U.S. Representative John Lewis of the Fifth Congressional District that included the site, and Senators Sam Nunn and Paul Coverdell of Georgia. Although the Bush Administration had funded $2.2 million for Park Service restoration work in 1992, the election of President Bill Clinton helped secure the necessary monies that the federal government appropriated in November 1993.[7]

As the Park Service completed local negotiations, the King Center, under the leadership of its newly elected president, Dexter Scott King, protested the planned visitor center and announced a competing proposal. The King family attempted to torpedo the land swap arrangement in order to get the site of the Martin Luther King Community Center for a Disney-like, "high-tech, virtual reality, interactive museum" called "The King Time Machine." Still in a conceptual phase, the King Dream Center as it came to be called, incorporated 3-D holographic recreations of King delivering famous speeches and virtually generated civil rights confrontations. The family had no funding in place for the estimated $40 to $60 million project but insisted on receiving the endorsement of the city and Park Service and securing the land. Nonetheless, the supporters of the Park Service plan stood firm as the land swap went through on August 16, 1994. As construction began on the visitor center in December 1994, Dexter King banned the Park Service from the Birth Home and the King Center complex. He issued a press release that explained "the history of the civil rights movement and the legacy of Dr. King shall not reside with the National Park Service, but shall forever remain in the care and custody of the King family." Already the family had won control over King's image and sayings. His real complaint focused on the visitor center, for the initial agreement had left the Park Service in a "support role"; but when it put "up something directly in competition" with the King Center, it had broken that agreement. The removal of the Park Service from the King Center properties forfeited a $534,000 lease agreement with the federal government, a serious financial blow, especially given that the center had run substantial deficits in eight of the previous ten years. A shortfall of $250,000 in 1991 tripled to $758,000 in 1993 but dropped down to $602,637 in 1994. Reports suggested the compensation paid Coretta Scott King declined with the deficit from $176,000 in

1992 to $114,922 in 1993, but the money woes convinced Coca-Cola and British Petroleum not to follow through on a scheduled $1.5 million pledge. As Dexter King confronted the King Center's finances, the Park Service proceeded with construction to meet its Olympic deadline.[8]

Unable to sway John Lewis and other supporters of the Park Service and unable to contend with the hoards of tourists expected during the Olympics, the King Center backed down. It renegotiated the use of the complex and allowed rangers to conduct tours of the Birth Home, crypt, and Freedom Hall. Dexter King explained, "It makes sense to let [them] do what they do best, that is deal with the public." He added, "Once the park service acknowledged that we had the legal right to interpret my father's legacy, we no longer had a problem. It was never really an issue over who was giving the tours so long as the message was consistent." Turning its attention to the "library and archive," the King estate signed multimillion dollar contracts to reprint King's books and secretly shopped around for a buyer of King's papers.[9]

Barely making the Olympics, the National Park Service opened its King National Historic Site Visitor Center in June 1996. In addition to the bathrooms, bookstore, large lobby, and offices for staff, the center contains an interactive display composed of six pods that recount segregation in the South, the King family and "Sweet Auburn," Martin Luther King's early leadership in Montgomery, his civil rights triumphs, his broad vision for reform, and his assassination in Memphis. Dividing the pods in half is "Freedom Road" on which monochromatic "lifecast" mannequins representing minorities walk up an incline to a picture window showing in the distance King's crypt. While putting a local spin on events, the Atlanta visitor center recounts the civil rights struggle from Montgomery to Memphis and emphasizes the triumph of the movement in a design and message similar to the memorials elsewhere.[10]

The memorialization of the civil rights movement in Selma, Alabama, began as a venture by veterans of the struggle; but as in Atlanta, it evolved into a federally supported initiative. Although local activists and the SCLC played a central role in the creation of the National Voting Rights Museum, the real force behind the Selma memorial is Congressman John Lewis, who annually returns to the site to recall this moment of glory and to emphasize the importance of the ballot. Seven years after Dallas County Sheriff Jim Clarke and his posse beat Lewis, Hosea Williams, and other black demonstrators at the foot of the Edmund Pettus Bridge in 1965, Lewis and fellow activist Julian Bond and F. D. Reese of Selma obtained a federal judge's order that allowed them to stage a reenactment. The 1972 protest launched an era of black empowerment in Dallas County. Since then, movement veterans have periodically returned to recall the Selma to Montgomery March.

With the collapse of cotton and the shift to beef cattle and other forms of agriculture and enterprise, Selma experienced an economic decline that city fathers addressed in the late 1970s and early 1980s by promoting historic preservation and tourism, featuring the city's antebellum mansions and post-bellum commercial district. In 1986 the Kiwanis Club staged its first reenact-ment of the Battle of Selma, an annual event that by 1998 attracted 15,000 people and raised $250,000 for charities and thousands more for the local economy, while emphasizing historical "authenticity." Selma's salesman, Mayor Joe Smitherman, who was in office during the civil rights demonstra-tions of 1965 and remains in office today, recognized the value of the voting rights reenactments for Selma's tourism industry. A local historian said of Smitherman, "He can do the reformed redneck segregationist almost better than anybody." The mayor once confessed from the pulpit of Brown Chapel African Methodist Episcopal Church, "My hands are as dirty as the others. I ordered the arrest of Dr. King. We were wrong. I did it. I'm sorry." In his thirty-five years in office, the mayor had worked hard to maintain racial peace while extending city services to the black side of town. But the firing of the first black school superintendent in 1990 almost brought down his adminis-tration while strengthening local resolve for a memorial to the movement.[11]

Voting rights marches had occurred in the late 1980s, but the 25th anniversary of the demonstrations brought thousands of people to Selma dur-ing the racial tensions of 1990. Lewis and Joseph Lowery of the SCLC co-chaired the Selma to Montgomery March Anniversary Committee, which oversaw the March 5 reenactment that included the firing of smoke bombs to simulate tear gas and the subsequent screaming of participants. One wag com-pared the dozens of journalists descending on the reenactors at the bridge crossing to George Wallace's state troopers. The audience included a who's who of black leaders, as Coretta Scott King, Hosea Williams, Jesse Jackson, Ben Chavis, and Dick Gregory addressed the racially mixed crowd of around 4,000. Local leaders welcomed the visiting black dignitaries as Smitherman dedicated a historical marker in a park beside the bridge. Writer Gay Talese, who had covered the original protests for the *New York Times,* returned to Selma to report on the reenactment and observed integration that led him to conclude: "It could be argued that Selma has changed more than any place in America in the past 25 years." Veteran John Lewis wanted to commemorate that change.[12]

In March 1990, Representative Lewis pushed through Congress the Selma to Montgomery National Trail Study Act, which authorized the National Park Service to determine if the 54-mile stretch of highway between Selma and Montgomery qualified as a National Historic Trail. After the Park Service submitted its report that the route met the criteria, Lewis introduced a bill in August 1993 to get Congress to designate the route a National Historic Trail. By 1995 Congressman Earl Hilliard, an African American from Birmingham, worked with Lewis to secure the passage of the act. In December 1995 Federal Highway Administrator Rodney Slater announced a $1.5 million grant to the Alabama Department of Transportation to develop the trail.[13]

When John Lewis returned to Selma in 1992, he joined other movement veterans in dedicating the National Voting Rights Museum that local activists, assisted by the SCLC, had created in a historic building at 1012 Water Avenue near the Edmund Pettus Bridge. Many of the veterans who periodically returned to Selma for the reenactments served as chairs and coordinators of the memorial. They established it "to offer America and the world the opportunity to learn the lessons of the past to assure we will not make the same mistakes in the 21st century and beyond. The museum's board of directors believes it to be a look back, but also a vision and reminder of what America can and will be." The National Voting Rights Museum took as its project the annual "Bridge Crossing Jubilee," combining the periodic ritual of the reenactment for voting rights with a weekend-long festival designed to attract tourists. A $2,000 grant from the Alabama Council on the Arts funded a "Bridge Festival" in April 1992 that served as a model for the National Voting Rights Museum's Jubilee as it combined crafts and food with musical performances on temporary stages set up along Water Avenue. The Jubilee added a beauty pageant and parade, and concerts by gospel groups and hip hop artists. By emphasizing elections, the museum attracted national politicians for the Jubilee, including presidential hopefuls Bob Kerrey and Jerry Brown. The museum's exhibits featured African American politicians from the first and second Reconstructions as well as memorials to the martyrs of the movement and a "Women's Suffrage Room." Indeed, black women played an instrumental role in creating the memorial, for Octavia Vivian, the wife of movement veteran C. T. Vivian, served as national curator of the museum; and in 1991 the Women of the SCLC erected a monument to movement martyr Viola Liuzzo on Highway 80.[14]

With the National Voting Rights Museum and the designation of the Selma to Montgomery National Historic Trail, Selma advertised the brutality of its racist past for tourism purposes. Chamber of commerce literature proudly juxtaposed the Greek Revival Sturdivant Hall next to Brown Chapel A.M.E. Church. It printed special brochures on Selma's "Legacy of Black Heritage." It assisted the National Voting Rights Museum with publicizing the Bridge Crossing Jubilee. With the National Park Service, it produced the Martin Luther King, Jr., Street Historic Walking Tour. It touted "Civil War Through Civil Rights," with promotional materials that offered tourists two reenactments: the Battle of Selma and the Selma to Montgomery March. Mayor Smitherman boosted his city in 1995 by joining John Lewis on *Oprah* and other TV talk shows. The Olympics sponsored the torch run through Selma, and Lewis and Smitherman carried the flame across the Edmund Pettus Bridge. By 1996 tourism generated $5 million for Selma. When President Bill Clinton announced that he would join Lewis in Selma on March 5, 2000, Smitherman exclaimed, "It is a great honor to have the president of the United States visit our historic city. . . . This will open doors for enormous tourism in our city."[15]

After years of delaying the project, Birmingham's black mayor finally attributed potential tourist dollars as convincing him to support the Birmingham Civil Rights Institute. The initial proposal to memorialize the movement in Birmingham came from the white racial liberal David Vann, who had played a crucial role in the negotiations that ended the spring 1963 demonstrations. In 1971 a coalition of moderate white and black voters had elected him mayor, but an egregious example of police brutality brought down his administration in 1979 and ushered in the era of Richard Arrington, who for twenty years served as Birmingham's first black mayor. Arrington's election reflected the local success of black empowerment. In the waning weeks of Vann's administration, the white mayor championed the commemoration of the fire hoses and police dogs as well as the biracial cooperation that had occurred since the racial troubles. The city council endorsed Vann's proposal for a study committee to determine the feasibility of a museum that local reformers also saw as a vehicle for urban renewal and tourism. Yet a year and a half passed before Mayor Arrington appointed the committee.[16]

The Birmingham Civil Rights Museum Study Committee began work in June 1981 with Vann laying out a proposal that the city implemented over the next decade. It called for the acquisition of the corner lot south of Sixteenth Street Baptist Church and west of Kelly Ingram Park as the site of the facility, which would collect materials on the movement and develop an activist agenda. Rather than a museum, the Study Committee proposed in October 1981 the Birmingham Civil Rights Institute as "an educational and research center" with "exhibitions, education, and archives" as its specific duties.[17]

The mayor and city council received the Study Committee's recommendations but failed to respond. Two years later Arrington won reelection as mayor, but the report still sat on the shelf. Then in 1984, Birmingham's black state senator, Earl Hilliard, proposed that Alabama build two institutes in Birmingham, one to memorialize the Civil War and the other to memorialize the civil rights movement. Politicians on Goat Hill killed the legislation, but advocates of the Birmingham Civil Rights Institute took heart. In November 1984, Arrington's executive secretary, Ed LaMonte, invited members of the Study Committee to meet with Hilliard and urban reformers to discuss the status of the report. Again Arrington delayed action until November 1985 when LaMonte made the surprise announcement that the city had $500,000 to purchase property for the proposed Institute.[18]

The change in administration policy allowed Arrington to reward his cronies and allegedly to line his own pockets. To oversee local work planning the Institute, Arrington hired his personal friend and business associate Tarlee Brown of the Atlanta architectural firm Milkey and Brown, which had already won several lucrative city contracts. Arrington asked Brown to coordinate the efforts of Marjorie Peters of MP Enterprises, who likewise received city work and was the mayor's personal friend. Court testimony later suggested that Peters told Brown that he "needed to show [his] appreciation to the mayor" by kicking back a quarter of all his profits. Brown claimed that at a March 1986 meeting with Arrington he agreed to the terms. The next month the city council allocated nearly $1 million and budgeted an additional $1.5 million taken from federal revenue sharing funds to finance the Institute. With the previous $500,000 lot, the city's investment reached nearly $3 million. The seed money in place, Arrington hired the nationally recognized minority architectural firm Bond Ryder James Associates, and it hired Brown and Peters.[19]

The mayor then appointed the Civil Rights Museum Task Force to advise the professionals in the design of the building. Arrington explained his newfound enthusiasm for the Institute: "I believe that the Civil Rights Museum has great potential for our community in establishing Birmingham as a tourist attraction." Echoing the urban reformer's "Master Plan," Arrington saw the Institute anchoring a civil rights district created to revitalize the Kelly Ingram Park area. He appointed to the committee several white racial liberals, including Vann and LaMonte; academic historians, including Horace Huntley of the University of Alabama at Birmingham and Marvyn Whiting of the Birmingham Public Library; and city planners, including Odessa Woolfolk. The Reverend Abraham Woods served as the only civil rights movement veteran on the committee.[20]

The mayor's initial plan allowed Bond Ryder James to conceptualize, design, and construct the actual building and exhibits without any real input by the local Task Force. Having designed the Martin Luther King, Jr., Center for Nonviolent Social Change, Inc., and renovations to the Schomburg Center among other projects, J. Max Bond felt comfortable proposing a standard museum blueprint that contained utilitarian exhibit space, offices, and gift shop. To woo the locals, Bond Ryder James had Marjorie Peters and Tarlee Brown schedule a "New York Workshop" in June 1986, where museum consultants came in to sell LaMonte, Whiting, and Woolfolk on the design. The trip included meals at expensive restaurants and Broadway entertainment. After the whirlwind visit to the Big Apple, the locals returned to Birmingham determined to wrestle control of the process away from the architects.[21] LaMonte asked the mayor to "slow down the development of a specific building" in order to give the Task Force time to develop a mission statement.[22] Supporting his executive secretary, Arrington gave LaMonte, Whiting, Woolfolk, and the other members of the Task Force veto power over the architect's use of space, the design of the thematic program, and the display of exhibits. Henceforth, local authorities determined the content of the Institute while working with the architects, museum experts, and exhibit fabricators hired by the city.[23]

Twice Mayor Arrington proposed bond issues to pay for the Institute, and twice Birmingham's voters rejected his plans, despite having a majority black electorate. In 1986 Arrington set aside for the Institute $10 million of a $65 million bond issue that also called for work on schools, sewers, parks, and sidewalks. On July 8, 1986, voters defeated the measure 23,281 against to 13,638 in favor of the referendum. Likewise, on May 10, 1988, Birmingham's electorate rejected for a second time the bond issue with its money for the Institute, even though African Americans comprised 65 percent of the electorate.

Having been defeated twice by the voters, Arrington decided to sell surplus city property and use the $7.2 million it generated to fund the Institute. By then Bond Ryder James, Tarlee Brown, and Marjorie Peters had spent the nearly $3 million previously set aside by the city.[24]

Giving the Task Force influence over the design and content of the Institute did not prevent the mayor's cronies from profiting by the project. In February 1987 Tarlee Brown allegedly kicked back to Arrington $4,000. When Bond Ryder James balked at giving Marjorie Peters money for supposedly promoting Birmingham's black heritage tourism program, she simply forged Max Bond's signature to an invoice and filed it with the city to collect $121,917. In response to Bond's questioning of the invoice, Tarlee Brown recommended that the three of them split the money. Bond refused. In response, Mayor Arrington replaced Bond Ryder James with Diversified Project Management (DPM) as the principal contractor, and its president routed the forged invoice through the city and paid off Marjorie Peters, who then left the project.[25]

Meeting with Arrington on July 11, 1986, the Task Force recapped the previous seven-year struggle to build the Institute. A consensus developed around the belief that the Institute should show "the success of Birmingham in dealing with civil rights" through "the resolution of conflict and struggle." Describing an "educational, cultural, and research center," the Task Force proposed a "living institution" that interpreted the events in Birmingham within a national and international context.[26] To conceptualize the exhibitory, the Task Force and Bond Ryder James encouraged the city to hire American History Workshop. Richard Rabinowitz headed the New York firm that had designed the United States Holocaust Memorial and the Center for Southern Folklore among other museums. Rabinowitz visited Birmingham several times, consulted with Woolfolk, Whiting, LaMonte, Vann, Huntley, and others, and gained their assistance in turning his rough draft into a formal thematic proposal. The final product, "Walking to Freedom: The Museum of America's Civil Rights Revolution," uses progressive history to recount the story of the movement. With elevated entrances, sloped walkways, and a domed foyer, Bond Ryder James designed a facility that complemented the Institute's thematic program. After a brief film introduces black Birmingham, the visitor explores galleries that represent life under segregation. Walking through "barriers" symbolizing the personal stings of racist attacks, the visitor enters the second half of the museum that recounts the civil rights struggle from Montgomery to Memphis by focusing on Birmingham. It culminates with a "processional" of monochromatic life-cast mannequins marching beside a life-size reproduction of James H. Karales famous photograph used in the opening credits to "Eyes on the Prize." Although a picture window looks out on Sixteenth Street Baptist Church where a bomb killed four black girls in September 1963, the visitor is pulled along by "milestones" that recount the story of black political empowerment. A concluding exhibit casts the gains in the context of the worldwide struggle for human rights.[27]

No sooner had the city authorized the letting of contracts to build the Institute than a scandal erupted. A federal investigation by the U.S. Attorney General's Office and the Internal Revenue Service subpoenaed materials from minority companies doing work with the city, including Milkey and Brown, MP Enterprises, Bond Ryder James, and DPM. Arrington refused to release records, dismissing the investigation as harassment by the Bush Administration. In 1991, overlooking the growing scandal, the city broke the ground bought in 1985 and announced the building of the Birmingham Civil Rights Institute in a ceremony headed by Arrington and the city's black leadership. Excluded from the event were the white racial liberals and academics involved in the Task Force and a black protest group that complained that the city had ignored the poor in the planning. A grand jury collected evidence for a year, then indicted Marjorie Peters in July 1991 for defrauding the city of Institute funds. Arrington responded, "To my knowledge, the services that we paid for were rendered." Confessing his guilt, Tarlee Brown plea-bargained and testified against Peters and the mayor, who was named by the Justice Department as an "unindicted co-conspirator." Arrington accused Washington of attempting to thwart his reelection bid for a fourth term. Indeed, the Peters trial started nine days before the mayoral election on October 8, 1991. The incumbent turned the investigation into his political platform by claiming the government had a "personal vendetta against him." Arrington used the charges of corruption to unify the black community behind his administration, easily defeating what had been seen as strong black opposition.[28]

The U.S. Attorney General subpoenaed the mayor's appointment calendar to corroborate the testimony of Tarlee Brown, but a belligerent Arrington refused to release it, claiming racism. The Attorney General then charged the mayor with contempt of court and threatened imprisonment. Wrapped in chains and handcuffed to Abraham Woods and Hosea Williams, Arrington retraced the route King took to jail in 1963 as the mayor marched by the construction site of the Birmingham Civil Rights Institute and past supporters waving signs that read "Racism is Corruption" on his way to the Federal Court-house. There authorities took him away for his first night behind bars in a minimum-security facility in Montgomery. Within twenty-four hours Arrington had released the calendar and returned home.[29]

While the U.S. Attorney General's office considered indicting Arrington, the mayor used the dedication of the Birmingham Civil Rights Institute to solidify his control over the black community. When Woods threatened to march on the Federal Courthouse during the September 1992 rededication of Kelly Ingram Park, Arrington calmed the crowd by describing the park as "a Place of Revolution that has given way to Reconciliation." As the pieces of the mayor's Civil Rights Cultural District fell into place, he milked each one to his political advantage. Arrington surrounded himself by veterans of the civil rights movement during the weeklong celebration that accompanied the grand opening of the Institute on November 15, 1992, and he gloried in the success of the Institute. It had taken thirteen years and $12 million dollars, but Birmingham could boast of an instant tourist attraction that was visited by 25,000 people in the first two weeks of operation.[30]

While on a smaller scale and budget, the Albany Civil Rights Movement Museum at old Mt. Zion also attracted tourists after it opened to great acclaim in November 1998. Like the other memorials to the movement, its bifurcated mission proposed to "commemorate the 1960s Civil Rights Movement in Albany and southwest Georgia so that it serves as an educational resource for the community, the nation, and the world." As in Birmingham, local funding paid for the facility and local white racial liberals played a leading role in its creation. Albany's memorialists galvanized around the potential sale of a move-ment church. The congregation of Mt. Zion Baptist Church had responded to urban decline by building a new sanctuary in the suburbs and boarding up the old historic structure that had hosted numerous mass meetings during the 1961–62 demonstrations. When the board of deacons placed a "for sale" sign on the property, Professor Lee Formwalt, a white historian at black Albany State University, and movement veterans McCree Harris, Bee McCormack, and A. C. Searles Sr. organized an effort to acquire the abandoned building as a memorial to the movement. The Albany City Commission, under the lead-ership of Mayor Tommy Coleman, appointed the memorialists to the Albany Movement Historical Commission, which approached the board of deacons of Mt. Zion with the request that they donate the church for a museum. Back in 1989 members of the congregation had attempted to get the church listed on the National Register of Historic Places. They struggled with the decision to surrender the structure, but "after much prayer and consideration, Reverend E. James Grant and the Board of Deacons and Trustees of Mt. Zion Baptist Church deeded old Mt. Zion to the Museum Corporation."

The sanctuary had fallen into a terrible state of disrepair. Determined to succeed, the memorialists applied for a grant from the Georgia Department of Natural Resources' Historic Preservation Division to stabilize the brick building. They incorporated their group as the Albany Civil Rights Movement Museum and received 501 (C) 3 status. With grant money, work "began in earnest" in the spring of 1994. Even that year's tragic flood of the Flint River, which devastated much of Albany, especially the black sections of town, failed to halt work—and in fact contributed to the substantial public support that the memorial received. In response to the flood, the Dougherty County Commission proposed a special sales tax that included $750,000 to fund the renovation of the church. Memorialists raised an additional $200,000 from the Miller Brewing Company, Proctor and Gamble, and other sources in the private sector. In 1997 the City of Albany added $250,000, bringing the total to $1.2 million, more than enough to cover the $850,000 cost to rehabilitate the building and the additional expense of developing exhibits for the interior. David Maschke, a local architect, oversaw the work that in nine months had restored the church to its 1960s appearance.[31]

The return of Freedom Riders to Albany in November 1998 announced the grand opening of the Mount Zion Albany Civil Rights Movement Museum and a weeklong "Jubilee Celebration." Dr. William G. Anderson, who in 1961 had served as president of the Albany movement and had invited Dr. King to participate in the demonstrations, joined the museum's C. W. Grant, Formwalt, Harris, Mayor Coleman, and others in cutting the ribbon that opened the facility. Anderson then joined Charles Sherrod and the Reverend Samuel B. Wells in leading a memorial march along the historic route taken to jail. The evening concluded with a singing lecture by Bernice Johnson Reagon, a native of Albany and veteran of the demonstrations who later took her vocal talent and interest in African American music into the academy, earned a doctorate, and a staff position at the Smithsonian Institute. Later in the week the Freedom Riders received keys to the city from the white mayor and greetings from the black chief of police. Also the "Jubilee Celebration" staged a reenactment of a mass meeting, a symposium of local activists discussing current racial issues, a roundtable discussion of civil rights historiography by scholars, and a concert by the remaining members of the Original SNCC Freedom Singers. Capturing the moment, reporter Rheta Grimsley Johnson observed, "Movement reunions are not unlike those of World War II soldiers. People swap battle stories, remember the ditches they once shared. But it's impossible to recapture the intensity of the moment. Time won't keep in a bottle. Even a Freedom Rider reunion becomes conferencelike."[32]

The efforts to memorialize the movement in Albany, Birmingham, Selma, and Atlanta—while spontaneous and independent—have resulted in similar outcomes. City and county governments and urban reformers assisted movement veterans and scholars in developing the memorials. In some instances, national museum consultants and the federal government participated in the planning. The goal of heritage tourism became a driving force as chambers of commerce advertised the racist past for tourist dollars. Indeed, black political empowerment made possible significant monies for the various initiatives. Consequently, the exhibits put local spins on the popular Montgomery to Memphis refrain, generating a common message. In fact, the contested past is less an issue than the controversy over purpose, for the memorials propose a bifurcated existence as both an interpretative museum and an agent for social change.[33]

Certainly the memorialization of the civil rights movement reflects a new collective memory of the South's recent past and an articulation of the region's civic ideology. In participating in the memorialization, movement veterans engage in nostalgia by recalling a golden moment of heroism and virtue. Reporting on the Albany reunion, Johnson recognized the ephemeral nature of the process: "Thank goodness for the music, the bridge to that passionate time. You can't mute the music, even with 37 years." Yet movement veterans often apply critical memory to the process whereby they evaluate the past revolution in light of present difficulties, hence the bifurcated nature of the movement memorials. Rituals such as the King Center's observance of the national holiday or the National Voting Rights Museum's annual Bridge Crossing Jubilee expand to address contemporary concerns while attracting the public with parades and festivals. Not content with simply creating a museum, the memorialists want to make their message relevant. Yet the very process by which the past is preserved and catalogued underscores the problems of cultural authenticity, for museums manufacture an interpretation of the past by placing on display artifacts taken out of context. Critics have long argued that museums house abstract and dead knowledge alienated from present reality.

Mayor Vann recognized this irony about the Birmingham Civil Rights Institute when he noted: "I've always said the best way to put your bad images to rest is to declare them history and put them in a museum."[34]

Unlike the occasionally contested renaming of streets in honor of Martin Luther King Jr., the civil rights commemorations have met for the most part with general acceptance as they come to symbolize a new ideology of toleration. Certainly the dynamics of heritage tourism have elicited a public support that few people would have dreamed of thirty years ago when Coretta Scott King initiated the process of memorializing the movement.[35]

NOTES

1. The forthcoming volume of essays, *No Deed but Memory: History and Memory in the American South* (Chapel Hill: University of North Carolina Press, forthcoming), edited by William Fitzhugh Brundage, addresses the evolution of historical memory in the region. The literature on historical memory has grown in recent years, but few books actually analyze the construction of memorials. The provocative study by Kirk Savage, *Standing Soldiers, Kneeling Slaves: Race, War, and Monument in Nineteenth-Century America* (Princeton, N.J.: Princeton University Press, 1997), considers the commemorations of the Civil War in public monuments and what this meant for race relations within the American collective memory. Although the war had abolished slavery, the monuments memorialized the heroism of average white soldiers, thus remaking the whiteness of the public space. That space itself is analyzed by Kenneth E. Foote in *Shadowed Ground: America's Landscapes of Violence and Tragedy* (Austin: University of Texas Press, 1997). Foote considers public sites where atrocities or other horrific acts occurred and how they are commemorated.

2. *Atlanta Journal,* 4 June 1968, 10 June 1968; *Atlanta Constitution,* 15 January 1969, 20 May 1973; *Atlanta Journal-Constitution,* 28 September 1969. Until the 1970s there were few indigenous African American museums; see Spencer R. Crew, "African Americans, History and Museums: Preserving African American History in the Public Arena," in *Making Histories in Museums,* ed. Gaynor Kavanagh (London: Leicester University Press, 1996). Like Emancipation Day and Independence Day celebrations, King Day became another commemoration. On black collective memory, see Genevieve Fabre, "African-American Commemorative Celebrations in the Nineteenth Century," in *History and Memory in African-American Culture,* ed. Genevieve Fabre and Robert O'Meally (New York: Oxford University Press, 1994); for background material on King's widow, see Coretta Scott King's *My Life with Martin Luther King, Jr.* (New York: Holt, Rinehart and Winston, 1969); and the *Atlanta Journal-Constitution,* 17 January 1993.

3. *Atlanta Constitution*, 16 January 1975, 17 September 1975, 4 April 1977, 27, 28, 29 July 1976, 4 April 1977, 4 October 1978. By 1976 the King Center had moved into temporary headquarters on the corner of Auburn Avenue and Boulevard but had left the papers at the Interdenominational Theological Center; see Dan Durett and Dana F. White, *An-Other Atlanta: The Black Heritage* (Atlanta: The History Group, 1975). A federal grant of $660,000 supported the child care center (*Atlanta Journal-Constitution*, 8 January 1984).

4. *Atlanta Constitution*, 4 October 1978, 14 January 1979, 9 December 1977; 17, 18 October 1979. $4 million of the $10 million building costs came from federal grants (*Atlanta Journal-Constitution*, 8 January 1984.

5. Public Law 96–428 adopted by the 96th Congress on October 10, 1980; National Park Service, *General Management Plan and Development Concept Plan*, 21 February 1986.

6. *Atlanta Journal-Constitution*, 9 January 1983, 8, 14, January 1984, 7 January 1985, 17 November 1985, 17 January 1986, 11 January 1995. The endowment drive attracted $500,000 from an Atlanta foundation and corporate support from Stroh Brewery Company.

7. National Park Service, *Martin Luther King, Jr., National Historic Site Land Protection Plan*, 1994 Update; National Park Service, *A Grand Endeavor for a Man with a Dream: The Story of Martin Luther King, Jr., National Historic Site and Preservation District* [1996]; *Atlanta Constitution*, 11 August 1994.

8. In April 1989 the board of directors appointed Dexter Scott King acting president of the King Center, and it elected him to the post in October 1994 (*Atlanta Constitution*, 5 April 1989, 22 October 1994). Dexter King approached neighborhood leaders regarding the King Dream Center in June 1994; see *Atlanta Journal-Constitution*, 11, 16 August 1994, 16 June 1996, and 1, 10, 14, 15, 21 January 1995.

9. *Atlanta Journal-Constitution*, 21 May, 16 June, 20 November 1996; on the King papers, see *Journal-Constitution*, 27 October, 14 November 1999; on the marketing of King, see *Journal-Constitution*, 12 January 1999; and on the Park Service facility fulfilling the needs of visitors, see 16 January 1999.

10. National Park Service, *A Grand Endeavor for a Man with a Dream.*

11. The closing of Craig Field by the military in the 1970s devastated the local economy; see Nicholas H. Holmes Jr., *What's Good about Downtown: A Handbook for the Economic and Aesthetic Revitalization of Downtown Selma, Alabama* (n.p., August 1979); *Selma Times-Journal*, 2, 3 August 1983; *Selma Showcase: A Magazine about Selma and Dallas County* 1, no. 2 (spring 1990), also 1998–99 edition; *Montgomery Advertiser*, 27 April 1998; *Selma Times-Journal*, 22–25 April 1999; *Atlanta*

Journal-Constitution 25 February 1990. The standard account of the civil rights struggle in Selma is David J. Garrow, *Protest at Selma: Martin Luther King, Jr., and the Voting Rights Act of 1965* (New Haven, Conn.: Yale University Press, 1978); on the significance of Selma in the life of John Lewis, see John Lewis with Michael D'Orso, *Walking with the Wind: A Memoir of the Movement* (New York: Simon and Schuster, 1998).

12. *Selma Times-Journal,* 28 February, 4, 5, 11 March 1990; *Montgomery Advertiser,* 11 March 1990.

13. *Selma Times-Journal,* 8 March 1990, 26 February 1995; National Park Service, *Selma to Montgomery Historic Trail Study* (n.p., [1992?]); *Atlanta Journal-Constitution,* 21 December 1995.

14. *Bridge Crossing Jubilee,* 5 March 1993, a tabloid published by the Southern Christian Leadership Conference for the National Voting Rights Museum. It lists co-chairs, Joseph Lowery and John Lewis; honorary chairs, Jesse Jackson, Coretta Scott King, James Orange, and Ben Chavis; national coordinators, C. T. Vivian and his wife Octavia Vivian; state chair, Alabama State Senator Hank Sanders; and local veterans of the 1965 march, Marie Foster and Albert Turner. See also *Selma Times-Journal,* 9 March 1992, and *Bridge Festival Edition,* a tabloid published 9 April 1992, by the *Selma Times-Journal.*

15. *Selma Showcase* (Selma, Ala.: Crossroads Visitor Information Center, 1998), 3, 10–11; "History Lives In Selma," "Selma: A Legacy of Black Heritage," and "Martin Luther King, Jr., Street Historic Walking Tour," brochures published by the Selma-Dallas County Chamber of Commerce; *Atlanta Journal-Constitution,* 20 June 1996; *Selma Times-Journal,* 17 February 2000; *Montgomery Advertiser,* 1 March 2000; *Atlanta Journal-Constitution,* 6 March 2000.

16. Jimmie Lewis Franklin, *Back to Birmingham: Richard Arrington, Jr., and His Times* (Tuscaloosa: University of Alabama Press, 1989), 92–133; *Birmingham Post-Herald,* 19 November 1992; city council resolution on July 29, 1980, Birmingham Civil Rights Institute Collection, Birmingham Public Library Department of Archives and Manuscripts, Birmingham, Ala.; City of Birmingham and Operation New Birmingham, *Master Plan for Downtown Birmingham, Alabama,* December 1980. Although Arrington suggested at the opening of the Institute in 1992 that "when David Vann first mentioned the idea of a civil rights museum, I became sort of enslaved by that idea," his actions suggest otherwise; for an account of the 1963 demonstrations, see Glenn T. Eskew, *But for Birmingham: The Local and National Movements in the Civil Rights Struggle* (Chapel Hill: University of North Carolina Press, 1997).

17. Richard Arrington to _____, June 16, 1981, BCRI Collection; David Vann, "Memorandum to Civil Rights Museum Committee: Concepts for

Consideration," n.d., attached to "Report of Civil Rights Museum Study Committee," 7 October 1981, BCRI Collection.

18. "Report of Civil Rights Museum Study Committee," 7 October 1981, BCRI Collection; Franklin, *Back to Birmingham,* 297–305; *Birmingham Post-Herald,* 23 February 1984.

19. *Birmingham Post-Herald,* 16 April 1986; *Birmingham News,* 5, 6, 25 September 1991. Arrington, Tarlee Brown, and Willie Davis of Arrington's staff formed ABD Marketing Corp., in 1985. City law authorizes the mayor to hire architects and project managers without going through the normal bid procedure because this work is considered professional service.

20. Arrington to Whiting, 6 May 1986; Mayor's Office to Birmingham City Council, 5 May 1986; Arrington to Whiting, 10 June 1986, BCRI Collection.

21. J. Max Bond to LaMonte, 12 June 1986, BCRI Collection; Marjorie Peters to Participants of Birmingham Civil Rights Museum Workshop, New York Workshop, 19 June 1986, BCRI Collection.

22. James K. Baker to LaMonte, 17 June 1986; Ann Kaufman, Minutes of Birmingham Civil Rights Museum Meeting, 21 June 1986, BCRI Collection; Arrington to J. Max Bond Jr., 25 June 1986, BCRI Collection.

23. Arrington to J. Max Bond Jr., 25 June 1986, BCRI Collection.

24. *Birmingham News,* 6 July 1986; Bond Issue of 1986 flier, Tutwiler Vertical File, Southern History Collection, Birmingham Public Library. In 1990 Birmingham's total population was 265,968 with 168,277, or 63 percent, African American. Woolfolk to BCRI Board of Directors, 12 March 1990; William Gilchrist to Woolfolk, 28 February 1990, BCRI Collection.

25. Art Clement of DPM testified that Peters told him she had forged the invoice in the "amount she needed to keep her business going." DPM helped Peters get the money. Previously DPM had hired Peters and paid her $84,000 for "political" or "nontechnical" work. See the *Birmingham Post-Herald,* 9, 11, 15, 18, 19 October 1991; *Birmingham News,* 6 September 1991; Woolfolk to Rabinowitz, 3 February 1988, BCRI Collection; *Birmingham Post-Herald,* 9, 11 October 1991.

26. *Birmingham Post-Herald,* 9, 11, 15, 18, 19 October 1991; *Birmingham News* 6 September 1991; Wodfolk to Rabinowitz, 3 February 1988, BCRI Collection; *Birmingham Post-Herald,* 9, 11 October 1991; Draft of Mission Statement, 20 August 1986, BCRI Collection.

27. Richard Rabinowitz to Ann Kaufman, 31 October and 13 November 1986. Rabinowitz estimated it would take him 39 days for a personal total of $29,250; Rabinowitz to Woolfolk and Task Force, 8 April 1987; American History Workshop, "Preliminary Exhibit Plan for the Birmingham Civil Rights Institute," 1 April 1987; American History Workshop, "Walking to Freedom: The Museum of America's

Civil Rights Revolution," June 1987, BCRI Collection; American History Workshop, "Walking To Freedom," BCRI Collection.

28. *Birmingham News,* 5, 6 September 1991; BCRI on Groundbreaking Ceremonies, 22 February 1991, BCRI Collection. Peters was indicted on July 26, 1991, for stealing $220,000 (*Birmingham Post-Herald,* 30 September and 9 October 1991; *Birmingham News,* 23 February 1991).

29. *Atlanta Journal-Constitution,* 23 January 1992; *Birmingham News,* 22, 24, 25, 26 January 1992; *Birmingham Post-Herald* 21 January 1992. As *Time* magazine recognized, "Equating the mayor with King is as bogus as comparing [Attorney General] Donaldson to Bull Connor. . . . The racial battleground is no longer black or white, but a murky gray, and Arrington's bizarre performance only adds to the confusion and frustration" (*Time,* 3 February 1992).

30. *Birmingham News,* 30 January 1992, 5, 8 February 1992; *Birmingham News,* 6, 15, 16 September 1992; BCRI attendance totals, November 1992 through March 1993, BCRI Collection; *Birmingham News,* 14 November 1992. In the winter 1993 issue of *Southern Changes,* Julian Bond wrote a wonderful piece entitled "History, Hope and Heroes" that looks at the first visitors to the Institute and what they wrote in a ledger used to record the comments of tourists.

31. Albany Civil Rights Movement Museum Web site (members.surfsouth.com/mtzion/); Albany Civil Rights Movement Museum, "The Grand Opening Souvenir Program 'Jubilee Week,' November 16–21, 1998"; an analysis of the Albany Movement may be found in the three essays published as a special issue of *Journal of Southwest Georgia History* 2 (fall 1984).

32. Albany Civil Rights Movement Museum, "The Grand Opening Souvenir Program 'Jubilee Week,' November 16–21, 1998"; *Atlanta Journal-Constitution,* 22 November 1998.

33. Of course, the similarities to the Lost Cause and the effort to memorialize the Confederacy cannot be overlooked. For analyses of this process, see Charles Reagan Wilson, *Baptized in Blood: The Religion of the Lost Cause, 1865–1920* (Athens: University of Georgia Press, 1980), and Gaines M. Foster, *Ghosts of the Confederacy: Defeat, the Lost Cause, and the Emergence of the New South* (New York: Oxford University Press, 1987).

34. On nostalgia and critical memory, see Houston Baker Jr., "Critical Memory and the Black Public Sphere," in *Cultural Memory and the Construction of Identity,* ed. Dan Ben-Amos and Liliane Weissberg (Detroit, Mich.: Wayne State University Press, 1999); on museums and cultural authenticity, see Didier Maleuvre, *Museum Memories: History, Technology, Art* (Stanford, Calif.: Stanford University Press, 1999); for a general discussion on the role of museums in society, see Stephen E. Weil, *A*

Cabinet of Curiosities: Inquiries into Museums and Their Prospects (Washington, D.C.: Smithsonian Institution Press, 1995).

35. Derek H. Alderman, "Creating a New Geography of Memory in the South: (Re)Naming of Streets in Honor of Martin Luther King, Jr." *Southeastern Geographer* 36 (May 1996): 51–69. Although the Albany Civil Rights Museum at Old Mt. Zion received broad support within both the black and white communities, the renaming of Jefferson Street as MLK Drive generated controversy; see the *Atlanta Journal-Constitution*, 20 February 1996.

PART VII

Back to the Future

A theme running through many of the preceding essays in this volume, as well as through Southern history generally, is that of the region as a place of vivid and perhaps rationally inexplicable contradictions. In "The Ambivalent South," Sheldon Hackney meditates on that phenomenon and suggests a way in which it might be better understood.

Southerners, Hackney argues, are not contradictory. But they are ambivalent. And that ambivalence is the product of a dual identity that is "fully American, yet is at the same time a dissent from America." It was shaped "by the structure of a society whose defining feature is biracialism and by a worldview growing out of the transcendence of various religious paradoxes in Protestant Christianity." Judged by material or economic benchmarks, the South and the non-South periodically grow closer together—sometimes close enough to eradicate any measurable difference in key areas of life. But the disappearance of one South has always been followed by the emergence of another rooted in the same dual identity that has made, and probably will continue to make, the South "both American and its opposite, both endorser and critic" and, under any guise, distinctive. That process, Hackney playfully writes, might best be labeled as the South's perpetual "molting . . . always in the process of shedding a skin, only to reveal another skin of original design covering the same beast." To be Southern, Hackney concludes, is "to be created in the conversation between the American identity and dissenting critiques of the American identity" and to embrace both—just as Christians embrace the dilemmas of their faith in the hope and belief that it eventually will lead them to salvation.

18

The Ambivalent South

SHELDON HACKNEY

Not long after the reelection of President Clinton in 1996, while the sore losers were picking through the rubble trying to figure out how such a faulted character could win, and when the press was feasting on the story about the hazing of the four women cadets who had rushed through the breach blasted in The Citadel by Shannon Faulkner the year before,[1] I was driving from Washington, D.C., to Charlottesville, Virginia, on the Interstate when I was passed by a car going very fast. This would have been unremarkable had I not noticed as the other car pulled away from me that it sported two stickers on its rear bumper. One read, "Don't blame me, I voted Libertarian." The other simply announced its loyalty to "The Citadel."

My mind was occupied the rest of the way to Charlottesville with the puzzle of how the same person could harbor such contrasting sentiments, the one envisioning a life minimally constrained by externally imposed rules, and the other symbolizing submission to the most rigorous military discipline. There is, of course, the time-honored idea that some heroes must give up their individual freedom in order to protect the freedom enjoyed by the whole society. I suspect, however, that the occupant of this particular automobile was expressing a different and less altruistic notion. He was adopting an oppositional stance, embracing two unfashionable loyalties in defiance of mainstream opinion, choosing an identity that set himself proudly apart from the herd-like majority.

It recalled to my mind the image of right-wing "militias" holding training maneuvers in the woods in camouflage uniforms while professing opposition to the authoritarian federal government, another instance of submitting to authority in order to oppose authority. The militias were attractive to a certain kind of person because membership allowed one to be super-patriotic and subversive at the same time. Such mirror-image identities, like opposing strands of DNA in the double helix, are satisfying solutions to the tensions of dual loyalties. In an analogous fashion, Southerners, both black and white, maintain an identity that is fully American, yet is at the same time a dissent from America.

One of the traditional puzzles of the historiography of the South, the Fermat's Last Theorem of Southern history,[2] is whether the South is quintessentially American with a few "peculiar institutions" that it chose to defend, or whether it has been a society whose structure, values, and ideals of behavior are fundamentally different from the rest of America. One could field a football team of distinguished historians on each side of this question.[3] It has been widely accepted that the idea of the South—the social construction of the South as the American "other"—has been created and used by both Southerners and Yankees for political, ideological, and psychological purposes.

Left unresolved is how so many serious scholars, citing convincing evidence, could reach opposite conclusions about the real-world South to which the socially constructed South must bear some relationship, however imperfect that relationship may be.[4] The solution is that the South is ambivalent; it is *both* American *and* the alternative American. The dual identity grows out of the double history of the South, and it fits comfortably within an identity shaped by the structure of a society whose defining feature is biracialism and by a worldview growing out of the transcendence of various religious paradoxes in Protestant Christianity.

Consider this illustration. In a series of seductive essays in the 1950s and 1960s, C. Vann Woodward wrote about the Southern identity as rooted in the un-American experiences of defeat, poverty, and the guilt of slavery and racial injustice in contrast to the nation's view of its own history as one of success, affluence, and innocence.[5] Woodward here was engaging in the old literary tactic of using the South as a counterpoint to the North.[6] His subject was actually the complacent American mood of the postwar era and the dangerous arrogance flowing from the myths of American invincibility and purity of motive. The experience of the South, being much more akin to the human experience of the rest of the world, should serve as an antidote to the delusion that America was a chosen people, exempt from the consequences of hubris. Had America listened and learned from the "irony" of Southern history, we might have been spared the tragedy of the war in Vietnam.

As it happened, the nation did not listen. The United States was led by a Southern president, a Southern secretary of state, and a Southern commanding general into a war that could not be won, over matters that were not central to our national interest. It was a foreign involvement that generated increasingly strong opposition at home, leaving scars that have not yet fully healed. Ironically, the most hawkish section of the country was the South, the same South whose white inhabitants were simultaneously conducting a campaign of resistance to the federal government's authority in the area of civil rights and justice for African Americans, women, and members of other groups that suffered from discrimination. Here we see the South in its dichotomous unity as both the land of super-patriotism and the locus of dissent.

The South's multiple personality is obviously causally connected to its being both a part of the national story and at various times an impediment to that story. White Southerners and black Southerners share the double history of the region even though they may experience their relationship to it in ways that are inverse to each other. The self-consciousness of the South as a single, distinct region of the country with common interests was created during the debates over the Missouri Compromise in 1820, solidified in the defense of slavery against the abolitionist crusade, martyred in the Civil War and Reconstruction, extended by the rise and reign of Jim Crow, fed by perceptions of exploitation at the hand of Pittsburgh or Wall Street or Washington, and then reactivated by the struggle to resist the civil rights movement of the 1950s and 60s. Through all of this, it is clear that the identity was called into being originally by white apologists for slavery to oppose perceived threats to the "peculiar institution" from the outside. An oppositional mentality is one of the legacies of the white South's insistence for so long on some form of racial subordination as the defining feature of the social structure.

Conversely, being black in the hostile environment of the South has involved complex strategies of allegiance and opposition. Southern blacks and whites have been locked in a mutually modifying embrace, shaping and being shaped by a society whose core element is its biracial nature.[7] Whether or not biracialism finds institutional expression in slavery, in segregation, or in some more fluid and complex public and private relationships, there is still a "twoness" about living in the South. Yes, there are Cuban Americans in South Florida, Mexican Americans in South Texas, Cajuns in South Louisiana, Chinese in Mississippi, and triracial communities in Virginia and North Carolina; but those and other complications don't yet challenge the formative power of biracialism in Southern culture.

The South, of course, is not the only part of the United States with a regional consciousness and a special history. We have stereotypical images of

New England, Texas, the West, and California, for instance. Those images, however, are rooted in times past, in certain events (like the Battle of the Alamo) or particular periods (like the transplantation of town-meeting Protestantism to New England in the Colonial period, or the settling of the Great plains in the nineteenth century by Europeans). The South, however, has a collective identity that was forged in a conflict with the rest of the nation, was fixed by the grim realities of the Civil War, and has been renewed not only by continuing defensiveness but by the filtering of common developments and experiences through an awareness of difference.

During two periods of our relatively brief national history, the South has been the site of the central domestic political conflict: from the Missouri Compromise of 1820 through the Civil War and Reconstruction, when the abolition of slavery dominated politics; and from the *Brown* decision in 1954 through the assassination of Martin Luther King Jr. in 1968, when the civil rights movement was ignited in the South and then spread geographically to the rest of the country and demographically to other oppressed groups.

The realignment of American politics that came as a result of the Voting Rights Act of 1965 and as a reaction to the social justice and countercultural movements of the 1960s still defines the American political scene. A hugely disproportionate number of the leaders of both national parties now speak with a Southern accent.

In short, unlike other regions, the South has played a major role in American politics, just as it has played a larger-than-life role in the American imagination. In the nonpolitical realm, the South has provided the nation with a scapegoat on some occasions, with compensatory "Song of the South" nostalgia that would ease the tensions of industrialization and legitimize an unjust racial order, with dueling images of Tobacco Road versus Tara, with a convenient "Other" who could bear guilt or carry utopian dreams as the psychic needs of the nation required.[8]

Despite its powerful and continuing presence, the South has been vanishing since Henry Grady began peddling his New South snake oil, one of the longest and most theatrical exits on record. In his presidential address to the Southern Historical Association in November 1999, Jim Cobb wryly and wonderfully tweaked the noses of those who have pronounced premature epitaphs for Dixie over the ensuing century and a quarter.[9] He went on to argue that it is the North that has disappeared, dissolved by the discovery in the 1960s and 1970s that the stereotypical sins of the South were shared by the nation. That, of course, threatens the South, because the South has existed as the foil of the North.[10] Left undecided is whether the South can exist without a utopianized North, and if so, what will be the identity of the post-North South?

There is a danger, however, in thinking that, just because the North has been exposed as harboring racial prejudice every bit as horrific as that found in the South, there is no real distinction between North and South. Anti-black feelings were rampant in the North during the antebellum period as well, but that did not make slavery less "peculiar" or less evil, nor did it prevent the Civil War. There is a fundamental difference between a society that contains racial prejudice, and a society that is fundamentally shaped by biracial consciousness, whatever the current balance of power or mode of race relations happens to be. In the South, biracialism has guided residential patterns, business practices, civic activities, leisure pursuits, political arrangements, and almost every thread in the warp and woof of society. It is a substratum of the South's being.

Whatever the disappearance of the North portends, scholars and journalists are sure to continue their debate about whether the South still exists.[11] One cannot deny that various indices of Southern distinctiveness continue to converge with the non-South so that it is increasingly difficult to distinguish the region statistically.[12] Median family income in the South is closing the gap with the national average, and the responses to survey questions about time-honored litmus tests of Southernness are revealing less regional variation.

For instance, when a national sample of adults in 1993 were asked how often they ate an evening meal together as a family while they were growing up, there was no difference between Southern and non-Southern respondents. In the same survey, there was no significant regional difference in church going, nor in saying grace before meals, nor in entertaining a person of a different race in one's home, nor in attitudes toward women working and the influence of that on the family, nor in attitudes toward pornography, nor in geographical closeness to relatives, nor in preference for family over friends for leisure-time companions, nor in attitudes toward military service as a qualification for elective office, nor even in attending a stock car race.

A 1992 poll asking whether the respondent favored racial integration, segregation, or something in between found 55 percent of Southerners and 58 percent of non-Southerners in favor of integration, and about 30 percent of both favoring something in between! Only when the question was about interracial dating and marriage did Southerners show more resistance to racial mingling, and that difference is still present in a 1999 survey. On the other hand, a survey in 1996 found similar responses from Southerners and non-Southerners to a question about the desirability of hate-crime legislation, and similar percentages in 1999 claimed that the racial composition of their neighborhood made no difference to them. Could it be that it is finally time to play taps for the Southern mystique?[13]

The reason for the interminable disappearing act is that the South actually is constantly disappearing, only to be succeeded by another South, also distinct but distinct in a different way. I think of this as the "molting South," always in the process of shedding a skin, only to reveal another skin of original design covering the same beast.

Now it is true that some of the persistent Southern identity is simply in the minds of Americans, North and South. For instance, in the same 1993 survey that found indistinguishable answers between Southerners and non-Southerners on questions about family behavior, there was this question as well: "In general, do you think Southerners are more loyal to family or less loyal to family than people in other areas of the country?" A majority of both Southerners (68%) and non-Southerners (56%) thought that Southerners were more loyal to family. Perceptions of Southern distinctiveness sometimes outstrip the reality.

A representative sample of adults were asked in the summer of 1999 whether or not their community was in the South. Of the eleven ex-Confederate states, only Texas (84%) and Virginia (82%) fell below the 90 percent level in respondents who believed their community was in the South. The suburbs of Washington and the Texas borderland are nibbling at the edges of Southern self-consciousness. Kentucky (79%) and Oklahoma (69%) remained as pretenders to Southernness, while other states that are sometimes referred to as "Southern" contained only minorities who thought of themselves as living in the South. West Virginia (45%), Maryland (40%), Missouri (23%), Delaware (14%), and the District of Columbia (7%). The idea of the South is alive in the minds of ordinary people.[14]

It is also true that the South still exists in the world of measurable differences and real human actions. The Federal Center for Disease Control and Prevention recently issued a report warning the public that obesity is a public health problem in the United States. The nation is fat and getting fatter, and the South is leading the way. Traditional Southern cooking might be part of the problem, but the "more likely reason for the greater increase below the Mason-Dixon line is a lack of exercise. Southerners are less likely to hike, ride a bike, walk or join a health club than people in the rest of the nation."[15] This is the sedentary South, which joins the lazy South, the militant South, the violent South, the demagogic South, and other exotic Souths on the shelf of national curiosity.

Another recent government study reported that the state of literacy in the country was not good, and it found the South particularly illiterate. Of the eleven ex-Confederate states, only Virginia had fewer than 20 percent of its population in Level One literacy (the worst category). All the rest had 21 percent or more of the population in Level One literacy. Of the non-Southern states, only California, New Jersey, New York, and the District of Columbia, all places with large numbers of immigrants and high levels of poverty, had 21 percent or more of their populations in Level One literacy. Tempting as it is to define the South as that part of the United States that is fat and dumb, that would be to confuse transitory symptoms with lasting identity.[16]

The current controversy about the Confederate flag flying over the South Carolina state capitol reminds us that the siege mentality, while no longer claiming a majority of white South Carolinians, is still aggressively alive. That was confirmed for me when I spotted a Confederate flag bumper sticker on a shabby pickup truck in Alabama earlier this year whose text read, "If At First You Don't Secede."

Tony Horwitz recently found enough Confederates in the attic to give one pause. Among the vibrant subculture of Civil War reenactments, and the popular market for Civil War symbols and memorabilia, he detects a continuing sense of grievance and of loss within a certain part of the white Southern population. Theirs is a proxy battle against big government, and the Confederate battle flag serves as a talisman against modernity.[17]

Even though pollsters have difficulty asking questions about racial attitudes that differentiate Southerners from non-Southerners, practicing politicians in the South know that racial attitudes still motivate a significant portion of the electorate in a way that is not true in the non-South. Cynthia McKinney, a black woman running for reelection to the U.S. House of Representatives in a redrawn white-majority district, played the reverse race card in 1998, appealing to the progressive whites in the neighborhoods around Emory University to demonstrate to the country that Atlanta was beyond racism. It worked. She was reelected.

On the other hand, Zell Miller, former Democratic governor of Georgia, told an audience of Southern historians in November 1999 that it had been a political mistake for him to try to purge the Confederate symbol from the Georgia state flag, not because he had changed his mind about the morality of the situation, but because he had rebalanced the political equation. He had expended huge amounts of political time, energy, and credibility on an issue that was merely symbolic and about which a majority of the white voters felt very strongly. It was counterproductive.

Miller's advice for white Democrats was to avoid the buzz-saw symbolic issues and talk about things government can do to improve the lives of ordinary folks, black as well as white. The formula for success is well known to white Democrats, he said. They must get ninety percent of the black vote and forty percent of the white vote. The implication is clear. Any issue tinged by race will chase enough white voters away to allow the Republicans to win.

Another way to think of the continuing presence of race in the thinking of the Southern electorate is to ask the question, "Why is the South the most Republican section of the country in presidential elections?" It is certainly not because the South contains a disproportionate share of the economic elite that benefit from Republican policies, though it is true that when the federal government first began to cater to the needs of people at the local level during the New Deal, it was intruding into the province of local elites in the South. The economic order was threatened as well as the racial order. The flip flop to the Solid Republican South after 1968 occurred because the Republican party came to represent resistance to the federal government's threat to the intertwined racial and economic arrangements of Southern society. The Republican party also represented a brand of self-reliance that struck a responsive chord in a region not far removed from its agricultural past.

Recognizing the difficulty of separating cause and effect, the transformation of the Democratic South into the Republican South also had something to do with the fact that the Religious Right is centered in the South. The Religious Right is dedicated to resisting the drift of our culture toward secularism, hedonism, and materialism. One of the large ironies of the present day is that the Religious Right has identified the Democratic Party as the sponsor of modernist cultural values. Thus, it has allied itself with the Republican Party, the party that prides itself with being the champion of free markets, capitalism, and technological progress—the very forces that inevitably undermine the values that the Religious Right seeks to preserve. It is not unusual to find that a major trend in American culture has generated its own negation; it *is* unusual to find both the thesis and the antithesis in the same political party.

As modern life has gotten more self-serving and pleasure-seeking, the opposition to it has gotten more Southern, even though Southerners participate enthusiastically in the materialism of modernity. This is another instance of double consciousness.

The function of religion in Southern life, however, is probably more subtle and more powerful than is suggested by the political activism of the black church or Pat Robertson's Christian Coalition. Protestant Christianity provides the unconscious cultural model for understanding the world and our place in it. We find our identities in the paradoxes of our theological assumptions, in the conversation between conflicting cultural commandments, in the dialogue between the opposing poles of the dichotomous choices we face in daily living. Believing Christians know Jesus both as Lord and as servant. They internalize the view of Jesus as both human and divine. These are overarching contradictions that believers embrace with no trouble. The Christian paradox that you cannot save your life except by giving it away is the example of Christ as well as the message of Christianity. The Christian promise that "the last shall be first" helps shape a worldview that is constructed on important contradictions.

The evangelical dilemma, then, is that we are all absolutely responsible for our sins and for the state of our soul, but we are powerless without the help of God to save ourselves. We are at the same time radically independent and abjectly dependent. We struggle to understand and to live life while caught in this pincers.

The secular analogy is that we are all expected by society to be responsible for our own well-being, but we are incapable by ourselves of sustaining ourselves. We not only are social animals, but we live in a modern society composed of intricate arrangements that make each of us dependent in some ways on each other—for a job, for police protection, for a market in which to sell the products of our hands and head, for a government that will educate our neighbors so they can also contribute to society rather than preying on us, for laws that will guarantee our ownership of all kinds of property against the rapacious designs of predatory individuals and organizations, for the provision of common goods like clean air and water, roads and bridges.

The resulting tension between individualism and organization is a central theme of American history, a running argument between Clint Eastwood and Bill Gates. It occurs in the South with a regional flavor, refracted by the biracialism that has shaped the Southern identity, an identity that is to be found in the cultural exchange between black and white, and between "just American" and "Southern American." Just as Christians embrace the dilemmas of faith, Southerners accept the paradoxes of their Southern identity.

The South is thus full of exemplary Americans and of alternative Americans at the same time. The American identity is multifaceted and changes over time; but whatever it is at any one time, the South is both American and its opposite, both endorser and critic. In short, Southerners, both black and white, live with contradiction.

To be Southern is to have had one's public identity formed in a biracial world, a world in which the interplay between black and white cultures has left each group profoundly influenced by the other. To be Southern is to be formed by a religious culture of compatible contradictions. To be a Southerner is also to be created in the conversation between the American identity and dissenting critiques of the American identity. To be Southern is to be ambivalent.

NOTES

1. Catherine S. Manegold, *In Glory's Shadow: Shannon Faulkner, The Citadel and a Changing America* (New York: Alfred A. Knopf, 2000).

2. For an unraveling of this metaphor, go to www.AMS.org/index/new-in-math/Fermat.html. Also see: www.groups.DCS.STAND.AC.UK/history/HISTopics/Fermat's_Last_Theorem.html.

3. See, for instance, Carl N. Degler, *Place over Time: The Continuity of Southern Distinctiveness* (Baton Rouge: Louisiana State University Press, 1977), especially 2–7.

4. See David L. Carlton, "How American Is the American South?" in *The South as an American Problem,* ed. Larry J. Griffin and Don H. Doyle (Athens: University of Georgia Press, 1995), 33–56. Carlton recognizes the problem, which is much to his credit, but provides an explanation that is only a partial solution because it does not account for the contemporary duality of the Southern identity

5. C. Vann Woodward, *The Burden of Southern History,* rev. ed. (1960; Baton Rouge: Louisiana State University Press, 1968).

6. See, for instance, C. Vann Woodward, *American Counterpoint: Slavery and Racism in the North-South Dialogue* (Boston: Little, Brown and Company, 1971).

7. An interesting exploration of the rootedness or sense of community that blacks feel about the South is found in James C. Cobb, "Searching for Southernness: Community and Identity in the Contemporary South," in *Redefining Southern Culture: Mind and Identity in the Modern South* (Athens: University of Georgia Press, 1999), 125–49.

8. The classic statement of a mythic South created to counterbalance certain motifs of national character is William R. Taylor, *Cavalier and Yankee: The Old South and American National Character* (New York: George Braziller, Inc., 1961). The Doubleday Anchor edition appeared in 1963.

9. James C. Cobb, "An Epitaph for the North: Reflections on the Politics of Regional and National Identity at the Millennium," *Journal of Southern History* (February 2000): 3–24. See also George B. Tindall's charming and suggestive essay, "Beyond the Mainstream: The Ethnic Southerners," in *The Ethnic Southerners* (Baton Rouge: Louisiana State University Press, 1976), 1–21. The first full treatment of Southern whites as an ethnic group is to be found in Lewis Killian, *White Southerners* (New York: Random House, 1970).

10. Some superficial confirmation of this interesting observation is provided by the National Collegiate Athletic Association. The four regions into which the men's national basketball championship tournament is divided are South, East, West, and Midwest. There is no North. In the women's tournament, frequently a harbinger, there is no South either, just East and West and their "Mid" twins.

11. Benjamin Schwarz, "The Idea of the South," *Atlantic Monthly* (December 1997), 117*ff.* My favorite empirical tracing of the existence of the South is John Shelton Reed, *The Enduring South* (Chapel Hill: University of North Carolina Press, 1974). Reed focuses on family, religion, and violence as distinguishing features.

12. John Egerton, *The Americanization of Dixie: The Southernization of America* (New York: Harpers Magazine Press, 1974). See also Peter Applebome, *Dixie Rising* (New York: Harcourt, Brace/Harvest Books, 1996).

13. All survey results cited here are from the Howard Odum Center at Chapel Hill, available on the web at www. IRSS.UNC.edu/data_archive/pollsearch.html.

14. Southern Culture poll of the Howard Odum Center. www. IRSS.UNC.edu: 80/data_archive/pollsearch.html.

15. *New York Times,* 27 October 1999.

16. *The State of Literacy in America,* available through the NIFL homepage (www.nifl.gov).

17. Tony Horwitz, *Confederates in the Attic: Dispatches from the Unfinished Civil War* (New York: Pantheon Books, 1998).

CONTRIBUTORS

Rod Andrew Jr. is assistant professor of history at Clemson University. He specializes in the history of the late-nineteenth and twentieth-century South and is the author of *Long Gray Lines: The Southern Military School Tradition, 1839–1915.*

Patrick H. Breen teaches in the history department at Providence College. He is also working on a Ph.D. from the University of Georgia, where his dissertation examines Nat Turner's Rebellion. He lives in Rhode Island with his wife, Catherine, and daughter, Mary Teresa.

W. Fitzhugh Brundage is the William B. Umstead Professor of History at the University of North Carolina at Chapel Hill. He has published on lynching and utopian socialism in the American South and has edited *Where These Memories Grow: History, Memory, and Regional Identity in the South.*

Michael E. Daly graduated in 1999 from Davidson College, where he collaborated with Professor John Wertheimer and others on the article published in this book. He has studied advanced Arabic and worked for the United Nations Development Programme in the Middle East. He is currently finishing a Fulbright Scholarship in Damascus, Syria.

Brian R. Dirck is assistant professor of history at Anderson University. He is the author of *Lincoln and Davis: Imagining America, 1809–1865* and is currently working on a new study of Abraham Lincoln's law practice.

Glenn T. Eskew teaches history at Georgia State University in Atlanta, where he has worked since 1993. His book *But for Birmingham: The Local and National Movements in the Civil Rights Struggle* received the Francis Butler Simkins Award given jointly by the Southern Historical Association and Longwood College. Currently he is at work on a collection of essays evaluating the recent effort to memorialize the civil rights movement through museums and institutes.

James O. Farmer Jr. received his Ph.D. from the University of South Carolina and is June Rainsford Henderson Professor of Southern and Local History at the University of South Carolina Aiken. His major research interest is in Southern religion and thought. His *Metaphysical Confederacy: James Henley Thornwell and the Synthesis of Southern Values* was reissued in 1999.

William R. Glass is professor of history at Mississippi University for Women, Columbus. He earned his Ph.D. from Emory University. He has published *Strangers in Zion: Fundamentalists in the South, 1900–1950* as well as articles on American religion in *American Presbyterians, American Baptist Quarterly, Jewish Social Studies,* and *Studies in the Social Sciences.* He is currently working on a biographical essay of A. T. Pierson and a book-length study of the efforts to reunite Northern and Southern denominations.

Sheldon Hackney is a historian of the American South. He is also the former president of Tulane University (1975–1981) and the University of Pennsylvania (1981–1993) and the past chairman of the National Endowment for the Humanities (1993–1997). He is currently professor of history at the University of Pennsylvania. Among his articles and books, *Populism to Progressivism in Alabama* won the Charles S. Sydnor Award of the Southern Historical Association and the Albert J. Beveridge Award of the American Historical Association.

Paul Harvey is associate professor of history at the University of Colorado at Colorado Springs. He is the author of *Redeeming the South: Religious Cultures and Racial Identities among Southern Baptists, 1865–1925* and is presently completing a manuscript titled "Freedom's Coming: Religion, Race, and Culture in the South from the Civil War through the Civil Rights Movement."

Joan Marie Johnson received her Ph.D. from University of California, Los Angeles and has published several articles on Southern women, race, gender, and reform. She edited *Southern Women at Vassar: The Poppenheim Family Letters, 1882–1916.* She is currently a scholar-in-residence at the Newberry Library, Chicago, where she is the recipient of a Spencer Foundation grant, studying Southern women and higher education.

Alexander S. Macaulay Jr. was born and raised in South Carolina. He graduated from The Citadel in 1994 and earned a master's degree in history from the University of Tennessee–Knoxville. He is currently working toward his doctoral degree at the University of Georgia.

James McMillin is the associate director of Bridwell Library and associate professor of American religious history in the Perkins School of Theology at Southern Methodist University.

Winfred B. Moore Jr. is professor of history at The Citadel. He is the author of articles on twentieth-century Southern history and the coeditor of four earlier books of essays.

Christopher Phillips is associate professor of history at the University of Cincinnati. He received his Ph.D. in history from the University of Georgia and is the author of several books on southern history, including *Freedom's Port: The African American Community of Baltimore, 1790–1860* and *Missouri's Confederate: Claiborne Fox Jackson and the Creation of Southern Identity in the Border West.* His current book project is a social-cultural history of the Civil War era in the Ohio Valley.

Kyle S. Sinisi is a graduate of the Virginia Military Institute. He received his Ph.D. from Kansas State University and is currently associate professor of history at The Citadel. He is the author of *Sacred Debts: State Civil War Claims and American Federalism.*

Emory M. Thomas was formerly Regents Professor of History at the University of Georgia and is currently Mark W. Clark Distinguished Visiting Professor of History at The Citadel. His books include *Robert E. Lee: An Album; Robert E. Lee: A Biography; Travels to Hallowed Ground: A Historian's Journey to the American Civil War; Bold Dragoon: The Life of J. E. B. Stuart; The Confederate Nation, 1861–1865; The American War and Peace, 1860–1877; The Confederacy as a Revolutionary Experience;* and *The Confederate State of Richmond: A Biography.*

Christopher Waldrep is Jamie and Phyllis Pasker Professor of History at San Francisco State University. He is the author of articles and books on the American South and legal history.

Peter Wallenstein teaches history at Virginia Polytechnic Institute and State University. His books include *From Slave South to New South: Public Policy in Nineteenth-Century Georgia* and *Tell the Court I Love My Wife: Race, Marriage, and Law—an American History.* His current work explores how black Southerners' struggled to desegregate public higher education from 1935 to 1970.

John Wertheimer is associate professor of history at Davidson College. In addition to his own research, which concerns the history of free speech and civil liberties, he frequently collaborates with Davidson College students on legal history research papers, including the one published in this volume.

David H. White Jr. is professor emeritus of history at The Citadel. He is the author of articles on American diplomatic and military history and is at work on an oral history of The Citadel class of 1942.

Kirsten E. Wood is assistant professor of history at Florida International University. She received her Ph.D. from the University of Pennsylvania. Specializing in gender and the Old South, Wood currently has in progress a book-length study of slaveholding widowhood. Wood has also published on the Eaton Affair and is looking forward to a new project on representation, broadly conceived, in the early republic.

INDEX